THE GATES
OF MEMORY

Saint Peter's University Library
Withdrawn

Saint Peter's University Library
Withdrawn

THE GATES OF MEMORY

MEMORY

Geoffrey Keynes

Oxford   New York

OXFORD UNIVERSITY PRESS

1983

Oxford University Press, Walton Street, Oxford OX2 6DP

London Glasgow New York Toronto
Delhi Bombay Calcutta Madras Karachi
Kuala Lumpur Singapore Hong Kong Tokyo
Nairobi Dar es Salaam Cape Town
Melbourne Auckland
and associates in
Beirut Berlin Ibadan Mexico City Nicosia

© Geoffrey Keynes 1981

First published by the Clarendon Press 1981
Reprinted 1982 (three times)
First issued as an Oxford University Press paperback 1983
Chapter 11, 'The First World War', was first published
(under the title 'A Doctor's War') in Promise of Greatness,
ed. George A. Panichas (New York: The John Day Co.; London:
Cassell & Co., 1968); previous publication of some other
sections of this book is acknowledged at pp. 64, 373, and 392. G.L.K.

All rights reserved. No part of this publication may be reproduced,
stored in a retrieval system, or transmitted, in any form or by any means,
electronic, mechanical, photocopying, recording, or otherwise, without
the prior permission of Oxford University Press

This book is sold subject to the condition that it shall not, by way
of trade or otherwise, be lent, re-sold, hired out or otherwise circulated
without the publisher's prior consent in any form of binding or cover
other than that in which it is published and without a similar condition
including this condition being imposed on the subsequent purchaser

British Library Cataloguing in Publication Data

Keynes, Sir Geoffrey
The gates of memory
1. Keynes, Sir Geoffrey 2. Surgeons—Great Britain—Biography
I. Title
617'.09'4 RD27.35.K4
ISBN 0-19-285130-6

Library of Congress Cataloging in Publication Data

Keynes, Geoffrey, Sir, 1887–
The gates of memory. (Oxford paperbacks) Includes index.
1. Keynes, Geoffrey, Sir, 1887– . 2. Surgeons—Great Britain—Biography.
3. Litterateurs—Great Britain—Biography. I. Title.
RD27.35.K49A33 1983 610'.92'4 [B] 82-19037
ISBN 0-19-285130-6 (pbk.)

Printed and bound in Great Britain by
William Clowes (Beccles) Limited,
Beccles and London

RD
27.35
.K49
A33
1983
c.1

Unbar the Gates of Memory: look upon me
Not as another, but thy real Self. I am thy Spectre

William Blake: *The Four Zoas*
Night the Seventh, lines 347–8

CONTENTS

ILLUSTRATIONS

I

ANCESTORS

MANY times I have been urged by friends, and even by publishers, to write an autobiography, but I have been unwilling to oblige because I always seemed to have better things to do. Usually the suggestion has been followed by the remark, 'You must have known so many interesting people.' It is true, I have and still do, but the suggestion sounds too much like performing an exercise in name-dropping, the most unattractive of all occupations, which no one enjoys. The writer of an autobiography must try to believe that other people will like to read about what he himself has tried to achieve, however imperfectly, and what people and things have engaged his interest. As regards people, it is not only 'interest' that has concerned me. I have found endless enjoyment in friendship, and that has played a great part in the fulfilment of what seems likely to be an unusually long life—though not, as will be seen, unusual in our family.

Among the persons of interest with whom I have associated an important figure has been my brother, Maynard Keynes, and this suggests that a short account of our common ancestry may not be out of place. My mother, Florence Ada Keynes, gave a brief history of the family in her small book of memoirs.[1] This was based on a preliminary investigation made by my brother when he was a King's Scholar at Eton College, and it has been carried further by my grandson, Simon Keynes, an historian and Fellow of Trinity College, Cambridge.

The name Keynes derives from a village in Normandy called Cahagnes, in the Val de Vire south-west of Caen. This had given its name to William de Cahagnes who had come to England with the Conqueror in 1066 at the behest of his over-

[1] *Gathering up the Threads* (Cambridge: Heffer, 1950).

lord Robert, Count of Mortain and half-brother to the Conqueror. The name appears as Cahanges or Cahainges in
Domesday Book, and among many variants the forms Kahaines
and Kaynes appear in the twelfth and thirteenth centuries; a
preference for the modern form Keynes emerges in the fourteenth century, though still pronounced to rhyme with
'grains'.[1] It is not that I feel any great satisfaction in claiming
descent from one of William's robber barons, but the survival
of a somewhat unusual name in direct male line from robber
baron, William de Cahagnes, to economic baron, John
Maynard Keynes, is of some interest.

After the Conquest, William de Cahagnes was assigned
numerous estates in England, chiefly in Northamptonshire
and Sussex, but also including outliers in Cambridgeshire and
Buckinghamshire. His principal estate was at Dodford in
Northamptonshire, and he is found as sheriff of that county
during the reign of William Rufus. Some of the land in Cam-
bridgeshire was at Comberton (given to William by Odo,
Bishop of Bayeux, 'but the men of the Hundred know not for
what reason', comments Domesday Book), and the rest was at
Barton, now almost a suburb of Cambridge itself. The tithes of
Barton church were given by one of William's descendants to
Merton Priory in Surrey, and on passing to the Crown at the
Dissolution were sold by Henry VIII to King's College,
Cambridge. The College still accepts responsibility for the up-
keep of the chancel, and so it came about that my brother, as
Bursar of King's College for some years, had a special interest
in this former property of his ancestors.

The lands of William de Cahagnes passed to his son Ralph,
who in turn begat three sons, Ralph, Hugh, and William, each

---

[1] The name is often mispronounced to rhyme with 'jeans', presumably by
(false) analogy with the modern pronunciation of 'key'; but 'key' was pronounced to rhyme with 'day', 'play', etc., at least until the end of the seventeenth century, and other English words like 'grey' and 'whey' preserve the
same vowel and pronunciation. Every one of the numerous places in England
bearing the family name has traditionally kept the correct pronunciation,
with the exception of the renegade 'New Town' of Milton Keynes. I have
made due protest in a letter to *The Times* (25 May 1973), but without any
effect.

of whom founded a separate branch of the family. Their surname became attached to several of the places associated with
the different branches, and most of the place-names still survive in this form to bear witness to the family's former owner-
ship of the land. Ralph inherited the estate at Dodford, but by
a fortunate marriage to an heiress he acquired additional
properties at Tarrant Keynston and Coombe Keynes (in
Dorset) and at Somerford Keynes (once in Wiltshire, but now
in Gloucestershire); further marriages contracted by Ralph's
descendants brought Ashton Keynes (in Wiltshire) and Poole
Keynes (in Gloucestershire) into the family, but the male line
gave out towards the end of the fourteenth century and the
various properties passed to others who had themselves married
Keynes heiresses. Memorials to this branch of the family are to
be seen in the church at Dodford, a small place now reached
from the main road to Daventry by steep and narrow ways:
these include a fine effigy in Purbeck marble of a reclining
knight, believed to represent Sir Robert de Keynes (died 1305),
and two effigies of women, one in wood (now sadly disfigured
by devouring worms) and the other in stone, believed to represent Sir Robert's mother Hawise and his brother's grand-
daughter Wentiliana, the last of the line.

Hugh, the second son of the first Ralph, inherited a share of
the Northamptonshire properties, but the branch of the family
that he established was based principally on the Sussex estates
of the original William de Cahagnes. These included Horsted
Keynes, where a church was soon built with stone seemingly
brought from Caen in Normandy, reproducing the proportions
of the church at Cahagnes (which was destroyed by the
Germans in 1944, lest the tower should serve as a landmark for
allied planes). The church at Horsted Keynes contains a
miniature effigy of a cross-legged knight, commonly believed
to be a heart-shrine commemorating a member of the Keynes
family who had died abroad on a Crusade. Another of the
Sussex estates was Tilton, at the foot of Firle Beacon. In the
1930s my brother acquired from Lord Gage of Firle Place a life
interest in the house and farm of Upper Tilton, and here he
died in 1946 in an area that had belonged to our family at the
time of the Domesday survey, over eight hundred years before.

His widow is still tenant of the house, though the land has reverted to Lord Gage.

Hugh's younger son married the heiress of Milton Keynes in Buckinghamshire and established another branch of the family, but both this and the Sussex line died out during the course of the fourteenth century and again the properties passed to families who had married into our own. It remained for Ralph's third son William to establish the branch from which the present members of the family are descended. He too inherited a share of the Northamptonshire properties, but his interests lay principally in the south-west.

It was this William who made a distinguished appearance on the national stage when, fighting for the Earl of Gloucester at the battle of Lincoln in 1141, he contrived to take King Stephen prisoner:

> The king's courage did not fail, but his heavy battle-axe gleamed like lightning, striking down some, bearing back others. At length it was shattered by repeated blows; then he drew his well-tried sword, with which he wrought wonders, until that, too, was broken. Perceiving which, William de Kahaines, a brave knight, rushed on him, and, seizing him by his helmet, shouted, 'Here, here; I have taken the king!' Others came to his aid, and the king was made prisoner.
>
> (Henry of Huntingdon)

It is surmised that the grateful Earl of Gloucester rewarded William for this act of 'gallantry' with one of his estates in Devon, now known as Winkleigh but formerly known as Winkleigh Keynes; I atoned for it myself by naming my youngest son after the king. The village still boasts a 'Keynes Castle', which turns out on inspection to be a large earthen mound much overgrown and difficult of access, but not unimpressive: in the words of a nineteenth-century local historian, 'It must have once been a place of great strength, and stood upon an oval mound, 144 feet across from north to south, and 104 from east to west, and 44 feet high, and it is still nearly surrounded by a deep moat.'

In the fourteenth century John de Keynes of Winkleigh married Isabelle de Wake, supposedly a descendant of Her-

eward the Wake, and the marriage brought further estates into
the possession of the family. These included Dowlish Wake in
Somerset, and the church there contains an elegant effigy of
Isabelle, as well as one of her grandson John de Keynes,
sheriff of Devon, portrayed resting peacefully on the top of his
tomb beside his wife Joanna. In the sixteenth century the
family moved from Winkleigh to Compton Pauncefoot in
Somerset, another property then recently acquired by marriage. The Keyneses of Compton Pauncefoot were clearly a
remarkable breed. One of them, John Keynes, came to blows
with David Dee, M.A., pastor of Sherborne in Dorset, and indeed, John assaulted him so effectively that it was not for six
weeks that Dee was able to speak loud enough to press his
charge.

Two of John's sons became Jesuit priests: one of them,
George (1553–1611), translated a *Roman Martyrology* which was
published posthumously in St. Omer in 1627 (second edition,
1667), and this was in fact the first family book which I had
opportunity to acquire. The family produced several other
Jesuit priests in the following generations, including a second
George (who sailed for the China mission in 1654 but died in
the Philippines four years later), Edward (who died in 1665
tending victims of the plague in London), and Charles (Professor of Logic at Liège). The most famous of them all, Father
John Keynes, was the alleged ringleader of those accused by
Titus Oates of complicity in the plot to assassinate Charles II,
but he managed to escape to the Continent, becoming Rector
of the Jesuit College at Liège in 1680 and Provincial of the
English Jesuits, 1683–9. He published *A Rational, Compendious
way to Convince, Without any Dispute, All Persons whatsoever,
Dissenting from the True Religion* (London, 1674), which I have,
along with a neat manuscript account of Oates's schemes and
its Jesuit victims written in French and presented to Louis XIV
by 'Jean de Kaines provincial'; the manuscript, formerly in the
library of the Duke of Newcastle, seems to be the author's copy
of the version sent to Louis, which was preserved in the
Bibliothèque Nationale but is now lost.

Fortunately, the Catholic convictions of the Keynes family
did not always take them as far as the Jesuit priesthood, and the

line continued through Father John's elder brother, Colonel Alexander Keynes. In a colourful career, Alexander served Charles I in the Civil War, and I have a document by which he was guaranteed safe-conduct through the realms of Louis XIV while discharging 'plusieurs commissions de grande importance au service du Roy son maître', signed by Louis and by his mother the Queen Regent. During the Commonwealth, Alexander was imprisoned and then banished, and after serving Charles II for a while on the Continent he gained a command in the Venetian army and was killed in a battle against the Turks. Alexander's activities, however, meant the effective end of his family's fortunes. The property at Compton Pauncefoot was sold in 1646 (I have the deed of sale, signed by Alexander's father Edward), and the remaining estates, now apparently centred on Radipole in Dorset, were sequestered under the Commonwealth.

But the Keyneses did not leave the ranks of the landed gentry without a struggle. Alexander's wife Sarah made a strenuous attempt to recover her husband's property after his removal abroad, claiming that she had been born and brought up a Protestant, that she had been forced to marry the recusant Alexander Keynes when only twelve years old, and that she now had six small children ready to perish; she claimed further that her husband had lately died on the Continent and that she should be entitled to her share of his property. She won her case, but soon afterwards it was discovered that her evidence of Alexander's death was forged, so she was arrested with her co-conspirators and Radipole was re-sequestered. Clearly not one to give up easily, Sarah subsequently petitioned Charles II and managed to gain £1000 'in consideration of the services and sufferings of her late husband'. The family's fortunes must have been at a low ebb when Alexander's son Henry accosted two men in a beerhouse in Wiltshire 'and, without any provocation, called them informing rogues, who deserved to have their brains beaten out, and then fell upon them and beat them out of the house, and would have killed them but for the company present'.

In the following generations the family passed into respectable obscurity, though it changed its religious spots and moved about more freely than it had before. Richard Keynes, son of Henry, and his numerous children lie buried in the churchyard at Wareham in Dorset. Richard's grandson, another Richard, moved to Salisbury, and this Richard's grandson, the fifth Richard in succession, became a Congregational minister at Blandford and was the author of several published sermons. I have found only one of these, printed in 1825. It is a powerful discourse on 'The beneficent Influence of Wisdom and Knowledge', concluding with 'the fact, the delightful fact, WISDOM AND KNOWLEDGE SHALL BE THE STABILITY OF THE TIMES'.

The Reverend Richard had several sons and four of them emigrated to Australia to found a prosperous line of large-scale sheep farmers centred on Keynton in South Australia, with whom we maintain friendly relations. Other sons, however, remained in England and probably account for the distant cousins who tend to appear in unexpected places. Some years ago, in conversation with the custodian of the Swannery at Abbotsbury, I was told of a colourful local character called Monty Keynes. The custodian pulled out of his breast pocket a photograph of Monty, who, it appeared, was a deep drinker and teller of tall stories, greatly prized by his friends.

The Reverend Richard's younger brother, John Keynes, stayed in Salisbury and was my great-grandfather. My grandfather, another John Keynes, was born in 1805, and as a young man took part in the family business of 'brush-making' —production, that is, of high-quality brushes. But he became more interested in horticulture and finally left the family business to be a professional horticulturist, specializing in roses and dahlias. He made a great success of his floral nurseries, though my brother always believed that he never kept any accounts at all—I do not know what evidence he had of this. Hanging in my bathroom is an illuminated 'Address to John Keynes Esq.' dated 9 November 1877 from the City of New Sarum, thanking him 'for the kindness, courtesy and efficiency with which he had discharged the office of Chief Magistrate during the past year'. He was certainly a popular figure in Salisbury and on one occasion entertained 10,000 citizens with an exhibition of dahlias at Stonehenge. He was twice married and my father, John Neville Keynes, born in 1852, was the only child of his second wife, Anna Maynard Neville.

I have no memories of my grandfather, as he died in 1878, several years before I was born. My grandmother Keynes had been brought from Salisbury by my father to live in Cambridge, at 56 Bateman Street near the Botanic Gardens, before I came on the scene. She lived alone with a small domestic staff and we were encouraged to visit her very often. She was compounded of kindness and affection, and we devoured innumerable Sally Lunn tea cakes at her table. She had a nice sense of mild humour and one of her favourite stories, as I remember it, was of a Congregational minister of her acquaintance who had occasion to offer up a prayer during a drought. 'Lord,' he said, 'please give us rain—drizzle drozzle, drizzle drozzle, for about a week.' My father took us to Bateman Street on most Sunday afternoons when we were in Cambridge and relieved the possible tedium of family conversation by reading to us from Dickens. He was a good reader and in this way we were guided through *David Copperfield* and other classic works with great enjoyment and benefit. My grandmother died suddenly in 1905 and I recall being taken up to her bedroom to pay my last respects. It was my first experience of a death in the family and, being young, I thought it was my duty to kiss the empurpled cheek of the dear departed. I can never forget the chill horror of the contact and have ever since avoided even seeing any of my relations after death. They should be remembered as they were in life.

My father had an elder half-sister who married a prosperous grocer and lived into her hundredth year. My eldest grandson, Adrian—his other grandfather was Lord Adrian of Cambridge —married one of her descendants, a fact totally unknown to us until some time afterwards. My great-grandson, Robert Keynes, therefore has a double dose of the right genes.

Having given a sketch of my brother's and my own male line of descent, I feel it would shew lack of balance if I ignored the features Maynard might have inherited from my mother's side. She was born, Florence Ada Brown, in 1862 and died in 1958 within a few days of her ninety-sixth birthday. Little is known of the early history of either of her parents' forebears, but she

had clear memories of her mother's father, David Everard
Ford, born in 1797 of a family living near Lancing in Sussex.
Her great-grandfather, David Ford, born in 1765, had, as she
related in her memoirs, 'an unpropitious start in life' owing to
the misdemeanours of his uncle and father. In order to avoid
the heavy import duties imposed by the government on al-
coholic liquors they had embarked on a large-scale business as
smugglers, landing the barrels on the beaches near Lancing and
hiding them in secret storage places on the Sussex Downs. In
January 1768 they had the misfortune to encounter the
excisemen and David's father was killed in the affray. Dr.
Johnson would have excused their action, defining 'Excise' in
his *Dictionary* (1755) as: 'A hateful tax levied upon com-
modities, and adjudged not by the common judge of property,
but [by] wretches hired by those to whom excise is paid.' For
this reason my brother felt a wry satisfaction in the thought that
his ancestor had been a convicted smuggler; but the boy
David was only three years old at the time and became unhappy after his mother had remarried. He therefore left home,
aged thirteen, to seek his fortune elsewhere, and in July 1776
recorded in his diary that 'I was placed by Providence in
London', with the surprising result that, instead of 'going to the
bad', as do so many adventurers in the metropolis, he 'went to
the good'. Encouraged by a legacy from his smuggling uncle,
he engaged in business with a hatter in Lombard Street. He
there had the wisdom to listen to good advice from his elders
and began training in a college for the Nonconformist ministry.
This led to his meeting and marrying Mary Everard, daughter
of a silk manufacturer belonging to the Baptist persuasion. He
had already obtained a charge in Long Melford in Suffolk, and
there he lived for the rest of his life as minister of the Congregationalist chapel. He lies buried under a large slab at one
side of the chapel where he preached.

Melford is only a few miles from where I now live and I have
often visited the chapel, with its plain but quietly attractive
appointments, and talked with the female minister living in the
adjoining manse. The inscription on David Ford's stone slab
has been badly worn by the hobnailed boots of the Suffolk
farmers and to my dismay I have been unable to find a stone-

mason competent to do the recutting. It is noteworthy that
David Ford was much interested in collecting fossils and, like
the young Charles Darwin, was tortured by misgivings as to
what bearing they might have on his religious beliefs. His
grandson, also David, followed him in the ministry at Melford,
but is not commemorated there.

The eldest son, David Everard Ford, also followed his father
in the Congregational ministry and settled at Lymington in
Hampshire in 1821. According to my mother's account he was
a formidable old gentleman, both in his looks and behaviour.
He had a massive frame and a handsome bearded face with
brilliant dark brown eyes surmounted by a shock of white hair.
He was usually clothed in a long frock coat and wore a tall silk
hat. He had a gouty leg, which made walking difficult. She remembered that at the age of six she had to go into his study to
be given a Bible from her father. Her grandfather was seated
in a remote corner of the large room and from behind his long
churchwarden pipe came a stentorian voice asking, 'Do you
love Jesus?' She wished to sink through the floor, but somehow
got herself across the room. In later life David Everard Ford
retired from the ministry and interested himself in hymnology,
which he afterwards rejected as too frivolous.

When about thirty-seven years old, David Everard Ford
married Jane Elizabeth Down, whose grandfather had been a
Langdon; he was in turn related to the Haydon family. These
alliances brought me my second name, Langdon, and a great-
uncle, Dr. Langdon Down. The Haydons reached back to John
de Haydon, a follower of the Conqueror, and took in on the way
Benjamin Robert Haydon, the historical painter, friend of
Keats and Coleridge. Dr. Langdon Down was an eminent
physician, whose special interest was mental deficiency. He was
the founder of a private home for patients with mental defects,
called Normansfield,[1] and was the first to describe the congenital mental defect formerly known as 'mongolism', now
changed to 'Down's syndrome' in deference to the feelings of
our Far Eastern friends. One of my Down cousins married an-

[1] Recently the subject of an investigation into maladministration following
its absorption into the National Health Service—without reflecting in any
way on the reputation of its founder.

other distinguished physician and neurologist, Russell Brain (afterwards Lord Brain), who succeeded Sir Henry Head at the London Hospital.

Our grandmother, Ada Haydon Brown, daughter of David Everard Ford, inherited some of his rather formidable qualities, with dark good looks and a strong mind of her own. During the South African war she annoyed her family by being, like some other Liberals, aggressively pro-Boer. While bringing up a large family, she ran a successful school for girls in Bedford. Dr. John Brown, whom she married in 1859, was born in 1830 of Scottish descent and brought up in Sweet Green, Bolton-le-Moors, in Lancashire. As a boy he loved to wander over the moorland, sleeping out on the hillside, very much as I did on the South Downs above Arundel when a medical student in London. John Brown was a bookish boy and, after his first employment in a solicitor's office, while also studying theology in the evenings with a Congregational minister, was apprenticed to a bookseller and printer. He was released from this when his employer died, and then matriculated at London University, gaining a scholarship at Lancaster Independent College. His next move was to Owen's College, Manchester, and while there he acted as minister to a Congregational meeting at Park Chapel, which he saved from extinction by organizing it as the nucleus of a properly constituted church. In the course of this he came to know the family of David Everard Ford and married my grandmother. John Brown had by then acquired a reputation as a brilliant theologian endowed with a witty mind and a sense of drama. These qualities combined to make him an effective preacher so that in 1860 he was invited to officiate as minister at the Bunyan Meeting House in Bedford, the centre in England for Congregationalism. There he reigned with great distinction as a preacher and Liberal politician for thirty-eight years, and until he retired and left Bedford in 1903. He died in London at the age of ninety-four. He had enjoyed his life with my grandmother for sixty-three years, and she also lived beyond the age of ninety.

When we were children the family always spent Christmas at the Manse in Dame Alice Street, Bedford. In those days Christmas was usually 'white', with a hard frost, and we practised skating on the Great Ouse River. The draughty Manse had no central heating and we enjoyed being out in the snow. There were no motor cars, lorries, or tankers to spoil the countryside and we knew how to live happily without them; my first experience of motoring was in a truck at Bedford offering a joy-ride for two or three miles for a fee of tuppence. Another first experience in Bedford was a visit to a circus with performing animals. On that occasion a lioness had been disobedient and done her performance badly, and I happened to witness her punishment. She had been shut up in a narrow cage and was being savagely prodded with a steel-pointed pole. Ever since that I have loathed seeing animals perform and have avoided the circus. It is not only cruel but an insult to the animals' dignity.

My grandfather Brown, though an intellectual puritan, had a great sense of humour and was a friendly companion. I was allowed to go freely into his study, where I became familiar with such objects as Bunyan's chair, his staff, and his small oak cabinet, all now preserved, together with his anvil, in the Bunyan Museum. Sunday was fully observed in the Manse, with family prayers before breakfast, ourselves kneeling at horsehair chairs or settees with the maids standing in the background. We were not even allowed to play Snap because it was 'a card game' and we had to attend the morning service at Bunyan Meeting. I can still see quite clearly my grandfather in his pulpit high above the congregation, with his white pointed beard, healthy pink face, and piercing blue eyes, preaching in his silvery voice to a rapt audience below.

As minister he naturally became deeply interested in Bunyan and his works, and after ten years of careful and enjoyable research he published in 1885 his *Life of Bunyan*; this is still the standard life, except for the revision in a later edition of a passage relating to Bunyan's confinement in a tiny prison on Bedford Bridge over the Ouse. When a tercentenary edition of the work was published in 1928, I contributed a checklist of John Brown's books and pamphlets, which included the classic study of *The Pilgrim Fathers of New England*, *Apostolic Succession in the Light of History*, and *Puritan Preaching in England*, all works of scholarship and wide knowledge. My brother felt an immense respect for his grandfather, though I think the elder author might have been puzzled by the signed copy of *Indian Finance and Currency* which he was given.

My father, John Neville Keynes, born and brought up in Salisbury, was educated first at the Cathedral School and then at a small private school, Amersham Hall, near Reading. There he came under the influence of Ebenezer West, a headmaster with very high standards, who produced a succession of re-markable pupils. One of them, Sir Buckston Browne, a surgeon, wrote in a letter to *The Times* in 1932 that 'Ebenezer taught the boys so to live that they "feared the grave as little as their bed" in the hope of "rising glorious at the Judgement Day", in the meantime it being almost essential to ultimate salvation that they should pass the London Matric. on their way through it'.[1] My father responded to the pressure and matriculated there at the age of seventeen with a scholarship in University Hall, where he worked diligently, up to twelve hours a day, for three years. He entered Pembroke College, Cambridge, in 1872 with a minor scholarship in Mathematics, but did not like this subject, and although gaining a foundation scholarship at the end of the first year, turned to Moral Science. He more than justified the change by becoming Senior Moralist in the Tripos two years later and Gold Medallist in Moral Science the next year in the London M.A. This was in 1876 and in the same year he was elected Fellow of both Pembroke College, Cambridge, and University College, London. He was clearly set for an academic life and there could be no doubt of his intellectual eminence. He lost much of his hair early in life and, as a small boy, I often found myself gazing in awe at his impressive bald head trying to picture to myself what was going on inside it. I concluded that there must be a constant churning of noiseless wheels to operate the complicated intellectual processes with which it was busy.

In 1876 my father started lecturing on Logic and Political Economy, supplementing his income by private coaching, but in 1880 he turned to administration, being appointed Assistant Secretary to the Local Examinations and Lectures Syndicate

[1] *Gathering up the Threads*, p. 45.

under G. F. Browne, later Bishop of Bristol. This was his ap-
prenticeship in administration, and in due course he became
Secretary to the Syndics, in 1892, and the next year Secretary
to the Council of the University of Cambridge. I have the impression that in this capacity he propped up for some years the
work of the acting Registrary, J. W. Clark, a distinguished
character but not a very efficient official, with the result that
when my father was appointed Registrary in succession to
'J.W.', in 1910, he carried on as Secretary to the Council, filling
both posts so well that in 1924 the two offices were permanently
merged under the title of Registrary. He then retired, having
reached the age of seventy-two. He had administered the affairs
of the University for thirty-three years and, though he would
not have admitted it (he was the most modest man imagin-
able), kept a long succession of Vice-Chancellors on the straight
and narrow path of duty. He was quiet and gentle and not a
man of many words. Sir Gerald Kelly, P.R.A., painted two
excellent portraits of him in 1927 and kept him awake during
the sittings with many amusing reminiscences of life in Cambridge, but Sir Gerald told me later that he extracted very
little information from my father in return—though I think
that may have been partly because he was given very little
opportunity to speak.

In his later years my father was pleased to recall that his first
pupil, of the few young students in Moral Science from Girton
and Newnham whom he coached, had been Constance Jones,
afterwards Mistress of Girton. In his speech at the presentation
of his portrait to Pembroke in 1927, he said of his experiences at
Girton: 'I well remember the trepidation with which I gave
instruction to this lady [Constance Jones], accompanied by the
click of knitting needles of Miss Bernard, then Mistress of
Girton, who in conformity with the conventions of those days
thought it unsuitable to leave us tête-à-tête.' These chaperones
served, I suspect, not only to preserve the proprieties between
teacher and pupil, but also to guard against loss of students by
romantic attachments that might develop between them.

Another pupil of my father's was the youngest student at
Newnham Hall, who had entered in October 1878. This was
Florence Brown, a shy girl of eighteen, whose intelligence soon

attracted the notice of Miss Clough, the Principal. Miss Clough, as my mother learned, had let it be known that Miss Brown's family had expressed a wish that Florence should not go out very much. How then did it happen that the promising student was snatched away from under the noses of the College authorities, to their very great annoyance, before she had completed her course? Miss Clough's efforts to protect her were in vain, and she and my father became engaged in 1880. Mrs. Brown told the young man it was very lucky that she approved of him; she would not have allowed her daughter to go to anyone she did not like.

The escape route for my mother had been the house in Brookside where the Bond family lived. William Bond was the founder of the large grocery in Trinity Street under the name Hallack and Bond, a first-class shop which has disappeared only in recent times. I have many early memories of visits to the Bonds' hospitable house, where they had a large conservatory for nurturing an array of monstrous chrysanthemums, then fashionably cultivated under the belief that 'big is beautiful', and of course the blooms had to be bigger than anyone else could shew. I did my best to admire them, but secretly found them rather repulsive. William Bond was a Congregationalist friend of Florence's father, as he had been of John Keynes, so that Florence was able to meet the young Pembroke don there without question. Henry Bond, the son of the family, who later became Master of Trinity Hall, was a close friend of my father's. When I was old enough to feel sympathy with older people, I did feel sorry for Henry Bond's sister, Minnie. She was by then an elderly spinster with a gentle charm, and must so obviously have been a candidate for my mother's position in 1880. But I was very, very glad she had not made it! I had no wish for a different mother.

My parents' engagement was prolonged, as was then the custom, and they were not married until 12 August 1882, at Bunyan Meeting in Bedford. We have my father's intimate diary for the 1881–2 period,[1] and it is plain that they were very

[1] All the later volumes, dealing mainly with University affairs, have been deposited in the University Library, where they may be consulted by approved historians.

happy lovers, though he sometimes tortured himself with the thought that he might not be worthy of his bride. When he married he had to resign his Fellowship at Pembroke because of the rule of celibacy. This had already been rescinded at some other Colleges, and Pembroke followed suit two years later; it was not until 1924, after forty-two years, that he was made an Honorary Fellow.

6 HARVEY ROAD

DURING his engagement my father had bought a ninety-nine years' lease of a newly built semi-detached house in Harvey Road, on land belonging to Caius College. At the end of the road to the east was Fenner's cricket ground. Not far away to the south were open fields where our butcher, Mr. Bulman, grazed his cattle. The house with its basement, three storeys above, and small garden at the back had no special charm or character. The architect had used the pallid local bricks—'corpse bricks' we used to call them—and the building was inevitably 'Victorian' in appearance, but it suited our unexacting standards. The staircases were very steep and my mother in her old age had fallen down the flight from her bedroom three times without serious injury before she died there after seventy-six years' tenancy.

The furnishings were undistinguished but comfortable, some having stood in my father's rooms in Pembroke. The walls of the rather dark dining room were clad in deep blue and crimson William Morris paper of such quality that, except for occasional patching, it never needed renewal. The pictures were conventional examples of period taste, the most clearly remembered being a large reproduction of Raphael's *Virgin and Child*, such as might have been seen in a hundred other homes of the same class. In the narrow hall was a print of Reynolds's *Garrick between Comedy and Tragedy*. The few oil paintings had been bought in Salisbury, by my grandfather Keynes. He had been advised by a Mr. Tiffin, regarded as an authority on contemporary art, but apart from a modest canvas by Morland, his purchases were of small interest. It was tantalizing to find many years later, when going through the letters of Blake's friend, John Linnell, that Tiffin had had some

My mother and father on their golden wedding day, 15 August 1932

interest in Blake's work and had asked Linnell to let him see the family collection. However, it is most unlikely that this would have led to any of Blake's pictures being bought by my grandfather.

Our home surroundings thus afforded no aesthetic stimulus of modernity or novelty to our expanding consciousnesses, though Maynard was fully exposed to the intellectual stimulus provided by our academic society. Home was all middle-class comfort and security, providing an ideal atmosphere for a highly individual intelligence like my brother's to develop, unfettered by parental dominance or prejudice. Our parents, as I now look back on them, had a lovable aura of perfect integrity and goodness without stuffiness or pomposity; they were affectionate without sentimentality, and were careful not to interfere with the personalities of their children, while always ready to foster any worthwhile interests as soon as they discerned them.

My father, in any situation of uncertainty, assumed a settled attitude of being 'prepared for the worst'—whether it was the uncertain result of an examination or, on one occasion, the long-overdue return of Maynard from an Alpine expedition with the celebrated climber Geoffrey Young and his brother Hilton. But Father was never really justified in pessimism over any of our careers. He always took a deep interest in our school work and set great store by our marks and position in class, and this stimulated a sense of competition, particularly in Maynard, who enjoyed his own capacity for learning and leaping ahead of the other boys. His relations with my father were very close and he was devoted to my mother throughout his life. There was never in our family any of the antagonism now so frequent between the generations.

Maynard was born on 5 June 1883, my sister Margaret followed in February 1885, and myself on 25 March 1887, rather less than four years after my brother. All my young days were therefore lived under the shadow of a far more forceful and intellectual character than my own. Not that Maynard was ever unkind or domineering; our relation was the natural result of the elder leading not so much by virtue of being a few years older as by inborn advantages of mind. We were not close friends and my view of him was more that of an eminent acquaintance to whom I looked up as a superior and somewhat distant being.

I have no memories of his taking part in nursery life, for he had passed out of this stage before I was old enough to be conscious of his presence. He moved in another sphere and it is impossible to imagine him under the dominance of a nurse or governess. He had the reputation in the family of having always been able to get the better of them in any argument, though being much too intelligent to be conventionally 'naughty'. My mother has recorded that his mind set itself difficult problems from an early age. 'Who invented Time?' he asked at the age of six. 'How did things get their names?' 'Just now', he said, 'my brain is wondering how it thinks. It ought to know.'

Although both our parents had been brought up in a sincerely held Congregationalist faith, my mother strictly so, at Harvey Road we enjoyed a more relaxed view of religious duties and observances. The whole family attended every Sunday morning the service at Emmanuel Church opposite Pembroke and listened to a highly intellectual sermon lasting for anything up to three-quarters of an hour. To me this seemed to be interminable and very tedious, though Maynard was usually attentive and at Eton in his teens he recorded in his diary the preachers' names and his opinion of their sermons, sometimes in forthright terms of indignation. He always felt an intellectual interest in religion, but at the age of seventeen or eighteen passed painlessly, as did my sister and I, into a natural state of agnosticism. None of us was subject to any kind of pressure in matters of religion, each taking his or her own course. Rather surprisingly, when we had all ceased to go to Sunday services, our parents followed suit, without any discussion or outward show of unease.

Maynard and I each went at the age of nine to St. Faith's day school in the Trumpington Road, where Ralph Goodchild was both founder and headmaster, but owing to the four years between us we did not overlap. Goodchild had a very high opinion of Maynard's abilities. He was, he said, 'head and shoulders above all the other boys both physically and mentally', for he was growing very fast. Goodchild was not at all

G.L.K. as a pretty boy in a lace collar, *c.* 1893

SAINT PETER'S COLLEGE LIBRARY
JERSEY CITY, NEW JERSEY 07306

Miss Ratcliffe's Dancing Class: Margaret Keynes, Geoffrey Keynes, Iris Morgan, Ruth Darwin. From a drawing by Gwen Darwin (Raverat) for her book *Period Piece*

surprised when Maynard became a King's Scholar at Eton in July 1897. The family waited anxiously for news of the examination results, my father having, of course, made up his mind to face failure. When the telegram came through announcing my brother's success we happened all to be standing together in the garden at Harvey Road. I well remember how, with a small boy's impulsive enthusiasm, I flung my arms round Maynard's neck, only to be pushed impatiently away. He was too old, being already fourteen, for such demonstrations of affection.

While my brother was pursuing his brilliant course through St. Faith's and Eton, I was making my more humdrum progress through a series of schools. The first was a 'kindergarten' for tiny children followed by a Dame's School under Miss Hattie Johnson, sister of the philosopher W. E. Johnson, but of these I have no memories. Then followed nearly five years at St. Faith's, where I was a very ordinary pupil. The incident I remember most vividly from those years was my being an unwilling witness of a boy being flogged in front of the whole school. I was deeply affected by the brutality of the punishment for what seemed to me a trivial offence. It appeared that this rather senior boy had been caught somewhere in the school precincts inciting two smaller boys to a competition to see who could urinate furthest up a wall. A gardener had overheard the words used and reported to the headmaster, who took a very serious view of the offence, which it seemed to me could have been dismissed with a reprimand and a smile. Many years later I found a charming wood engraving of about 1790 by the great artist Thomas Bewick, of Newcastle upon Tyne, illustrating a similar incident in which the two boys are standing at the edge of a pond, the competition being in distance rather than height.

The Border War: wood engraving by
Thomas Bewick

(It will be seen that one of the boys is wearing a Scottish bonnet and that the other has an English cap; I am told that the scene is sometimes known as 'The Border War', but have been unable to find out if it was ever used in a book.) What Bewick had regarded as a harmless joke, the Victorian schoolmaster magnified into a major offence demanding brutal punishment.

Harvey Road was obviously named to commemorate the residence in Caius College of Dr. William Harvey as an undergraduate at the end of the sixteenth century, but I am sure it had no influence on my choice of a medical career, or on my special interest in Harvey's life and works. The decision was made very early in my life. My mother remembered that she had found me on the nursery floor at the age of three making a close study of a book with diagrams of the circulation of the blood, and I am convinced that this was the true origin of my choice. It never changed or even wavered, relieving my parents of any uncertainty in directing the course of my education. As a small boy, my only parlour trick that had any success was an impersonation of our family physician, Dr. Wherry, a tall man with a long melancholy face and manner. I do not blame him for not diagnosing a serious abdominal condition when I was about ten years old. I remember vividly the pain and persistent vomiting, uncontrolled by the physician, who declared after my recovery that I had narrowly escaped 'an attack of jaundice'. 'Appendicitis' was unknown before 1900, and only became generally recognized after King Edward VII had to postpone his Coronation because of an operation for appendicitis with an abscess. Not long before, I had heard about the tragic death of R. A. Neil, a Fellow of Pembroke, from general peritonitis due to the same cause. My own trouble lay dormant for fifty years until it endangered my life by an unusual complication, identified at operation.

During our childhood the long summer holidays were the most important event in our lives, routine being replaced by life, lasting for six weeks, in the country. During my infancy the holidays were spent at Overstrand on the Norfolk coast, but of this I have only the vaguest memory. By the time I was six we were going much further afield, and for four years in succession went to Lealholm Hall, a totally self-sufficient farm in a hamlet above Glaisdale, about ten miles from Whitby, in an area of Yorkshire surrounded by unspoiled moorland.

My parents shewed the best of good sense in making this choice. For me, at least, there was never a dull moment. I was utterly happy, taking part in all the farm activities. Mrs. Redman, the farmer's wife, was childless and treated us with affectionate care; she even allowed us into the dairy to admire with greedy eyes the pans of creamy cream and to help with the butter- and cheese-making in a churn. We had full knowledge about the calving of cows and had learnt the Facts of Life without surprise or shock. After trying vainly to milk the cows, however, I had to admit that my sister could do it much better

Geoffrey and Margaret in a Victorian drawing room at 6 Harvey Road, *c.* 1895

Margaret and Geoffrey at Lealholm, 1895

G.L.K. looking for trout in the beck at Lealholm, 1895

—she seemed to be a natural milkmaid, which was allowable in a girl.

The poultry wandered all over the farm and had no settled place for laying their eggs, or rather, they settled it themselves. Mrs. Redman knew all the hiding places where eggs were likely to be found. When meat was wanted they slaughtered one of their own animals humanely and when a sheep had been skinned, Mrs. Redman herself would reduce its carcase to joints of meat. There was a blacksmith's shop for shoeing the splendid farm horses and a wheelwright in the person of Old Willie, Mrs. Redman's father, who superintended the shrinking of new iron tyres on to the wheels of the great waggons when the old ones were worn. Apart from that, he mostly sat about smoking his pipe and watching the others with critical eye.

At a large pond close by I could watch the ducks and drakes performing their normal functions, and I can remember seeing two young cousins standing on the edge doing exactly what Bewick had drawn in his wood engraving. We kept out of the way of the geese; they hissed and were the only unfriendly beings about the farm.

Half a mile away there was a piece of wild woodland with a beck running through it where we could create little lakes by damming up the stream. If I were alone I would sometimes catch small trout in the beck, using the traditional tackle of a home-made rod and a bent pin transfixing a worm. The bait was landed on the bed of the stream and I would stand motion-less until it was taken; the fish was then suddenly jerked out on to the bank before it knew what had happened.

In the evenings I would sometimes go with a young farm hand to see what rabbits we could find in the cruel snares set in the morning; but a more productive source of rabbit meat was a large warren in the corner of a field near the house, where the animals could breed as fast as they liked, apparently never learning that the small hut in one corner was a hide which Mr. Redman with his gun could reach unseen, to pick them off unerringly the moment they peered out of their holes.

The grand event of the season was always the harvest. The farmer had one rather primitive horse-drawn mowing machine with a rotating fan to push the stems towards the cutting knife, but more was done by reapers who knew how to keep their scythes swinging rhythmically by the hour, only relaxing as they approached the final swathes, ready to chase the rabbits as they tried to escape their doom by rushing out of the last remains of standing corn. Marvell's poem had come to life if only I had known it. We helped by plaiting girdles of straw to bind the sheaves and then stooking them as fast as our strength allowed, while the Real Men laughed at us. At the morning break, Mrs. Redman and her maid would bring urns of tea out to the field and rich buttery scones, still warm and speckled with raisins, known as 'fat rascals'. After dark we could sit in one of the large barns adjoining the great threshing machine, worked by a hidden engine, to listen to a singsong by the men while they twisted straw into dollies in traditional fashion. I recall our astonishment when, one evening, one of them produced a large and elaborate bird-cage made of the same material. I would not attempt to write a full-scale description of this annual event because it might seem to compete with the late Herbert Read's long account of an almost exactly similar experience, over a longer period, in his essay 'The Innocent Eye' (included in his book *The Contrary Experience*, 1963). Read, writing with the perceptions of a poet, has documented the experience with a child's clear-eyed enjoyment of unsophisticated pleasures.

It was during this period that, at the age of about nine, I began to take an interest in entomology, that is, in collecting butterflies and moths and in studying their life histories. My childish enthusiasm soon attracted my father's attention and led him to extend his natural instinct for 'collecting', hitherto focused only on postage stamps, to include butterflies. This was greatly to my advantage, since he did not grudge adding some of his pocket-money to mine so that we could acquire all the apparatus necessary for the hobby. Not far from our home in Cambridge was Mr. Farren's shop, which announced that its proprietor was 'Furrier and Taxidermist'. I did not know the meaning of these strange words, but soon understood that he could supply everything a boy's heart could desire in the pursuit of natural history. His charges were moderate and were an-

Aurelians in Yorkshire on a hot day, August 1897

nounced with the most wonderful Cimebridgeshire accent I had ever heard. To hear him drawling out the names of villages, such as Babraham, was a great joy, and he was always generous in his business dealings. Sometimes I saw in the shop a boy with a curiously sleepy appearance owing to his inability to raise his eyelids properly (doctors name this 'ptosis'); the appearance was most misleading, for the sleepy-looking boy became, as Sir William Farren, F.R.S., one of the leading mathematicians and physicists in the country and of immense value to the wartime science of aeronautics.

My father's munificence eventually provided a full supply of boxes containing the necessary sizes of setting boards, silver pins for impaling the insects we collected, chloroform for stupefying them, nicotine for killing them, glass-bottomed pill boxes to take them home in, and so on. Some refinements in technique came later, in a large-scale enterprise covering much of Europe; but Lealholm saw the beginning, with the rather dangerous cyanide 'killing bottle' and its menacing smell. The butterflies of the moors were hard to catch; easier prey were the plentiful caterpillars of the splendid Emperor moths, Oak-eggers, Drinkers, and other large moths for breeding in properly built cages. After dark came the exciting pastime of finding moths in a state of inebriation on the patches of 'sugar' —a sticky mixture of molasses and beer laced with the attractive scent of aniseed—previously spread on trees and gateposts.

I have sometimes wondered whether this form of collecting may not have implanted in my young mind a moral lesson. Ever since I was a boy I have been filled with disgust by the sight of a drunken man and though not myself an abstainer I have never been anywhere near the brink of drunkenness. If my friends over-indulged themselves, I found the spectacle to be a pitiful loss of control and dignity rather than amusing, as it usually seems to be to others. I have learned that the greatest part of ill health in the population at large is due to the self-inflicted wounds suffered from alcohol and tobacco, twin social ills which common sense seems to be unable to influence or check. My brother Maynard is said to have remarked near the end of his life that one of his chief regrets was that he had not drunk enough champagne; but this was not to be taken to mean that he had ever wished to be tipsy. My impression is that he never drank much alcohol in any form; he only regretted that he had neglected one of the best sources of moderate enjoyment. As a medical student I was judged to be 'unclubbable' because I never joined in public-house sessions to drink beer in happy brotherhood. I have never been able to drink except when thirsty; then it is most enjoyable. Perhaps my 'aversion' (to use a psychotherapeutic term) began with watching stupid moths suffering capture and death through indulgence in alcohol.

Even if the suggestion of moral gain from entomology is unfounded, there can be no doubt of the value it had in training my hands for the delicate manipulations needed for success in my later career as a surgeon. I was taught from the beginning not to waste butterfly life by spoiling them. The greatest care and attention had to be devoted to the art of spreading and fixing their wings on the setting boards where they were left until their bodies had dried out.

By the time I was fourteen and about to go off to public school, I was beginning to extend my interests beyond butterflies and moths, though not giving them up. I had found another boy with similar tastes, Ivor Evans, living on the other side of Harvey Road, and we decided to start issuing a periodical, *The Enthusiast*, which flourished from May 1901 to May 1904, twelve numbers. Most of the informative text was written in my hand; it was fully illustrated with photographs and drawings, many in colour, some of them done by a third boy whose talents lay in making copies from books and other sources.

Ivor and I were mainly reporting the results of our own expeditions. We covered birds (Ivor's father, A. H. Evans, was one of the leading ornithologists of his day), entomology, geology, and archaeology. We were much encouraged by Professor McKenny Hughes, Woodwardian Professor of Geology, who each year used to conduct a party of young people in brakes and on bicycles for a long day on the Roman Road, in those days a perfect unofficial nature reserve, unspoilt by intensive cultivation or motor bicycles. Ivor's and my activities could only be carried on during the school holidays, but we wasted no time and ranged over the country in all directions. One of the most productive places was Monk's Wood, where we could find the rare Black Hairstreak (*Thecla pruni*). This piece of ancient woodland was then surrounded by a large area of fallow land which made it an exceptionally productive hunting ground for naturalists. Monk's Wood has now been constituted an official nature reserve with an associated research station.

Another quite extraordinary site was the pit at Barrington, only seven miles from Cambridge, where gravel and clay for brick-making were excavated. The site had been a swamp, or perhaps an eddy in a large post-glacial river, where the bodies of all kinds of animals accumulated during the Pleistocene era, some 70,000 years ago. Their bones were scattered among the deposits laid down on the river bed waiting to be collected by boys fascinated by the perfection of their only semi-fossilized state. They had only to be washed and soaked in a warm bath of diluted carpenter's glue to form museum objects of worship. The workmen sometimes put aside the beautiful hippopotamus teeth to be traded for a shilling each.

Better still, enterprising boys were allowed to dig for themselves and to take away what they could find. I was the proud donor of a rhinoceros skull to the Woodwardian Museum in Cambridge, where for many years it could be seen in a glass case, until it was replaced by a better specimen obtained when the authorities chose before it was too late to excavate in a systematic way for these wonderful treasures. I had the bones and horncores of the huge prehistoric ox, *Bos primigenius*, the jaw of a cave-lion, and innumerable other specimens. Ivor Evans had found the skull of an elk and, best of all, the whole lower jaw of an outsize hippopotamus with all four ivory tusks intact, each nearly two feet long. This made an impressive photograph for the pages of *The Enthusiast*.

On one occasion I was invited by Dr. Lloyd Jones, a friendly practitioner in Cambridge, to help him rescue the complete skull of an elephant, found at Barrington by a labourer in his employ. One curving ivory tusk six feet long was extracted intact, but the main part of the specimen, since we could not command the right technique, crumbled to a thousand pieces in our hands.

One serious embarrassment was the size and weight of our prizes, which were difficult to bring home on bicycles. Sometimes we travelled by rail to Foxton, the nearest station to Barrington, and once, when we had missed the last train home, anxious parents sent a fly[1] to pick up two weary boys carrying heavy bags of bones, which they would not have abandoned under any circumstances. For days after these expeditions the whole house in Harvey Road would smell strongly of carpenter's glue.

A third much favoured site was the one just above the large chalk pit at Cherry Hinton. The pit itself was an excellent nature reserve and in the area above it were the rather mysterious 'War Ditches'. These were an irregular system of Romano-British trenches the lower strata of which were rich in fragments of rough pottery decorated with patterns in white, red, or blue paste—slip-ware, I think it was called. Sometimes we found human bones, and once I found a large rounded lump of clay such as is used as a support when pots are fired in a kiln, shewing that some of the pottery was made on the spot.

On one occasion I accompanied a party of older antiquaries on a visit to Grime's Graves, the neolithic flint mines near Brandon. We were equipped with picks and shovels, though I cannot tell what we were expected to achieve, since the flint mines were thirty feet in depth. All I remember is throwing a shovelful of earth over Howard Marsh, the Master of Downing and Professor of Surgery, and picking up a large palaeolithic axe head with the white patina suggesting that it had lain there for millennia before the flints were mined.

My companion in most of these exploits, Ivor Evans, afterwards went his own way apart from mine, becoming a noted anthropologist, working chiefly in Borneo. I don't remember his taking any part in the rescue of medieval pottery when the excavations were being made for the underground lavatories in the Cambridge market-place. I was able to piece together two almost complete specimens of the handsome large jugs with twisted handles, their upper parts covered with a beautiful

[1] A 'fly', or sometimes 'growler', was the term for the horse-drawn four-wheelers which plied for custom in the streets of Cambridge, or could be hired from Spicer's stables.

green glaze. No one seemed to have any interest in them at the time, except a friend who was a humble assistant in the Museum of Archaeology. But I was pleased to find out many years later that a friend of my own age, whom I met in 1934, Lawrence of Arabia, had been doing exactly the same thing at the same time in Oxford.

My early butterfly collection was augmented by a younger Cambridge friend who was a technician in the zoological laboratories. He would come along at intervals with specimens of the magnificent 'Large Copper' butterfly (*Lycaena dispar*), a species that had been extinct since 1850, saying they had come from an old collection he knew of made in the fens. This may well have been true and I would persuade my father to give him a few pounds for them. I have sometimes wondered whether the 'old collection' may not have been in the laboratories where my friend worked, and where they had a great many specimens, not very well looked after; he was a kind young man who knew I would be a better custodian and wanted to help me. If this was so, I am very grateful to him and no one need have any regrets: the butterflies having long since been returned in excellent condition to the University department whence they may have come.

3

RUGBY SCHOOL

In March 1901, when I reached the age of fourteen, I was aware that my father had been for some time consulting handbooks with information about the merits of the public schools. I had heard mention of the rather alarming name of Giggleswick in Yorkshire. This did not sound at all friendly and I was relieved when the wheel of chance came down on Rugby—anything rather than Giggleswick.

In September 1901 I was despatched to Rugby, being put in a train in the charge of a slightly older boy, Armie Chase, younger son of the President of Queens' College, later Bishop of Ely. Chase had already entered the school and thus was able to introduce me to the peculiarities of Rugby. I had, of course, read the alarming book, so well known as *Tom Brown's School-days*, and was uneasily wondering what rough trials I was to experience.

The cross-country train, then useful but long since abolished, landed us at Bletchley Station where we had to change for Rugby. The wait there helped, on this occasion and always afterwards, to alleviate the new boy's apprehensions by the certainty of witnessing the express train to London from the North roaring at full speed between the platforms. The huge steam engines in full action were objects of beauty and terror of which we never tired. A favourite short expedition for many Rugby boys was going to a vantage point near the railway where several of these glorious monsters were due to pass. Then came the train to Rugby, which had to negotiate what I believed to be the longest tunnel in England. At last we were decanted at Rugby with many other boys, most of whom were accustomed to facing a new term at school and were happily greeting their friends, thus accentuating my loneliness.

For some reason I was not admitted at once to the large house at School Field, so called because it was on the very edge of the school Close with its playing fields and fringe of elms. My first term being spent in a smaller house, I was thus exposed by stages to the full experience of life in a large public school.

In January 1902 I duly arrived at School Field under the housemaster William Parker Brooke. He was a kindly man, but without any particular understanding of, or special sympathy with, the minds of adolescent boys, and my feelings towards him were and remained indifferent. He was known as 'Tooler' Brooke because, as I always supposed, he habitually jingled coins in his trouser pocket. His wife, 'Ma Tooler', was a much more colourful figure. She had a loud, rather harsh, voice and an alarming manner. She undoubtedly had the remains of great beauty, but she looked much older than she really was owing to a myriad of tiny wrinkles criss-crossing the fine skin of her face. She had little sense of humour and seldom laughed, ruling the house with strong good sense. I quailed before her for several years, but in the end came to love her very dearly.

Being a timid boy, I did not make friends easily and at first tended to stick by the side of Armie Chase, who had brought me to Rugby. But it was not long before I began to fall under the spell of Rupert Brooke, son of the housemaster. His position was obviously awkward. Would the other boys feel he had been put there to spy on them and report to his father? In truth he was at School Field because his health was thought to be uncertain; he was 'delicate', liable to catch any ailment that might be around—as was indeed illustrated too tragically when he died of a bacterial infection in 1915—and his mother wanted to have him under her eye while he was at school. His preparatory school had been very near Rugby, presumably for the same reason. And throughout our time at Rugby no suspicion of him ever arose. Everybody liked him and knew that he would never do anything disloyal to his friends.

Rupert might indeed have given his father useful advice. There was one 'boy' in the house who had matured abnormally early and should not have been left among a throng of ordinary boys eager to learn. He held what were known as 'Bible classes', but I was never drawn into these gatherings and so do not know whether I lost or gained. Maybe he only imparted knowledge of things which the other boys' parents should have told them; maybe there was more in it than that. I never found out, but I do not think I lost much, having learnt all the important Facts of Life from my early observations on the Yorkshire farm.

Rupert, though a few months younger than I, was much wiser and more clever, and he soon became the friend to whom I turned with complete confidence and admiration. I was at first unaware of the physical beauty for which he afterwards became so famous. He seemed somewhat overgrown, with cropped hair and rather bowed legs, which earned him the nickname 'Bowles' among his friends.

With this friendship I should have been very happy in School Field had it not been for systematic persecution by another boy of my year. He was a violent and ruthless character with great strength whom I couldn't possibly have overcome in battle. If the little hero had stood up to the bully, it would not have been of any avail. He did not do me any serious injury, but used more subtle, cat-and-mouse tactics causing me much misery, no doubt just what he intended. Later at Cambridge we were in the same College, but there we ignored one another. I was astonished some forty-five years later when he suddenly turned up, uninvited, at my country house, wishing as it seemed to have another sight of the boy, now recently honoured by the Queen with a knighthood, whom he had once so much despised. We had a friendly conversation in which he revealed that he was then acting as a prison visitor. I did not probe into how he had spent most of his life, but it seemed that his character had changed. He was now occupied in trying to help people less fortunate than himself and possibly regretted the cruelty he had seemed to enjoy as a schoolboy. Neither of us referred to this and we parted, never to meet again.

At Rugby I was now seeing more of Rupert Brooke than of anyone else, while sharing a study with a stout, good-natured boy, Hugh Russell Smith. We made up a cheerful trio, Brooke providing most of the entertainment with a flow of hilarious nonsense. Thus we climbed up the school in parallel until we found ourselves working in the same form, known as The Twenty, under a great classical scholar, Robert Whitelaw. Brooke was at the top of the form and I was stationed firmly at the bottom, knowing that I was to be transferred in the next term to the sixth form as a science specialist, working only at physics and chemistry. But at the moment it was mostly Latin and Greek, with some English. Brooke and I often worked together in his study, where I would assume the humble task of looking up the words in the dictionaries so that he could provide the more intellectual result of a good translation. After his death I inherited the two massive volumes, Liddell and Scott (Greek) and Lewis and Short (Latin), and have used them constantly ever since, stirring memories each time I have pulled one from the shelf.

While sitting at the bottom of Whitelaw's form I tried to appear to be an industrious scholar by often writing notes during lessons. Our much respected teacher was always in utter despair concerning the apathy and stupidity of his pupils, and would reward them with satire and abuse. I therefore had much fun in writing in my notebook a verbatim report of the barbed remarks that fell from his lips, together with a good deal of saliva, on his front bench. On one occasion he treated us to an almost continuous harangue which kept my pencil busy. It was addressed primarily to one harmless boy, but was turned at intervals on to the whole class:

(*To F.A.W.:*) ' "What sort of a dative?" and he stands dumb again.' (*Asks another question.*) 'Now he stands dumb again.' (*Repeats this seven times.*) 'He doesn't try to answer. I don't believe for a moment you don't know what it means.' (*Turns to top bench.*) 'Oh goodness, is there any mortal thing they know at this top bench!—He stares at me as if he had never seen or heard it before. What's the good of staring at me like that? You are a terrible person in your manners and way of construing. Don't stand still and be dumb.—They don't see why they should exert themselves to translate well. Why should they?—I'll give you something to write if you go on like that. I cannot do with it—could anybody ever go through such torment, not only to myself, but to the whole place. Oh, stupid creature! Not taking the trouble to attach any meaning to what I'm saying. Intolerably stupid!'

Rupert Brooke was Whitelaw's godson, and perhaps for that very reason was a frequent target:

(To R.C.B.:) 'At the bottom of the Adriatic! More appropriate to say it's at the bottom of the sea!'
    'You do like to have everything vague, don't you? You like to have it all in a nice haze.'
    'Oh, you're a dreadful person! You *are* so careless.'
    'Of course you knew it wasn't the answer I wanted.'
    'Oh dear, what *do* you know.'
    'Your mind is so inert.'
    'You are perfectly incorrigible, you tiresome boy.'
    'You are beyond endurance. You are intolerable for sheer carelessness. I can only repeat the formula "You're losing all capacity for doing work".'

And so on. I was too far away to attract much notice and I had only two sentences addressed to me: 'I really thought you had some sense of decency' and, 'You science people come here thinking you know everything.' But his blue pencil was red-hot when he read and marked my written offerings; '18, bad.' '12!! write analysis 5 pages.' '16, bad, *v. bad*—you must take notes.' (I did, but not the ones he meant.) 'Terrible, write 5 pages analysis.' '13, only meagre.' It was never the same twice, but then came, '26, meagre indeed—not half learnt—but not foolish (like some).' This was praise indeed, and I was delighted. I knew he really liked me, since he continued to ask me to breakfast at his House for several terms after I had left his form. We all loved him for his enthusiasm and his genuine efforts to educate us.

By the time he was seventeen Rupert Brooke had distinguished himself in every way. He was a natural athlete and was given his school colours in both the cricket eleven and the rugby football fifteen. He was good at any game he cared to play, whereas I hated cricket and was humiliated by having to play in the lowest House team, known as 'Remnants'. Rugby football I enjoyed if I was allowed to play outside the scrum, but was not good enough to be able to play in the House team. I sometimes dreamed vainly of getting my 'cap', so that I could sport coloured velvet headgear with a gold tassel, but there was no hope of that. Brooke did not despise me for this inferiority and never had the least vanity in regard to his own prowess.

He had by now blossomed into his adolescent beauty with a perfect complexion, surely inherited from his mother, and golden hair with a reddish tinge. He was writing more poetry and getting some of it printed in school magazines. Impressed by this sign of genius, I began collecting and keeping everything he produced, the natural beginning of my bibliographical instincts with, I felt sure, a worthy object. At the same time he was trying to educate me to appreciate other greater poets. While walking in the country he would declaim Swinburne's verses which he tended to imitate, and did me much good. We cultivated a taste for the drawings of Aubrey Beardsley and an admiration for 'decadent' literature and art. He had chosen to let his hair grow to an inordinate length, declaring that it was his duty as a poet, though it flapped around his face on the football field. This was in defiance of school regulations and custom, but no one among either school or staff wished to complain of his eccentricities; in him they seemed wholly delightful. When he reached the sixth form he wore a 'puff' tie made of black silk, all to boost his self-conscious role as poet and intellectual—though I, knowing him better than most, was aware of his occasional descent into phases of deep depression and self-abasement. He was putting on an act, which we all enjoyed and encouraged.

I was not so dazzled by my friendship with Rupert that I did not make other friends. One in another House was Claude Fryer, son of a farmer from the Cambridgeshire fens. Fryer Senr. was a scientific farmer who prospered by supplying seeds of various kinds of grasses rather than ordinary crops; his son had been trained from an early age to know the delights of entomology, and was able to teach me much of those mysteries to which I was already addicted. He was even well versed in knowledge of the microlepidoptera, the smallest moths, and had discovered in a pond near Rugby the uncommon insect, *Acentrobus niveus*; its larval life was spent inside the stems of water plants, and when the moths were ready to emerge they crawled up out of the water, the male with snowy white wings, the female without any wings at all. Claude somehow always knew exactly when this was going to happen, so that we could go to watch the insects appearing in large numbers.

A boy in another House had been fortunate enough to catch a specimen of an extremely rare immigrant sphingid moth, *Deilephila livornica*, of which he made a skilful coloured drawing; this I was allowed to reproduce with my secretarial report of the entomological section of the Natural History Society—my first experiment in editing (1905). I had joined the Society in my first term and was always active in its affairs.

In the holidays I stayed with Claude Fryer and his family at Chatteris, and we spent many nights collecting the fenland moths, sometimes with the help of a lamp, as they flew among the reeds in the dykes, or were attracted to a white sheet illuminated by another acetylene lamp. As the chill of night drew on the stream of moths usually tended to tail off and might even cease. Yet we were willing to stay on watch at least until one o'clock in the morning, because there was always the chance that one or two specimens of a very drab little moth called *Hydrillula palustris* might turn up even at that late hour; such was its habit, and it was worth waiting for, since it was supposed to be very rare (possibly owing to its arriving so late at the lure that most collectors had not the patience to wait for it) and commanded a price of £3 or £4 in the entomological market. Recently the myth of the rarity of *palustris* has been rudely challenged by Mr. R. P. Demuth, who has shewn that it is widely distributed and can be quite commonly found (*Entomologist's Record*, 1979, p. 54).

Staying at Chatteris was attractive for another quite different reason. Claude's father owned some fields in the parish of Somersham not far from Chatteris where ploughmen had in the past turned up Roman coins and pottery. Recently a labourer digging for gravel in the same area had found other signs of Roman occupation, and my eager enquiries resulted in my

being allowed to conduct an archaeological investigation on
my own account with Claude as assistant. In the course of a few
days' work this produced a remarkable assortment of 'finds'
made of glass, metal, bone, and pottery. The most remarkable
of these was an unusual bone 'shet knife' (as it was called by
the locals who came to watch), that is, a clasp knife, bound with
bronze at one end, perfect except for the rusted blade; another
was a fine coin of the Emperor Magnentius of about the year
A.D. 350, bearing on the reverse a Christian *chrismon*, a symbol
formed on the *chi-rho* with α and ω on either side. We had been
clearing out a late Romano-British rubbish pit never before
disturbed.

I wrote a detailed account of the finds and their significance,
drew a map of the waterways to which the site was related,
photographed most of the finds, and entered the result in the
competition for a special prize offered at Rugby School for an
essay on any subject of interest. My essay was submitted to Dr.
F. J. Haverfield, the greatest living authority on Roman
Britain, and was approved by him because I had stuck to the
facts and refrained from putting forward any wild theories
(this was, of course, because I had not enough knowledge to be
able to frame any theories). I was duly awarded the prize.

This made Rupert very cross, and he complained in a letter
that for his poem 'The Bastille', which had just been awarded
the annual prize, he had been given £3, whereas 'a farrago of
pseudo-archaeological Roman(?) rubbish fetched a pound
more'. In fact I was given £7 and secretly agreed with him,
having greatly admired his poem; but he approved my buying
with my prize money two large volumes of the *Collected Works
of Aubrey Beardsley*, though I did not have the courage to take
them up to the Headmaster for his approval and signature. My
essay, fully illustrated, was printed as a Supplement to the
Report of the Natural History Society for 1905. This was my
first publication with its own title-page and filled me with pride.

When Claude Fryer left Rugby he went to Cambridge and,
after winning distinction there, undertook to live alone on the
island of Aldabra in the Indian Ocean for several months, while
investigating the plants, animals, birds, and insects. He also
made observations on the formation of the group of atolls, of

which Aldabra was the chief, and concluded that Darwin's theory of the formation of coral islands by their having been built up on land which had sunk below the surface of the sea was not tenable for Aldabra. It was clear to him that the group had formed on rocks which had risen from the sea bed a thousand fathoms below. In spite of this Fryer was faced with the same problem as Darwin: to explain how the giant land tortoise came to be there. For this he could find no answer. Like Darwin, he made his extremely interesting Report to the Linnaean Society, who published it in their *Transactions* for 1911. Later he became Consulting Entomologist to the Government and received a knighthood as Sir John Fryer. I had lost touch with him long before this, but it was interesting to see the heights to which his schoolboy hobbies had led him. This was probably the result of his knowledge of mosquitoes and their relation to the spread of malaria. He had taught me their names, *Stegomeia* and the rest, while being bitten during our night watches in the fens.

4

AURELIANS ON THE CONTINENT

HAVING begun to take an interest in entomology, with my father following suit, we were in fact becoming lepidopterists. I regret that we could not have called ourselves 'Aurelians', a name based on the Italian word for 'chrysalis', or 'pupa', as they did in the eighteenth century, but I did not become familiar with that name until many years later when I acquired from David's bookshop in St. Edward's Passage a fine copy of Moses Harris's book, *The Aurelian* (1778), with its splendid hand-coloured plates of lepidoptera.

Having spent four successive summers at Lealholm Hall in Yorkshire, we then went for several following years to Tintagel, on the north coast of Cornwall. This was enjoyable enough, with its romantic castle, its medieval Post Office buildings, and its golf course on the cliffs. But the Aurelians were unsatisfied, and in 1905 my father decided to widen our horizons by taking us to Switzerland. A continental tour thereupon became the regular pattern for seven years—we went several times to Switzerland, twice to the Pyrenees, once to Hungary, and twice to the Tyrolese Alps. My father would read the reports by other Aurelians in the entomological journals, correspond with the authors, and plan our journeys carefully so as to be in the right places at the right times. We usually found what we wanted and took our pastime very seriously, making it a semi-scientific pursuit, and doing it in such a fashion that the results would be of historical value, illustrating for later Aurelians the distribution and range of variation of butterflies in relation to their locale.

Our techniques were directed to keeping each specimen in perfect condition. After being caught in a butterfly net the insect was transferred to a glass-bottomed box of a size to suit the species, where it could be examined to see that it was of the right kind and in a condition to make it worth keeping. If not, it was set free. The chosen victims were put in a satchel, where they would respond to the darkness by staying quiet instead of battering themselves to pieces on the walls of their prisons. Back in our hotel rooms in the evening we set about the slow work of preserving them. Each insect was stupefied by a drop of chloroform introduced into its box on a wisp of cotton wool, and then re-examined to make sure that it was worth keeping; if not, it was allowed to recover from the anaesthetic and re-leased next day. If worthy, its thorax was pierced with a needle carrying a tiny amount of nicotine to ensure that it died pain-lessly. It was then transfixed with a silver pin, which would not corrode, and set, while it was still limp, on a cork setting board of suitable size, the wings being fixed in the correct position under slips of paper. They remained in this position until the paper slips were removed after we had returned home, the setting boards being carried in strong wooden boxes to ensure that they suffered no damage in transit. The whole process was slow and the delicate manipulation was all done with special forceps. When the specimens were unset each one was provided with a paper label, transfixed by the pin through the insect's body, giving the locale and date collected, with the initials of the Aurelian responsible. Only in this way could the specimens be made of value as a collection for later reference.

My father bought from cabinet-makers the best obtainable mahogany cabinets with air-tight interchangeable drawers for display of the specimens. These were kept at Harvey Road as long as my parents were alive, chiefly for the enjoyment of the grandchildren. Eventually the cabinets were transferred to the Cambridge University Museum of Zoology as a reference col-lection available to anyone who might be interested. In every country of Europe sophistication of the countryside tends to exterminate wild life, especially the insects, and in years to come collections of this kind will form the only record of former times.

The objects of our study took us to many out-of-the-way places; they were to be found not only in the hot river valleys, but also on the high Alps up to the snow line, in the wildest spots. We usually avoided the tourist centres, so that it was possible to have the full enjoyment of our surroundings with the added interest of making a valuable collection. Our earlier expeditions to Switzerland took us to various parts, from the Rhône Valley and the Bernese Oberland to the Engadine; the last, in 1908, was centred on the route to the Simplon Pass over the Alps. In 1907 and 1909 our experience was widened by travels in the Pyrenees from west to east.

The last family expedition was to Hungary, this being perhaps the most interesting of all. It entailed stopping in Vienna, where I first became entranced by the art of Pieter Bruegel the Elder. The room in the National Gallery filled with his greatest paintings has never dimmed in my mind's eye, and led me in later years to the formation of a remarkable collection of the splendid etchings after Bruegel's drawings, which could be bought in London for astonishingly low prices. The collection when put on show at the Fitzwilliam Museum in 1969 exactly filled the Print Room with its sixty-five prints.

The journey from Vienna by boat down the Danube from Belgrade through the Iron Gates to Orsova was exciting, and a stay in Herculesbad was rewarding for the Aurelians. On one occasion we crossed unknowingly into Romania, where we were greeted on high arid land with an attack launched by savage sheepdogs, which rushed over the grass screeching at us with the greatest ferocity. Fortunately we had been warned about this and advised that the only action needed was to stoop down as if to pick up a stone. This was most effective, and we watched the brave guardians of the sheep themselves fleeing in apparent terror. We were rewarded for our courage by being able to record a form of blue butterfly previously found only in Turkey. On the way to this neighbourhood I had a sight of the fabulous *Polygonia Vau-Album*, a gorgeous relation of our humble tortoiseshell. Fortunately the specimen was out of reach of my net and I have always been glad that this rare insect survived to reproduce its kind.

On another level I can never forget the splendours of Buda and Pest with their two connecting bridges across the Danube, especially when seen lit up at night. A wild area on the outskirts of the city, named Svàb-Hegy, provided the Aurelians with yet another rich experience. After twenty years' activity as an Aurelian I have sometimes made the claim that I could recognize nearly every species of European butterfly while on the wing. No doubt this is an exaggerated boast, but expresses some of my gratitude to my father for giving me so much enjoyment.

It was our practice from 1905 onwards to record our experiences each year in the pages of *The Entomologist's Record and Journal of Variation* for the benefit (we hoped) of other Aurelians. A very old friend, Michael Chalmers-Hunt, whom I first met when he was working in Francis Edwards's bookshop in Marylebone High Street, is now editor of *The Entomologist's Record*. We have shared many expeditions nearer home, though he has never yet, as promised, succeeded in shewing me the Purple Emperor (*Apatura iris*) on his English throne (usually, I believe, a dead rabbit or a heap of dung).

Among the other Aurelians whose acquaintance we culti-vated the most eccentric was the Revd. G. H. Raynor. He lived near Maldon in Essex and devoted his life to breeding thousands of the common Currant Moth (*Abraxas grossulariata*) in order to produce a startling array of aberrations in the markings on their wings. This could have been an important experiment in genetics, a branch of science then in its infancy, but he was not moved by scientific motives. He seemed to feel only the wish to have a larger number of freaks in his cabinets than anyone else. He directed that after his death all the evidence was to be de-stroyed. It was a most laborious procedure and we could but wonder how much of his time was devoted to care of souls and how much to his researches. His parishioners were expected to provide him with the large quantity of gooseberry-bush leaves needed for his armies of caterpillars. He kindly invited us to spend a night in his house where he seemed to live a rather ascetic life. The weather was cold and his elderly wife was shivering, but if she suggested lighting a fire he would not allow it, saying that 'a coal fire vitiates the atmosphere'.

Near the end of the Michaelmas term of 1905 at Rugby I came

up to Cambridge to sit the entrance examination to the University, perhaps with a hope of winning some distinction. I came in company with Rupert Brooke and Russell Smith and all of us succeeded in this aim—Rupert gaining a scholarship in classics at King's College, Russell Smith doing the same at St. John's, and myself being given an exhibition at Pembroke, my father's old College. Perhaps my name gave me an advantage, though I like to think the distinction may have been due to an essay I wrote on Darwin's theory of natural selection. Natural history being my special interest, I had read *The Origin of Species* and retained enough in my head to impress the examiners.

For many years our family had enjoyed an acquaintance with the Darwin families, the children of Sir George, Sir Horace, and Sir Francis, the three tribes associating with one another in preference to any outsiders. A catalytic agent, however, was present in the friendly shape of Aunt Bessie Darwin, who gave every year a large dancing party for the young children of Cambridge academics. As a small boy I had endured dancing classes in company with Sir George's younger daughter Margaret. One of these classes is pictured by Gwen Raverat in her book *Period Piece* and I suppose must be accepted as a fair shewing of what happened, though I doubt if the costumes are correct. In any case I took no pleasure in dancing and suffered much embarrassment in the process of finding partners at the parties; in fact I sometimes found myself gravitating towards the girls who were becoming 'wallflowers' through lack of attraction, and might be willing to sit out the dances. I did not mind talking to them.

When the Cambridge ordeal was over, I stayed for a month at home in Cambridge. It had been decreed that I should spend a little time in Germany, my parents believing that a knowledge of the German language would be of more use to me in a medical career than French. This proved to be a very great mistake. Throughout the rest of my life many of my holiday periods were spent in France where I was dumb, and none in Germany where I could have talked fluently; nor did I find any reason for reading German medical literature.

However, on 1 February 1906 I was despatched to Lahr-in-

Baden, in the Black Forest not far from Freiburg. There I spent five months, most of the time in the home of an elderly couple who came from Prussia and were believed to speak the best German. They were unspeakably bourgeois, very kind and cheerful, though I was sometimes bewildered by their standards of behaviour. If I ever turned my plate around at table in order to reach my food more easily, they held up their hands in horror and told me I must never do anything so rude. But they liked their food, particularly the hateful sausages and sauerkraut, which I ate with difficulty.

The best days were when we set out on a '*forellen ausflucht*', walking some distance into the Forest to find a pleasant inn, where we could each choose our own trout, swimming in a tank outside. The fish were then caught and served up, perfectly cooked, for our meal. The route to the inn lay at first along a road bordered by cherry trees laden in the summer with luscious fruit. Herr Kaufmann would always remember his first walk along the road and would stop beside a particular tree and announce, '*Hier bekam ich leibweh*', with guttural chuckles.

I could find hardly anyone I really liked in their limited society. There was a nephew, a mild youth of my own age, with whom I tried to make friends. After some weeks' acquaintance I rashly addressed him with a familiar '*Du*', instead of the more formal '*Sie*'; he turned on me in astonishment and asked if I really wished to be on '*Du*' terms. A cousin was far worse. He was a year or two older and was set to give me some tuition in the German language. He immediately ordered me to read a life of Bismarck, an instruction met with passive resistance. He had already cultivated the abrupt address of an army officer belonging to a superior race and aroused in me an undying hatred. My lessons did not prosper. I preferred to read Goethe's *Wilhelm Meisters Lehrjahre* and would tease Frau Kaufmann by asking what was the meaning of words such as '*Frauenzimmer*', which I was too innocent to understand.

I cannot forget one occasion when we were having a family reading from a book of which I do not recall the title. We came to an exclamatory passage ending '*Deutschland, Deutschland! Über Alles!*' At this point I broke in with '*Ach nein, hier ist ein*

Drückfehler! Est sollte "England, England! Über Alles!" sein.' It was meant as a joke, but was received with a stony silence.

During the spring and summer my best times were spent bicycling in the neighbouring country and in the Forest to the banks of the Rhine. In the spring the great river had overflowed its banks and it was exciting to watch the water swirling through the trees. This freedom enabled me to make a wide study of the butterflies of the district, and to compose a detailed report for *The Entomologist's Record*.[1]

My five months in Germany had been a time of uncomfortable alienation from my family and friends, among people none of whom I really wished ever to see again. It was not only the sensation of their being *foreign* to my general outlook on society at home; nor was it merely having to hear and talk a language which I found ugly, though not too difficult to learn. My chief solace had been a series of, to me, extremely entertaining and comforting letters from Rupert Brooke, and these had served to accentuate the feeling of moral and intellectual stuffiness, from which I was about to escape. My sister Margaret had a very similar experience during her exile to Wittenberg.

Now, at the beginning of July 1906, I was to join my parents in Basel on our way to the Swiss Engadine, and then to go back to Cambridge. Before me lay the attractive prospect of three or four years of university life, the carefree prelude to a future fulfilment in the profession of surgery. I never consciously envisaged how exacting and responsible it was bound to be. I knew only that it was what I had pledged myself to do.

---

[1] Vol. xix, no. 4, 1906.

5

CAMBRIDGE FRIENDS

WHEN I entered Pembroke College in October 1906, my first acquaintance was with another freshman, Sydney Roberts, who already had some connexion with my family. We remained friends for life. He stayed in Cambridge, finding his place in the Cambridge University Press, first as assistant, then rising to the position of Secretary to the Syndics, that is, as University Publisher. The eighteenth-century flavour of Sydney's highly individual personality was greatly enjoyed by his friends and colleagues; naturally he was an authority on Dr. Johnson and his circle. He completed his career as Master of Pembroke, having been for many years a Fellow of the College, and was awarded a knighthood in 1958.

Some years earlier his first wife had been one of my surgical patients and had rewarded my efforts on her behalf by making a good recovery. I have inevitably experienced this particular relation with so many of my friends that I have been able without trouble to overcome any embarrassments that might arise. It has been one way of cementing friendships that I have valued.

Another of my earliest friendships at Pembroke—one which happened spontaneously, almost at sight—was with Maurice Perrin, like myself a medical student. He was a handsome, heavily built man, a valiant oarsman and with very good wits, though a bit too lazy always to do himself justice in his academic career. Ours was a steady friendship based simply on mutual liking and respect; we pursued parallel careers at University, St. Bartholomew's Hospital, and the Royal Army Medical Corps through the First World War, and were never very far apart until his untimely death in an aeroplane crash after the Armistice of 1918.

I sometimes stayed with Maurice at his home in Bushey, north of London, and found myself in a strange family. His father was a merchant in the City, his sister was a promising art student studying modelling and sculpture, while his mother was apparently quite dumb. The household was run by a maiden aunt. We would sit through breakfast without a single word being spoken, a situation which the Perrins evidently regarded as quite normal—it appeared that Mrs. Perrin had not spoken for several years—and then we would all go our several ways. I always regret that I was not present on the memorable occasion when Mrs. Perrin came down as usual to breakfast, announced: 'I'm all right now', and began to talk. The aunt was summarily dismissed and Mrs. Perrin took charge. She never stopped talking, unless she was asleep, until the day of her death. It was as if some psychological log-jam had suddenly broken up, with a complete return to normality. I have not encountered a more extraordinary transformation of personality, but I never learnt the full story of how the condition had developed or why it had so suddenly ended. Mrs. Perrin was a most kindly and affectionate old lady as I knew her in later years. She was heart-broken at the loss of her son, my very close friend, and liked to see me, though I was embarrassed whenever I met Maurice's wife, whom he had married during the war, who would give me verbal messages from him.

During my first year at Cambridge I saw much of Rupert Brooke. He did not take kindly to University life at King's College, but thought of his lost boyhood at Rugby, and turned to the friends who had come to Cambridge with him. Sometimes I would collaborate with him in trying to win prizes for poems in the competition columns of the *Westminster Gazette*. If one of these required a translation from the German I would provide it and share the guinea if Rupert's poem was successful. On one occasion (27 January 1907) I found on my breakfast table in Pembroke a manuscript note headed 'Sunday 1.30 a.m.':

For two hours I have been trying the translation. This is all I have produced, and I fear it's not very literal. R.C.B.

A Comment

God gives us, in earth's loveliness,
   His own great song book, it is stated.
We stumble through (and have to guess
   To whom or what it's dedicated!).

On first perusing, how we yearn to
   Mark every song! But soon, my friend,
The only page we want to turn to
   Holds two best words of all, 'The End'.

But, since we've got to read it through,
   Let us, as true philosophers,
Sit down, and critically review
   God's *very* minor book of verse.

One poem I've underlined—the best—
   (There's all sorts in God's poetry book!):
But of the lot I most detest
   God's vulgar lyric 'Rupert Brooke'.

And, if you're lenient, and declare
   The faults & merits pretty equal,
At least you'll join my hearty prayer
   'Dear Author, *please* don't write a sequel!'

Another friend who became one of the most important figures in my life, until his death in 1967, was Cosmo Gordon. He was a year or two older than I and had come up to King's from Rugby; he had been a member of the Headmaster's School House there, and I had known him only by sight. We met in Cambridge at the house of Charles Sayle, an assistant in the University Library, who had young friends in many of the Colleges and liked them to meet one another in his house.

Cosmo Gordon was the only son of Arthur Gordon, laird of Ellon in Aberdeenshire, and was related to the Marquess of Aberdeen, but in his modesty was ashamed of this aristocratic connexion, although he was proud of his Scottish ancestry. He was already shaping as a scholar by virtue of his growing knowledge of medieval manuscripts, and was a friend of Montague Rhodes James, a Fellow of King's and the greatest living authority on such manuscripts.

I did not share in this august society, but did profit from Cosmo's knowledge of early books such as were to be found at low prices on Gustave David's bookstall in Cambridge market-place. David would sit there in all weathers grumbling at his fate, but always treating his customers, largely undergradu-ates, with generosity; if he had bought a book cheap he would sell it cheap, a most unusual attitude in the second-hand book trade. David became a very well-known 'character' in Cam-bridge and many people eminent in later life have registered their gratitude to the old man.

Cosmo was able to teach me much about bibliography and seventeenth-century literature, in which I was beginning to take an intelligent interest. Rupert Brooke had taught me to appreciate the poetry of Dr. John Donne and I soon began to concentrate on finding copies of his works. When I fixed on Sir Thomas Browne as one of the greatest literary artists, as well as being a doctor, and therefore to be collected, Cosmo was sym-pathetic and helpful, and for some time we shared a Browne collection. In 1908 he and I boldly sent a joint letter to Sir William Osler, Regius Professor of Medicine in Oxford Uni-versity, reputed to possess the largest collection in existence of the works of Sir Thomas Browne. Osler responded in character-istic fashion and soon we found ourselves staying as guests in his house, known in Oxford as 'The Open Arms', with the library and its historical treasures thrown open to us whenever we liked to go there. I had acquired another true friend in one of the greatest physicians of our time, who combined clinical skill with a degree of historical scholarship such as I could only hope to imitate as far as I was able.[1]

Cosmo's and my collaboration over Sir Thomas Browne could not last, as I was a much more assiduous collector than he, and I had to carry on alone in my resolve to make a com-plete assemblage of Browne's works and associated books. It was inevitably some sixty years before this was accomplished. I

[1] The full story of this friendship and an account of Osler as I knew him are given in an appendix to this volume.

had announced that the collection was to be bequeathed to Winchester College where Browne had spent his school days, but later, after I had been unexpectedly elected a Fellow of the Royal College of Physicians of London in the wake of Sir Thomas Browne himself—a time-lag of about three hundred years—I changed my mind and gave it to the Physicians' College where I judged it would be more accessible and of greater service to scholars.

Cosmo and I found our tastes and interests were always in harmony and I came to love his particular sense of humour and gentle goodness, as well as to respect his unusual style of scholarship and general culture. Indeed, it now seems to me in retrospect that I derived over the greater part of my life a more continuous delight in his company and influence than from any other—though it is extremely difficult to assign relative values to so many friendships enjoyed through so long a life.

We were neither of us athletes and I suppose would have been numbered with the 'aesthetes' rather than with the 'hearties' by the standards of the period. But neither were we quite 'aesthetes'—we had no affectations and regarded ourselves as ordinary persons, going our own unremarked and unremarkable way, enjoying what we regarded as the simple joys of reasonably intelligent people. Having no interest in organized games, and lacking the physique to make us oarsmen, we preferred to take our exercise in Sunday walks around the Cambridge countryside, mostly in the fenland, commonly regarded as 'dull' and not worth anybody's notice. A wide sky and a horizon unbroken by any kind of lump (except the one glorified by Ely Cathedral) is denigrated by the word 'empty', especially when one recalls the quite amazing displays of Aurora Borealis seen during the fenland nocturnes I have described above.

Occasionally we covered considerable distances on foot and I remember with special pleasure a Sunday in June 1908 when we took an early train from Cambridge to Ely. From there we walked nine miles towards and along the eastern bank of the Old and New Bedford Rivers enclosing the Washes, an area of land created in the seventeenth century to contain the flood waters from the sea and the drainage of water from surrounding higher ground with a system of dykes and waterways, and now recognized as one of the most valuable bird reserves in the British Isles. The great embankment stretching for twenty miles from Earith to Denver Sluice was wearing a dazzling yellow coat of buttercups as far as the eye could reach, reflecting the sunshine of a perfect day. We took a bathe in the stream and loitered on our way back to Ely where we were not surprised to find that we had missed the last train to Cambridge. We took a light meal at the Cutter Inn near the river and resigned ourselves happily to walking the sixteen miles along the bank to Cambridge through the lovely moonlight of a night almost as bright as the day, cuckoos shouting at us in a chorus of approval all the way. We arrived in Cambridge about 3 a.m., wearily satisfied that we had covered thirty-four miles on foot, though with less panache than my small mongrel dog who chased cats in the deserted streets of the town with immense zest. Dogs never go straight and he must have covered at least forty miles on the way.

We slept for the remainder of the night in Cosmo's tiny lodging, known as 'The Doll's House', in Little St. Mary's Lane opposite Pembroke. I felt it was my duty to report next day to my Tutor to explain why I had been out of College for the night. F. E. Hutchinson was an easy-going man and did not interfere with my life as an undergraduate—in fact I hardly ever saw him, and took it as a compliment that he seemed to think I could manage my academic career without his help. He afterwards became Master of the College and I have sometimes wondered whether he should not have taken more interest in the obscure undergraduate nominally under his direction. However, my entrance Exhibition was converted at the end of my first year to a Foundation Scholarship, so perhaps he was taking more interest than I realized.

On another occasion during a summer vacation Cosmo and I were camping for a second season in a field on the north bank of the Great Ouse River opposite to the village of Overcote. Beyond our field was a small inn owned by Mrs. Hemingway, whose customers came by a ramshackle chain-ferry across the water. We asked our apple-cheeked hostess for some eggs, which she gave us with the reassuring statement, 'You 'ad some last year and you shall 'ave some this'—not specially memorable words, though they come to my ears as a clear echo from seventy-five years ago. We had hired a light outrigger vessel—a boat with one sliding seat for sculling, while the other crew steered—from a boatyard in Huntingdon and one day, having glanced at a map, decided to make an expedition by water to King's Lynn in Norfolk. We were soon to learn how rash we had been.

It was easy to scull to Earith where we could join the New Bedford River running from there in a straight line under a high embankment parallel to the Old Bedford River. What we did not know was that the New Bedford was tidal right up to Earith and that it would have been beyond our strength to scull against the tide. But by undeserved good fortune the tide happened to turn in our favour just when we arrived at Earith and we were able to scull rapidly with the tide for twenty miles along the river to Denver Sluice. Had the tide turned when we were halfway there we might have got into difficulties. As it was, we were able to leave the tidal waters and go up through the lock at Denver to the river Ouse.

Our boat was a beautifully built craft, but it seemed very light and frail when we had to enter the cavern of the huge lock, built to take the largest barges. The water had to be let in very slowly lest we should be swamped. When we reached the level of the Ouse we found that at high tide the water outside was ten feet above it and at low tide twenty feet below it. Having reached the upper level we put up our tent, cooked our sausages, and turned in for the night. Next morning, well instructed by the lock-keeper about tides, we went down through the lock to the tidal waters and sculled at good speed to King's Lynn. For the last part of the course our frail craft was being tossed on the choppy surface of the widening river and we were being swept rapidly out to sea by the tide, but we steered towards the high quay above us and I was able to grab hold of a rope on a large buoy and so get safely moored alongside. We landed and made a first acquaintance with the old Dutch town and its fascinating buildings before returning to the quay to board our boat again and to scull comfortably back on the returning tide to Denver, to camp for a second night on the bank of the Ouse.

On the morning of the third day we decided to go up the slow waters of the Ouse past Ely as far as the junction with the river Cam, where the Ouse became the Old West River. On the fourth day we made our way along this relic of the original course of the Ouse, before the Old and New Bedford Rivers had been cut, but the ancient water course had been so neglected for three centuries that sometimes we had to use our oars as poles in order to push the boat through the dense growth of water plants obstructing the disused stream.

Slowly we made our way back to Earith, whence we could scull comfortably home to Overcote and Mrs. Hemingway, tired and sunburnt but with the satisfactory feeling of having covered about a hundred miles of East Anglian water courses by our own efforts aided only by favourable tides—better we thought than slaving in a College Eight on the river at Cambridge.

Another favourite pastime in vacations, suiting Cosmo's and my tastes to perfection, was staying in cathedral cities. Salisbury (being my 'home' city) was our most frequent choice, our habit being to lodge in the Close Constable's house over the arched entrance to the cathedral Close. The Close must be the largest and the most beautiful in England, ringed with fine houses of various periods. On our first visit we made friends with the head Verger and thereafter always had the complete liberty of the building, Henry James's 'blonde beauty', with its pale stone structure offset by numerous almost black marble pillars from the Purbeck quarries of Dorset. The cathedral seems to me to have special attractions in being all of a piece, having been built comparatively quickly after the monks had moved from the Abbey of Old Sarum near the city, being much troubled by the military encamped above them and by the cold winds to which they were exposed.

The spire of the new cathedral was well built and had never, as had so many others, fallen down. We delighted in climbing up inside the spire by means of the fourteenth-century scaffolding, still in perfectly sound condition, up to within fifteen feet of the great weathercock. There we could open a small wooden window, known as 'the weather door', and look out over the city and its neighbourhood. We did not attempt to go out through this to climb on stanchions to the platform above; that we left to the steeplejacks. Anyway, the Verger had forbidden it—the only thing we were not allowed to do. We made long walks over the surrounding country, usually seeing the top of the Tump, that is, the cathedral spire, looking at us over the brow of high ground near the city, announcing that we were nearly home. There were several second-hand bookshops in Salisbury providing books of interest at the give-away prices then customary.

Several times too we stayed in Wells, in the Vicars' Close, a narrow street with early terraced houses on either side, close to the cathedral. Another favourite stopping place was Muchelney Abbey in Somerset, part of it inhabited by a caretaker, who would allow us to sleep in the Abbot's chamber with its great carved stone fireplace and oak fittings.

I stayed a number of times with Cosmo at his parents' home, Ellon Castle, in Aberdeenshire. The actual 'castle' was represented by a mouldering tower near by, the house being a modest medieval building with some pretentious eighteenth-century additions. The garden below a high tower had a grove of fifteen grand yew trees planted about 1715,[1] but was otherwise simple. Sometimes we would go fishing for salmon and sea trout in the river Ythan, and once I induced Cosmo to help me search for a peculiar beetle found only in the nests of Scottish moles, which was wanted by my Cambridge friend, Claude Fryer. We were able to find plenty of moles' nests on rough ground in the Ythan valley, the litter in them infested with the beetles.

This unusual quest is associated in my mind with a natural phenomenon on the coast called the Buller, or *bouloir*, of Buchan. The inhabitants knew it more familiarly as 'the Pot', and we went to look at it. Cosmo averred it had been described by Dr. Samuel Johnson as being 'a rock perpendicularly tubulated'. Dr. Johnson had just had breakfast at Ellon, so Cosmo ought to have known. Boswell called it a 'monstrous

---

[1] C. A. Gordon, 'Yew Trees at Ellon Castle, Aberdeenshire', *Scottish Forestry*, April 1957.

cauldron' and so it is—a huge circular hole at the edge of the cliff, two hundred feet deep and nearly a hundred feet wide, with a narrow rim on one side. A footpath could be followed all the way round. Either the path must have been wider two hundred years ago than it now is, or Johnson was a very brave man. He trundled round it, Boswell writing afterwards that it alarmed him 'to see Dr. Johnson striding irregularly along', finding it himself 'somewhat horrid'.[1] I remember starting to follow Dr. Johnson, but found the circuit so frightening that I believe I turned back, though having 'a good head for heights' in general. Johnson devoted three pages to a description of the Buller, 'which', he said, 'no man can see with indifference, who has either sense of danger or delight in rarity'. (I felt both.) Johnson, more enterprising than we were, insisted on going down to the sea and penetrating by boat into the Pot through the small opening by which the sea entered. When inside he felt a sensation of 'insurmountable confinement'.[2]

Every time I went to Ellon we never failed to visit the small, but almost complete and romantic, ruinous castle of Tolquhon (pronounced To'hon), where we felt sure we could identify the little stone chamber where the Owd Laird sat doing his accounts. In the last years of Cosmo's life he lived at Insh, at the foot of the hill at Dunnideer (the Hill of the Oak Trees) with vitrified forts and a ruined castle built by Edward I in 1296 with fifteen earthworks encircling it. Thence we radiated out over a large area to see every carved Pictish stone that was known and could be photographed.

Another friend, whom I had met in Charles Sayle's house even before I entered the University, was A. T. Bartholomew. His parents had burdened him with the names Augustus Theodore, but he was always known as 'Theo' to his friends—an attractive abbreviation which suited him. Born in 1882 and thus five years older than I, he was a member of a family well known in London for their craftsmanship as cabinet-makers. Educated as a grammar school boy at Bishop's Stortford, Theo decided very early in his life that his work must be connected

---

[1] *Journal of a Tour to the Hebrides with Samuel Johnson* (1785), p. 104.
[2] *A Journey to the Western Islands of Scotland* (1777), pp. 38–41.

with books. Sheer persistence on the part of his widowed mother helped him in 1900, at the age of seventeen, to attain a humble position in the Cambridge University Library, and there he remained for the rest of his life. Having established himself in the Library, he became an undergraduate in the University and was able to do enough work in his spare time to take an ordinary degree.

In due course, without attracting any special attention to his remarkable qualities of mind and character, he became one of the most valued servants of the University. During the First World War his defective eyesight kept him from military service, and, working unobtrusively in the Library, he found himself almost in the position of Deputy Librarian. The Librarian, F. H. Jenkinson, was devoting himself to the task of collecting the printed ephemera of wartime, leaving Theo, among a depleted staff, to carry on the day-to-day administration, at which, owing to his acute intelligence and hatred of muddle and disorder, he proved to be most effective. His imperturbable temper and wide knowledge made his small room in the Old Library a constant place of call both for readers and other members of the staff. He was deeply devoted to the rambling rooms of the Old Library in which he had grown up, but he was no antiquary or sentimentalist and when plans for the New Library were in the air he welcomed them, making many suggestions in the planning which are embodied in the present building. Out of Library hours he gave a great deal of help to Sir Adolphus Ward, Master of Peterhouse, and to J. W. Clark, the Registrary, in carrying out their literary work. His eye for craftsmanship directed his attention to book design and production and to typography, working in association with Bruce Rogers, the American typographer, while he was in Cambridge.

Theo combined to a remarkable degree the qualities of human sympathy and common sense. He could enter into the lives and interests of anyone with whom he established a close friendship, and his shrewd, matter-of-fact, humorous and tolerant outlook on life attracted all those in whom he chose to take an interest. It will already have been obvious how much I owed to him as friend and mentor. Every visit to him was something 'special' and one went away having gained more than one had given. Theo's 'sanity' was a byword among his friends—until the apparently impossible thing happened. In 1926 he suddenly plunged into a deep pit of melancholy, from which it seemed he could never recover. He had for so long been giving so much more than he received that his psychic reserve was exhausted, his proverbial sanity had gone. His friends were in despair. Nevertheless a drastic course of psychotherapy resulted in his making a complete recovery, so that the last years of his life were the happiest he had ever known. But sadly, in his fiftieth year, he developed an incurable form of high blood pressure, from which he died in 1933. When he died I wrote an appreciation of his life and personality, too long to reproduce here, which was published in *The Cambridge Review*, 28 April 1933.

Through Theo my wife and I in later years had made great friends with Henry Festing Jones, who would entertain us with endless stories about the oddities of his friend Samuel Butler, author of *Erewhon*, among other books of less appeal. From 'Enrico', as Festing Jones was known, Theo had inherited the office of Literary Executor to Samuel Butler, some of whose copyrights were still valid. He had given a great deal of help to Enrico in writing his two-volume life of Butler and in making the complicated index to the book, and when Theo died he passed on to me, in association with Brian Hill, another friend, the duties and emoluments of Butler's executors. Brian Hill and I did not expect very much income from this office. We received a small amount as editors of a volume of *Letters between Butler and Miss Savage* (1935). Butler's novel, *The Way of All Flesh*, published posthumously in 1902, had still two years' copyright to run when we agreed to allow a Penguin edition to be published, thinking little of its prospects. We were agreeably surprised to learn that royalties were due the first year on a sale of 400,000 copies; but the copyright then expired and the return could not be repeated.

With the duties of executor came a handsome glass-fronted bureau holding a large collection of Butler's books, with manuscripts and other relics in the drawers, also Enrico's gold signet ring inscribed on the inside as a gift from Butler, which

I have habitually worn. Some manuscripts we sold to American collectors; Butler's early typewriter we sold as a 'museum piece'. His painting stool I am afraid had its legs cut down so that it could be used as a bedside table. Butler's soap dish was a problem. I think it just got lost.[1] A pair of ballet dancer's shoes was given away to a suitable applicant. A number of paintings in watercolours were given to St. John's College, Cambridge, but I still have two very good oil paintings by Butler of Italian scenes, never recognized by anyone as his. My associate executor having died in 1978, the bureau with its contents has now gone to St. John's College. The ring will go there in due course. I wonder who will wear it?

[1] Nicolas Barker has reminded me that I had contributed the humble soap dish to an auction sale in aid of the London Library in 1961; it made £8.

6

HENRY JAMES IN CAMBRIDGE

THEO BARTHOLOMEW had been a participant, with Charles Sayle and myself, in an episode of June 1909 which proved to be one of the most memorable events of my life in Cambridge. I reproduce here my published account[1] of the episode:

> On New Year's Eve 1907 three friends met in Cambridge to 'see the New Year in'—Charles Sayle, Theodore Bartholomew, and myself. The gathering was at the house of the eldest of the trio, Charles Sayle, Under-Librarian at the University Library, who lived in a small house, No. 8 Trumpington Street, squeezed in, almost invisibly, between its larger neighbours. Here Sayle, a bachelor, delighted to entertain his friends, mostly undergraduates and younger dons; and many first meetings leading to close friendships took place in the small upstairs sitting room. On this occasion it was out of term, but the three friends were all Cambridge residents, Bartholomew being an Assistant Librarian, and myself a Pembroke undergraduate in my second year. Towards midnight Sayle suggested that each of us should choose someone to whom he would like to send a New Year's greeting in admiration of his achievements, to be signed by all three. The choice was difficult and time before the clock struck twelve was short. Sayle, representing an older generation, chose George Meredith; Bartholomew, a great reader of more recent literature, chose Henry James; and I, a medical student interested in the latest scientific

---

[1] *Henry James in Cambridge* (Cambridge: Heffer, 1967). I recorded the account twice on radio, with Douglas Cleverdon as producer and with the late Carleton Hobbs taking the part of the novelist; 'Hobbo's' lovely voice and acting added greatly to the success of the broadcast.

novelties, chose Elie Metchnikoff, whose theories on old age and rejuvenation were then attracting much attention.

Three postcards sending greetings were soon written, signed, and posted in the pillar-box just outside the house; the party broke up about 1 a.m. to await results. Results were meagre. Meredith and Metchnikoff gave no sign whatever, but to everyone's delight a few days later a letter of acknowledgement came from Henry James:

Lamb House, Rye, Sussex

My dear Charles Sayle,
My dear A. Theodore Bartholomew,
My dear Geoffrey Keynes,

I am extremely touched & very grateful & all responsively yours,

HENRY JAMES

January 2nd 1908

Encouraged by this evidence of active goodwill the senders dared to follow the New Year's message by an invitation to visit Cambridge, but this was not successful; if there was any answer it has not survived.

The meeting on New Year's Eve was to be an annual event and on the second occasion, in 1908, the names for greetings were again discussed. Sayle's choice was A. E. Shipley (elected Master of Christ's in 1910). My choice was Rupert Brooke, my school friend and contemporary, then at King's. Bartholomew naturally repeated his choice of the year before, since it had been acknowledged, and this time the greeting was accompanied by a second invitation to visit Cambridge, though it was hardly expected that the great man would condescend to accept.

Rupert Brooke, who was with his family at Rugby, replied:

School Field, Rugby
Jan. 2

Thank you all very much. I am glad you did not address it Rupert Brooke, Switzerland, as seems to have been your first thought. It would probably have found me, of course; but not certainly.

Who were the other immortals this year, I wonder? H.J., Metch, and little Wells last year, I think. G.M. [? George Meredith], Stephen Coleridge [leader of the anti-vivisection-ists at this time] and Miss Pankhurst [the militant suffra-gette] this year, I feel.

RUPERT

Henry James was now splendidly responsive:

Lamb House, Rye, Sussex
January 4th 1908[9]

My dear Cambridge Three,

Yes, I really will come this year—about the May time, I promise myself, & your renewed demonstration of how I shall like it is meanwhile most sustaining. Everything & everyone—in the way of 'first aid'—failed & betrayed me in 1908; but *this* shrouded figure seems just to unveil charmingly propitious eyes, to which we must artfully, all together, still further endear ourselves. We shall receive the sign, & you will live until then gallantly in the thoughts of yours all im-patiently & gratefully,

HENRY JAMES

Encouraged by this warmth of expression, I dared to ask the Master if he would perhaps, during his visit, address an undergraduate Society at my College. His reply, as might have been expected, was unfavourable:

Lamb House, Rye, Sussex
February 24th 1909

My dear Geoffrey Keynes,

All this is very kind of you & of the other gallant Two, & I can only blush to be so unworthy of it. Alas, it isn't possible to me to prepare a paper to read to you within any calculable period; I am very poor at the preparation of papers at any time, & happen to be, for all this year to come, committed & pledged to work, tangled up with obligations & complica-tions, that leave me no margin of leisure at all. So we mustn't talk of that, please, beyond my thus thanking you all three, very cordially, for the faith in me which prompts such lordly visions, such greatly imagined things. However, don't let that faith dwindle, by reaction, by the shock of my confessed inaptitude to anything [any] doubt of my great desire to bask for a day or two in the light of your three-branched candle-stick. Be a little patient with me & I shall come, though I won't even then inflict my *continuous* presence on either of you: I shall put up at the most convenient inn—but, on the other hand, or at the same time, shall markedly & publicly & incorruptibly prefer your triune company to that of any other set of persons whatever. Pardon meanwhile my feeble failure to oblige in the Pembroke matter, and find a reason for doing so in the fact that I shall, instead of that, be occupied with something much more to the purpose—the purpose of your taking time to listen to it, or otherwise assimilate it. I renew to you all my friendliest remembrances & am yours most truly,

HENRY JAMES

Plans for the visit gradually matured and the next letter made definite proposals:

Lamb House, Rye, Sussex
March 29th 1909

My dear Triumvir,

It's the most charming idea—that is, making my little visit June 11th is; & I beg you all (I like so that 'all'—such an affluence of favour, yet without the taint of popularity!) to understand that I will gladly make it—your proposal—suit me. I have expected to be in town from May 1st to the end of the 1st week in June, & now I will stop over to the 11th for so beautiful a reason & come straight thence on that after-noon. So much for time. I only venture to make the most apologetic amendment as to place. Nothing could touch me more than your putting houses, in the Spanish manner, at my feet, but if I shan't seem too basely unappreciative it will suit me best that you kindly bespeak for me a good room &, if possible to be had, a sitting room at the ancient inn. It may be—that moment—for aught I know—your Commemora-tions week, or whatever name you give (pardon my indecent vagueness) the high festival—& rooms at inns much over-peopled. But by engaging it weeks ahead, the shelter I so invidiously invoke—may I not be able to count on it? This then is what I shall ask you very kindly to do. You see I am a more tattered & battered old person than you perhaps suppose & subject to interlunar swoons. But save during those discreet eclipses I shall be, my dear Triumvirate,

Yours most truly,
HENRY JAMES

It would, perhaps, have been better if his request for the privacy of rooms in an inn had been granted; but Sayle's kind importunity bore him down and he next wrote:

Lamb House, Rye, Sussex
April 20th 1909

My dear Charles Sayle,

The doctor put me to bed (for a temporary ailment now overcome) at the moment your most kind letter arrived, & I have but just got on my feet again & recovered the use of ink. 'The way of it', as you say, is that you are extraordinarily kind, & as luminous as kind, & that the only trouble, further, then, that I shall give you on the fateful 11th June will be to allow me to cross your own hospitable threshold on arriving & to accept most gratefully the shelter of your roof. You speak as if your own absence from the scene, for much of the time, would naturally operate as a main attraction with me—but, while duly noting that seductive fact, I don't despair of inducing you to cohabit a little! Let me thank you all then again with all my heart & repeat over my hand & seal that you may count on me at 8 Trumpington St. A very decent, sober, temperate, peaceful, accommodating inmate will you find yours most truly

HENRY JAMES

As the Day approached a programme of events was drawn up by Sayle and submitted to the prospective guest for his approval. He returned this with the items marked: '*Delighted*', 'Enchanted', 'Re-delighted', 'Re-enchanted'. A suggestion of going to a Sunday afternoon service in King's College Chapel was marked 'Suitable—that is, most favourably affected', but this was not in the end carried out. The accompanying letter was as follows:

> Reform Club, Pall Mall, S.W.
> May 20th 1909

My dear Charles Sayle,

You are all magnificent & I am dazzled, overwhelmed—deeply affected. I subscribe to everything, delight in the prospect of everything, give myself up to you to do with me whatever best suits your convenience—on which, indeed, *through* everything, I shall keep my eyes jealously & devoutly fixed. I shall have to tear myself from you on the Tuesday a.m.—& I exhibit the one invidious preference for Tea in one of your gardens (oh delirium!) over even the sight of your contending crews. But for the rest I am of each & all of you the grateful slave, & have gluttonously marked with rapturous accent the items of the list you have so kindly enclosed. I bless you all in fondest anticipation & am yours, all, more than cordially

> HENRY JAMES

P.S. I am in town for 3 or 4 weeks, & expect to be *here* till the 11th. I have a small perch here.

The final word was in reply to an invitation to dine on one evening with the University Registrary, J. W. Clark:

> Reform Club. June 10th 1909

My dear C.S.

Just a belated word to mention that I shall of course be most happy to dine with my friend Clark whatever the whereabouts—especially as you are to be of it. Till tomorrow then —as soon as possible after 6.15. But what a temperature!

> Yours,
> HENRY JAMES

Friday, 11 June, dawned at last and the triumvirate met

Henry James at 6.19 p.m. at Cambridge station. James had
written on 5 June to A. C. Benson: 'I go to Cambridge next
Friday, for almost the first time in my life—to see a party of
three friends whom I am in the singular position of never
having seen in my life.' The meaning of 'almost' qualifying
'the first time' was at first obscure, since it was fully understood that this was the first time he had set foot in Cambridge.
In fact he had paid one brief visit there in 1878 or 1879.[1] On
the present occasion he was conveyed in a cab to 8 Trumpington Street, where dinner was served before going to a concert
in the Guildhall. The music consisted of pieces by Parry,
Stanford, Mendelssohn, and Wagner, but it was not an exciting programme and James was frankly bored. Conversation continued afterwards at 8 Trumpington Street until
midnight and was remembered afterwards as amusing and
very pleasant. Among the subjects discussed were the poetry
of Walt Whitman, James maintaining that it was impossible
for any woman to write a good criticism of him or to get near
his point of view. Had the concert been more enlivening it
would have been a good beginning to the whole episode, but
one unfortunate feature made itself felt almost from the first
moment. Delight in James's style of conversation was always
enhanced for his audience by his habit of ponderously
groping for the right word at every turn of phrase with interminable mumblings and interjections. This worked so much
on Sayle's kindly and helpful nature that he was unable to
resist the impulse to suggest the word that he felt sure must
be the *mot juste*. Invariably the suggestion was wrong and the
word was waved aside, but Sayle proceeded imperturbably
to offer another suggestion at the next opportunity. The other
members of the triumvirate were agonizingly aware of the
mounting irritation suffered by their distinguished guest, but
Sayle was unable to restrain himself, and it was afterwards
felt that this was, perhaps, an important factor in forming
James's decision to leave Cambridge a day sooner than he
had originally intended.

[1] This visit he first described in *Lippincott's Magazine*, April 1879; it was
reprinted in *Portraits of Places* (1883), under 'English Vignettes' and again
in *English Hours* (1905 and [ed. Lowe] 1960).

In spite of this unfortunate lapse in tact by James's chief host, breakfast at 8 Trumpington Street on Saturday, 12 June, was a most pleasant meal. Later in the morning he was taken by Sayle to see King's Chapel and the University Library. Bartholomew was seen working in his compartment in the Library and James, looking at him through the glass partition, remarked: 'Il n'est pas gâté by this view.' At one o'clock an anxious undergraduate (for it was an unforgettable occasion in the life of so youthful a host as myself) was preparing to welcome him to luncheon in his rooms in Pembroke. The company invited was formed, rather oddly, of R. C. Punnett, Professor of Genetics, Sydney Cockerell, Director of the Fitzwilliam Museum, and Rupert Brooke. There is no memory of the topics of conversation, but there is no doubt that James fell at once under the spell of Rupert Brooke. He was the only new acquaintance made by James during the Cambridge episode to become a friend thought worthy of several subsequent meetings in London.

After luncheon James was taken by Cockerell to the Fitzwilliam Museum, where he seemed much interested, and, over the displayed manuscripts, talked with great admiration of Byron and Tolstoy. At four o'clock there was a gathering in the lovely long Combination Room at St. John's, J. W. Clark, Francis Cornford (later Professor of Greek), and H. F. Stewart, Dean of Trinity, being invited to meet James, and after tea there was a memorable perambulation through Queens' College to see the famous gallery in the President's Lodge and other charming rooms. A vivid memory remains of Henry James (a true American in his reactions to the splendours of a medieval University) pausing to look up at Erasmus's tower to exclaim, with hands raised in wonder, 'How intensely venerable!' The afternoon's sightseeing clearly gave James the greatest delight and there were no complaints (as he had indicated in his letter of 20 May that there would not be) at having missed a view of the May Races on the river. In the evening James dined with his triumvirate at the Union, and he was taken to see a play at the A.D.C. Theatre. He had anticipated much enjoyment from this, as the play (*The Return of the Prodigal*) was by his friend St. John

Hankin, but it was a long drawn-out disappointment, and the chief pleasure for his hosts was James's conversation during the intervals. I drew him on to the subject of H. G. Wells, for whom he still, at this date, had great admiration. He declared that *Kipps* was the best novel of the last forty years. He talked also about modern plays, summing them up with the opinion that most of them should be neither acted nor read.

Sunday, 13 June, was ushered in by breakfast with Maynard Keynes in King's. It is quite certain that on this occasion Henry James did not enjoy himself. He was bewildered by the clever scintillating conversation that eddied round him (this was confirmed by Maynard Keynes himself), and told afterwards of the incomprehensible utterances made by the Laughing Philosopher, as he called Harry Norton, one of Maynard's circle, who habitually followed every remark he made with senseless laughter and giggles. Thirty years later, in a review of Sir Edward Marsh's *A Number of People*, Desmond MacCarthy pretended to recall his memories of this occasion. It is quite plain that they were almost wholly inventions since they do not at all agree with the facts; nevertheless they are amusing enough to bear repetition and no doubt record, in a fictional setting, MacCarthy's impressions of the episode. He was a late arrival at the breakfast party and as he entered the room saw

Henry James still sitting at the table, with a cold poached egg in front of him bleeding to death upon a too large, too thick helping of bacon, and surrounded by a respectful circle of silent, smoking, observant undergraduates. I saw again his bright, hazel-grey, prominent eyes signalling distress to me in the doorway—a latecomer but an old acquaintance—and the flustered eagerness of his greetings. 'Tell me,' he said, as soon as we were outside, 'tell me about these remarkable young men, from whom, for some years past I have received a most flattering annual invitation. The beauty of this gorgeous summer, the remembered beauty of this august place, and, to be frank, also a small domestic upheaval not unconnected with plumbing, has at last induced me, as you perceive, to respond. I naturally expected to provide the fox, *to be* the fox, if I may compare myself to so agile and wary an animal, but I never foresaw that I should have also to furnish the hounds, the horses, the drags, the dog-carts, the terriers—in short the whole paraphernalia of a meet!'

MacCarthy then shews James asking 'Who was the long quiet youth with fair hair who sometimes smiled?' and being told it was Rupert Brooke—though in fact James had already met Brooke the previous day. When told by MacCarthy that he wrote poetry, which was no good, James is reported to have said, 'Well, I must say I am *relieved*, for with *that* appearance if he had also talent it would be too unfair.' MacCarthy says that later he asked Brooke what James talked about, and was told, 'He gave me advice; he told me not to be afraid of being happy.' There is so much fiction in the rest of the story that it is impossible not to be suspicious of the truth of the last sentence. It seems more probable that James gave this advice at a much later meeting—if, indeed, he ever gave it at all.

After this uncomfortable experience James returned to the less exacting company of his triumvirate, luncheon being at 8 Trumpington Street, with Desmond MacCarthy and Cosmo Gordon of King's added to the group. The weather was perfect and the party sat after their meal in the little walled garden at the back of the apparently almost non-existent house. James's conversation was brilliant, the best that his visit to Cambridge elicited, including a description of Carlyle lecturing and a vivid impression of Lady Ritchie, 'her style, all smiles and wavings of the pocket handkerchief'. James talked to MacCarthy and Sayle of J. K. Huysmans and Pierre Louÿs, dismissing them both with opprobrium. At 5.30 James and MacCarthy went to call on Sir George Darwin at Newnham Grange. Sayle and Cosmo Gordon accompanied James to dinner with J. W. Clark, where there was great talk about Racine, Molière, *Hernani* and *Marion de Lorme* (by Victor Hugo), accompanied by 1847 port. The party came back to another gathering in Sayle's garden for coffee, being joined there by Rupert Brooke, Steuart Wilson of King's, and George Mallory of Magdalene. James's talk included a discussion of dancing and he told us also of the frontispieces to be added to the new edition of his works.

Monday, 14 June, was another lovely day, and after breakfast one of us suggested taking our guest on the river in a punt. Accordingly, towards midday, his bulky form was disposed on the cushions of a punt, hatless and completely at ease. The process of pushing off from the landing stage was marred when Sayle dropped the pole with a crack on the large, shiny, yellowish dome of James's bald head. Fortunately no serious harm was done, and Rupert Brooke, who had joined Sayle and myself for this enterprise, then assumed the task of poling the punt. Henry James enjoyed the unaccustomed experience to the full[1] and an unforgettable image of him remains, lying comfortably on the cushions and gazing up through prominent half-closed eyes at Brooke's handsome figure clad in white shirt and white flannel trousers (for shorts were not worn by undergraduates in those days). This floating idyll lasted for more than an hour, while little conversation was possible, and the party then went to luncheon in Bartholomew's rooms at Kellet Lodge, Tennis Court Road, being joined by Cosmo Gordon. After the meal a final gathering assembled in Sayle's garden for coffee, including Desmond MacCarthy and Francis Thompson of Pembroke.

James had made a rather sudden decision to leave that afternoon instead of next morning and he was seen off by the triumvirate in the 4.35 train, the cab in which he left 8 Trumpington Street seeming to be piled with an extraordinary number of hats considering the shortness of his visit. At the station James conducted a delicious and inimitable leave-taking, during which Sayle must surely have still been

---

[1] In his description of Cambridge in 1879 James had written rather disparagingly that the 'scantily-flowing Cam appears to exist simply as an occasion for these enchanting little bridges—the beautiful covered gallery of John's or the slightly collapsing arch of Clare'.

suggesting the suitable words, though no accurate memory of this remains.

So ended a memorable episode, which Percy Lubbock has somewhere stated that James summarized by saying that he had 'met hundreds and hundreds of undergraduates all exactly alike'. Sydney Cockerell also recalled that James wrote to someone that he had been entertained at Cambridge 'by young men whose mother's milk was barely dry on their lips'; he had probably expected to be entertained by more senior University dons. Yet his three hosts had not gathered an impression that he was in any way discontented. In discussions afterwards the visit was decided to have been on the whole a success. Except for the King's breakfast party their guest had obviously enjoyed almost everything in varying degree, with the river voyage as a suitable climax to the succession of events.

The 'Collins' arrived at 8 Trumpington Street on 17 June:

> Reform Club, Pall Mall, S.W.
> June 16th 1909

My dear Charles Sayle,

I want to send you back a grateful—a graceful—greeting, & to let you all know that the more I think over your charming hospitality & friendly labour & (so to speak) loyal service, the more I feel touched and convinced. My three days with you will become for me a very precious little treasure of memory—they are, in fact, already taking their place, in that character, in a beautiful little innermost niche where they glow in a golden & rose-coloured light. I have come back to sterner things—you did nothing but beguile & waylay—making me loll not only figuratively, but literally (so unforgettably—all that wondrous Monday morning) on velvet surfaces exactly adapted to my figure. For their share in these generous yet so subtle arts please convey again my thanks to all concerned—& in particular to the gentle Geoffrey and the admirable Theodore, with a definite stretch towards the Rupert—with whose name I take this liberty because I don't know whether one loves one's love with a (surname terminal) *e* or not. Please take it from me, all, that I shall live but to testify to you further, and in some more effective way than this—my desire for which is as a long rich vista that can only be compared to that adorable great perspective of St John's gallery as we saw it on Saturday afternoon. Peace then be with you—I hope it came promptly after the last strain and stress and all the rude porterage (*so* appreciated!) to which I subjected you. I'll fetch and carry, in some fashion or other, for you yet, & am ever so faithfully yours

HENRY JAMES

P.S. Just a momentary drop to meaner things to say that I appear to have left in my room a sleeping-suit (blue & white pyjamas—jacket & trousers) which in the hurry of my departure & my eagerness to rejoin you a little in the garden before tearing myself away, I probably left folded away under my pillow. If your brave House Keeper (who evaded my look about for her at the last) will very kindly make of them such a little packet as may safely reach me here by parcels' post—she will greatly oblige yours again (& hers)

H.J.

The pyjamas were duly restored to their owner but with the embarrassing addition of a necktie, which did not belong.

The Athenæum, Pall Mall, S.W.
June 20th, 1909

My dear Sayle,

I thank you kindly for sending me back my poor old night-clothes with which I am ashamed to have burdened you—but only a pressure of occupations has let me continue dishonestly to retain without protest or rectifications the black necktie included in the parcel under the impression I had left that too, but to which I have no claim. I wish I *had* a just one! So I return *that* elegant armament—I don't know where found (I didn't spy it in my room)—which will have been forgotten by some other guest. I continue to cherish my fond impression & recollections of you all & am yours most truly

HENRY JAMES

Seven months later Sayle had again, unwisely, attempted to produce the Master on a public occasion, this time for the Charles Lamb dinner of which he was one of the chief promoters.

Lamb House, Rye.
Feb. 8th, 1910

My dear Charles Sayle,

Don't think me a great brute—or rowdy—for (1st) inflicting on you these poor pencil-strokes (after having been rather dismally ill for a month or more, and now only fully convalescent & incapable of a sturdy pen;) and (2d) for frankly, even if ungraciously, pleading my terror & inability in respect to engaging to dine with your delightful company a year hence & on a fixed date. There is much to be said about this—more than I can really go into in this disqualified condition: but the great fact is *this*, that I have, alone, the very *religion* of being vastly unamenable to dinners that have about them even the very faintest tinge of publicity or oratory. Such is my obstinate & impracticable & utterly consistent habit; & when one has for years so gracelessly conducted one's self with offence to toasted friends & eschewal of flattering opportunities & rudeness to those one has really *otherwise* much honoured the only decency is to be consistent to the end & not give one's whole awkward but at least uniform past away by a fatal deviation. Take it from me therefore with all charity & indulgence that I *can't*, absolutely and positively can't, have the honour of accepting the so kind invitation of the Ch. Lamb Society for Feb. 10th 1911. Express my perversity to them, please, as inoffensively & worshipfully as possible—I wish I were in a better state to express it myself.

I am getting better—but it is slow & a little dismal, & am as yet a limp rag. I was unwell when I wrote you at the New Year—& then got worse & after a vain struggle had quite to collapse for a while & am still under control of Doctor &

Nurse, who forbid me any but the shortest scrawls. This is why I must be all ruefully & regretfully yours & all my (& your) good friends,

HENRY JAMES

For the whole of 1910 James was the victim of deep mental depression and after the death of his brother, William, he remained in the United States until September 1911. He then immediately began to pick up again the threads he had abandoned in England, the next, and last, letter to Charles Sayle being certainly occasioned by his wish to meet again with Rupert Brooke.

Lamb House, Rye, Sussex.
October 1st, 1911

Dear Charles Sayle,
Will you very kindly address & post the enclosed for me? I have but very lately returned from a year's absence from England—& like to embrace this occasion of attesting to myself (& to you) that such damnable distances have abated & that I am by so much nearer those happy associations of which your genial house was nearly thirty months ago the centre—& remains such for fond memory.

Yours all faithfully,
HENRY JAMES

James did later meet Brooke on several occasions, at 10 Downing Street, and elsewhere, as he recalled in his letters to Sir Edward Marsh written in 1914 and 1915, while expressing his admiration for the War Sonnets and his profound grief at the poet's death. 'I have been spending unspeakable hours over it—heartbreaking ones, under the sense of the stupid extinction of so exquisite an instrument and so exquisite a being' (6 June 1915). His Introduction to Brooke's *Letters from America* was the last writing that he did before the stroke which, on 2 December 1915, ushered in his final illness. So, his Cambridge visit coloured his last lucid hours, recalling how 'during a short visit there in "May week" or otherwise early in June 1909, I first, and as I was to find,

RUPERT BROOKE AETAT. SUAE XXIV

Rupert Brooke: pencil drawing by Gwen Raverat, 1910

very unforgettingly, met him. He reappears to me as with his felicities all most promptly divinable, in that splendid setting of the river at the "backs"; as to which indeed I remember vaguely wondering what it was left to such a place to do with the added, the verily wasted, grace of such a person, or how even such a person could hold his own, as who should say, at such a pitch of simple scenic perfection.'

7

DISCOVERING WILLIAM BLAKE

I THINK it must have been during my second year at Cambridge, 1907, that an event took place which profoundly affected my life. I was walking along the west-side pavement of Trinity Street and passing the bookshop, now long defunct, of Elijah Johnson, when I happened to raise my eyes to an upper level of his window. There I saw on a shelf two prints which immediately riveted my attention. They were quite unlike anything I had ever seen before, and for me had a quite extraordinary quality, which has held my admiration ever since. It is now impossible exactly to describe what it was in these designs from William Blake's *Illustrations of the Book of Job* that had so great an effect on me. I can only suggest with hindsight something of what it may have been. One of the prints was the first plate of 'Job with his Family' sitting in the sunset of a complacent life; the other I cannot now identify. The designs were imaginative, yet precise in the technique of their engraving. They were unconventional, yet obviously deeply felt by their inventor. They were not pretty, but had a solemn beauty of their own. For some such reasons I was immediately smitten by a deep interest in the artist, though I had not heard of him before. Rupert Brooke had not preached to me about Blake as he had about John Donne. My feelings had arisen spontaneously and I proceeded to find out more about him.

I read Gilchrist's *Life of Blake* and Swinburne's *Critical Essay*. In his first edition of 1863 Gilchrist had called Blake '*Pictor Ignotus*' and, though revealing a great deal of value, had tended to patronize and sentimentalize the man, while failing to attach much value to Blake's major works known as the Prophetic Books. Swinburne, on the other hand, evaluated all his poetry, including the difficult symbolic works, which had

reduced Gilchrist to admitting that for him they had little
meaning. The Rossetti brothers added to Gilchrist's book a
text of some of the poems, but treated them with little respect
and believed they could 'improve' them. In 1905 Dr. John
Sampson had provided for the Oxford Standard Authors a
scholarly text of the shorter poems, some torn out of their
context and far from complete.

There was obviously much work to be done on Blake, and
the realization awakened my instincts as an amateur bibliographer, already beginning to be focused on John Donne and Sir
Thomas Browne. I was helped by Sir Sydney Cockerell,
Director of the Fitzwilliam Museum, who was a friend to all
our circle; none of that circle shared my unconventional taste
for Blake, though they did not discourage me. Most of them
tended to agree with Gilchrist that Blake was, after all, a bit
mad. I forget when I wrote the first page of the *Bibliography*—it
was anyway to be a long haul and, as will be seen, it was not
published until fourteen years later.[1]

Meanwhile other friendships were developing. In 1907 Maurice
Perrin and I were both elected members of the select Natural
Science Club and got to know the younger scientists in the
University—E. D. Adrian, Geoffrey Taylor, Clifford Dobell,
Charles Darwin (grandson of the great naturalist), V. H.
Mottram, A. V. Hill, who later married my sister Margaret,
and others. I was not noticed by any of the senior Fellows of
my own College, but I was content with the friendship of at
least two of my seniors, Sydney Cockerell and, above all,
William Bateson, then *ad hoc* Professor of Genetics.

The latter's lectures were not part of the syllabus for students
of Zoology, but I was excited by the new ideas just then coming
to the surface as 'Mendelism', of which Bateson was the leading
exponent in England, and so went to hear him. I would boldly
go up to him after his lectures and question him, and would
even lend him drawers of specimens from our family collection
of butterflies to illustrate genetic variation, particularly those

---

[1]An account of the various stages in my work on the Blake *Bibliography* will
be found in the appendix to this volume entitled '*Religio Bibliographici*'.

shewing the blue variations of the usually dark brown female Chalk Hill Blues (*Lycaena corydon*), of which I claimed to be the first discoverer on Royston Heath. I foolishly published a paper about them in *The Entomologist's Record* which brought all the dealers to Royston, seemingly bent on exterminating this rare form of butterfly by ruthlessly taking hundreds of specimens for sale. By good fortune they did not quite succeed in this enterprise, because the gene producing the variety was carried by the males, not by the females in which it appeared and which were therefore the dealers' chief prey; but it did undoubtedly reduce the numbers to be found on the Heath.

Soon I was a regular visitor at the Batesons' house in Grantchester. Bateson was generally regarded as a somewhat formidable character, but I found him to be full of intellectual interests, great fun in conversation and, to my delight, a collector of the works of William Blake—indeed he was the possessor of one of Blake's most startling colour prints shewing 'Satan Exulting over Eve'. It hung in his dining room, so that I could sit opposite and gaze at it throughout the meal. At Grantchester I would also meet other interesting seniors, particularly medical ones: I remember best Sir Henry Head, neurologist and Physician to the London Hospital, and Sir Wilmot Herringham, Physician to St. Bartholomew's. I also became devoted to Bateson's wife, Beatrice, whom he sometimes treated rather roughly. I recall being with them at some party when Beatrice was hesitating to break the conventions by smoking a cigar. He snapped at her, 'Beatrice, don't be so sheepish.' He thought that people should assert themselves boldly, as he did in his scientific battles, and relished Max Beerbohm's description of the self-assertive artist, Sturge Moore, as 'a sheep in sheep's clothing'.

Although I had so many friends in other Colleges, I did not wish to be left out of things in Pembroke. I joined the College discussion society, known as 'The Martlets', the name derived from the three sparrows on the College coat of arms. I contributed one or two papers to the Society's deliberations though these were not, I think, of any distinction. My main achievement was in inducing H. G. Wells to address the Society, and

later Hilaire Belloc. From an early age I had regarded Wells
as master of the 'science fiction' of the day. In 1898 my brother
had given me a copy of *The Time Machine*, and I had read this
so many times that I think it headed my list of books for rereading. I enjoyed all Wells's novels—*The War in the Air, The
Food of the Gods, The First Men in the Moon, The Invisible Man,
Boon*, and the rest. I never got to know their author intimately,
but was amused to find myself playing tennis with him at
Lady Warwick's house near Dunmow. He had a disappoint-
ingly insignificant personality, with an unpleasant high-
pitched voice which seemed to depreciate the value of everything
he said.

Though I was not really interested in Wells's socialism, I
even read his sociological books—these with Rupert Brooke's
approval. Rupert had joined the Fabian Society, and I had
followed suit, partly to please him, but principally because I
wanted to hear Bernard Shaw, who was about to visit Cambridge. The younger people at Cambridge with whom I was
becoming ever more involved tended to be politically slanted
in a socialist direction. These were Katherine Cox, then at
Newnham, and the four daughters of Sir Sydney Olivier,
Governor of Jamaica—Margery, Daphne, Brynhild, and
Noel. The centre of the circle was, of course, Rupert Brooke,
with, rather confusingly, Justin Brooke, who was not related to
Rupert, though he had a brother named Rupert, whom we
never met. Justin brought with him a Frenchman, Jacques
Raverat, always called 'Jakes'. Both at Emmanuel College,
they had come from the co-educational school Bedales, then
thought to be a very daring experiment and generally disapproved.

It had certainly not done Justin Brooke any harm. He was
one of the several sons of the successful grocer and tea merchant,
founder of the company of Brooke Bond, whose commercial
empire now dominates the world of tea. There never was a Mr.
Bond and the first Brooke with his five sons constituted the
whole firm. Justin had an extraordinary capacity for success in
whatever he touched. He came from Bedales boiling over with
interest in Elizabethan drama and music. He was determined
to change the reputation of the theatre in Cambridge, then at

a low ebb, and so came to found the Marlowe Dramatic Society.

Rupert Brooke has very often been given the credit for the theatrical revival in Cambridge, though Justin was the only begetter. His enthusiasm infected all of us and sometimes we could be seen gathered in a field singing Elizabethan part-songs conducted by an eager Justin. Later, when Rupert had taken up his residence in Grantchester, there was much bathing by both sexes in the river, and we were designated by Virginia Woolf as 'Neopagans', though we were scarcely unconventional enough to merit this name.

The drama we took very seriously indeed. Marlowe's *Dr. Faustus* was the choice for our first production, with Justin as Faustus and Rupert as Mephistopheles. I have the first poster announcing the new theatrical venture. It has several names of performers who were about to astonish the University world. Two of them were H. St. J. B. Philby and myself! Of Philby I have no memory at all and doubt if he ever appeared on the stage. For myself, as a founder member of the Society, there is little to be said. I was given the very small part of the Evil Angel, which I did so badly that I was never asked to act again. Instead I became Secretary, with a variety of humble tasks.

Our principles were very high—no scenery, no names of actors on the programmes, no curtain calls. We were determined, under Justin's direction, to revive Elizabethan drama in England in an unadulterated form, and to some degree that is what we did. Somehow the influence of the very amateur Marlowe Society did infiltrate the world of theatre, no doubt helped by the surprising number of distinguished professional actors and producers who gained their first experience in the Marlowe Society productions. The production which lives most vividly in my mind is that of *Richard II*, the first Shakespeare play we attempted, with Reginald Pole, unkindly nicknamed 'the Duchess' by his friends, in the name part. Reginald, a nephew of the well-known director William Poel, led a most moving rendering of the play and I can still bring back the sensation of being almost in tears at rehearsals.

A production in which I took no part, owing to my being in

Switzerland with my father, was *Comus*, done in the grounds of Christ's College as part of the Milton Tercentenary celebrations. Francis Cornford took the name part with success and afterwards became engaged to Frances Darwin (daughter of Sir Francis) who had been doing much work behind the scenes —a delightful 'spin-off', as it would now be called, from the Society's activities, and unusual, in that University regulations did not then allow any students from Newnham or Girton to join theatrical societies. *Comus*, given during the summer vacation, was an unofficial affair, and it was allowable for Sabrina and The Lady to be impersonated by girls from Newnham and for others to be drawn in. Rupert Brooke had a major part in the production owing to Justin's unavoidable absence, and also acted the part of the Attendant Spirit. He did not have a good speaking voice on the stage and was not an impressive actor, but this particular characterization he could carry off by his appearance. His costume was so exiguous that when he used it later at a fancy-dress party he found he could not sit down with decency—or was this another costume worn when he appeared in a Greek play as a Herald who did not have to speak? I am not sure.

Jacques Raverat, who had come with Justin Brooke to join our circle, had been sent to Bedales by his father in order, it was said, to give him 'a good business education'—the last thing most people would look for under the tutelage of J. H. Baddeley, whom Bedalians called their 'Chief'. But Raverat *père* was himself an unusual businessman. When I stayed with Jacques at his father's splendid country house at Prunoy, I found that the old man was a strict vegetarian and a believer in the principles of Metchnikoff, who had set about conquering old age by the help of the Bulgarian bacillus. At Prunoy we were expected to breakfast off a bowl of yoghurt. Nothing else was offered. It was served in an elegant bowl and was delicious, but in those days was rather 'advanced' as a social habit. Probably M. Raverat was right about Bedales; we had only to look at what the school had done for Justin Brooke, a born businessman as he afterwards proved.

Jacques came to Cambridge as a student of advanced mathematics, not as an undergraduate. He had the strong build and dark complexion of a French peasant, with very good wits and a sympathetic nature. He became a great friend to us all, very 'down to earth', to use an overworked cliché, with a highly cultivated mind. He was a little older than the rest of us and the intellectual superior of all of us except for Rupert Brooke, and so a wholly good influence. He seemed to have little interest in mathematics, though his analytical mind had no doubt been sharpened by this discipline. I felt great affection and respect for him and much enjoyed staying with him at Prunoy and thus getting my first view of the Yonne countryside and of noble churches such as Auxerre, to which we walked across country, and Chartres.

It was a great grief to us all when Jacques suddenly suffered a breakdown—a maniacal episode which came on him while travelling with a skiing party to Switzerland. For a long time the true cause of his illness was misunderstood. It seemed to be a mental instability, with a weakening of his immensely strong body, so psychological treatment was tried. When orthodox methods seemed to fail, he was put under the care of an unorthodox practitioner of Coué's treatment by 'suggestion'. This man was quite confident he could cure his patient and at first seemed to succeed; but the improvement only happened to coincide with a temporary phase in the slow progress of the dreaded neurological disorder, multiple sclerosis, from which Jacques ultimately died. The onset of the disorder was, it seems, most unusual and misleading.

I stayed with Jacques at Loquirec on the coast of Brittany, where his doctor was taking his holiday, during his phase of improvement. Jacques was slightly unsteady on his legs but otherwise looked in good health; we sailed and bathed on, and in, the great Atlantic rollers characteristic of that coast. Jacques was a powerful swimmer by comparison with my feeble efforts and we felt confident that he was on the road to recovery. I found that sailing a small fishing boat was exhilarating; plunging from the top of one roller down into the trough and then climbing safely to the top of the next one was most exciting. At the same time we caught many mackerel. All this seemed to prove that I was 'a good sailor', but disillusionment followed when we dropped anchor and started fishing for flat fish on the bottom. We were then at the mercy of the sea instead of riding triumphantly over it and I quickly became extremely seasick, demanding to be taken back to shore at once.

8

GEORGE LEIGH MALLORY

ANOTHER friendship of this period was one of the most inspiring, for a few years, that I have ever enjoyed. I believe that I must first have met George Leigh Mallory of Magdalene College at Charles Sayle's 'menagerie', as his social gatherings at Trumpington Street were called. Mallory, son of the rector of the parish of Mobberley, near Chester, was a serious youth, more interested in ethics than in religion. He was fond of argumentative discussion and had an interesting mind though he was not outstandingly clever. He had a younger brother, Trafford (of whom more later), and two sisters, Mary and Avie, the latter having great attraction. He had been in College at Winchester and came up to Cambridge the year before me. Soon after entering he had made friends with Arthur Christopher Benson, a senior Fellow (and later Master) of Magdalene, author of so many volumes of reflective essays, all rather alike and popular, though never leading the reader's mind in any particular direction. Benson suffered greatly from attacks of depression and George would make efforts to draw him back to life.

I have deliberately referred to George as a 'youth' rather than as a young man because he looked for so long like a senior schoolboy, with good looks in the Botticelli style, rather than an adult, with the build of an ideal athlete unspoilt by over-development in any part. To many people this was his chief attraction, but I found that behind this façade was an enquiring mind with an intellect not so far superior to mine as to prevent our arriving at a complete understanding. He was widely read and had some ambitions as a writer, but one did not have to know him for long before finding out that the real passion of his life was mountaineering. A master at Winchester had encouraged this and had taken him on several adventures in the Swiss Alps, so that he was already a trained expert in the science and art of climbing, whether on rocks or ice slopes. George was a fine oarsman and in his third year at Cambridge was the successful captain of his College eight, but he was not of the 'hearty' sort and came naturally into our circle; Rupert Brooke and he liked one another well enough, though I was the only one who entered for a time into his passion for climbing. If I had been to Switzerland or the Pyrenees then it was for an entirely different purpose, and I had seldom been above the snowline. But I listened to George's persuasive account of rock climbing in Wales and agreed to go with him to Snowdonia.

We tried to entice Rupert and one or two others to join our enterprise, but succeeded only with an older friend of George's, Hugh Wilson of King's. In September 1907 we set out equipped with rucksacks, hob-nailed boots, ropes, and bicycles (known at the time as 'bog-wheels'). We found quarters in a small farmhouse, Gwern-y-gof-Isaf, on the mountain slopes above Capel Curig, which cost me £3.9.1½ for full board and lodging, with laundry, for nearly a fortnight. Each day we cycled down to the inn, Gorphwysfa, at Pen-y-pass, deposited our bog-wheels, and trudged the two miles to the foot of the rock faces. We had already bathed before breakfast in the stream above our lodging, but usually bathed again in the lake, Llyn Llydaw, before and after climbing.

Rock climbing demands knowledge of technical rules to be obeyed for safety, but is also an art depending on good balance, a level head, and no tendency to panic. At first everything depends on the leader who must command the absolute confidence of the other two or three on the rope below him. Each time a climber moves the rope above him must be securely belayed, that is, hitched over some convenient knob of rock to take the weight of the climber if he slips. Our party relied only on boot nails and fingertips for holds on the rocks; fingertips soon develop slightly swollen pads which help the climber hold on to the irregularities of the rocks. It never ceased to surprise me how small the holds could be and yet give secure support to the clinker nails on our boots, and for padded fingertips. We never used iron pitons driven into the rock face for holds. We regarded such artificial aids as violating the true spirit of the game, unless to overcome difficulties that would have made a climb quite impossible. George had never thought of carrying pitons, though I believe they are now in common use. This may be because some of the available rock faces have been so often assaulted that many normal holds have been worn away since I tried my novice fingers on them more than seventy years ago. We were sometimes making new climbs, without knowing it, and the number of possible climbs on any given rock face is limited.

As novices we were guided by George up Tryfaen, the usual peak for learners, though even Tryfaen has claimed its victims. After one day's practice we climbed most often on the face of Llywedd, doing two or even three ascents on one day. There certainly can be no better way of enjoying total exercise of the body. By the end of the second day every separate muscle was pleasantly aching, but this quickly passed off, giving place to a sensation of physical fitness such as I had never known before.

A climbing diary which we wrote up each evening before resting our well-exercised bodies recorded our difficulties and achievements. Most climbs afforded at least one sensational episode, as my diary account of what happened on Tuesday 17 September will illustrate:

H. S. W[ilson], having dreamt all night that he was in a gully and having several times woken to find himself looking for footholds in the ironwork at the end of his bed, stayed at home, amidst the jeers of his stronger (less imaginative) companions. They set out with a good deal of swagger about 9.45 a.m.

With the help of bog-wheels we soon reached Ogwen Cottage and at once started towards Glyder Fawr. We began the climb up a heathery passage on the slabs to the left of the Introductory Gully; no difficulty was found until we were compelled to traverse to the right, where we met a hard rectangular corner. This was ascended by means of three ledges: the first of these was easily gained by a stiff pull on the right; the second was abandoned on the right after a long struggle, but was eventually gained on the left by a small ledge for foothold, with grass and heather handholds; the third was reached more easily by ascending for six feet and traversing leftwards; this ledge was an overhanging grass cornice just large enough to hold two. On the left just within reach was a pillar of rock affording a good handhold at its top, but this could not be properly gripped without leaving the ledge, nor was there any foothold whatever; the latter was supplied by the second man's hand for the leader's right foot, who then managed to pull himself up so that his left hand rested on the pillar's summit, while the right hand groped vaguely and vainly for a hold above. At length sufficient roughness was found to preserve his balance while the right foot was cautiously lifted to the top of the pillar, estimated to be nine inches broad. The chief difficulty was now overcome, but thirty feet of steep, and by no means easy, rock had still to be ascended before anchorage could be obtained.

It was now the second man's turn to leave the ledge, which he did, but he was unable to progress without considerable aid from the rope. The remainder of the climb was over easy rocks, though a sensational chimney was climbed further up, which might have been avoided. Lunch was then consumed and an easy traverse was made to the foot of the Central Gully. The first part of this ascent was of an unpleasant character, the holds being smooth and wet and sloping downwards. About half-way up, a traverse was made to the left into a subsidiary groove, and this was not so difficult, though the holds were still not satisfactory. In this manner the Cave Pitch was reached, and after some deliberation G. L. K[eynes] wedged himself into the cave, thus obtaining a secure anchorage. G. H. L. M[allory] then set to work to climb the left wall, which he did by means of a very small hold for the left foot and a right handhold under the Chockstone [which roofed the cave]. By the latter he was able (presumably through his great strength) to pull himself up— there being no other foothold whatever—until he could get his left hand over the top of the Chock-stone, where the hold by God's grace proved good. Relying on this, his right hand found a similar hold, and with his legs swinging out, a short struggle brought him breathless to the top. Meanwhile the second man, curled up in the cave, was equally breathless with anxiety, being only able to see the leader's legs kicking wildly in mid-air, and knowing that if he fell he must fall twelve feet before the rope could take effect. He was soon reassured by the complete disappearance of the legs, and it was now his turn to overcome the Chock-stone; but his task was made easy by the presence of the rope and the knowledge of the handhold on the top of the Chock-stone, which in the leader's case had been only hypothetical. The climbing after this was of little interest, being characterized chiefly by the wetness of the grass holds.

The descent was made down very pleasant screes on the west of the mountain, and we then returned to Gwern-y-gof-Isaf to find the remains of an enormous lunch, which soon returned in its entirety from Bettws.

There were many interesting 'pitches' during the remainder of our Welsh season, but too full of technicalities to be of general interest. The diary has been perused by historians of the fraternity and they have probably extracted anything of novelty.

In September 1908 George and I repeated the experience in the Lake District instead of North Wales. Hugh Wilson was not available, his place being taken by two other more skilled climbers, Porter and Gibson. We had accommodation at the Wastwater Hotel, not so attractive as our little Welsh farmstead; the main room was hung with portraits of the climbers who had lost their lives on the neighbouring crags and often festooned with puttees hung out to dry. But the climbs were superb, nearly all well known to generations of climbers and fully documented, including one episode, alarming to me, on Scafell. We had been doing the regular climbs on Kern Knotts and were finally faced with the Eagle's Nest Arrête, famous for its dangers—so famous, indeed, that even George decreed that Gibson and I should leave him at the foot of the climb and go without him by an easier way to the top and from

The second ascent of Gibson's Chimney on Scafell, 22 September 1908. Mallory and Porter (in white shirt) above; G.L.K., dimly seen at the bottom, about to begin the ascent

there let down a rope for his safety. Our route took us longer to complete than had been expected and when we reached the summit we were shocked to find George already there. Tired of waiting, he had climbed the crag without the reassurance of the rope. He had no doubt of his competence to do what others had done before him and so demonstrated his utter fearlessness.

Clearest in my memory is the North Climb on the Pillar Rock, including the Savage Gully with a really frightening 'stomach traverse', that is, crawling face down along a narrow ledge with half one's body hanging over empty space (Gibson and myself), or with a 'hand traverse', that is, using fingers only without any footholds at all, by George. The climax of our adventures was a climb on Scafell Pinnacle, including an ascent called 'Gibson's Chimney', climbed only once before by Gibson. He it was who, poised on an opposite crag with a camera, recorded our ascent, George and Porter half-way up and myself below about to start.

George has sometimes been criticized for taking relatively unpractised climbers up such difficult ascents. I did not feel that any complaints were justified. A good leader goes up first and can inspire confidence in those on the rope behind him. Confidence breeds skill, which cannot be acquired without it. That was how George's pupils escaped injury.

Early in 1909 I was for a short time in Wales with Mallory. Robert Graves, in his autobiographical book *Good-bye To All That* (1929), notes that we stayed in the Snowdon Ranger Hotel at Quellyn Lake, and continues:

It was January and the mountain was covered with snow. We did a little rock climbing, but went up some good snow slopes with rope and ice axe. I remember one climb the objective of which was the summit; we found the hotel there with its roof blown off in the blizzard of the previous night. We sat by the cairn and ate Carlsbad plums and liver-sausage sandwiches. Geoffrey Keynes, the editor of the Nonesuch Blake, was there; he and George, who used to go drunk with excitement at the end of his climbs, picked stones off the cairn and shied them at the chimney stack of the hotel until they had sent it where the roof was (p. 98).

My grandsons have been amused to find my name appearing in Graves's entertaining but unreliable work, which they read when it was a set book in their classrooms. Graves said that 'George was one of the three or four best climbers in climbing history'. This may have been true, but I have no memory of his being 'drunk with excitement' after any of his climbs. Edmund Blunden in a review of Graves's book (*Time and Tide*, 6 December 1929) gently exposed the author of this 'slipshod prose' as boastful and inaccurate. In the first edition of *Good-bye To All That* Graves had also deeply wounded Siegfried Sassoon by publishing without permission, and so violating his privacy, part of Sassoon's verse letter written from hospital shortly after he had been wounded in the head in July 1918. Copies of the edition were withdrawn soon after publication, making those containing the verses (pp. 341–3) into 'collectors' pieces'. I have seldom met Graves, the great poet, since that encounter, though we were both at Pen-y-Pass in the spring of 1914 with a party gathered round Geoffrey Young, the most famous climber of an earlier generation.

I had never aspired to accompany George and Geoffrey Young on Alpine adventures, though George had tried to persuade me to make the experiment. In July 1913 Jacques Raverat and I agreed to do this and were recommended as novices to begin with the high-altitude traverse from Arolla in the Engadine to Chamonix, and to engage as guide the famous Adolph Knübel, the usual companion of Geoffrey Young himself. We could not of course be in safer hands, and were not going to risk the conquest of any peak. We did in fact reach Chamonix without mishap, spending two nights in Alpine huts, though not without real danger. It appeared at the very beginning of the traverse that Knübel had assumed that any Englishmen recommended by Young would already possess the ordinary skills. When we came to the first ice slope, he judged it would not be necessary for us to be roped, and so my first experience as a real Alpinist was to follow him across the terrifying slope without the reassurance of a rope, putting my feet in the small steps cut by Knübel with his ice axe. Even worse was Jacques's difficulty in keeping upright owing to the slight ataxia which was, so far, the only symptom he shewed of the multiple sclerosis later diagnosed. We were lucky, but I have to admit that I was very much frightened at the time.

George Mallory finished his fourth year at Cambridge in 1908, but stayed on for a while in lodgings looking for a career. In June he took part in the Henry James episode described above, but at the end of July I wrote to him: 'I would have liked to see you again, and the pool would have been a good place for the purpose. Anyway, that's that, and the end of you from a Cambridge point of view—not a very pleasant reflexion. Do you realize that you have gone down?'

After failing to fill a much-desired post as a master at Winchester College under the Headmaster, Montague Rendall, George went as a master to Charterhouse School near Godalming in Surrey. I stayed with him there a few times and he seemed happy, but it was well known that he was a failure as a pedagogue. I was told that it was always easy to guess where George was holding his classes by the noise that was coming from the room. He did not believe in a disciplinary relation between master and pupils, but preferred to fraternize with them. This was perhaps partly inevitable because he still looked so absurdly young. To his annoyance the parents of the boys usually took him for another schoolboy. Graves said the boys despised him for his attitude, though a few, including Graves himself, found him a very good friend.

In July 1914 George married a very lovely wife, Ruth, daughter of the architect Hugh Thackeray Turner, but soon afterwards the First World War broke out, and I did not see him again until Armistice Day 1918. I became godfather to his son John, who had the celebrated violinist Jelly d'Aranyi as godmother. John, born on 27 July 1920, for some years devoted himself to Buchman's Oxford Movement, but eventually became an engineer, working in South Africa, with a large family.

George Mallory's share in the Everest expeditions is a matter of history. In his younger days he had claimed that the satisfaction in mountaineering lay in aesthetics, and compared it rather extravagantly with the pleasures of great music. I grant that all scenery looks better from the top of a mountain than from any other aspect, and coming to the summit, even in Wales, always gives the climber a sudden revelation of great beauty. But to me the chief satisfaction in climbing lay in the feeling of having conquered a piece of Nature's rugged face by one's own efforts.

Whatever George may have dreamed of mountains and aesthetics, his famous answer to the question, 'Why do you want to climb Mount Everest?', 'Because it's there', seems to me to betray that it had become an obsession, a psychological fixation. He had held himself as partly responsible for the death of seven Sherpas, killed in an avalanche during the second expedition, and before going on the third, fatal, attempt, he admitted that he hated leaving his wife and children. Shortly before starting he said to me that what he would have to face would be more like war than adventure, and that he did not believe he would return alive. He knew that no one would criticize him if he refused to go, but he felt it a compulsion. The situation has its literary counterpart in Melville's Captain Ahab and his pursuit of the White Whale, Moby Dick.

I have talked over the final phase of the Everest climb with Noel Odell, the man who, from two thousand feet below, glimpsed for the last time through a break in the mists the tiny figures of Mallory and his companion, Irvine, moving strongly upwards about six hundred feet from the summit. It is my belief, based on my knowledge of George's character, that he did struggle to the top—then, exhausted by his efforts, probably made without the help of oxygen, was swept by the wind with his companion off the bare face of the rocks while attempting a descent even more perilous than moving slowly upwards. His commitment to his task gave him the proportions of a hero.

After we had lost George, my wife and I became friends with his widow, Ruth, as close a friendship as I had enjoyed with him. We rejoiced at her second marriage to the artist, Will Arnold-Forster, but then, alas, she came to me as a patient with a complaint needing a very serious operation. This was successfully performed, but some time later she died from an obscure secondary cause, which was never explained. There

George Mallory: oil painting by Duncan Grant, 1912

had been no recurrence of the disease. The life of a surgeon can sometimes be very hard, as Rowlandson's drawing, 'The Doctor's Despair',. which came to me from my brother's collection, dramatically illustrates.

'The Doctor's Despair': drawing by Rowlandson

—◆◆◆—

9

MEDICAL TRAINING

THREE years spent at Cambridge as an undergraduate cultivating a variety of interests were not wasted. At Rugby it was noticed that I spent more of my time on school work than the average boy and earned the title 'studious Keynes'. This was not bestowed on me through the admiration of my schoolfellows, but rather in scorn. It was not natural or quite decent to be interested in learning and I was not clever enough to absorb knowledge without industry. The school had not given me any instruction in biology. 'Science' was understood to cover only elementary chemistry and physics, obviously the basic subjects which had to be endured, with mathematics in the background; the last subject was somehow antipathetic to my cast of mind and aroused active resistance. However, I managed to acquire enough of all these disciplines to achieve the minor scholarship I had at Cambridge, which gave me the advantage of being allowed to spend the whole of my time in College rooms with an oriel window overlooking Trumpington Street from almost opposite Little St. Mary's Lane. Here I could read in peace and comfort while the chief part of my scientific education was spent in the laboratories. My main tripos subjects were zoology, anatomy, physiology, pathology, and chemistry. The value of lectures varied with the personality of the lecturer. I was told that the elementary physiology lectures were a waste of time, because the lecturer, a very distinguished scientist, was not respected, so that they became a bear garden. I did not attend one of these lectures, but never missed any laboratory work in any of my subjects, and was justified by gaining a first class in the tripos examinations, for an honours degree.

The College authorities expected that a student who wished

to spend a fourth year at Cambridge would take a second part in advanced study of a subject such as physiology. However, in agreement with Maurice Perrin, I had set my sights on the conquest of the Primary Fellowship examination of the Royal College of Surgeons, success in which would give me a great advantage when I went on to pursue my medical studies in a London hospital. Consequently I had to leave College, and found delightful lodgings at 7 Fitzwilliam Street, almost opposite the house where Charles Darwin had lived while wasting his time on unacademic pursuits. There I settled down for an enjoyable year of work and play, if that is the right word for close study of the lives and works of William Blake, Dr. John Donne, and Sir Thomas Browne. Aided and abetted in my studies by Theo Bartholomew and Cosmo Gordon—Cosmo being then engaged in cataloguing the Sandars Library of rare books in the University Library—I was able to lay the foundations of a special knowledge of these authors and to apply it in booksellers' shops and at Sotheby's sale rooms in London.

My plan of making bibliographies was beginning to take shape. In addition to my friendship with Sir William Osler, I had formed a close relationship with the elderly artist and playwright Graham Robertson, owner of the largest collection in England of pictures and drawings by William Blake. As usual the method of direct approach was met with immediate friendship and many visits to Robertson's houses in Surrey and London gave me greatly increased knowledge of Blake and his works. Robertson, a survivor from the artistic and literary circles of the Nineties, was a wonderful raconteur and anyone who has read his book, *Time Was* (1931), can guess how entertaining his unprinted reminiscences would have been. He lived on to a great age and I was still visiting him during the Second World War, when he was paralysed and speechless, but still able to enjoy being given the latest news of the Blake world. After his death his executor, Kerrison Preston, gave me his copy of Oscar Wilde's *Happy Prince*, inscribed by the author 'To Graham for his dancing'. Robertson had been a devoted friend and admirer of Ellen Terry and I was afterwards able to steer his portrait of her to the National Portrait Gallery. He would talk of her extraordinary charm and beauty both on and

off the stage, whereas I can only remember her as the Nurse in
Romeo and Juliet, still lovely but, owing to her impaired memory,
able only to provide her own words rather than Shakespeare's
—without any loss of effect.

Graham Robertson had begun his career as a Blake collector
in 1896 by acquiring the startling painting in tempera of 'The
Ghost of a Flea'. Being well endowed with bequests from, it was
believed, numerous maiden aunts, he was able to buy in the
sale rooms any important work by Blake that turned up, until
the walls of every room in his two houses glowed with the pictures still unregarded by other collectors, including nearly all
the great colour prints. Unfortunately their owner, though
himself an artist, did not appreciate the damage that could
result from exposure of watercolours to direct sunlight. He
liked to have them all where they could be seen and enjoyed
rather than hiding them away in drawers, with the consequence
that a few lost much of their original quality.

The sale-room prices for Blake were then still very moderate,
though out of my reach in the 1920s and 1930s. When one of
Blake's masterpieces, 'Satan smiting Job with Sore Boils', one
of his last three pictures in tempera, using a new and faultless
technique, was sold in London in 1911 for £150 and offered
by a dealer for £350, I implored my father to lend me the
money, but he was not impressed, saying, 'Blake is a cult.' He
would not go beyond a useless £200. If I had told him that as an
investment the picture would yield a 500 per cent return, he
would not have believed me. Fortunately it was bought by a
generous American lady, who gave it to the Tate Gallery and
so it was saved for the nation. However, I could console myself
by acquiring smaller masterpieces, such as the woodcut illustrations to Thornton's Virgil, for which booksellers were then
asking three guineas. Already, before 1914, I had twice been to
look through the Blake collection owned by the Linnell family
and kept intact in a house in Redhill, Surrey; it could not be
sold, I was given to understand, until 'Aunt Sarah' had passed
away and there was no knowing when that might happen; but
it was still possible to buy from the family's stock a set of the
seven prints for Dante's *Inferno* for seven guineas, and that was
within my means. I could also turn over at Redhill the 102

'Satan smiting Job with Sore Boils': William Blake

'The
Circumcision':
William Blake

watercolour and pencil drawings for the *Inferno*, all quite bewilderingly beautiful, and safely stored away from the light of day.

But all this had nothing to do with my progress towards a professional career. In October 1910 I had completed four years of exciting mental development, with interests along many lines in literature and art; now I had to choose a medical school in London for further professional education in medicine, so much more exciting than the purely academic work I had had to do hitherto. Unfortunately I failed in the Primary Fellowship examination of the Royal College—I was successful in physiology, but inadequate in the ordeal of exposure to the savagely searching questions asked by experienced and sometimes rather alarming surgeons, who wanted to know how much a frightened young man could reproduce, from his only partly trained memory, of details of topographical anatomy, much of which had seemed to him to be of little or no practical importance. Some fortunate students possessed the kind of memory which could store the required knowledge for a short time, just long enough to carry them through the examination with success. I was not one of these, and had to accept failure, with the prospect of making another attempt in the future.

I felt humiliated by failing this examination, and, in a state of depression, decided to go for a long walk by myself. This was to start from Gloucester, going northwards through the West Country, then striking eastwards from Hawes Junction towards Whitby, with the intention of ending at Lealholm Hall, with all that it had meant to me twelve years earlier—a kind of return to the womb of my happy childhood. Soon after leaving Gloucester I fell in with a man travelling by pony cart (up to sixty miles in a day, as he said, though I did not believe him). He told me that one need never go thirsty in the West Country. Any farmhouse would always provide a draught of home-brewed cider on request and free of charge. This proved to be true of the generous farmers' wives on whom I called. I carried on my back only a blanket, a small spirit stove for boiling eggs, and a copy of Fielding's *Tom Jones*, for I was travelling straight

across country and sleeping rough on the Yorkshire fells, behind a wall if it did not rain, in a barn if it did.

The weather was fine, though colder at night, and I kept to
my resolve, except at Rievaulx which was so beautiful that I
paused for a night's lodging under cover. On the fourth day I
hoped I might reach Rosedale Abbey, but the thought of
Lealholm Hall urged me on faster and faster, until I came at
about six o'clock to Lealholm to fall into Mrs. Redman's ample
arms and find rest for tired feet. It was still the remembered
Paradise. Old Willie had been gathered, but all else was
exactly as it used to be. I followed farmer Redman on his
rounds, I bathed in the beck, and the food was delicious.
Primary Fellowships could be forgotten and I luxuriated for
several days before going south again to camp with Cosmo
Gordon at Overcote.

The choice of a medical school had not been difficult, because
my uncle, Sir Walter Langdon-Brown, was senior physician on
the staff of St. Bartholomew's Hospital in Smithfield, just outside the walls of the City of London, and he naturally wished
me to enter there. The hospital (to be hereafter known as
'Bart's') also had the attraction of an unbroken history of
nearly eight hundred years on the same site, having been
founded by the monk Rahere in 1123, on land given him by
King Henry I. Maurice Perrin and I made our decision to go
together to Bart's and we could not have made a better choice.
I had been well trained in zoology at Cambridge and I easily
scored an open scholarship at the hospital; it only remained to
find somewhere to live.

The conventional area offering lodgings for students at that
time was Bloomsbury, and my mother and I made an exploratory expedition to the forbidding London squares to see what we
could find. After viewing many rooms and blowsy landladies
we were in despair; nothing seemed to be tolerable to our
country eyes. I then began to tell my mother how Cosmo
Gordon and I had often been to look at the beauty of North
Street, behind Dean's Yard in Westminster, with its enchanting
Queen Anne houses. It is now Lord North Street and inhabited
almost entirely by Members of Parliament; even then it was a

particularly choice enclave between the Houses of Parliament and Westminster Abbey. We walked along the street admiring the lovely early eighteenth-century frontages with their elegant steps up to the 'period' front doors, and iron stands for the torches of the link boys, and realized that this was not for me —or was it?

We retraced our steps down North Street and turned round the corner into Cowley Street. Almost immediately we saw in the window of No. 14 a notice advertising lodgings at twenty-five shillings a week; we only had to ring the bell, speak to the pleasant young woman who opened the door, and engage the two delightful panelled rooms on the first floor in which I was to live for the next three years. The houses were of the same date as those in North Street, though with less grand fronts. My landlord was a cabinet-maker, who had already provided my sitting room with a fine glass-fronted bookcase exactly suited for my embryo library. The only sound at night was the chiming of Big Ben, to which I soon became accustomed, and even by day it was as quiet as could be desired, there being hardly any traffic. It had all been an 'act of faith', richly rewarded. The daily journey to Bart's could be made on foot or by tram along the Thames Embankment to Blackfriars Bridge and so to the hospital. Sensitivity to surroundings had been perfectly satisfied.

The life of a medical student at hospital can be pleasantly quiet if he chooses to be lazy, or tiringly exciting if he chooses otherwise. I gave my whole being to it; at last I was doing something real, dealing with human beings and learning fast what is meant by suffering. Soon I was attached to a surgical 'firm', that is, working in a group of about eight students under one of the Senior Surgeons in the two wards, male and female, where his patients lay, taking clinical histories, examining patients, trying to diagnose their complaints based on as yet insufficient knowledge, and finally summoning up courage to announce an opinion before the surgeon and the other students. Sometimes, of course, some help might be afforded by a kindly house officer. I had decided at an early stage that the essential basis of learning was to see as many patients as possible, whether in wards or in outpatient or casualty departments. When the firm was on duty for the whole twenty-four hours, I would attach myself to the House Surgeon and follow him wherever he went, watching whatever he did, sometimes until far into the night. He knew how to handle patients, both adult and juvenile. His was an example to follow and he did not mind my tagging on.

In those days an interesting episode in one's training was the month spent doing duty 'on the District', that is, attending the deliveries of babies in the houses of people living in the district near the hospital. I protected myself by spending a fortnight beforehand at the City of London Lying-in Hospital so that I should know something of the mysteries of obstetrics before going out alone on the District. I managed to achieve my required number of deliveries (twelve or twenty, I forget which) without any serious trouble. It was always possible to call for the help of the Intern, a fully qualified man, from the hospital in any case of real difficulty. I encountered only one such, a patient who faced me (rather a contradiction in terms) with a breech presentation—that is, the baby chose to arrive bottom-first instead of head-first, as usually happens. This I handed over to the Intern for him to manage more expertly than I could have done. A more entertaining aberration was that of a very buxom and powerful young woman who, as the climax of her first labour came on, insisted on getting out of bed and sitting on a chamber-pot. The combined efforts of her mother, the qualified midwife (or 'gamp'), and myself failed to get her back into bed and, when she finally stood up, there was a pink and healthy infant squalling in the pot. She had managed the delivery in her own way quite successfully.

During my obstetrical training I had made friends with a student named Dick (though really Reginald) Morshead, to whom I became much attached, a quiet and reserved person. Through him I met his younger brother, Owen, whose friendship became an important feature of my life until his death. Sir Owen Morshead was not an important public figure, but in private was an incomparable friend by reason of his charm and wit, accompanied by his knowledge and appreciation of everything that is good in all the arts. He would observe his fellow men and women with a penetrating but kindly eye, and describe them so delightfully that to possess his friendship and affection gave me confidence in my own personality. When his brother first introduced him to me during a visit to Bart's, Owen was a young cadet at Sandhurst, and he bowed over my handshake with a natural courtesy most unusual in someone of his age.

During the First World War he was an army liaison officer, tearing about the front on a motor bicycle with a fearlessness and efficiency that earned him a D.S.O. and a Military Cross. After the Armistice he returned to civilian life and gravitated back to his Cambridge College, Magdalene, where he was in due course appointed Pepysian Librarian, an office which he fulfilled with distinction not so much because of bibliographical expertise as through wise and sympathetic administration. In this capacity he attracted the notice of Queen Mary, consort of King George V, and at the first opportunity she secured his services as Librarian and Archivist at Windsor Castle. This was a very happy position for Owen, full of interest and responsibility, with the added enjoyment of friendship with the Queen. He was an amused observer of the royal style of life, though embarrassed by his failure to live up to the pleasures of the royal table. Each year he was invited to stay for several days at Sandringham, and each time he was overcome by the richness of the food. King George was much concerned by this, and whenever Owen had to retire to his bed would say, 'I can't understand his being ill. *It's all our own cream.*' This became a favourite quotation in our household.

My wife and I stayed in Owen's house at Windsor and were given a fascinating private view of the Castle and its contents when the royal family was not in residence; I was able to have a leisurely sight of the Leonardo da Vinci drawings and to investigate the drawings by William Blake. Later, when Owen had retired to Sturminster Newton in Dorset, we would go with him on visits to the churches in the county. He had organized a Dorset Historic Churches Trust to help in the upkeep of the buildings, having formed a full knowledge of their needs by personal investigation. He died in 1977 at the age of eighty-three.

Inevitably, at Bart's, there were long periods of waiting between calls for duty; these I filled by writing an essay for a Medical College prize offered for a study of any individual of importance in the history of medicine. I chose the outstanding figure of Sir Astley Cooper, surgeon to Guy's Hospital at the end of the eighteenth and in the early nineteenth centuries. This did not break any new biographical ground, but I found the subject interesting; moreover the examiners liked it and awarded me the prize, with which I bought a copy of the English Bible, 1903, printed in six volumes by Constable for David Nutt, half-bound in red niger morocco—not an adventurous choice, but quite sensible.

Three years as a medical student had confirmed my determination to become a surgeon rather than a physician. I was sorry for the physicians. They had hard intellectual work judging the patient's personality and arriving at a diagnosis by observation of signs and symptoms, but, that done, there were but few really specific drugs and the 'doctor' could only try to create the best circumstances in which natural processes could enable the patient to cure himself; whereas a surgeon, having diagnosed, proceeded to cure the patient by the skill of his own hands, a much more positive satisfaction for the medical man. A surgeon is a craftsman, basing his craft on a wide knowledge of human structure and biology, always gaining by experience of the results of his work. I once suggested to my eminent uncle, Sir Walter Langdon-Brown, that a surgeon had a much greater responsibility than a physician, literally carrying the matter of the patient's life or death in his hands. My remark was tactless and made Sir Walter very angry. He had written an important and progressive book, *Physiological Principles in Treatment* (1908), which seemed to me to support my point—he was, quite correctly, helping Nature in an indirect way to remove the responsibility still more from his own shoulders. I was, of course, quite wrong in making the comparison at all, and I should not have presumed to exalt my brash self-confidence over his intelligence.

Meanwhile I was not neglecting my literary interests. At home in Cowley Street I would close all medical textbooks at ten o'clock and turn to my work on Blake until Big Ben an-

nounced that it was midnight. I had been regularly spending
Saturday afternoons in the Reading Room of the British
Museum and accumulating the material for the massive
Bibliography which was to appear in 1921. In 1913 it was being
written for the third time, the first and second versions having
been condemned by Dr. John Sampson, Librarian to the
University of Liverpool.

Dr. Sampson has been forgotten now except in Liverpool
where he is regarded as a great literary pioneer. He had started
life as a lithographer and printer, working with 'a noisy hand
press', as I am told, in the old Liverpool Corn Market, earning
only a pittance from this skilled labour. For years he consorted
mostly with the local gipsies, learning their language so that he
could record and translate their poems. His volume of gipsy
poems was later (1931) published by the Oxford University
Press, with a coloured frontispiece by Augustus John, also a
lover of gipsies.

Dr. Sampson's 1905 text of the lyrical poems had made him
the chief authority on Blake, so clearly I had had to go to see
him; and though he was known as an eccentric character and
a stern critic, he was very kind to me. He had perceived the
merits of Blake's poetry many years before, and was ready to
help my stumbling footsteps towards the proper recognition of
Blake as one of the greatest English poets and artists. I found
him in his Library embodying the authentic presence of a
Dickensian savant and Man of Letters. Somewhat obscured
by a cloud of tobacco smoke, he sat, a heavy figure with a florid
countenance, hunched in an armchair at a great desk covered
with papers, a gold-rimmed pince-nez dripping off his nose over
a wide waistcoat scattered with portions of food that had not
reached his mouth, but with a kindly grey eye. He told me
plainly where my work was defective and how it might be
emended, dismissing me with his blessings, though condemning me to write the whole bibliography yet again.[1] I
treasure the letters he afterwards wrote me and cannot forget
his generosity in giving me his copy of Donne's *Poems*, 1639, with
contemporary annotations—for other work on Sir Thomas

---

[1] See Appendix, p. 380.

Browne and John Donne had also been going slowly forward, and copies of their books were trickling into my bookcase, mostly from bookshops in the Charing Cross Road.

I was pursuing other interests as well in these first London years. My Cowley Street lodging had no second bed or spare room, but there was a couch in the front room where guests could sleep. Rupert Brooke was living in the Old Vicarage, Grantchester, when he was not abroad, and I did not see much of him. Sometimes he came to London for a night, however, and we would go to see the Russian Ballet. Diaghilev's company was performing at the Royal Opera House, Covent Garden, throughout the season of 1911. I still have the programmes and so can be certain that I repeatedly saw Nijinsky dance his best parts, in 'Le Carnaval', 'Le Pavillon d'Armide', 'Les Sylphides', 'Scheherazade', and 'Le Spectre de la Rose'. Sometimes Rupert and I sat up among the gods in the gallery, far, far away from the tiny figures on the stage, but it was the thrilling introduction to a passion which occupied a great part of my aesthetic life for so many years after 1918. It is Nijinsky in 'Scheherazade' and 'Le Spectre de la Rose' that I fancy I can recall most vividly from things seen sixty-eight years ago; but it is difficult to be certain that it is genuine recall, having seen the same ballets at intervals since that time.

10

HOUSE SURGEON

DURING the latter part of 1913 I had passed the qualifying examinations for the Royal Colleges, and some parts of those for the Cambridge M.B. I had also won the most desirable prizes at Bart's, the Brackenbury Scholarship in Surgery and the silver medal for Operative Surgery. These ensured that I would be able to choose whichever 'firm' I wished for my appointment as house officer. My choice, naturally surgical, was the unit in which I had served as dresser when I first came to Bart's. I was accepted by the Senior Surgeon and I was sorry in the end that he had done so, for my Chief was not a person that I care to remember. He was a sound conventional operator of no great distinction, but he was vain and bad-tempered. His conversation consisted entirely of stories telling how he had scored off someone else. Every House Surgeon who worked for him was told he was the worst he had ever had to endure. He always blamed and never praised. The excellent house officer from whom I had learnt so much, being blamed for some supposed clumsiness, retorted, 'What d'you mean? D'you think I'm a bloody octopus?' That was the best way to deal with a bully, though not a method I was capable of imitating.

On one occasion we had a real 'scene'. A patient had been brought down to the operating theatre because she was thought to have an abscess in her chest and this had to be explored by probing with a needle and syringe until the position of the trouble was found. My Chief made several attempts to do this, but having failed, he finally gave up and went away. I was left thinking what course it was my duty to take in the patient's interest. The procedure was not an 'operation' in the full sense of the word and usually a surgeon on the staff of the hospital would ask his House Surgeon to do it for him. If our patient now went back to the ward she would be no better than before and another attempt would have to be made, probably by myself. I therefore decided it was my duty to try again at once, hoping I might be more fortunate than my Chief. There was no question of any particular skill being needed. As it happened I was immediately lucky in finding the abscess cavity, which was drained. I hoped my Chief would be pleased, but I had misjudged him. When I met him next day his face was dark with rage and he was so angry that I feared he might dismiss me from my post and put my whole career in danger. The patient, however, soon recovered and the affair seemed to be forgotten.

In October 1913 I had left my lodgings in Cowley Street and occupied a room at the top of a house in Brunswick Square, Bloomsbury, because, as House Surgeon at Bart's for the following year, I should have to spend much more of my time in the hospital—in fact for the second six months, as senior house officer, I should be in residence there. Living in the Brunswick Square house at the time were Adrian Stephen, Virginia Stephen, and Duncan Grant; probably for this reason it has often been supposed that I belonged to the famous Bloomsbury group. In fact I make no claim to this. I did, of course, know all of them slightly and very much liked Duncan Grant, but I was not recognized as 'belonging' and did not wish to be. I respected Vanessa Bell, disliked her husband Clive, who was always 'shewing off' in a noisy way, and did not know Adrian at all. Saxon Sydney-Turner I had no way of knowing as he never opened his mouth, and I sometimes wondered why he was there at all. Harry Norton (Henry James's 'laughing philosopher') annoyed me by his presumably clever nonsense and more particularly by his saying to me that my father was 'an old fly-by-night'; what that meant I did not know, but anyway it was offensive.

Virginia Stephen I hardly knew, though it was with her that I had closer relations, while she was more or less unconscious. I came back one evening from the hospital to find the whole house in a state of consternation because Virginia had been found insensible in her room, having just made her first attempt at suicide by means of a large dose of a narcotic drug. They had tried to get Sir Henry Head by telephone, because she had recently been seen by him as a patient for depression. It was obvious to me that it would be more practical to get as soon as possible a stomach pump, that is, a long rubber tube and funnel with which to wash out her stomach, so as to get rid of any portion of the drug that had not been absorbed. Leonard Woolf and I dashed through the street to Bart's in a taxicab waving aside the policemen (in the then absence of traffic lights) shouting 'Doctor! Doctor!' if they tried to stop us. However it was that we accomplished our task, we succeeded. The stomach pump was fetched. Sir Henry Head (whom I had met first at William Bateson's house near Cambridge) and I spent part of the night washing out our patient's stomach, the distinguished physician and myself on our knees at her bedside. I can recall, as we lifted the patient on to her bed, my admiration of the slender beauty for which she was famous, and, in retrospect, the realization that this took place before she had written any of her novels. We can now know what literature would never have existed had our efforts failed.

Many years later I suggested to Leonard Woolf that perhaps I deserved some token of gratitude for my action. Leonard, whom my wife and I regarded as our best friend in the Bloomsbury group, agreed and gave me the holograph manuscript of Virginia's long essay with the title, 'On Being Ill', published by the Hogarth Press in 1930. This document has special attractions because Virginia commonly composed her work on a typewriter, whereas this one is written in her own hand, with many corrections, in her violet ink. Also, when the essay was published in a small edition, hand set and signed by the author, she sent me a copy with corrections in the last sentence. It seems I had criticized another sentence, since I have two letters from her, the second of which I have permission to quote, with astonishment at my presumption:

52 Tavistock Square, W.C.1
26 Oct. [1930]

Dear Geoffrey,
    I have only altered a few words near the end—though I

know there's a whole sentence crumpled up some where. But if I begin, there will be no end, so I give you full liberty to re-write it for me!

Yours ever,
VIRGINIA WOOLF

My room at the top of the house in Brunswick Square was quiet enough, but I had little opportunity to work there. I had furnished it in very simple style with reed matting on the floor, a few second-hand windsor chairs and other necessities with, as far as I remember, only one picture on the walls. This was by Stanley Spencer, known to his friends as 'Cookham', from the name of his native village from which throughout his life he could never really separate himself. The picture, painted in 1911, was called 'John Donne Arriving in Heaven'. It had been lent to me by Gwen Raverat,[1] who with her husband Jacques had adopted Cookham, when he first arrived at the Slade School of Art with his brother Gilbert, and had given him advice and paid attention to his physical welfare, particularly in relation to his teeth, which seemed to have erupted in an unsightly double row. I did not have any part in the dental surgery that was required. I must have met the painter in 1913, though it was only after 1918 that I came to know him better.

The picture on my wall shewed four figures stepping, at various angles to the horizon, into Heaven and was known in the family as 'The Penguins', but I found that I enjoyed its oddities. Cookham's brother-in-law, Richard Carline, in his book *Stanley Spencer at War* (1978), says that the picture 'always took a pre-eminent place in his [Stanley's] estimation'; he described it as 'more directly from my imagination than any I have ever done'. 'I have always loved reading Donne,' he told an Oxford audience in 1923, 'though I understand only a little of it.' A sermon 'about going to Heaven by Heaven', he interpreted as meaning that 'Donne went past Heaven, alongside', and 'getting a broadside view of it'. 'As I was thinking like this,' Spencer explained, 'I seemed to see four people praying in all

---

[1] Elder daughter of Sir George Darwin, wood-engraver, and recorder of her childhood memories in *Period Piece*, 1952.

'John Donne Arriving in Heaven': oil painting by Stanley Spencer, Slade student, later R.A.

directions. I saw all their exact relative positions all in a moment. Heaven was Heaven everywhere, so, of course, they prayed in all directions.' He sold the painting to Jacques Raverat for two guineas and said he 'had been inspired of late'. At a later date the picture was again lent to me by Gwen Raverat's daughter, Sophie Gurney, and it hung in my Brinkley house for several years.

I cannot now remember exactly when I first met another artist, Eric Gill, whom I came to know well, but it must I think have been early in 1912, probably at the Cornfords' house. Gill was by then well known as an authority on lettering and typography and was just beginning to establish himself as a sculptor. I was attracted by his general attitude to the arts, and his view of himself as a craftsman rather than as an 'artist', and decided to visit him at Ditchling Common, where he and his family lived in a kind of commune with Douglas Pepler; together they ran a small business as printers of small books and wood engravings. In 1912 I was accustomed to making long walks on the South Downs at weekends, sometimes sleeping out in the open. Cosmo Gordon and I arrived late one afternoon at Ditchling Beacon on the Downs and then raced down the slopes to call on Eric Gill in the village below. He was not expecting us but gave a warm welcome and was anxious to give us something stronger than tea to drink. The pub next door was not open so he approached the publican from over the garden wall and came back with a bottle of 'four-ale', with which we assuaged our thirst. It was double-brewed beer, half-way to eight-ale, usually known as 'audit ale'—a drink too strong for stomachs such as ours except in small quantity. I have never met with four-ale since drinking it at Ditchling, but can never forget how deliciously it went down our throats under Eric's direction. Neither have I forgotten the difficulty we had in eating the very hard baked bread prepared by Mary, Eric's dear wife. Eric believed in living the hard way and she had to work in primitive conditions. That visit was the beginning of a delightful friendship lasting until his death in 1940. He and I used to regard ourselves as fellow craftsmen, he carving the outlines of the human form in stone, I moulding the shapes of the secret organs within.

Rupert Brooke also liked Gill's work and had acquired early in 1912 a small image of a 'Mother and Child' about six inches high. This appealed also to me but I wanted something larger and I asked him to make me a similar subject of a considerably larger size. On 30 September he wrote to say:

I've made you a carving of a 'Mother and Child'. But following your instructions to make it as big as possible (in reason) I've made it of such a size and have consequently taken such a time over it as to make me feel that if you can run to the £15 (instead of £10 or £12) you spoke of I'd be glad. I'm sorry but you have only to say no if you don't care to go to the £15 & I'll do another one smaller. Then again you may not like the thing & so do not want it at any price. Will you come and see?

I found I liked the stone very much indeed and only suggested he should cut some lettering round three sides of the plinth below. He approved the idea, writing, 'The cost of such an addition wd. be so little that as in the case of "this 'ere tortoise" there wd. be no charge for it.' So my sculpture bears on three sides of the plinth the message ESURIENTES IMPLEVIT BONIS ET DIVITES DIMISIT INANES, cut in Gill's characteristic letters. It was delivered complete in the same month, September 1913, and I have had undiminished enjoyment from its beauty ever since. The charge of £15 seemed to me absurdly small in 1913 and now almost unbelievable. Being one of the earliest of Gill's sculptures it does not have the stylization which he developed later. It seems to me that in its simple and unaffected style it is quite perfect.

A year or two later, when George Mallory was getting married, I decided to give him a carving by Gill in relief of two boys boxing. It had been in Gill's workshop for some time and he, in a fit of boredom with seeing it there, had painted the figures in bright colours, one red, the other yellow, with a dark blue background. I was sorry he had put on the paint and Gill wrote in March 1915:

I doubt if the paint wd. come off v. satisfactorily. It would be sure to stick in the pores of the stone a good deal. However if

'Mother and Child', by Eric Gill, commissioned 1912

necessary I cd. have a try. About the price. I don't know what to ask. War is war & I must snatch at any chance of selling things—besides I'd like you to have the stone. At the Goupil Exhib^n it was priced at £42 but that was absurd. What wd. you think of £20? Let me know. I wd. consider any offer from you.

So I paid £20 for the stone, George agreed with me about the colours, and after the Armistice scraped as much of the paint as he could off the figures, leaving the blue background. We both liked the result, though it was perhaps an act of vandalism. After the tragedy of Everest Ruth Mallory had no place for the heavy stone and returned it to me. It has now found a place in the house of my youngest son.

All through the war Gill wrote me a series of letters, interesting, amusing, and affectionate, but after he moved to Capel-y-ffin in Wales in 1924 I was out of touch with him. In 1928, when he had returned to England to live in a small commune at Pigotts, near High Wycombe, my wife and I became frequent visitors at his final home. His views on religion, politics, art, and industrialism, together with his life style, were original and deeply felt, but always humane. Above all he was a dedicated artist-craftsman of absolute integrity. He had a good deal in common with Blake. But I was worried and annoyed by his addiction to cigarette smoking. He seemed to be unable to work without having the foul 'fag' hanging from his mouth. I don't remember that I ever warned him of the possible dire result, as I have so often annoyed my friends by doing, but I was not surprised when a persistent cough was found to be due to a cancer of the lung. When Gill asked my advice, I could only tell him that he must face the necessary operation. I was not the craftsman who exercised his skill in the effort to save him—it was not 'in my line'—and the operation could have been completely successful had not his already damaged heart proved unequal to the strain. He was a very real artist.

In 1914 I was so much occupied with my work at Bart's that I can have had little time for bibliography, yet the last touches must have been given to the *Bibliography of Dr. John Donne*, for it was accepted for publication by the Baskerville Club of Cambridge, as their second (and last) book, and I delivered the script to J. B. Peace, the University Printer, in 1914. He listened to my amateur views and prejudices in favour of Caslon Old Face type, and using as many 'swash letters' as possible in headlines and elsewhere. But the outbreak of war deprived me of any further part in the production of the book, and the first copy was delivered to me early in 1915 at the hospital at Versailles where I was working.

THE FIRST WORLD WAR

In August 1914 I was halfway through my twenty-seventh year. Young people of my age had lived through the late Victorian and Edwardian times with a sense of complete physical security, and most of us had never given a thought to the possibility of our being involved in a European war. On 4 August I was enjoying a holiday from my work as a senior house surgeon at St. Bartholomew's Hospital, London, camping with a group of friends on the Cornish coast at Manaccan, a village on the south side of Falmouth Bay. We received the news of the declaration of war with Germany with astonishment almost amounting to incredulity but soon had to face the fact, and everyone arranged to return at once to his home. I went back to Bart's and decided without hesitation to offer myself to the War Office for enrolment as a junior officer in the Royal Army Medical Corps. The decision was influenced partly by my not being happy with my Chief (he did not discourage me), but more by a conviction that Great Britain would win the war, that it would not last long, and that the experience must not be missed. Since medical officers were noncombatants, there was no element of heroism in volunteering for the Army. 'War' did not suggest unnamed horrors, but to a young surgeon meant useful employment in his own profession while doing his duty for his country.

Formalities at the War Office were soon completed, and on 16 August I reported with the rank of lieutenant R.A.M.C. to my unit, a base hospital at Woolwich. Some equipment still had to be bought in London, and on 18 August I chanced to meet Rupert Brooke near my rooms in Bloomsbury. He gazed at my uniform with envy and almost with despair. Like many other young men, he was having great difficulty in deciding in what capacity he ought to serve. For me the decision had been quick and easy. My military inexperience was almost total—a week in camp at Aldershot in the Rugby School cadet corps a few years earlier had not encouraged a military outlook, yet it was not difficult to fit into the framework of an Army medical unit, where everyone but a few senior officers was as innocent as myself. My brief diary tells me that on 20 August the Germans occupied Brussels and that I (fortunately) failed to buy a sword in London. Active service was held to have automatically abolished most ceremony, and even details of uniform could be decided by each individual. In common with Maurice Perrin from Bart's I decided to have a tunic of khaki drill, corduroy riding breeches, and skiing boots reaching to just below the knee, thus getting rid of the constant nuisance of winding on and unwinding puttees, though these were the regulation wear.

On 22 August the unit left Woolwich, by train, for South-ampton Docks and embarked the next day on a dirty cargo boat bound for Le Havre and Rouen. The ship's progress up the Seine was enlivened from the banks by cheering crowds composed entirely of women, children, and old men, to whom

G.L.K. (centre) camping with friends at Manaccan on the Cornish coast, 4 August 1914

our troops responded with songs and countercheers. The ship docked at Rouen on the evening of 24 August, twenty days after the declaration of war, and our equipment was unloaded with a view to the hospital's being established in tents near the town. Casualties were arriving by train in large numbers by 28 August but were taken to other units. On the following day I was detailed to superintend the digging of latrines, a foretaste of the realities of war, but next morning it was reported that the Germans were marching on Paris. We were instructed to re-load everything on to the ship as quickly as possible and to return down the Seine to Le Havre. We knew little of what was happening at the front, so could live only for the moment and obey orders. One of the regular officers tried to frighten us by assuring us that the ship would be 'peppered with bullets' on our way down the river, but our eventual retreat was very much like our arrival, though there was noticeably less enthusiasm on the river banks. The ship did not, in fact, leave Rouen until early on 2 September, when the Germans were (erroneously) reported to have reached Amiens. We spent the next day steaming round Cape Finistère out of sight of land, while many of the officers and troops became patients with violent gastroenteritis. On 4 September we found ourselves near Saint-Nazaire in the estuary of the Loire, and it was several days before we knew where we were to go. Meanwhile, our equipment had been unloaded on to the quay, and time was occupied by taking parties of men down to the sea for bathing, where they surprisingly attempted to observe the conventions with underpants, handkerchiefs, or even puttees. For several nights I slept under the stars or, when it rained, under a small groundsheet. On 10 September our equipment was hopefully loaded on to a train, and next day definite orders were received to proceed to Versailles. This sounded improbable after the rumours that had reached us in the previous week; but it turned out to be true, and by the evening of 13 September we knew that we were to establish our hospital at Versailles in the Hotel Trianon Palace. After so many nights spent on the iron decks of a ship, on the ground, or in luggage waggons, the news seemed improbably good; but it proved true, and so ended the prelude to a doctor's war.

Maurice Perrin and G.L.K., Lieutenants R.A.M.C., August 1914

The hotel, situated just outside the gates of the palace of Versailles, could easily be adapted for use as a hospital, the large salons forming admirable wards. For two days I was busy planning and fitting up an operating theatre, until on 16 September two patients were admitted. One of them, under my care with a compound fracture of the leg, died the next day, the first indication of the lethal nature of wounds received on the richly manured ground of northern France and Flanders. We had been instructed not to interfere with apparently clean bullet wounds, experience of the South African war at the turn of the century being the only evidence available to the senior R.A.M.C. officers of how to deal with penetrating wounds. We soon learned, however, of the difference between wounds sustained on the clean South African veldt and those contaminated by European mud. Anaerobic bacteria lurking in the soil were responsible for the gas gangrene which proved to be one of the chief causes of death among those men who reached a base hospital alive. By 17 September, patients were arriving in hundreds, many of them having spent several days on the way from the battlefield of Mons. Hospital trains had been improvised from French *fourgons*, or cattle trucks, and the condition of the men posed many problems to our inexperienced judgement. Common sense was the best guide, but 'doing our best' was often distressingly inadequate while we learned the lessons of war surgery by trial and error.

For the next four months I worked at Versailles, steadily gaining experience of how to deal with the wounds of modern warfare. The question of amputating limbs raised the most perplexing and frequent of all problems. Reluctance to perform a mutilating operation, when nonperformance might cost the patient's life, created a difficult situation for an inexperienced surgeon. His seniors could give little help. The officers' ward was put in my charge, though the responsibility was no greater than if the patients had been private soldiers. The conditions were the same for all.

The work was uneven in intensity, the arrival of ambulance trains from the front naturally increasing the pressure for a time. Always a large proportion of the patients could be sent on to England after a short stay in hospital, or returned to duty.

Consequently there were leisured periods when we could visit Paris, explore the beauties of the palace and the Petit Trianon, go riding in the park, or, best of all, make friends with the French pilots at the neighbouring airfields of Buc and Saint-Cyr. All my early experience of flying was gained in this way, my first flight being in a Blériot monoplane. Later flights were in the primitive Farman biplane, where one sat exposed in a sort of open-sided basket, and in the more advanced Caudrons and Moranes. I even enjoyed coming down from 5,000 metres in a spiral descent on edge, followed by an almost vertical dive. It all seemed safe enough, even in the aeronautical dawn of 1914. One of these visits provided the additional satisfaction of taking a salute from Georges Carpentier, the greatest pugilist of his day, though his face was the flattened image of his profession rather than the handsome hero of popular legend. More than once I met my brother Maynard in Paris, where he was investigating French finances.

The proximity of the hospital to Paris naturally brought many interesting visitors. Not only were there official visits from the surgical consultants such as Sir George Makins and Sir Anthony Bowlby—the latter from the staff of my hospital and so particularly welcome—but also from unofficial visitors such as Lord Robert Cecil, Sir Frederick Treves, Prince Arthur of Connaught, and, of most interest to me, the great Elie Metchnikoff, pioneer in the study of rejuvenation by surgical operation and of the prevention of ageing through diet.

There were thus many amenities, and life was far too comfortable to constitute real experience of war. It was, therefore, not too unpleasant to learn on 6 February 1915 that I had been detailed by the C.O. for duty on an ambulance train. I accordingly left next day for Boulogne, having enjoyed a last evening in Paris at a revue, *Paris quand même*, at the Folies Bergères. For nearly six months I was to endure the peculiar conditions of life with two other officers on a constantly moving hospital. My bed-sitting room was an ordinary first-class compartment in a train composed mainly of second- and third-class carriages for sitting patients and of *fourgons* adapted for stretchers to carry those more seriously ill or wounded. Headquarters were at Boulogne, but we had to be ready to move at a moment's notice to any part of the front in France or Flanders. Often orders came during the night, and the first question to ask on waking in the morning was: 'Where are we?' So I became familiar with many railway stations—there was seldom time to investigate the towns or countryside around them. The number of patients carried on each journey varied between 100 and 400. During my turn of duty in the train we carried nearly 19,000 patients. Medical duties were usually restricted to ensuring that the wounded men, who had already been attended in a field ambulance or casualty clearing station, travelled as comfortably as possible with the help of sedative and analgesic drugs. Frequently they had to suffer violent jolts during shunting operations, occasionally so violent that couplings were smashed. Sometimes the engine driver was placed under arrest when he seemed to have been guilty of extremes of negligence or incompetence. We feared that men with fractured limbs would be subjected to unjustifiable pain or risks by the antics of callous drivers.

Usually the patients had been fully cared for before being sent on by train to the base hospitals, but on one occasion (12 March 1915), during the battle of Neuve-Chapelle, the train was ordered to go close to the front line near Armentières and take on casualties who had barely received first aid. The journey to Boulogne was spent working under great difficulties, even the coaches meant for lightly wounded men having to be filled with patients who had to lie down, many of them desperately ill. Several died during the journey or even before the train started to move. This was a distressing introduction to dealing with casualties coming straight from the battlefield. Yet on the whole, life on an ambulance train was fairly easy once we were used to the extreme irregularity of our existence. More than ever we lived in the moment and were largely unaware of what was happening beyond our limited horizon. On 27 April, I had news of the death of Rupert Brooke three days earlier in the Aegean, and I began to be more aware of the fate which was to kill the majority of the friends of my generation at Rugby and Cambridge.

On 24 July, having worked all night with a complement of 364 patients, I received the news at Boulogne that I was ordered to join the 7th Field Ambulance in the 3rd Division. After a day spent at Boulogne with my future brother-in-law, Lieutenant Charles Darwin, I left for Bailleul in a supply train. The next morning a London bus helped me on the road in a search for divisional headquarters, and I finally found my new unit in a field near Poperinghe. The town was under intermittent bombardment, though on 29 July ten of fourteen shells failed to explode. I was now more definitely at the front than hitherto and found myself going about my duties on horseback, though my only previous experience of riding had been to find myself on a horse bolting across Salisbury Plain towards Stonehenge.

My posting to the 7th Field Ambulance proved, however, to be only a brief interlude, my real destination being the 23rd Brigade of the Royal Field Artillery, which I joined on 5 August. A year had passed since the declaration of war, but it was only now, while engaged at close quarters with the enemy, that I realized how gently I had been let down into the cauldron of war. The 23rd Brigade, R.F.A., was stationed in the Ypres Salient, the gun emplacements being in front of the walls of the town beyond the Lille Gate. The area was under constant shell fire from three directions. The brigade H.Q. was in small dugouts in a field near Kruisstraat on the south side of Ypres, about half a mile from the walls. Every hedge was occupied by guns, large and small. The ground was pitted with shell holes, and several shells exploded in the field close behind us during the first evening; but the situation was regarded as fairly peaceful by my four companions, the colonel, the adjutant, the orderly officer, and the interpreter, a son of the governor of Calais.

As medical officer, I found to my astonishment that I was attended by a batman, a medical orderly, a groom, and three horses. The animals lived in the waggon lines, some distance further back, but were brought up to headquarters whenever I had to go anywhere other than the three batteries. At other times, when we were out in a rest area or moving to a fresh station, they were essential, and I found that my life was spent largely on horseback, a totally unexpected experience and most enjoyable. Though quite uninstructed in riding, I fell off only once, when my horse fell in attempting to jump a wide ditch from a slippery takeoff, giving me a severe concussion. When we were in action, I took sick parades at H.Q. and at each of the batteries, doing my rounds on foot along the walls of Ypres. I often rode off to the waggon lines and the ammunition column, where I saw sick parades in my consulting room (a converted pig-sty) and ensured that general sanitation was adequate.

Ten days after my joining the brigade, my posting was confirmed, so it seemed that I would do, and this gave me immense satisfaction. Not only were my nerves unruffled by the exceedingly dangerous position in which we lived, but also I was becoming closely attached to my companions, who received me as their equal in spite of my utterly unmilitary outlook—so obviously that of a civilian in uniform and a noncombatant. On one of my visits to a battery I sat in a dugout on the edge of a railway embankment with the major in command, while shells were thudding into the other side of the embankment. I noticed to my surprise that the major was trembling and dripping with sweat. Shell bursts were my daily lot, but none of the shells seemed to be meant for me. Frequently they would burst a hundred yards beyond our dugouts among some empty gun emplacements, and occasionally it seemed sensible to dodge behind a tree when we heard them coming; but usually we took no notice. If the enemy chose to bombard an abandoned gun position, it was none of our business. One of my favourite entertainments was going to watch the 17-inch shells roaring into Ypres with a noise like an express train and making huge craters among the ruins. This nonchalance was natural but was not to be confused with courage. It was plain inexperience. My friend, the sweating major, knew more about it than I did, as I subsequently discovered.

Occasionally there was a quiet day, and on one of these (24 August 1915) I walked into Ypres and straight through to the central square. Every house was in ruins, but the streets had been swept clear of debris. At the time, in mid-morning, it was completely deserted except for an occasional messenger on a bicycle hurrying through as though pursued by a ghost. The lovely medieval Cloth Hall was fearfully battered, but the walls remained with one brave little pinnacle of the central tower still standing. Frescoes on the walls of the upper floors were hanging in space. The neighbouring cathedral was even more devastated, though the tower was still erect, surrounded by huge shell craters. The bones of the last ten centuries were sticking out of the ground and a charnel house odour filled the air. I took two blue Flemish tiles from a fireplace in one of the houses in the square as a memento. A few days later, when the mail had just arrived, I was enjoying the perusal of a new *Bibliography of Dr. Samuel Johnson*, sent from Oxford by Sir William Osler, when I heard a shell coming. I looked up to see the last turret of the Cloth Hall actually falling after a direct hit.

Even this did not suggest to my mind the idea of a personal missile with my name on it. That came on the next day, 12 September. German aeroplanes had been active overhead for two days, and we had certainly been very careless about getting under cover when they were around. About 10 a.m. several shells came over as usual to the end of the next field, and we took no notice, though the last two did come nearer. At lunchtime we were thinking of our usual alfresco meal, when we heard another shell coming and realized from the different sound that it was going to land among us. It was too late to move, and I turned to watch it hit the ground ten yards away. It was an 8-inch shell, and by all the rules I was instantly killed. Instead, I saw a fountain of mud and debris shooting up into the air and attempted to hide under a wooden ledge fixed to a tree as a sort of sideboard, hoping to escape the mud as it came raining down again. No one was hurt, for the ground was so soft that the whole force of the explosion was dissipated upwards while the fragments were buried in the soil. The enemy had, in fact, ranged accurately on our headquarters, and it was time to run to some neighbouring dugouts, where we crouched until the shelling stopped. Orders had been given to all ranks to evacuate the site, but soon I was summoned to the telephonists' dugout, where three men had chosen to remain. A direct hit had been the price of disobedience, and every trace of the bodies of the men above their waists had vanished. It seemed in a way foolish to worry about what remained; but it was felt that their legs had to be given decent burial, and so I carefully extracted as much as I could and summoned the padre to perform his part. In those few minutes I had learned my lesson. I was no longer a civilian in uniform but was suddenly almost a soldier, though very much afraid.

On 23 August a German aeroplane dropped a typewritten message near us in a bag weighted with sand:

An das 16 Flying-Corps (Poperinge)

Nachdem wie aus der von Ihnen abgeworfenen Meldung zu ersehen ist, unsere erste Meldung leider nicht in ihren Besitz gelangt ist, versuchen wir nun zum zweiten Mal Sie über Kapitän Pike zu benachrichtigen.

Pike wurde am 9·8 von einem unserer Flügzeuge im Luftkampf heruntergeschossen, und ist kurz nach der Landung seiner Verwundung erlegen. Er hat also einen schönen Fliegertod gefunden und wurde mit allen militärischen Ehren auf einem Kirchhof hinter unserer Linie beigesetzt.[1]

At this date, the courtesies of civilized warfare were still being observed, though we usually referred to the enemy as the Huns, without much feeling of personal enmity in spite of experiencing narrow escapes from death many times each day.

Near the end of September 1915, I was given fourteen days' leave in England, returning to the daily round in the salient on 6 October. A fortnight later the brigade moved back to a rest area. The casualties in our brigade had not been serious during my three months in the front line, but there could be no question of the wisdom of giving the troops a prolonged rest from the continual tension of static warfare in an extremely hot corner of the front. On 30 November, I was provided with a new medical orderly in the person of an ex-cotton master who had worked with 800 men under him in Russia. He was able to help greatly in the organization of my medical inspections and

[1] After we had seen the message dropped by you, our first message unfortunately failed to reach you; we now try for the second time to inform you about Captain Pike.

Pike was shot down in air battle by one of our aircraft on 9 August and, soon after reaching the ground, died of his wounds. So he met with a fine airman's death and was buried with full military honours in a churchyard behind our lines.

sick parades, and I began to take lessons in Russian. Meanwhile, there was more free time, and I rode widely around the country, visiting friends in other units and learning something of what was happening on other fronts beyond our own. Our rest was to last until just after Christmas, and on 16 December I rode to Dickebusch Lake, only two miles from Ypres, which was to be the next station for our brigade.

Three days later, after the sound of very heavy firing at the front line, we became conscious of a strong smell of chlorine. The Germans had made their first gas attack north of Ypres, the discharge lasting one and a half hours, but it had failed, even though followed up by a heavy bombardment with gas shells. We were under orders to stand by, but as few Germans were able to leave their own trenches, no reinforcement had been necessary. We were provided with ludicrously inadequate gas masks—just a pad of cotton wool wrapped in muslin—so it was fortunate that the concentration of gas proved to be so light.

On 20 December, while still on my rounds, I found that my horse was being followed by a magnificent deerhound, which appeared to think I was his owner. Indeed, I proudly assumed the part and astonished the officers at the next battery headquarters by appearing with this retinue. The battery major possessed a small terrier bitch, and my magnificent gentleman immediately did the honours by lifting his immense hind leg and saluting the top of the officers' mess table with a generous flow of urine. This was taken in good part, and my deerhound followed me home, sharing my bed for that night. This glory could not last, and next day a messenger came from the mayor of Poperinghe to collect the Earl of Feversham's dog.

Christmas was celebrated with the customary dinner, for which a remarkable collection of bottles had been assembled, yet no one was noticeably drunk, perhaps because no one had forgotten that we were to move into our new action stations at Dickebusch next day. Two days later the relief of the 40th Brigade, R.F.A., had been completed, and I was able to take stock of my new surroundings in the *brasserie*, a large building close to the lake, round whose banks the gun emplacements had been fixed. The building was so large that it must have been

visible from the German lines and could have been easily
destroyed by gunfire. We were convinced that its survival was
due to the fact that the owner was in communication with the
enemy, though there was never any proof of the truth of this
uncharitable belief. Nevertheless, we were thankful that our
winter quarters provided a sound roof overhead, and we chose
to forget that it might have been at any moment destroyed with
ourselves inside.

Though more than sixty years have passed, the name
Dickebusch still stirs memories of events as vivid and moving as
anything that has ever happened to me. After four months I
was beginning to realize how deeply my life was bound up with
the welfare of the officers and men of the brigade. It had been
difficult to feel much personal devotion to a hospital temporarily situated in a French hotel or to an ambulance train with
its perpetually changing load of patients. The relation of a
medical officer to an artillery brigade in the front line was
intensely personal—a noncombatant sharing all the dangers
and interests of an Army unit which on active service knew
nothing of spit and polish, but was rich in the qualities of
courage, friendship, and determination. I could not really enjoy
the music hall songs they perpetually played on the gramo-
phone in the officers' mess; after my long academic training at
the university and hospital I had innumerable interests which
none of them could share, but their fine humanity under the
conditions we all had to endure was irresistible.

The positions of our gun emplacements and headquarters at
Dickebusch were much nearer the trenches than they had been
in the Ypres Salient. We were overlooked by captive balloons
and aeroplanes and might even be seen from lookout posts on
the ground. Except that the enemy refrained from destroying
our great *brasserie*, life was made more frightening by the
frequency of shellbursts. I had to give up Russian lessons with
my medical corporal; it was impossible to concentrate on the
unaccustomed alphabet and syllables with constant speculation at the back of my mind: where will the next one fall? For
six and a half months the tension was unbroken for me except
for a brief spell of leave in England. Occasionally a small shell,
or whizbang, hit the *brasserie*, one falling while some troops

were in the divisional baths established in one end of the capacious building. All the men ran out naked but soon preferred to risk the arrival of another shell inside—it was 25 March 1916. There were many other excitements. Mines were sprung under neighbouring trenches, local battles swayed to and fro, and it was sometimes satisfactory to see a few hundred prisoners being escorted to our rear. There were frequent dog-fights in the air over our heads, fifteen or twenty machines sometimes taking part. Anti-aircraft fire was usually ineffectual, the technique of ranging on moving targets being undeveloped. Occasionally a machine was seen to crash, with cheers from the ground if it was thought to be German. Falling fragments of anti-aircraft shells were another frequent hazard, though it was seldom that any injury resulted. Although the individual batteries were often shelled, the German gunners were usually inaccurate, and our casualties were not very heavy. Often I would notice that the enemy was ranging on one of our batteries and would watch from behind a tree to see if my help was likely to be needed.

On one occasion, when I happened to be in my dressing station near the *brasserie*, a message came that a gunner had been wounded and was lying beside his gun at the edge of the lake. Would I, please, come at once? I then experienced a feeling which it is hard to describe. It was my duty to walk immediately with stretcher-bearers from a position of comparative safety to a gun pit, which was being accurately shelled every few minutes. I ordered my legs to take me there, but at first they refused to move. My mind was equal to the ordeal, but another part of my brain declined to pass on the necessary instructions. I soon succeeded in reaching the position, having fallen flat several times on the way when shells were heard approaching. It was only about 200 yards to go, but the cerebral conflict involved in doing anything so contrary to nature caused a most strange sensation. Was this 'cowardice'? When I reached the gun pit, the gunner was almost dead, and nothing could have been done to save him.

Earlier in the year I had recorded 25 January as 'a bright but terrible day'. A German aeroplane came over about ten o'clock to range a gun firing at one of our batteries with 8-inch shells.

Eleven times it came over, dropped a starlight signal, and returned to report, always keeping about 500 yards beyond the range of the nearest anti-aircraft gun. About two o'clock the shells were falling faster around the battery, and finally one landed in the middle of a group of officers standing outside the billet where they lived. This shell killed five men altogether, including the major in command and the French interpreter, whose father, the governor of Calais, had visited the unit only an hour earlier. I attended as best I could to each of them, but all were terribly mutilated and were dead or dying. I felt it my duty to report at once to the colonel. I found him walking in the garden of the *brasserie* and went through the motions of a clumsy salute—I was never able to achieve the smartness of a proper military salute. Though hardly able to speak, I told him that he had lost five men, including the finest soldier in the brigade, the battery commander. He said nothing. We were both on the point of tears, and it was hard to maintain the stiff upper lip proper to the occasion. Far greater tragedies were happening elsewhere all the time. The long-drawn-out horrors of Passchendaele were to take place not far away; but the pattern of war is shaped in the individual mind by small individual experiences, and I can see these things as clearly today as if they had just happened, down to the body of the major's terrier bitch (the same that had been saluted by the deerhound) lying near her master.

During the second week in February, 1916, the brigade was to move back to a rest area twenty miles from Boulogne, and I was given a few days' leave. Less than a month later the brigade returned to Dickebusch to find various buildings in the neighbourhood had been destroyed, though the *brasserie* was still only slightly damaged. Life at Dickebusch continued on an ascending scale of terror. We suffered many casualties, and it was a great relief to be allowed to go again to a rest area on 15 April for a fortnight. Soon afterwards rearrangements in the divisional artillery deprived our brigade of all three batteries, so that for a short time I was almost unemployed. It seemed to me to be an appropriate moment to apply for a posting to a casualty clearing station—that is, a tented hospital at a suitable distance from the front line, able to give full surgical and medical treatment to men brought in by the field ambulances. Patients could sometimes be landed safely in hospital within an hour of being wounded. The brigade, as I had known it for so many months, was disintegrating owing to reorganization, half the officers with whom I had been most friendly had been killed, and I longed to be doing a more professionally useful job. First aid and sick parades were all that a medical officer in the front line could expect to find ready to his hand, and this could not satisfy for very long a young man who knew that his vocation lay in some branch of major surgery.

The reorganized artillery remained in Flanders for another two months, but towards the end of June rumours ran strongly that we were soon to move south into France to take part in the great battle of the Somme. Our move began on 1 July, and six days later we had reached the Ancre, a tributary of the Somme. On the way I had seized the opportunity of visiting a Casualty Clearing Station (C.C.S.) at Heilly, where a surgeon from Bart's was working, and had arranged with him that Sir Anthony Bowlby should be asked to have me posted to this unit. As so often happens in real life, it is knowing the right people that counts, and it was this that now provided the key to the actual beginning of my career in surgery. This could not, however, happen at once, and early on 7 July I was watching from the ridge near Carnoy one of the many attempts to capture the notorious Mametz Wood. I can still see the little black figures advancing towards the blasted trees. Later in the day I watched similar figures, this time running in the other direction while shells fell among them. These were probably prisoners being rounded up after the capture of Contalmaison, but, as usual, we, being on the spot, knew little of what was actually happening. While eating breakfast that day, I was hit on the shoulder by the only missile that actually found me throughout the war, but it was a spent shrapnel bullet, which failed even to penetrate my raincoat.

We were now living under very different conditions from those we had endured for so long in Flanders. We were in the middle of one of the great battles of the war, and armies were in movement. We found ourselves on the crest of a ridge in a

G.L.K., Captain R.A.M.C., 1916: later Surgical Specialist Major, R.A.M.C.

line of what had been German trenches with very little food and no shelter. Deep dugouts were there in plenty; but they were occupied by dead Germans, and we had to do the best we could on the surface of the ground. It was a good vantage point for watching the line of battle, but the noise of guns of every kind firing over our heads and from all sides was distracting; premature bursts caused some casualties. Three divisions of cavalry were at hand, ready to go through the anticipated breach in the enemy line. On 12 July a German prisoner told us that they were beginning to realize that the game was lost but thought that they would still put up a good fight—as indeed they did.

Gradually our artillery moved forward, and on 17 July we were in Montauban Alley, a trench just in front of the village of Montauban with a view from Mametz to Delville Wood of evil memory. At nine-thirty that evening we had just finished our supper of bully beef, when suddenly small shells began whistling over our heads at the rate of thirty or forty a minute, making no detonation as they hit the ground. Our gunners were at first completely mystified; but presently a shell fell near us, and it became apparent that these were a new form of small gas shells. We were in a shallow trench, and while the other officers were putting on their gas masks, I thought it better to climb up into the open air, where the concentration of gas was much lighter, and so escaped with only a mouthful of gas. One man was badly gassed, and I had to carry him half a mile to a collecting post. By then I was so exhausted that I had to rest there for two hours.

When I returned to my unit, it was getting light and raining, but the shelling continued until after four-thirty. We reckoned that at least 30,000 shells had been used and began to look around to see what effect they had had. My first unpleasant impression was that only by a miracle had I escaped stepping during the night on one of the many German dead bodies, which lay about in the long grass where they had been for several days, their faces pitch-black and decomposing. It appeared that the bombardment had been aimed at a neighbouring crossroads, where we found the way blocked by dead mules and horses, some disembowelled by direct hits. I noticed one of our men sitting at the roadside; he was bolt upright but had no head, again the result of a direct hit. As a gas attack, however, it had been a failure in spite of the enormous expenditure of material. Larger shells now began to fall very close, and I rigged up a tiny shelter in a trench with a roof of corrugated iron and sandbags. The protection was mainly of psychological value, for I was only 200 yards from the crossroads. One shell fell within ten yards of my flimsy hiding place. There were more and larger gas shells, so that I became thoroughly gassed and almost incapacitated, though there was little I could do in any case. Meanwhile, battles in the air were occurring at frequent intervals and provided exciting interludes.

On 22 July we moved forward again, our headquarters being situated between two 6-inch howitzer batteries, with another close behind. It would be difficult to imagine a more unpleasant situation or a more likely target for the German guns. I spent the afternoon preparing some sort of dugout which would provide a pretence of safety. Then at last came the message that I was to join a C.C.S. forthwith at Heilly, and was with profound relief that I made my way to Carnoy and so by stages during the night to Heilly.

I had been in the front line for only a few days short of a year, for most of the time in one of the hottest sections of the trench warfare in Flanders. I was spiritually and physically exhausted and felt that I had earned at least a spell of more creative work away from the front line. I learned later that the colonel of my artillery unit had recommended me for a Military Cross, at that time the most coveted decoration a young officer could be given. I did not get it—no doubt there were many others who deserved it more—but the recommendation was enough by itself to assure me that nothing had been shirked, so that I could concentrate for the future with a good conscience on my professional work, while living in comparative safety and fair comfort.

For the remainder of the war I was able to practise surgery on a huge scale in casualty clearing stations in France. From my first day at Heilly I was allowed to perform abdominal operations under the supervision of my future Chief, George Gask, who, after the war, initiated at Bart's the first professorial surgical unit in London. I began to feel that I had achieved my life's ambition, though I had not anticipated that it would be under the abnormal conditions of a world war.

After a month at Heilly I was instructed to rejoin the artillery in the front line and actually left for Amiens and Doullens, but fortunately my surgery had made a sufficiently good impression to earn a reversal of the order, and I was now told to join a C.C.S. at Edgehill, near Dernancourt, a ridge overlooking the town of Albert with the well-known 'hanging Virgin'; the effigy on the cathedral had been damaged by a shell and left projecting horizontally from the roof, where it remained, a bizarre landmark, for two years or more. The operating theatres were in tents where a vast amount of life-saving surgery was performed on those men too severely wounded for immediate despatch to the base hospitals. Those who remained in the C.C.S. were kept only as long as was needed to make them capable of transfer to the base. Many died and got no further. The survivors formed a constantly changing population in our wards, surgical success being measured not only by survival but also by the shortness of their necessary stay under our care.

Work was continuous, but naturally varied in intensity according to the sequence of events at the front line. The hospital was too far from the front line to be in danger from enemy shells, but the sound of the guns was the incessant background of our lives, and we could often anticipate the arrival of casualties by noting the increased intensity of the bombardment; this sometimes reached a level that had to be heard to be believed. While there were days of comparative inactivity, at other times the surgical teams had to work for an indefinite stretch of time, limited only by the number of patients to be attended. I have vivid memories of one occasion during a major battle when I was working for twenty-one hours. After three hours' sleep I had to operate continuously for another twenty-one hours. That night I happened to be orderly officer and was called up after only three more hours' sleep. My physical state was such that I was at first unable to stand, and it took some little time before I could collect my faculties in order to carry out my immediate duties.

Meanwhile, the newly developed technique of blood transfusion was being increasingly used. I learned more than one method during a visit to an American C.C.S. from Harvard University and thereafter applied these, using chiefly the technique based on the use of sodium citrate to prevent coagulation of the donor's blood. The donors were chosen by preliminary blood grouping of both patient and prospective donor, a procedure which was still a novelty. Official encouragement took the form of allowing a fortnight's extra leave in 'Blighty' (England) to the donors chosen from among the lightly wounded men. Potential donors lined up eagerly for the test—rejection was regarded almost as a slur on their integrity, the scientific aspect being incomprehensible to the average soldier. Transfusion naturally provided an incomparable extension of the possibilities of life-saving surgery. Trained anaesthetists were scarce, and often I dispensed with their services. A preliminary transfusion followed by a spinal analgesic enabled me to do a major amputation single-handed. A second transfusion then established the patient so firmly on the road to recovery that he could be dismissed to the ward without further anxiety. At other times I was greatly distressed by the state of affairs in one large tent known as 'the moribund ward'. This contained all the patients regarded by a responsible officer as being probably past surgical aid, since it was our duty to operate where there was reasonable hope of recovery, rather than to waste effort where there seemed to be none. The possibility of blood transfusion now raised hopes where formerly there had not been any, and I made it my business during any lull in the work to steal into the moribund ward, choose a patient who was still breathing and had a perceptible pulse, transfuse him, and carry out the necessary operation. Most of them were suffering primarily from shock and loss of blood, and in this way I had the satisfaction of pulling many men back from the jaws of death.

The necessity for this rather surreptitious work on my part and the intermittent activity of such intensity that the standard of treatment would obviously be lowered argued that there was some lack of organization. The whole medical service had inevitably been improvised at the start of the war on a scale previously unknown, and it took some time to adjust the available skill to suit the circumstances. During the year 1917 this adjustment was taking shape, and presently the medical higher command was warned of impending battles, and surgical teams, consisting of operating surgeon, unqualified assistant, and anaesthetist (often a specially trained nurse), were assembled at the clearing stations likely to be most heavily involved. Eight-hour shifts of duty could then be instituted by day and night, thus avoiding the extremes of exhaustion previously experienced. I was sent on many of these expeditions, taking with me the transfusion apparatus which I had evolved. This worked so well that it became the standard apparatus in Great Britain for twenty years after the war—though it is now to be seen only in medical museums.

For eighteen months I was engaged in this exciting and often rewarding work, gaining extraordinary surgical experience from thousands of operations of all types from minor injuries and fractures to abdominal, thoracic, cranial, and even cardiac emergencies. The training was in a way unsatisfactory, since it was easy to slip into bad technical habits through the urgency demanded by the work. Sheer physical and mental tiredness must have taken its toll, though it was hard to admit this form of shortcoming. Novel problems constantly presented themselves, mostly surgical, but sometimes of quite a different kind. One of these was the admission to the ward under my care of Prince Friedrich Karl of Prussia, a second cousin of the Kaiser Wilhelm and a nephew of the Kaiserin. He had been shot down in an aeroplane, a bullet passing through his abdomen and out through his back, perforating the intestine and injuring lumbar arteries and nerves on its way. The intestinal injury was operated on by a consulting surgeon, and the Prince seemed for several days to be making a good recovery. He was an embarrassment to the authorities, being related to the English royal family. His cousin, Prince Arthur of Connaught, was sent to visit him, though he came with obvious reluctance. The Intelligence Department thought this might be an opportunity to extract important information from the German prince. Accordingly, a bi-lingual British officer was disguised as a wounded German and placed in the bed next to the

Prince so that he could engage him in conversation. It thus became my duty to carry out each day behind a screen an imaginary dressing of the bogus German officer. I resented this attempted deception being practised on my patient. He was a fine-looking young man with the brilliant blue eyes peculiar to the royal families of Great Britain and Germany. It was impossible not to admire him and to regret that he should be treated so dishonestly, and I have to admit that I was pleased to learn that nothing whatever of military value had been extracted from him by our spy. He was sent on to the base, after about ten days, apparently well, but died soon after from a secondary haemorrhage from the injured lumbar vessels.

The area behind Albert was, as I have said, relatively quiet, but there were alarms at night from enemy activity in the air. Almost every evening soon after dark several German Goliaths would become audible. These were large bombers immediately recognizable by the peculiar beat heard in the roar of their two engines. They dropped their bombs with impunity, since night flying by our fighters was impracticable, until one memorable night when we at last heard a fighter coming to our defence. We saw his tracer bullets ripping into one of the Goliaths, which fell in flames. All the other Goliaths within sight or hearing immediately fled back to their bases, and we heard no more of them for some time.

Our minds and hands were so fully occupied with our work that we hardly ever thought about the end of the war. War, more or less static, had become a normal state of affairs until on 21 March 1918, rumours came to us that the enemy had effected a wide breach in the Allied lines to the south and that our forces were swinging around in retreat. To me, at any rate, the idea that the Allies might be defeated had never presented itself. Ultimate victory was certain, even though the conflict might continue well into a fifth year. Now suddenly the air was full of doubts. On the next day two German fighters, Messerschmitts, appeared out of the clouds and sprayed our camp with bullets from only 200 or 300 feet over our heads. No one was hurt, but it was clear that the incredible had happened.

For many months I had been receiving antiquarian booksellers' catalogues from England and had often had books sent over to me in France. I still have a copy of Sir Thomas Browne's *Pseudodoxia Epidemica*, 1669, containing the note: 'Sent off from Edgehill, Dernancourt, near Albert 21 March 1918, the day of the great German offensive. It passed through Albert on 22 March, the last day on which the post could be sent that way.' We were instructed the same day to evacuate all our patients immediately by ambulance train to the base and to make ready for our own departure. We left our camp on foot on the evening of 25 March, and I spent the night of my thirty-first birthday tramping across country towards Doullens. Another officer and I were detailed to make sure that none of our hospital staff dropped by the wayside. Many of the men were in the C-3 category—that is, unfit for active service—and so enlisted as hospital orderlies. It was with great difficulty that we persuaded some of them not to sit down in their tracks, though somehow all of them did reach their destination. It was galling to be sternly rebuked in the middle of the night by a red-tabbed staff officer on horseback for not keeping our men in proper ranks. He did not understand that many of them could barely walk, and I did not attempt to enlighten him. So we trailed into the citadel at Doullens next morning. I was utterly exhausted and collapsed on to a stretcher to sleep for nearly eighteen hours.

Fortunately the German offensive proved to be the final effort of despair. It reached its natural term with a large salient denting our lines, but with the Allied defences not seriously broken. Our hospital on the Dernancourt ridge became the front line soon after we left, but we were already getting to work again, with such material as we had managed to salvage, in the citadel at Doullens, a fortress of such strength that no bomb could penetrate into the dungeons where we laboured. Casualties poured in, and there was no time to wonder what was happening elsewhere. One day I was operating on a man whose genitals had been mangled by a fragment of shell when I became aware that I was being watched intently by a visitor. I looked up and saw it was King George V; I tactfully gave no sign of recognition and concentrated again on what I was doing.

The succeeding months saw the closing phases of the war with the Allies advancing relentlessly to victory. Soon after the episode at Doullens I was transferred to another C.C.S. as a fully fledged surgical specialist with the rank of major. In these days pneumonic influenza was killing thousands of men who had come safely through the hazards of war; I can never forget the sight of our mortuary tents with the pathetic rows of bodies of the men killed by one of the most lethal epidemics ever known.

On Armistice Day, 11 November 1918, I was with a surgical team at a C.C.S. near Cambrai. George Leigh Mallory, then in charge of a railway gun, was visiting me and shared my tent for the night. Together we witnessed that extraordinary scene, when the whole front in France seemed to be occupied by maniacs, letting off flares, Verey lights, and every other form of demonstration they could lay their hands on. Engines whistled and hooted. Discipline had temporarily vanished. We all thought we had seen the last of war. I could not foresee that twenty-one years later I should again put on uniform, this time blue instead of khaki, and spend six years as consulting surgeon to the Royal Air Force.

12

MARRIAGE TO THE DARWIN FAMILY

An important event not mentioned in the course of my narrative of the First World War was my being given special 'marriage leave' in May 1917 and my wedding in Cambridge with Margaret Darwin on the 12th of that month. It may seem rather indecent to record in print such an intimate affair as getting engaged, but I feel it is permissible as my wife described it in detail in her speech at the celebration of our Golden Wedding, this being afterwards printed as a small keepsake for the occasion.

But I must go back a few years to tell how it came about. During my four years at Bart's I had become so completely immersed in my hospital training that I had all but lost touch with Rupert Brooke and knew nothing of his now well-publicized emotional entanglement with Ka Cox. On looking through my letters to Ka, returned to me after her death, I find that I was writing to her in a progressively more affectionate manner during this period. In fact I may as well reveal at once that I 'proposed' to her twice, the first time in 1912, on the second occasion in August 1914 just before leaving for France.

It was not until long afterwards, when I read Christopher Hassall's life of Brooke, that I came to know how my first proposal to Ka had affected Rupert when he and Ka's friends became aware of it. He was then in a rather equivocal position with regard to his love for Ka. He was not moved by any feeling of jealousy, and it is quite impossible for me to quote what he wrote to Ka about me.[1] Ka's refusal of me settled the matter, and clearly I had to look elsewhere.

I had, of course, been acquainted with Margaret Darwin all my life, though it was not until the summer of 1908 that we

[1] *Rupert Brooke: A Biography* (1964), p. 364.

Margaret Darwin, 1912, from a pencil drawing by Gwen Raverat

became close friends. In that summer Sir George Darwin and Uncle William Darwin had jointly rented for a family holiday a crumbling Jacobean mansion, Vaynor Park in Montgomeryshire, and I was invited to stay there for about a fortnight. As Margaret described in her own autobiographical book, *A House by the River*, we would go on long cross-country walks, sometimes reading aloud from Housman's *Shropshire Lad* as we went.[1] This cemented our friendship and, without my knowing it, aroused feelings in my companion of a much more serious kind—though the social customs of the time (we were both Victorians) did not allow her to give the least sign of what she was experiencing.

We met many times during the next six years, and after my final rebuff by Ka Cox and my departure for military service in France and Flanders, my thoughts turned back to her and we began a regular correspondence. I was still writing affectionate letters to Ka, but in due course my other correspondent assumed the greater importance. I sent both of them specimens of the pretty lace handkerchiefs made by village maidens in Flanders, but somehow the one sent to Margaret 'took' more successfully than the other one, and so the situation developed in the obvious direction. The soldier in France needed a 'friend' at home and it naturally came about that during a ten days' period of leave in England we became engaged. Margaret had been working since the beginning of May 1916 with a secret unit at the Admiralty, deciphering German messages in code, and I had arranged to see her for the last time at her lodging in Fulham, before going back to France. As she described the scene in her Golden Wedding speech:

> The evening passed and Geoffrey had begun to say it was time he went or he would lose the last bus, when suddenly he got up, went over to the window and threw it wide open, to my amazement, for it was a bitterly cold night. The gale that swept into the room apparently gave him courage to propose which he did there and then. Shortly afterwards we were sitting together on the back of a sofa when it toppled over and sent us sprawling on the ground. So his proposal,

[1] Our enjoyment of Housman's poetry was lasting; see below, p. 255.

which needless to say I had accepted, ended in helpless laughter.

We spent the last but one day of my leave at the house of William and Beatrice Bateson in Merton, south-west London, where Bateson directed the John Innes Botanical Research Institute. I bought a ring next morning and Margaret and I met in Trafalgar Square and walked to Green Park, where the fog was so thick that I could hardly see the finger on which I was to put the ring. We decided to be married whenever I could get leave for the purpose. I applied for special leave in February 1917, but was refused on the grounds that there was too much activity at the front; however I was unexpectedly allowed to go on 10 May. Margaret was hastily summoned from the Admiralty and we were married two days later at St. Botolph's Church in Cambridge. I was in uniform, which made it seem a bit more romantic. Margaret's father, Sir George Darwin, had died in 1915, and the bride was given away by Uncle Leonard Darwin. My brother Maynard was best man. Aunts Etty and Bessie were there with Lady Darwin and Gwen and Jacques Raverat, so that Darwins were well represented; Keyneses were comparatively few, except for my parents and sister Margaret.

We spent our honeymoon at Uncle Leonard's Surrey house, Cripps's Corner, in Ashdown Forest. The weather was very hot and an incident, much treasured by my family as an example of how cruel a newly wedded book collector can be to his young wife, then took place in the neighbouring town of Tunbridge Wells. There were several bookshops in the town, notably one run by an ex-clergyman called Barnard. He had many seventeenth-century volumes of interest to me, so that I had to spend a long time going round the shelves. The heat inside the shop was even greater than outside and presently my wife began to feel faint; full of sympathy I took her to the door of the shop, placed her comfortably on the doorstep in the open air so that she could rest and recover, and then went back into the shop to complete my survey. Very kind and sensible, it seemed to me.

Another visit was to the small town of Horsted Keynes, where the church has the tiny effigy of a knight reputed to represent an ancestor who died in the Crusades. The honey-moon was a great success, but was far too brief (only a week) to be genuine. We had to have another one three years later at Padstow in Cornwall to make up for the deficiency—though on that occasion we foolishly took with us a bachelor friend, whom we both liked, but whose presence was a grievous mistake.

It has to be explained that anyone who married a Darwin of our generation was sure to find before very long that he had be-come allied, not with an individual as he naturally supposed, but with a family group comprising three generations, held together by their deep veneration for Charles and Emma Darwin, as the unchallenged patterns of what it meant to be a 'Darwin'. The grandchildren had not known the great scientist, as he had died before most of them were born. He was always referred to as 'C.D.' and his image was present in their minds almost as an actual presence through the reminiscences provided by his sons and daughters and by their familiarity with the house and garden at Down in Kent where he had lived and worked. Besides this legendary aura there were the strongly developed mental characteristics, inherited through the generations and still to be seen in the generations following our own.

Darwins have an endearing innocence, along with modesty, absolute integrity, and unselfconsciousness. The passion for truth and accuracy which characterized the whole life's work of C.D. can always be recognized, sometimes combined with imagination and artistic skill—as seen in my wife's sister, Gwen, the artist, and her cousin Frances, the poet. It is hardly necessary to add that the Darwin intelligence is of a high order. The numerous members of the two generations that I knew best were so well adjusted to one another by their similarity of character that they formed a closely knit group to which it was a privilege to be admitted. Jacques Raverat and I would some-times pretend that we were being overwhelmed by this family exclusiveness and that we should form an anti-Darwin league to defend our individualities, though we were secretly aware that our own standards were greatly benefited by the close association, and we soon came to share the enjoyment of know-

ing all our wives' relations, young and old. They were all delightful in their different ways. Aunt Etty (Mrs. Lichfield) was
a favourite among the elders, perhaps because Margaret and I
were able to stay with her at her home in Surrey and witness the
characteristics which make chapter VII the most entertaining
(if that be possible) of all the chapters in that marvellous book
Period Piece. We could actually join in the 'wholesome and
exhilarating sport' of hunting the stinkhorn (*Fungus phalloides*)
in her woodlands.

Our closest associations were with Margaret's sister, a fine
artist and a woman with a fine and masculine mind. Gwen
Raverat's skill and originality as a wood engraver and book
illustrator rival that of Bewick (she admitted she would like to
have been Mrs. Bewick); she is less celebrated as a painter in
oils of landscapes and portraits, but many of these are highly
prized by members of the family—her painting of a scene in
Studland was the first picture I ever bought (in 1912) and I
have her portrait of her husband Jacques, as strong and convincing a likeness as can be desired.

It would be quite improper for me to attempt any glosses on
the incomparable *Period Piece*, in which Gwen Raverat relives
her own childhood, for my wife's book, *A House by the River*
(1976), supplements *Period Piece* as autobiography. Gwen
supplied portraits of her parents, uncles, and aunts, not only in
words of wit and insight, but also in line drawings, some of great
beauty and all, as I can testify, so true to life that it is hard to
believe that they were in fact nearly all done from memory. I
had the satisfaction of reading the manuscript of *Period Piece* as
it came in sections hot from the writer's pen—I have claimed
the distinction of having invented the title, though I believe
there is at least one other claimant—and at the end announced
to my wife: 'This will be a bestseller.' The opinion has proved
true in so far as the book has been such a steady seller that
135,000 copies have been sold (to 1979), and it is almost as well
known in the United States of America as it is in England. That
occasionally a member of the Darwin family may be a little
deficient in a sense of humour is suggested by the fact that when
the author's brother, Sir Charles Darwin, read the manuscript
he gave it as his opinion that the book was not worth publishing,

whereas most people find it so funny that it can be read with enjoyment again and again. Sir Charles had a sense of responsibility, if not of humour: as an outstanding mathematician and physicist, he had a part in the production of the atom bomb, and was one of the few scientists to give a clear warning to the politicians of what the consequences of using the bomb would be. He also gave a warning, in his book *The Next Million Years* (1952), of what would happen to the human race if the population continued to increase at the current rate. Anxious not to be alarmist, he used the word 'million' on his title-page, but admitted afterwards that he should have said 'thousand' or even 'hundred'.

Among the Darwin clan my wife's cousin Frances was also a close and much loved friend. She had married Francis Cornford, classical scholar and Fellow of Trinity College, after they had worked together in the Marlowe Society production of Milton's *Comus*. It was a perfect union of a serious scholar with an unworldly poet; Frances spent a large part of her life searching for possessions temporarily mislaid. She and Rupert Brooke naturally coalesced and would tease one another regarding their relative merits as poets. Her verses tended to be short, often epigrammatic. She and her school, Rupert once wrote to Eddie Marsh (25 February 1912):

> . . . are known as the Heart-criers, because they believe all poetry ought to be short, simple, naïve and a cry from the heart. . . . They object to my poetry as unreal, affected, complex, 'literary', and full of long words. I'm rewriting English Literature on their lines. Do you think this is a fair rendering of Shakespeare's first twenty sonnets if Mrs. Cornford had had the doing of them?

TRIOLET

> If you would only have a son,
>   William, the day would be a glad one.
> It *would* be nice for everyone,
> If you would only have a son.
> —And, William, what would you have done
>   If Lady Pembroke hadn't had one?

If you would only have a son,
　　William, the day *would* be a glad one.[1]

Frances Cornford had characterized Rupert in her too well-known epigram:

YOUTH

A YOUNG Apollo, golden-haired,
　　Stands dreaming on the verge of strife,
Magnificently unprepared
　　For the long littleness of life.[2]

She afterwards regretted this kindly-meant tribute, realizing how it had trivialized him in the eyes of the world. I was delighted when, among her manuscripts deposited in the British Library by myself and others, I came on an unpublished version of a poem expressing her real feelings about him; it was written in May 1915 shortly after his death:

RUPERT BROOKE

CAN it be possible when we grow old
And Time destroys us, that your image now
Clearer than day to us—the image of you
Who brought to all serenely like a gift
The eternal beauty of youth—as tho' you'd lain
A moment since in English grass by the river
Thinking & dreaming under the fresh sky
When May was in the hedges. Can it be
That this,—your hair flung back—your smile which kept
A kind of secret sweetness like a child's
Tho' you might be most sad—the whole of you—
Must when we die in the vast air of time
Be swallowed like a candle? Nothing left
To the enamelled hard revolving world
(Full, full forever of fresh births & deaths
And busyness) of all you were?
　　　　　　　　　　　Perhaps
A thousand years ago some Greek boy died,

[1] *Letters of Rupert Brooke*, ed. Keynes (1968), pp. 361–2.
[2] *Poems by Frances Cornford* (Cambridge, 1910), p. 15.

So lovely-bodied, so adored, so young,
Like us they grieved & treasured little things
(And laughed with tears remembering his laughter),
And there was friendship in the very sound
Of his forgotten name to them. But now?
Now we know nothing, nothing is richer now
Because of all he was. O friend we have loved
Must it be thus with you?—and if it must be
How can men bear laboriously to live?[1]

When the 'Great War', the 'First German War', whichever you choose to call it, ended on 11 November 1918, I was soon sent back to England, but was not demobilized at once. Many of us were compelled to remain in uniform so that we might work at the military hospital at Woolwich to gain experience in the rehabilitation of the many injured men convalescing all over the country. I found rather dreary lodgings in Blackheath, from which I could bicycle to Woolwich. Our first child had been born in Cambridge during the time of the retreat of 1918 while my wife was in a state of anxiety concerning my survival; it lived only a few hours. Now, in 1919, another one was on the way, to be born later in the year in our flat in Fulham. Our first son Richard proved to be an entirely Darwinian character, both physically and mentally, and became in the fullness of time a Fellow of the Royal Society and Professor of Physiology at Cambridge.

Before his birth I had at last been able to discard my uniform and had been appointed second assistant in the new professorial surgical unit at Bart's, the first of its kind to be started at any teaching hospital in London, or, indeed, in England. An interesting experiment in education, the units, later both surgical and medical, were headed by Professors who worked full-time in the hospitals, renouncing private practice and its sometimes large emoluments for an academic (though still

[1] A revised version of the poem is included, under the title 'No Immortality', in her book *Autumn Midnight* (1923), p. 18. The poem was reprinted for me in December 1978 by Simon Rendall at his Cygnet Press, together with an unpublished serio-comic poem by Rupert and another tribute by Virginia Woolf in a letter to his mother.

Aunt Etty (Mrs. R. B. Lichfield) with Richard (Professor R. D.
Keynes, F.R.S.) aged 3 in the garden at Gomshall

clinical) life and a modest income. The head of the surgical
unit at Bart's was George Gask, one of the Senior Surgeons to
the hospital. I had not worked under him as a student, but
when I was attached to the casualty clearing station at Heilly
where he was Consulting Surgeon during the battle of the
Somme, in 1917, we had become fast friends. Although I still
lacked the higher qualifications in surgery which in normal
times would have been demanded for any holder of such an
office, Professor Gask had sufficient faith in my qualities to
wish to have me as a member of his team.

George Gask was an ideal Chief, and I could not have been
happier anywhere than I was with him. As well as acting as
assistant to the Professor, and to his assistant surgeon, and
taking part in all the clinical and teaching work, I was put in
charge of the unit's pathological laboratory, where we carried
out routine clinical tests and the microscopic examination of
specimens from the operating theatres. But although I had had
an enormous experience of clinical surgery in France, and had
attained the title of Surgical Specialist in the R.A.M.C., with

the rank of major, I was not really a fully trained surgeon. A cloud still on the horizon was the absolute necessity of passing the Primary Fellowship Examination at the Royal College of Surgeons of England. I had already failed once, in 1910, and knew how unequal my cast of mind seemed to be for the kind of test I would have to face.

The authorities at the College were prepared to take a sympathetic attitude and to offer what they regarded as easier terms than were customary to those candidates who had been caught up in Army service, as I had been, for more than four years and who had perhaps lost touch with the student's attitudes towards purely academic work. Encouraged by this concession I carried on with my work in the surgical unit and gave what time I was able to spare to academic anatomy and physiology. The result shewed that this was not enough. I failed again—this time not, as before, in one subject but in both. My humiliation was more complete than after the first attempt. I was told that a number of distinguished surgeons had suffered the same fate in the past, but had nevertheless overcome the obstruction by persistence; yet I was not reassured.

My Chief then decreed that, before the next examination was to be faced, I must spend three months working only for the examination, giving up my work for the unit to a deputy. I complied with this plan and after completing the physiological examination papers and viva voce confrontation, felt I might not have done too badly. It was the anatomical viva voce that still terrified me. I knew that this was silly, yet could not argue myself into a better frame of mind. A friend interested in psychiatry, then in its infancy as a medical speciality, recommended a young practitioner of his acquaintance who he thought might help me. At the first interview—*after* I had done the anatomy papers—he began questioning me about my dreams. I was immediately able to tell him of a vivid dream I had experienced the previous night. I had become aware of a large enemy aircraft overhead (this being obviously a memory of wartime experience); it had a numerous crew, one of whom I had seen dropping a small brass object which I must forthwith find somewhere in the grass if I was to survive. My psychiatrist was delighted, as I had given him exactly the lead he wanted. 'Of course,' he said, 'the crew of the aircraft represent the anatomy examiners and the brass container was the test you are about to have. You immediately found it. Obviously you are already approved by your papers and you need have no more anxiety.' I was foolish enough to believe him and went to the final confrontation in a mood of complete confidence, to find myself in the presence of a friendly colleague with whom I had worked in a casualty clearing hospital in France. I have often wondered whether he had been 'tipped off' by my Chief to let me through, for he asked me about my family, found that my eldest son had recently been born, and led on from that point to an elementary discussion of the infant's dentition. Nothing could have been easier. I had found my brass container, and I didn't have to ask what it contained.

I then decided to enter for the final test for the Fellowship of the Royal College of Surgeons, the F.R.C.S., at the first opportunity. For two years my life had been centred on the theory and practice of surgery, and it did not occur to me to start reading textbooks to cram in more knowledge with which to outwit the examiners. Perhaps I was supported by the feeling that I had still not lost the brass talisman which had taken me through the previous test so easily. Yet I was surprised, after I had been successful, to be told by the Senior Surgeon of Bart's and my former Chief, then President of the Royal College, that I had scored the highest aggregate of marks among the whole body of candidates.

This pleasant news gave me, I fear, a somewhat swollen head. I at once entered the next examination for the degree of M.Ch. (Master of Surgery) at Cambridge University. This is generally regarded as the stiffest test in the United Kingdom, failure being the rule following the dropping of a single 'brick'. Inevitably I dropped my brick in the clinical test and failed. I can still see in my mind's eye the patient's tongue exhibiting a flattened example of a harmless growth which I idiotically diagnosed as a syphilitic lesion. I deserved to fail and felt guilty when, many years later, having nearly completed a seven years' stint as Examiner in Surgery at Cambridge, I found myself Chairman of the Board and conducting an examination for the M.Ch. The candidates would not have known of my unworthiness to be in that position, but I was not unnaturally embarrassed by a feeling that I would like to let them all through. A year or two earlier I had been worried about a candidate who had seemed to find my (as I fondly imagined) kindly manner so frightening that he rolled off his chair unconscious. On that occasion the Board let him pass, for after all he had not answered any questions wrongly, and my colleagues acceded to my plea for mercy.

After my failure to achieve the M.Ch. I chose to believe that those particular letters after my name were a luxury rather than a necessity, and that I would not try again—in fact would never again submit myself to any humiliation of that kind. Yet Fate has seemed to provide a cornucopia of academic lettering to compensate for my abstention. When I presented myself for the degree of M.B. (Bachelor of Medicine) at Cambridge, a candidate was required to offer a thesis for approval before he could graduate. The title of my thesis was 'The Diagnosis of Gunshot Wounds of the Abdomen', based entirely on experience of the subject during the war in France. One day during a chance meeting, the Regius Professor of Medicine, Sir Clifford Albutt, nudged me in the ribs and said *sotto voce* that if I would submit my thesis for the degree of M.D. instead of M.B., I would be given it. So I became a Doctor of Medicine without further effort. In later years six universities have given me unsolicited honorary doctorates—LL.D. from Edinburgh, Litt.D., or D.Litt., from Oxford, Cambridge, Sheffield, Birmingham, and Reading—enough to satisfy the greediest searcher after academic distinctions especially when capped by the Fellowship of all three Royal Medical Colleges—F.R.C.S., F.R.C.P., F.R.C.O.G. and, in July 1980, reaching a climax by election to the Honorary Fellowship of the British Academy, F.B.A.

It was different for the next generation. After training at Trinity College, Cambridge, my third son, Milo, insisted on becoming a student at Bart's, where I was still a member of the staff, and decided to become a surgeon. He had little difficulty with the Primary and Final Fellowships of the R.C.S., and plunged immediately into the toils of the M.Ch., Cambridge, which he achieved on his second attempt. He also attained the

M.D., Cambridge, without a nudge in the ribs from the Regius Professor of Medicine. In the Primary Fellowship examination he had been passed by the same surgeon who had been so kind to me thirty years before. But again he did not have to be helped like a lame duck over the stile. At the moment I have a grandson, Gregory, who is going through the same mill and learning the hard way. When he challenged the examiners in anatomy at Cambridge he had all the more intricate details of the human body at his fingers' ends, but failed because the questions turned out to be so absurdly easy. The next time he was able to laugh at them. I can only sit and admire the younger generations cocking a snook at what I found so hard to do.

13

RUPERT BROOKE TRUSTEE

WHILE I was settling into the completion of my training as a surgeon I was at the same time picking up the threads of various projects laid aside for the duration of the war—though even the war had not interrupted them entirely. The publication of my *Bibliography of Dr. John Donne* early in 1915 had, for the time being, settled that particular obsession, which had originated, as I have recounted, in Rupert Brooke's influence over my literary interests. His death in April of that same year from septicaemia, in a French hospital ship on his way with the naval battalion to Gallipoli, had cut that, to me, very important relationship out of my life, and I felt that there could be no compensation.

Mrs. Brooke had by now lost all of her three sons: the eldest, Dick, had died of pneumonia in 1907; Alfred, the youngest, whom I had not known well, was killed in France in 1915. Their father, our housemaster at Rugby, had died before reaching retirement, his place being taken for a whole term by Rupert, a reluctant schoolmaster, torn away from his developing life at Cambridge. For a few years Rupert had been taken up by Sir Edward (Eddie) Marsh, who had introduced him into London society, centring on No. 10 Downing Street and Prime Minister Asquith's family. Rupert enjoyed the intellectual atmosphere, in which he moved so easily, and the beginnings of his reputation as a poet, which came with the publication of his first volume of poems in 1911. His sudden death in the Aegean soon after the publication of his famous War Sonnets, the solemn valediction by Winston Churchill in *The Times*, underlined by the quotation of the sonnet 'If I should die' in a sermon by Dean Inge at St. Paul's, the wave of national mourning for the romantic figure of the beautiful young poet cut off in his prime—all combined to create the Rupert Brooke 'legend' which has now persisted in one form or another for sixty-five years.

I have mentioned the difficulty some young men, such as Rupert Brooke, had had in 1914 in deciding how best they should serve their country. Brooke's War Sonnets, written in that year, expressed patriotic sentiments which were undoubtedly genuine and reflected the feelings of most young people at the time, but these poems did not glorify war (as some hostile postwar critics have insisted) or place their author among the later 'war poets'; he had seen no active service and had no opportunity of knowing what war really meant to those who took a direct part in it. True war poets, such as Siegfried Sassoon and Wilfred Owen, wrote only in horror at war's obscenities and with pity for its victims.

After his death Eddie Marsh, who had idolized Brooke and exploited him socially (with the kindest intentions) during the last years of his life, constituted himself his literary executor and biographer, to the dismay of Brooke's mother. Immediately after Brooke's death Marsh had edited a second volume of his poems, *1914 and Other Poems*, no doubt with Mrs. Brooke's knowledge and assent, and in August 1915 wrote a memoir of his friend with the intention of publishing this also. It was submitted to Mrs. Brooke, who objected strongly to its publication and insisted on many changes. No agreement could be reached until 1918, when a form of the memoir was published with the *Collected Poems*, preceded by two short 'Introductions' written in April of that year, the first making it plain that Mrs. Brooke had not approved the memoir even then and the second that the bewildered author felt he ought to rewrite it entirely, but had found it impossible to do so.

From 1916 onwards various tributes to Rupert Brooke as a poet had appeared in print, the most notable being an essay by Edward Thomas in *The English Review* for June 1915, a characteristic Preface by Henry James to Brooke's *Letters from America* (1916), and a lecture given by Walter de la Mare at Rugby School in 1919. But it was Marsh's memoir that made the greatest impact on the mind of the public. An elegantly written trifle, it was totally inadequate as a portrait of its subject, but served to satisfy the immediate public curiosity with an impression of an ineffectual young aesthete, who sought to attract notoriety by publishing poems, many of which were intended to shock by their unpleasant realism. Brooke's unmanly physical beauty was often taken as an indication that he was probably a homosexual and therefore to be despised. His patriotism was regarded as sentimentality and his talents as a brief efflorescence which would soon have been quenched by the realities of life. It had, of course, been far from Marsh's intention to produce any such impression. He had been deeply attached to Rupert, as he was to many young men, but lived himself in a sexual no-man's-land whose equivocal aura pervaded the memoir and contributed to the Brooke 'legend'. Mrs. Brooke had probably sensed this even though she might not have been able to put it into words, and was quite right to feel that the pretty sketch should never have been printed.

Her instincts having told her that Marsh's idolization of his subject was misleading, whereas her son's earlier friends, who had known 'the largest part of him', had never spoken, she had indeed turned to Dudley Ward and myself to undertake the task; but both of us had had to refuse our help at the time, owing to our wartime commitments—Ward as an economist employed in the Treasury, and myself as still in the Army Medical Service. Marsh had appropriated the greater part of the Brooke archive, comprising a large number of manuscript poems, letters, and related material; but I had the many letters Rupert had written me and manuscripts he had given me, and continued to feel a special obligation to his mother, who until her death in 1931 treated me almost as a son; I and my wife were both devoted to her.

Inevitably memorials to Rupert Brooke of a visual kind began to proliferate. A bust in the Poets' Corner in Westminster Abbey was suggested but rejected. A plaque of marble with a portrait in relief was designed and made in 1917 by Havard Thomas, an American sculptor, with a War Sonnet inscribed below in lettering cut by Eric Gill. Installation of the plaque in Rugby School chapel was delayed until March 1919, when an elaborate ceremony was organized with de la Mare's lecture and an unveiling by Sir Ian Hamilton supported by Colonel Freyberg together representing the officers who sailed with Brooke for Gallipoli, Sir Ian having been Commander-in-Chief of the ill-fated expedition. The medallion, based on one of the profile photographs by Sherril Schell, was much too pretty for my taste, lacking the dignity due to an individual of Rupert's stature. Mrs. Brooke made me and my wife her chief supporters on this occasion and I was set to carve the sacrificial chicken at the luncheon before the ceremony.

The memorial erected in Horse Guards Parade in April 1925 was of another kind, commemorating the Royal Naval Division rather than an individual, but it was associated with Brooke by having one of his War Sonnets inscribed on it and by being unveiled by Winston Churchill, who spoke of his poetry. I was a spectator at the ceremony but have little memory of the appearance of the memorial. It vanished before the Second World War because the ground where it stood had to be occupied by part of a kind of fortress needed for the security of government in case of enemy invasion, and has never been replaced.

The final unveiling was on the Greek island of Skyros in 1931, where a bronze statue was placed on a platform in the village instead of at the rather inaccessible site of Brooke's grave at the other end of the island. I did not see this until 1949 when on an organized tour of the Greek islands. It had been intended that the ship's company should visit the grave itself, but this proved to be impossible owing to its distant location. In the event the sea was so rough that only a caïque with four persons on board was able to reach the beach. I was one of the four and was to lay a wreath at the foot of the statue in honour of Rupert Brooke and give a brief oration. We had been met on the beach by a company of Boy Scouts who ran ahead up the steep path to the village. The memorial statue on its platform proved to be a solid symbol of youth and beauty, an abstraction, in the shape of a nude figure of a very different build from that of the hero it commemorated. When we reached it we found the same company of Boy Scouts, now not in friendly greeting but carrying placards saying ENOSIS and RUPERT BROOKE DIED FOR LIBERTY. The village schoolmaster then appeared and delivered an insulting speech against their enemies, the British. I could only lay down the wreath in embarrassment and retreat with the other three back to the ship. The wrong moment had been chosen for our gesture.

When Brooke's mother died in 1931 she chose to ignore Eddie Marsh's claim to be executor and in her will named me as Literary Trustee for the Estate, together with Dudley Ward, Walter de la Mare, and Jack Sheppard, Provost of King's. The other three tacitly accepted that I should assume responsibility, as the only active trustee, and it was my duty to claim the custody of the archive held by Eddie Marsh. I had always been on friendly terms with him and I enjoyed his witty conversation, but I was of no consequence to him. We frequently met in theatre foyers during the interval of a play or ballet; I think of him as never looking at me during our desultory conversations, but with his head raised, his monocle roving round the assembly to see if he could find someone of more importance. Yet he met my embarrassing claims with friendly grace and handed everything over to me without complaint.

So it came about that I found myself in the position of administrator of a valuable literary property, with control of the copyrights of the published and unpublished material. In 1931 there was no call for positive action beyond ensuring that the copyrights were not infringed by publishers, playwrights, or film-makers. The sales of the available editions of Brooke's poems went on at a steady rate, maintained until the present time (1979). Many hundreds of thousands of copies, now approaching a million, have been distributed by the publishers. Brooke had bequeathed the royalties from his poems to three other poets, Walter de la Mare, Wilfrid Wilson Gibson, and Lascelles Abercrombie, and after their several deaths the moneys went to the Royal Literary Fund. As the years pass the copyrights of the poems have mostly run out, though the income from them has in part been replaced by a share of the royalties from Christopher Hassall's *Rupert Brooke: A Biography* (1964), and from my edition of the *Letters of Rupert Brooke* (1968).

I had long been contemplating the latter project, as the best means of discrediting the legend by providing a truer picture of Rupert, and beginning in the 1930s had collected a large number of his letters, written to a variety of friends and representative of most sides of his character. There were a great many to Ka Cox—obviously too many and needing judicious selection—but none of those written to Noel Olivier, his youngest flame, who never would allow me to see them. I seemed to her to represent the 'publishing rascal' so effectively portrayed in Henry James's *The Aspern Papers*, though the ancient heroine of that story was at the end of her days, whereas Noel was at the beginning. I understood her reticence, and feeling that the omission of her letters would probably not greatly matter decided to go ahead without them. My co-trustees were not all as convinced as I was of the necessity of attacking the legend, but all, including Dudley Ward, made their letters available to me for selection.

During the next twenty years I did much work, helped by Robin Skelton, himself a poet, working since then at Leeds and later as Professor of English, at Victoria University, Vancouver. By 1955 I had made what seemed to me to be a satisfactory selection of letters to make a book of about 700 pages. Richard de la Mare, son of Brooke's friend and a director of the publishing firm of Faber and Faber, gladly undertook the publication. The book was set up in type by the Cambridge University Press and galley proofs were distributed to the other trustees. As Dudley Ward had welcomed the project and given me all his letters I had not thought it necessary to send him the typescript, but when he had read the proofs he announced that the book 'completely misrepresented' the writer of the letters and must not be published.

It was well known that Ward sometimes held views which seemed unaccountable to other people, but in this case he appeared to be so strongly persuaded of his own opinion that I felt unable to argue the matter; he was very ill at the time with heart trouble. The publishers were as bewildered as I was by Ward's objections. After much discussion it was decided with Fabers' agreement that Christopher Hassall, poet and librettist, should be asked to write a biography of Brooke with full use of the letters then in proof; meanwhile the type of the *Letters* was to be kept standing for an indefinite time. So the matter was resolved in a way that turned out to be the best possible.

Christopher Hassall, from a drawing by Joan Hassall

Hassall, who became a very dear friend, devoted himself to his task with all the powers of his mind and completed a careful and sympathetic account of Brooke's life. He died suddenly before his book was printed, and so it fell to me to see it through the press. I was filled with admiration as I read it. On its publication the biography was well received as a balanced account of a complex personality prevented from reaching its full flowering, though of extraordinary promise. Hassall's book also led to a demand for more knowledge of Brooke. Dudley Ward having died, I could now satisfy this demand by publishing in their original form the *Letters* of which the type had been standing for eleven years. It seemed that I had succeeded in getting the extent of the selection about right—not that any reviewer conceded this to the editor's credit, but as many of them complained that I had not provided enough letters as criticized me for printing too many. And the two books, the life and the *Letters*, have served to discredit the Rupert Brooke legend and to establish a truer valuation of his wholly masculine character and mind.

With the agreement of the other trustees I had edited Brooke's *Poetical Works* (1946), taking the opportunity to add a considerable amount of juvenilia to the canon. I compiled a full *Bibliography* of Brooke's writings in 1954, which has been twice reprinted with revisions, and I am now (1980) considering a new (third) edition of the poems with further additions of verses written in satirical and lighter vein or incorporated in letters. Three trustees have been appointed to fill the places of those who have died—two poets, Jon Stallworthy and Andrew Motion, with Peter Croft, scholar and librarian at King's College, in charge of the Brooke archive.

One further benefit from my trusteeship was my connection with Walter de la Mare, whose delightful friendship was for many years a bequest to me from Rupert. He had taken me to see Jack (as de la Mare preferred to be known) when he was living in Anerley, a London suburb, as an ill-paid literary journalist, and thereafter I visited him many times in his different homes as his fortunes improved. Best of all were the times when my wife and I would make our way to his apartments in a house in Montpelier Grove, Twickenham. He would talk in inimitable fashion for as long as we cared to stay. We both felt a high regard for much of de la Mare's poetry. I keep on my desk a copy of his poem 'Farewell' ('When I lie where shades of darkness'), which my wife kept on hers, and his conversation had for us much of the same quality. We once made an attempt to recapture a fragment of its charm by writing down shortly after leaving him as much of it as we could recall, but found it very difficult to reproduce the delicate texture of a poet's mind as he hovered over the problems of time and space on which he loved to speculate. My cousin by marriage, Lord Brain, tried with some success to do the same thing in his small book, *Tea with Walter de la Mare* (1957). As a physician and a neurologist with a special interest in psychology, he was better equipped to capture the flavour of so fleeting an experience.

Walter de la Mare, 1920

14

LITERARY WORK

JUST before the outbreak of war in 1914 I had been working on a study of William Pickering, pioneer in publishing attractive though inexpensive books, beginning in 1821, and first user of cloth bindings for his volumes in place of the fragile paper boards then almost universal. I had also looked around for a seventeenth-century writer to take the place of Dr. Donne. My choice had fallen on John Evelyn, the diarist. His diary was well known and he was recognized as a pioneer in the study of forestry, his work being enshrined in *Sylva* (1664), a classic in its own speciality; but all his other books, covering a wide range of subjects, had been ignored, although, as I had suspected, they were of great intrinsic interest. I had compiled a preliminary 'hand list' of Evelyn's works and had it printed in a small private edition as a basis on which to work. Theo Bartholomew agreed to act as watcher of the home market for Evelyn's books while I was away from England. I could still have booksellers' catalogues sent to me in France, as the British Expeditionary Force was well served by the Field Post Office, though the catalogues naturally reached me a few days after they had appeared on the breakfast tables of rival collectors in England. However, those collectors remained so pleasantly unaware of the attractions of Evelyn and his books that Theo and I were able to make a good start at forming an Evelyn collection. Thus it happened that I carried on my back during the Great Retreat of 1918 both the Pickering and Evelyn lists on which two of my later books were founded. All my other possessions had seemed for a time to be lost on the other side of the front line, though they reappeared some weeks later, having been whisked away in the last train to leave the hospital siding before the Germans arrived.

My Pickering interest brought me into contact with Stanley Morison, the great historian of typography, and with Oliver Simon, director of the Curwen Press; together they published *The Fleuron*, a typographical periodical, and Morison asked me to write a monograph on Pickering for publication from the office of *The Fleuron*. I gladly undertook this work, to comprise a memoir of Pickering with an eclectic catalogue of his publications. It was attractively produced by the Curwen Press and published in 1924, giving a start to a fashion for collecting the publications of Pickering, whose taste in literature was as commendable as was his flair for inexpensive book design. He was later to be seen as the forerunner of Francis Meynell, founder of the Nonesuch Press, whose first Nonesuch book was published in 1923, the year before the appearance of my Pickering monograph.

In the meantime my most recent literary interest, John Evelyn, was developing. With Theo Bartholomew's help I had acquired a good idea of Evelyn's status as a literary figure in 1921. His diary was esteemed as an historical document, though always less so than the racy and amusing diary covering a few years of the life of the civil servant Samuel Pepys. Evelyn's diary covered a much longer period, but he was a virtuous, and therefore a somewhat dull, character, less effective as a source of knowledge about the Court and character of King Charles II. His piety and sententious manner were so much disliked that little attention had been paid to his good sense, veracity, and highly cultivated mind, and the diary had not been seriously considered as needing re-examination. Both Pepys and Evelyn were bibliophiles, but whereas the Pepysian Library in Magdalene College, Cambridge, was well known and constantly mentioned in scholarly literature, no one had ever taken the trouble to find out about Evelyn's library or his stature as a collector.

It was plain that we must go to the fountainhead, Wotton House in Surrey, still inhabited by the Evelyn family and housing the library. It happened that Theo and I were both acquainted with Captain Evelyn Broadwood, a director of the Broadwood piano-making company, but also a cousin of Miss Joan Broadwood, living at Wotton as companion to Mrs.

Evelyn and curator of the library. It appeared that through most of the nineteenth century no stranger had been allowed to visit the library because of the supposed depredations made by William Upcott, the scholar chiefly responsible for editing the diary in 1818. It is probable that the losses suffered by the library were due chiefly to the irresponsible Lady Evelyn then in charge at Wotton, but the suspicions aroused by Upcott persisted and Evelyn's diary had not been examined by any independent witness for over a century.

Provided with the necessary introduction from Captain Broadwood, Theo and I went to Wotton in 1921 and were received by John Evelyn, a collateral descendant of the original owner, and Mrs. Evelyn, with their children, a girl and two boys, Jack and Peter. They were all most friendly. Mrs. Evelyn was more interested in breeding pedigree cattle than in books, but John Evelyn took up eagerly the points we wished to emphasize, with the result that he allowed the manuscript of the diary to be transferred to the Bodleian Library in Oxford for ten years, so that a complete and accurate transcription might be made. Miss Broadwood satisfied my interests by giving me a free run of the library under her guidance.

This was only the first of many visits; sometimes I was accompanied by a photographer so that I could make records of manuscripts, bindings, and portraits for use in my projected bibliography. I was allowed to borrow Evelyn's Library Catalogue of 1687 and other manuscripts for transcription, two of which were later published for me by the Nonesuch Press. Evelyn's *Instructions for the Gardener at Sayes Court* was easy to read; the other, *Memoires for my Grandson*, written by Evelyn in the tiny crabbed hand of his old age, was in parts exceedingly difficult to decipher, but proved to be a fascinating record of his life's experience. Sir Edmund Gosse, in a review of the book, greatly approved the phrase in my Preface referring to 'the admirable fussiness which impelled [Evelyn] to give such small details of how a country gentleman should conduct his life and affairs', with much good advice to the boy on how to regulate his own life. Francis Meynell had the little book set up in Fell type at Oxford, to make one of the most attractive of all the volumes carrying my name. It was given the distinction of a leading article in *The Times* and there was a scramble by the readers to buy up the limited number of copies.

I worked intermittently at the Evelyn bibliography during the next fifteen years and gradually built up an almost complete set of the books Evelyn had written and translated. His own library was oddly deficient in these, and his descendants had sometimes bought copies which had belonged to other people to fill the gaps. I used my Evelyn material for lectures given to the Bibliographical Society of London and for two Sandars Lectures at Cambridge University; the complete work, *John Evelyn: A Study in Bibliophily and a Bibliography of His Writings*, was printed at Cambridge and published jointly by the Grolier Club of New York and the Cambridge University Press in 1937.[1] These books had directed attention to the interest and value of Evelyn's library, deposited by Jack Evelyn at Christ Church, Oxford, and when it was to be sold at auction by the Evelyn family in 1978 desperate attempts were made to acquire it for the nation; but these failed owing to Government apathy, and it was scattered to the four winds.

Meanwhile—Evelyn's *Diary*, extracted from Wotton House in 1921, had been transcribed and retranscribed in Oxford and had been handed to Dr. Esmond de Beer for the preparation of a new edition by a modern scholar. Dr. de Beer and I worked in parallel, each helping the other when occasion offered, though my debt to him heavily outweighed his to me. The complete *Diary*, edited with consummate skill, was published in six volumes in 1955 by the Clarendon Press.

Throughout the period covered by work on Evelyn and others I was also collecting the numerous books published by Thomas Fuller, B.D., the whimsical author of *The Holy and Profane State* (1642) and *The Worthies of England* (1668), with a view to the ultimate compilation of a bibliography on my usual pattern. Fuller was regarded as a rather lightweight historian and sermonizer and most of his books were easy to find at low prices, but when my collection was nearing completion I found that an Oxford scholar, Strickland Gibson, was already well advanced along the same path, having encouraged his class in Bibliography to exercise their wits in 'doing' Fuller. This re-

[1] See Appendix, p. 388.

lieved me of having to assume the burden of the technical analysis of the books. Instead I was allowed to contribute a long Introduction on Fuller and his books, together with a portrait-frontispiece and many of the illustrative blocks made from title-pages, to Gibson's book, published by the Oxford Bibliographical Society in 1936.

I had made an unheard-of bibliographical discovery relating to Fuller in 1922, when I had purchased for 25 shillings from an Exeter bookseller an excellent copy of the first edition, 1639, of Fuller's *History of the Holy War*. I noticed some weeks later (as the bookseller clearly had not) that the binder had inserted as protective endpapers unfolded waste sheets of another book, which proved to be Shakespeare's *Poems* of 1640. It was pure serendipity that a book printed in Cambridge, bound (as was shewn by the 'rope marks' on the leather of the spine) in Oxford, and provided with inserted leaves from a book printed in London, should have landed in my appreciative hands. Since those happy days Fuller has come to be appreciated at his full value and his books have disappeared from the market.

In the years immediately after the First World War I had kept up my interest in Sir Thomas Browne, and some of my spare time while working for a few months in 1918–19 at the Woolwich Hospital, was occupied in writing a small book describing a manuscript Commonplace Book compiled by two of Browne's daughters. This I had bought for three guineas from a London bookseller during the war and found to be of great literary interest. It included a copy of an unknown passage on 'Consumptions' intended for their father's *Letter to a Friend on the Death of his Intimate Friend*, published posthumously in 1690. I was afterwards able to restore the new passage to its proper place when editing Browne's *Letter* for an American publisher in 1971. The *Letter* was to me one of Browne's most remarkable compositions, being a clinical report on one of his patients converted into a literary masterpiece by one of the greatest of English prose writers. I had my account of Browne's daughters' manuscript printed in 1919 in an edition of fifty copies by the Cambridge University Press. The edition was under the supervision of Bruce Rogers, the leading American typographer then working at Cambridge, who became a valued friend practising a technical craft always of great interest to me.

The first postwar years also saw the completion of my *Bibliography of Sir Thomas Browne*, begun in Cambridge in 1908 and published by the Cambridge University Press in 1924. To my sorrow it appeared a few years too late to be seen by Sir William Osler, who had written me a postcard on his deathbed asking plaintively *when* was it going to be finished. I could only reply by dedicating the book to his dear memory.

After 1918 I was picking up the threads of my bibliography of William Blake, abandoned in 1914 when the third version was nearing completion, and was again in communication with William A. White and his librarian, Henrietta Bartlett. She had been helping me with recording many of the copies of Blake's Illuminated Books in the possession of White and other American collectors. White was an influential member of the Grolier Club of New York, itself the best-known association of bibliophiles in the United States, and it was no doubt due largely to his support that the Grolier Club offered to publish the Blake *Bibliography*, previously rejected (with good reason) by the University Presses of Cambridge and Oxford. I gladly accepted the offer and when the Club's Secretary wrote to ask what my fee for the work would be I replied rather sententiously that there would not be any fee, the work having been done not for money, but for love of Blake. This surprised the Trustees so much that they immediately sent me a cheque for £2,000 with instructions to proceed with the production, in any manner that I chose, of an edition of 250 copies of the book, with the right to distribute 25 copies in Great Britain. This exceeded my wildest dreams, and I set about getting the book printed with enthusiasm. The first step was to agree on a contract for printing by the Chiswick Press; the next was to arrange with Sir Emery Walker for making the numerous illustrations in collotype and colour; and the third to visit Wookey Hole in Somerset to order a special making of handmade paper by the paper mill established there. The edition of 250 of this massive and handsome volume, published in 1921, proved to be much too small to satisfy the demand and it was soon sold out.

This pioneer work of Blake research, followed by the publication of the first approximately complete and accurate edition of Blake's writings, by the Nonesuch Press in 1925, together heralded the explosion of Blake scholarship and general appreciation which has been seen during the last fifty years. My work on Blake naturally brought me into contact with other people sharing my interest. Foremost among these was Laurence Binyon, Keeper of Prints and Drawings at the British Museum, himself a poet, and Max Plowman, author of an illuminating book on Blake for beginners, with whom I had long discussions on the difficult matter of Blake's punctuation in his Prophetic Books. His own markings were so casual and imperfectly formed that, as we agreed, it was better to supply consistent editorial punctuation than to attempt to interpret Blake's marks as he left them. This American purists have tried to do, though in fact they are guessing too, but with more confusing results than given by our rational method.

My *Bibliography* encouraged Mona Wilson, half-sister of my friend Hugh Wilson of King's College, and just retired after a distinguished career in the Civil Service, to write a new biography of Blake. I helped her as much as I could and her *Life of William Blake* (1927; revised edition 1971) has taken its place as the best biography since Gilchrist's of 1863 and 1880. Gilchrist's work can never be superseded, since he had the advantage of knowing several of Blake's friends, but he made no pretence of being able to understand Blake's mind as revealed by his poetry. Mona Wilson did much to fill this gap, and her book still has a position of authority. When she expressed a wish to give me something in recognition of my help I allowed her to pay ten pounds for a Blake print offered just then at Sotheby's. This turned out to be a unique and unrecorded first state of the magnificent engraving of 'Job and his Comforters'. The print had been trimmed and mounted on a stretcher but responded to the attentions of a skilled restorer, and is a fine example of what could in those days be found by a collector with a little more knowledge than the average dealer.

The three-volume 1925 edition of Blake's writings was a handsome and comparatively expensive book which would be out of the reach of the younger students of Blake's poetry, and I persuaded Francis Meynell to undertake a more modest edition, made less expensive by omitting variant readings and early drafts; this standard text of Blake, published in 1927, became the first of the Nonesuch 'Compendious Series' of English authors, issued in unlimited editions, and was many times reprinted with revisions up to 1939, when it was taken out of my hands. I later prepared a new one-volume text, published by the Nonesuch Press in 1957 and in 1966 reissued by Oxford University Press; constantly revised, this Oxford Standard Authors edition remains in print and a steady seller to the present day.[1]

In the 1920s I made an almost complete collection of the novels and related books of Jane Austen, my great literary heroine, including a first edition of Goldsmith's *Animated Nature* (1774), the first of the eight volumes containing her signature dated 1799, and all with the bookplate of her uncle, James Leigh Perrot. It is known that Jane was staying that year with her uncle and aunt in Bath. The Goldsmith volume had appeared with two others in a catalogue sent out by the bookseller C. Howes, of Hastings. It was priced at five guineas, and I had rather casually ordered it by post, not really believing that it could be genuine at that price. I had quite forgotten about it when a large parcel arrived a fortnight later. My astonishment and delight can be imagined by those who are alive to the pleasures of owning 'association copies'. (I always warn visitors who wish to see my books to open each volume at the very beginning, that is, by lifting the cover before looking at the fly-leaf. They will then so often see what they least expect, the author's presentation inscription or the signature of some other person of interest.) The other two books offered by Howes had been bought, one by Virginia Woolf, the other by R. W. Chapman, editor of the Oxford University Press edition of Jane Austen's *Collected Works*. My collections can also boast of two independent editions of a pamphlet published in Bath and Taunton, giving an account of the trial of Mrs. Leigh Perrot for the alleged offence of shoplifting a card of lace. The unfortunate lady, in the opinion of R. W. Chapman a victim of blackmail, was acquitted.

[1] A second edition was published by Oxford University Press in 1968.

Soon afterwards, in 1929, my *Bibliography of Jane Austen* was published by the Nonesuch Press. Francis Meynell designed the format and binding of the volume so that it closely resembled any one of the first editions of the novels in their original boards. The bibliography contained facsimiles of the half-titles as well as the title-pages, a luxury very seldom supplied, and revealed to many collectors, I am sorry to say, that their treasured first editions had been 'improved' by having the original half-titles, so regularly removed by binders, replaced with others taken from copies of the second edition—a practice which annoys the booksellers as much as it does the collectors. When later my youngest son, Stephen, married the daughter of Senator Knatchbull Hugessen of Montreal, he brought us into a connexion with our loved author, for Mary Hugessen was the great-great-niece of Jane Austen through her grandfather, Lord Brabourne, and Jane's favourite nephew, Edward, who took the name of Knight.

I had first met Francis Meynell in 1923. The Nonesuch Press had published its first book, *The Love Poems of John Donne*, in that year and had used in the binding the same decorated Italian paper that I had chosen for my copy of the Donne *Bibliography*. This seemed to be a signal and encouraged me to go uninvited into the basement of Birrell and Garnett's bookshop, in a street off Shaftesbury Avenue, where I was told the Nonesuch Press worked. They were about to publish an edition of Donne's *Paradoxes & Problems*, and I was prepared to offer my services as an editor, able to add to this edition material probably unknown to them. My offer was accepted and so began a wonderful friendship lasting for more than fifty years, ending only with Francis's death in 1975. He told me that I had produced, in whole or in part, sixteen books for the Nonesuch Press. I had a finger in a great many more besides. Francis moved his office soon afterwards to a house in Great James Street, Bloomsbury, which lay on my way home to Hampstead from Bart's Hospital, so that I could call in to see what he was doing and give opinions on design if asked for them.

My visit to the Nonesuch basement soon brought me another friendship when I was introduced in those surroundings to

Stephen Gooden, an artist-craftsman who seemed to be, as a copper-plate engraver, in direct line of descent from Dürer and Blake. He worked as master craftsman entirely from his own designs with great originality and beauty of line. His personality and outlook on life were also refreshingly original and unconventional. He, with his Irish wife, Mona, lived very much apart —he was so much engrossed in the very slow techniques of his creative work that he had little time for idle gossip, though he was always a most witty companion. He pretended to dislike children, but came with us on many seaside family holidays. There he would make entrancing sand sculptures of crocodiles for our pleasure and grief as we watched them being washed away by the sea, or would carve figures on the crumbling face of the Dunwich cliffs, which would last a little longer.

He was content with a modest income derived from his engraved work, always ready to oblige his friends with a personal bookplate designed to suit their tastes. The simple plate he made for me was characteristic of his wit: it shews a nude maiden seated at the top of the cartouche holding chains fastened round the necks of serpentine beasts on either side. When I asked him for an interpretation of his symbolism, he explained that there were two schools of thought—one that the figures represented Medical Science curbing Plague and Pestilence; or, if you preferred, that they shewed Civilization controlling Medicine and Surgery. Either view was relevant to my life's work, and so suitable for my books.

Steve's first published works were illustrations for the Nonesuch *Anacreon* and he made many other book illustrations, the best being his title-pages and his head- and tail-pieces for the splendid Nonesuch Bible and Apocrypha. His work was necessarily on a small scale and has never received the recognition it deserves, though he became a Royal Academician and was employed by Queen Mary to engrave heraldic bookplates for the royal family. Steve's was perhaps a minor form of artistic creation, but he brought to it a highly inventive mind and a superb craftsmanship. I bought from him prints of his entire output with innumerable 'early states', shewing how he built up his designs on the copper. The collection will find its ultimate home in the Fitzwilliam Museum, Cambridge, so that

Stephen Gooden, R.A., *c.* 1930.

this rare artist's whole creation can be seen in one place.

My published books sometimes brought me an unexpected bonus of friendship. In August 1922 I had a letter from a stranger telling me that when he was thirteen he had bought for three shillings in Wolverhampton a small volume without a title-page, which turned out to be an early edition of Donne's *Devotions*. He was now fifteen and having recently won a prize for Literature at Winchester College he had spent the money on Donne's *Poems*, *Life*, *Selected Sermons*, and my *Bibliography*; could I help him by identifying the edition of the *Devotions*? (It was the first, 1624.) The letter went on:

> I am so enthusiastic about the Devotions that I am trying to 'edit' them by transcribing them, writing notes, & an introduction. I don't know if you think that my youth is a fatal handicap to my success; I don't think I lack the little intelligence, the familiarity with Donne or the enthusiasm for him which seems to be needed. Do you think (supposing that I don't do it too badly), that such a book would have any chance of success? It is a great ambition with me.

There could be only one answer to this appeal. We made an assignation to meet on the steps of St. Paul's, where I encountered a small boy with a large bowler hat down on his ears and, lower down, a wide and friendly grin. Together we went into the cathedral to look at the effigy of Dr. Donne in his shroud, the only monument saved intact from the burning of the old cathedral in 1666 and now standing on an urn in the south aisle of the choir. Thereafter I lent the future Warden of All Souls College, Oxford, the other editions of the *Devotions*, so that he might compare the texts, contributed a 'Bibliographical Note', and made the necessary arrangements with the Cambridge University Press. The book was published in 1923, when the editor, John Sparrow, was sixteen, and it was for many years the standard edition of Donne's remarkable book. That all happened nearly sixty years ago, sixty years during which my friend's 'little intelligence' has consistently given me far more than I have given him.

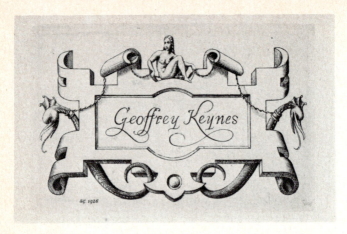

Bookplate for G.L.K. by Stephen Gooden, 1926

Stephen Gooden's emblem of the craft of engraving (1932), known to
Blake as 'Engraver's Hurry'

15

BART'S HOSPITAL

ALL this literary and bibliographical work may suggest that I was not taking my professional career too seriously, but in fact that would be far from the truth. My acquaintances have constantly remarked to me, 'I can't think how you can have found time, etc. etc.' I have answered that it all depends on how you use your time. There is always time for something you really want to do if you don't waste any—by 'waste' I mean sitting in front of the television, playing bridge, reading newspapers (except *The Times* and even that in moderation), and so on. Booksellers' catalogues can be read at the breakfast table. Punctuality for all professional engagements is essential; this depends on good organization, which affects everything else throughout an active day. Such a day should not infrequently be concluded at the theatre or the ballet, for there is always time, too, for life's major enjoyments.

It is true that the ordinary weekday life of a surgeon gives him little or no time to spend with his children. Only Sundays and the all too short holiday breaks are available for them. My sons have often complained that I neglected them during their childhood and I cannot deny this. But I can assert that Margaret and I never went abroad during the summer holidays; we always rented a house on the east coast, or in Dorset, or in Cumbria, taking the whole family with us, sometimes adding one or two young relations or godchildren, with a friend of our own generation.

To be a godfather is a somewhat equivocal position for one of my agnostic philosophy, but it was understood in our circles that the office did not have much to do with God. The most remarkable of the scatter of godchildren I acquired was John Rupert, the eldest son of Francis and Frances Cornford. He

John Cornford, aged 13, 1929

was a strong handsome boy with a dark complexion and a shock of black hair. He had a precocious intellect and it was easy to find books as presents which he would appreciate, such as Grote's *History of Greece*. But he soon became a rebel and I recall his exclaiming, when he was about twelve years old and saw a copy of the *Times Literary Supplement* on my table, 'Oh, I see you read that rag!' John had plenty of physical courage and I remember watching him diving through the largest Atlantic rollers on Chesil Beach in Dorset. He was strong-willed and no godfather could have diverted his drift into the ranks of the Communist Party, culminating in his death in the Spanish Civil War in 1936. He left behind him a considerable body of poems worth the reading and a son James, inheritor of his father's interest in sociology, being given at an early age a pro-fessorial chair in Edinburgh University and later working as political adviser to the Liberal Party.

At Bart's in the 1920s I was working with intense enjoyment in surroundings which commanded the devotion of everyone who came under their influence. With its history of good service over eight hundred years and still carried out within the noble buildings designed and built by Gibbs about the middle of the eighteenth century, the hospital had an aura unequalled by any other teaching hospital in London. It had a distinguished staff and a body of students who could be trusted to carry the name of their Alma Mater with distinction to all parts of the world. Like every other hospital in those days it was run as a charity, depending on the public for its funds—though in fact, owing to its age, it had hidden resources in scattered properties amounting to several millions of pounds. This created oppor-tunities for research paid for by what was known as a 'dis-cretionary fund', which gave exceptional opportunities to the members of the scientific staff.

Although I felt myself to be already an experienced surgeon because of the enormous amount of major surgery I had done in France, I was now, as second assistant to George Gask in the professorial surgical unit, in a subordinate position; but this did not trouble me. The surgery of trauma, that is, of men wounded in battle by bullets or high-explosive shells, is one thing: the

surgery of clinical disorders in civilian life is quite another, re-
quiring much more knowledge of pathology and craftsmanship,
and I still had a great deal to learn from older men of far wider
experience. In one area, however, I possessed much more
knowledge and experience than my elders. That was in the new
awareness of the possible value of blood transfusion in clinical
practice.

In 1914 the key factors in making the procedure practical
and safe were unknown. In 1907 the four main blood groups
into which human beings may be separated had been identified.
Using blood from the unsuitable group might be useless or even
fatal. Even if blood of the suitable group were used there would
remain the practical difficulty introduced by the liability of
blood to clot in the tubes through which it had to pass and so
put an end to the transfusion. Attempts had been made to do
'direct transfusions', that is, from donor's artery to patient's
vein, but this was technically very difficult to do and made it
impossible to know how much blood had passed. The second
key problem was solved by an American in 1914, when it was
shewn that clotting could be completely prevented by mixing
the donor's blood with the correct amount of a dilute watery
solution of a harmless chemical, sodium citrate. Owing to war
conditions these relatively simple facts had not been taken up
and applied in Great Britain, though by 1917 some American
surgeons had become familiar with them.

It so happened that soon after I had been transferred to a
casualty clearing station, or field hospital, in France I had paid
a visit to a similar unit staffed by volunteers from the Harvard
Medical School, in order to be instructed in this new technique.
I returned to my own unit filled with enthusiasm and determination to exploit to the full its obvious benefits, proceeding from
the fact that so many of our patients were suffering primarily
from loss of blood and traumatic shock, for both of which blood
transfusion would be a sovereign remedy. I had been shewn by
the Harvard team how to receive the donor's blood into a
conical glass flask already containing the sodium citrate solution, the mixture being then pumped into the patient's vein. I
soon modified this apparatus by adding to the delivery tube a
drip-feed by means of which the operator can control by sight

the rate at which the transfusion is given. The device worked perfectly and as an adjunct to surgery in saving the lives of our patients its value was almost beyond belief.

When I joined the surgical unit at Bart's I was astonished to find how seriously this extraordinary therapeutic advance was undervalued. Nowhere in London was any effort being made to organize a transfusion service. I had considerable difficulty in persuading my own surgical chiefs to allow me to give transfusions to patients on the operating table while they were undergoing serious operations involving much loss of blood. There were plain reasons for believing that the patient would be much helped by having the blood replaced as soon as possible after it had been lost, but my superiors were afraid my activities would 'get in the way' of the operators. However, giving such transfusions soon became a routine procedure.

There were also endless scientific wrangles about whether there might not be other kinds of fluid, such as gum arabic in solution, which would be of the requisite viscosity and therefore as effective as blood. Some patients were found to experience trivial reactions to the transfusion, shewn by a slight shivering fit with a mild and temporary rise in temperature. These were attributed to a variety of causes, such as some impurity derived from the rubber tube used for the transfusion, or, as was believed by a number of surgeons, more probably caused by the sodium citrate solution; but I never believed in this explanation, and, since the mild reactions appeared to do no harm, continued to use the citrate as anticoagulant. In due course the laboratory workers proved that human blood might vary somewhat in its chemical constitution, the variations being due to the subgroups now recognized as being normally present in blood, thus removing any objection to the use of citrate.

I tried to spread knowledge on the subject of blood transfusion among the public at large by publishing papers about it in 1920 in journals such as *The Athenaeum* and *Discovery*, and through various articles in *The Lancet* in 1920-2. Other surgeons were using transfusion to some extent, but not nearly as widely as its advantages demanded. Sometimes I would be invited to go to other teaching hospitals to demonstrate the technique, and to meet the demand for more general information I published through Oxford Medical Publications in 1922 the first textbook on the subject ever printed in Great Britain, which began with an historical sketch of the subject. *Blood Transfusion* made no great stir, but it sold off steadily; it was never reprinted because it was soon out of date owing to the growth of scientific knowledge and clinical experience. In 1949 I published a second, much larger, textbook on *Blood Transfusion*, myself contributing only an extended 'History of Transfusion', the technical parts being written by eight experts in the various aspects of the subject. This was translated into Spanish, but has long since been superseded by far more extensive works. The volume had contained the first family tree shewing the inheritance of the four blood groups found in fifty individuals of four generations of Darwins and Keyneses, the only ones not included being my wife's grandparents, Charles and Emma Darwin, who had both died long before. The charts shewed that the inheritance proceeded by strict Mendelian principles, encouraging me to predict the great advances which would result from the application of those principles to the science of anthropology.

As my work in blood transfusion became known I was being called upon more and more often by surgeons and physicians for help in treating their patients in private practice. In order to provide this service I found it necessary to organize a small panel of medical students among my acquaintance at Bart's to act as blood donors. I had determined their several blood groups, so that no mistakes should be made, but commonly the situation was one of urgency, so that most of my donors belonged to group O, the so-called 'universal donors', whose blood was compatible with that of all four groups. If the patient's blood group had to be determined before I could summon the donor by telephone too much time might be lost. For hospital patients, donors were usually sought among relations or friends and this sometimes resulted in serious delay. There was a popular and natural belief that the blood of a close family relation would be more acceptable than unrelated blood, though this had no scientific basis. It was thought too that the act of giving blood possessed a measure of heroism. It was essential that the medical profession should persuade the public that it was an act of generosity, not heroism. The donor was not running any risk whatever; in fact he often felt benefit after being let blood.

The necessity for some sort of organization for the supply of blood donors was brought to the notice of a Red Cross worker, P. L. Oliver, when in October 1921 he received from King's College Hospital a request for a donor. Oliver, a public-spirited and imaginative man, responded by founding the London Blood Transfusion Service. Working from his house in south-east London, he organized this service by finding individuals willing to give their blood; their blood group having been registered in Oliver's office, they could be contacted by telephone and directed where to go for service. At Oliver's request I acted as medical adviser to his organization, seconded by my friend H. F. Brewer, pathologist at Bart's. Brewer did most of the work, examining the suitability of the volunteers as donors and determining their groups. I continued for many years to publish articles on transfusion and to address medical meetings; on 22 October 1927 I gave the first broadcast appeal for donors, entitled 'A Call to Save Life', from the London station of the BBC on Savoy Hill (LO I). This set the seal on the principle that all blood donors in Great Britain were unpaid volunteers, which they remain, as almost nowhere else in the world, to this day. The London Service was the foundation on which, during the Second World War, Sir Lionel Whitby organized the present system of Blood Banks in all parts of the country, by which an adequate supply of blood can be sent to any hospital at any time.

Blood transfusion was only one of my special interests as a surgeon. Soon after joining the surgical unit at Bart's I was appointed by Gask's recommendation as second surgeon to the City of London Truss Society, a charity operating for more than a century in Finsbury Square. For ten years I began my day's work there at 9 a.m., examining patients with hernia in its various forms and fitting the necessary appliances needed for their relief. My senior in doing this work, another Bart's surgeon, was so consistently unpunctual that I had usually seen all the patients by the time he arrived, enabling me to see the maximum number by myself—up to a thousand each year. The surgical treatment of hernia, particularly those of the inguinal variety, a very common congenital defect, was apt to be regarded by surgeons in general as an uninteresting operation not calling for much technical skill. The chiefs were in consequence ready to turn the operation over to their juniors. I rejoiced in this because my familiarity with so many patients both in hospital and outside had convinced me that the surgical treatment had been found 'uninteresting' because it had been everywhere reduced to a routine, a conventional dogma. The condition in fact presented a variety of clinical differences, especially related to the patient's age and so the state of his tissues, the surgery needing variation in its technical details if later recurrence—notoriously all too frequent—was to be avoided. This was particularly true of the serious emergency known as strangulated femoral hernia. Here the conventional operation could be almost guaranteed to produce a recurrence, of which I saw many in my office in Finsbury Square. A little technical ingenuity and anatomical knowledge could avoid this.

In addition I encountered a great many patients coming regularly to Finsbury Square with huge hernial defects resulting from weakness of the scar tissue following the repair of the abdominal wall during some major abdominal operation. The condition was both distressing to the patient and very difficult to control with whatever form of belt or other appliance devised by the makers of these expensive remedies was tried. It was evident that the surgeons previously in charge of these patients had not thought it possible to repair the defects with further surgery. I felt sure that this attitude was wrong, and I took many such cases into Bart's for operations, sometimes heroic, designed to relieve their discomfort.

During my first visit to the United States, before 1930, I watched American surgeons at work in a number of surgical clinics, including the celebrated Mayo Clinic at Rochester, Minnesota, the Johns Hopkins Hospital in Baltimore, and Dr. George Crile's clinic at Cleveland, Ohio, and carried home a determination to profit by their example. The first fruits of this was an extensive use of a kind of plastic surgery by which the patients' own tissues were used as material for sewing up the large defects I have described. By the use of a special instrument it is easy to obtain a long strip of strong fascia from the sheath of the muscle on the outer side of the thigh. This material is much more likely to be accepted by the patient's other tissues in forming a soundly healed repair such as the situation of my patients demanded, than could be achieved by using less acceptable 'foreign bodies', such as silk, catgut, nylon, or even metal wire which had often been employed with uncertain, or even disastrous, results.

That first American visit was made in the company of Thomas Dunhill, a surgeon on the staff of Bart's from whom, in the course of twenty years of close association, I learnt far more than from any other colleague.

George Gask, while planning his strategy in 1920 for the establishment of the new kind of academic surgical unit, had taken the bold step of introducing into the rather inbred staff of the hospital a newcomer from Australia whom he had met while they were both serving as Army consultants in France. Thomas Dunhill had started life with no material advantages, serving for some years as assistant in a chemist's shop in order to earn enough money to pay for a medical education. After qualification he served on the staffs of two hospitals in Melbourne, and by 1907 was able to begin private practice as a surgeon. He had already taken an interest in the diseases of the thyroid gland, and then proceeded to pioneer the successful surgical treatment of toxic goitre, a condition in which overactivity of the thyroid gland was claiming many victims. Medical treatment was not effective and many patients became so ill that surgery proved lethal. Working in Melbourne, Dunhill had overcome the dangers by good management and skilful surgery combined with the use of local analgaesia instead of the usual general anaesthetics, ether and chloroform.

By the time he came to work in Bart's he had perfected his thyroid technique, although his reputation had not become known in other countries. He had published records of his work in Australia, but the physicians in England were unable to believe his claims. He was suspected of 'cooking' his results and used to tell of an experience at a dinner party when on his first visit to London. His neighbour on one side had begun by saying: 'It is quite certain that your cases of exophthalmic goitre are much less severe than those in England.' The neighbour on the other side did not speak at all while they were having their soup, but towards the end of the fish course found himself able to say: 'I am driven to the conclusion that surgeons are not candid in the statements they publish.' By 'surgeons' he meant Dunhill and by 'not candid' he meant telling lies. When Dunhill started working at Bart's they soon found that he was a surgical perfectionist and that his integrity was absolute. Visitors flocked to watch him at work in our operating theatre until it became difficult to work peacefully in the atmosphere needed for the concentrated attention we had to give to what we were trying to do.

Dunhill did not limit himself to being a thyroid specialist. He was a general surgeon in the true sense, exceptionally competent at all forms of surgery, whether abdominal or orthopaedic. I assisted him at hundreds of operations both in hospital and in private. Tension was always high, but I found it easy to work with him and with much practice we functioned almost like a single brain.

It was not surprising that he soon acquired a large private practice including attendance on the royal family. It was strange that with his other qualities he did not possess the faculty of lucid exposition. Although he enjoyed the company of students he knew that he was not very good at teaching them, and, equally, writing did not come easily to him. When speaking there was not time to seek out all the right words. A characteristic sentence uttered when under stress in the operating theatre ran: 'Tell Miss Thing to put the thing in the thing.' Nevertheless his written contributions were effective, being terse and direct. He confessed to me that when he first came to England he felt diffident and uneasy with us owing to our supposed greater culture, yet he could quote long passages from Browning's poetry without hesitation. He died in 1957, at the age of eighty-one.

My early association with Sir William Osler had brought me another friend from overseas, an American, Harvey Cushing, the world's leading surgeon in the field of the brain and nervous system, working at the Harvard Medical School. He was also a dedicated book collector in the medical field and wrote the authoritative life of Osler. We once had Cushing as a guest in our Hampstead house. He was a lean active man with a ferocious temper when in the operating theatre, but with great charm outside it. As a guest he was an early riser and went out before breakfast into the garden, a larger area than is common in London, with three steep terraces. There he was unlucky enough to meet my third son Milo, aged six or seven, who at once insisted on giving him a ride on a ramshackle go-cart assembled by himself and his elder brothers. This ended in our distinguished guest being deposited dangerously on his head at the bottom of the slope, luckily without serious injury.

My closest American friend was John Fulton, Professor of Physiology at Yale, book collector, medical historian, and biographer of Cushing. He suffered from demonic intellectual activity and, with the help of six secretaries, fell alas exhausted into a comparatively early grave. The combined Cushing and Fulton medical libraries now form one of the most important assemblages of this kind in America. Fulton's and my collections of the works of Robert Boyle, author of Boyle's Law concerning atmospheric pressure, and of *The Sceptical Chymist*, are, I suppose, two of the most complete in existence; we were rivals but did not quarrel. He took charge of the bibliography of Boyle, a most difficult task, and I was free to concentrate on other lines.

16

BALLETOMANIA

PREOCCUPATION with my professional duties did not prevent my being continually occupied with other 'cultural' activities. I was gradually building up a modest Blake collection as well as a library of English literature and medical history. Another growing passion was ballet, centring on Diaghilev's productions in London. I had never forgotten my experiences before the war with Rupert Brooke, and the performances by Nijinsky which we had seen together. Ballet was about to assume a much greater place in my life owing to the family association with my brother's wife, Lydia Lopokova.

Until that time Maynard had taken very little notice of me; for this I was sorry, as I felt a great admiration for him. Then in the summer of 1925 he unexpectedly invited me and my wife to go with him to see a performance of 'The Sleeping Beauty' ballet at Covent Garden. He told me that it was to introduce me to a sight of one of the Russian dancers, Lopokova, who was taking the part of the Lilac Fairy. I was delighted at his making this approach and still more to be taken round to the stage door in order to visit the dancer in her dressing room and given to understand that Maynard intended to make her his wife. Their marriage took place soon afterwards at a Registry Office, the only spectators being a large crowd of curious sight-seers on the pavement outside.

After my brother's death I was reading some of his letters to a friend, Duncan Grant, when I came on the sentence: 'Geoffrey is quite hopeless.' This seemed a harsh judgement, though the context of his remark shewed that it was justified. He was writing in 1907 from Luchon, a resort among the foothills of the Pyrenees, and was in the company of our family, but was nevertheless feeling lonely. With Duncan he could enjoy

Lydia Lopokova, by Picasso, 1919

conversation on a more imaginative level than any of us could provide. He was cultivating an aesthetic appreciation of the arts which the company of an artist could feed, but for which his younger brother was indeed 'hopeless'. My thoughts were centred on my Aurelian pursuits. and could contribute nothing of interest to Maynard's mind. He had been mistaken to come on this family holiday and he never made the same mistake again.

But the addition of Lydia's society was quite another matter. I loved her at sight and she loved me. Maynard's attitude changed immediately; from that time onwards he became a kind and affectionate brother. Margaret and I were constant guests at his house in Gordon Square, Bloomsbury, and at his country home at Tilton, in Sussex. Sometimes Maynard and Lydia were there, perhaps with their friends such as Sam Courtauld or Wittgenstein. Near by at Charleston were Clive and Vanessa Bell with Duncan Grant, whom we much loved when apart from the other Bloomsburyites. Often we had Tilton to ourselves, with Logan Thompson, the farm manager, next door, and used it as a weekend refuge until 1932, when we rented our own farmhouse in Suffolk.

Lydia was the most enchanting friend, always bubbling over with high spirits and delightful nonsense. There are many anecdotes of her (sometimes outrageous) remarks and eccentric behaviour. She brought joy to us all, especially to Maynard. They were a completely devoted couple. After she had come into my life my balletomania became more acute than ever. She took me behind the stage with Diaghilev's approval and introduced me to many of the dancers. Occasionally I would find myself trapped there after the curtain had been raised. This led to my seeing 'L'Après-midi d'un Faune' from an unusual angle. The people in the auditorium see the performance entirely in profile; watching from the wings I saw it on edge, so to speak, with the lovely ballerina Danilova peering over my shoulder. I never went behind without kissing the hand of the majestic Tchernicheva, wife of Grigoriev, the company's *regisseur*, but there was always the language difficulty.

Memories of Nijinsky were aroused by Serge Lifar, a very good performer, though without the extraordinary qualities of

Lopokova in action in the garden at Garsington, *c.* 1926

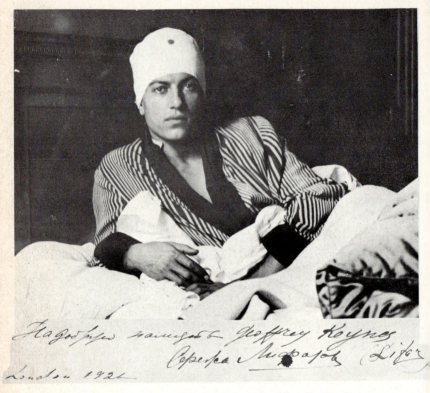

Надобрую память Geoffrey Keynes
Серёжа Лифарь (Lifar)
London 1926

Serge Lifar, a leading member of the Diaghilev Ballet Company,
recovering from an injury suffered while leaping off the stage at
Covent Garden Opera House, 1926

his prototype. On one occasion, after seeing him appear for the first time in London in 'L'Après-midi d'un Faune', I went up to Lifar's room to give my congratulations and found myself sitting on one side of his dressing table with Diaghilev himself, a terrifying presence, sitting on the other. I heard Boris Kochno, his attendant spirit, explaining to Diaghilev that I was Lydia's brother-in-law, but, having very little French, was struck almost dumb myself. Before I left I managed to blurt out, 'Il était prédestiné pour le Faune, n'est-ce-pas', receiving a vigorous nod of approval from the Presence. So I escaped unharmed. Another time I got Lifar to sign a photograph of himself recovering from an injury he had suffered when leaping off the stage into the wings. Diaghilev had had it published in *The Times* so as to get full publicity for the incident.

Best of all were Lydia's appearances as prima ballerina in all the classical ballets. I witnessed these so many times that I can still picture her in detail in my mind's eye—as Colombine in 'Le Carnaval', the Doll in 'Petrouchka', as the tiny figure triumphing over the powers of evil in 'The Firebird', as the can-can dancer with Massine in 'La Boutique fantasque' (this she sometimes repeated partnered by Maynard at parties in Gordon Square), perhaps above all as the leading lady in 'The Good-humoured Ladies'.

I found a special friend in Sokolova, alias Hilda Munnings, with whom there was no language barrier. She was a great favourite of Diaghilev and one of the most important of the company in spite of her nationality—a splendid ballerina, taking all the chief parts when called upon and, like the great Karsavina, free from attacks of jealousy and tantrums. Margaret and I often met Sokolova at supper with Lydia at Gordon Square after the performance. I was able to help her when she suffered from a whitlow, an acute infection of a thumb—so painful an affliction that I could never understand how she managed to dance in spite of it. I also visited her in hospital when she had undergone an operation.

Sokolova was devoted to Lydia who, as she says in her memoirs, was, like herself, without jealousy and always cheerful and amusing in any circumstances—unlike many of the company. She confirmed what Lydia told me of herself, that she

Lydia Sokolova, a member of the Diaghilev Ballet Company, *c.* 1925

was not in the real front rank of classical dancers—there was one classical ballet step she was never able to master—but owed her great success to her capacity for comic effects and her intelligence as an actress as well as a ballerina.

I spent so many evenings at Covent Garden that I was sometimes dragged out of my seat at the Opera House by a whispered message that I was wanted on the telephone. This usually meant that I had to leave the theatre to give a blood transfusion at some nursing home or private house. It was all in the day's work.

In 1927 my balletomania and admiration for the works of William Blake suddenly coalesced. I had recently acquired a fine copy of Blake's *Illustrations of the Book of Job*, a series of twenty-one engraved plates published in 1825 when he was an old man, yet constituting a masterpiece of creative art unique in England. The designs were commonly regarded as actual illustrations of the Bible story, but in 1910 Joseph Wicksteed, with whom I had long been closely associated through our common interest in Blake, published a study of his *Job* in which he revealed that the engravings really constituted a spiritual drama based on the Bible story, though telling Blake's own version of a man subjected to a series of severe trials by a malignant Satan, with the acquiescence of a pitying Jehovah, and ultimately brought to a realization of his worthlessness and his true position in the universe. Wicksteed's study revealed innumerable beauties of detail in the designs, as well as explaining why they seem so pregnant with meaning although the observer has been unable to take in all that they convey. Looking at the designs in 1926 it came to me that the groupings and gestures of the figures were asking to be put into actual motion on stage and, accompanied by dramatic music, could be fashioned into a new kind of symbolic ballet. It would not be easy to organize, however: stage designer, choreographer, and composer had to be brought to a common understanding and enthusiasm for Blake's purpose and a theatre manager had to be found willing to risk the financial undertaking.

My first appeal was to an artist, my sister-in-law, Gwen Raverat. She took my point and together we sat down to hammer out episodes and groupings to form a scenario covering enough of the series to suggest Blake's meaning to an audience unfamiliar with his eccentric designs. Several of them, such as 'Behemoth and Leviathan', representing war by land and sea, and 'Jehovah answering Job out of a Whirlwind', could not be shewn on a stage and had to be omitted, though the majority were amenable.

We had long discussions on the most suitable composer and finally chose Dr. Ralph Vaughan Williams, who we felt would be likely to have sympathy with Blake's symbolism and individuality, and who—perhaps most important of all—was the much-loved cousin of the Darwins and Wedgwoods, and therefore easily accessible. Gwen had made watercolour drop-scenes and small figures for assembling on the stage of a toy theatre, so that we could shew him the actual scenes we had devised. He was immediately struck with the possibilities, and was soon so fired with enthusiasm that he became rather difficult to control. He wished to introduce features having no connexion whatever with the designs, whereas it was my determination that the entire conception should be unadulterated Blake. No compromise was possible. Ralph was a formidable, but generous, opponent and gave way with good grace. At one point he wrote a letter to Gwen telling her that I had made my objections to his proposals 'in sorrow rather than in anger', so that he had to agree with me. He started immediately to compose music of a grandeur befitting the subject. He expressed, however, a great dislike of dancing 'on points', an essential feature of classical ballet, which made him feel ill. We agreed there should be none of this, and to his calling the production 'A Masque for Dancing' instead of a ballet.

The next move was to find a choreographer, and a company to stage the ballet. My first idea was to put it before Diaghilev. Gwen translated our scenario into French and I sent this with a set of reproductions of Blake's plates through Lydia to Big Serge in the hope that the novelty of the idea might attract him. I assumed that he would know and admire the quality of Ralph's music. The answer came back that the Masque was 'too English and too old-fashioned'. He kept the reproductions and I could see distinct traces of Blake's influence in another biblical ballet, 'The Prodigal Son', produced by Diaghilev in his next London season.

I thought Diaghilev's criticism was quite unjust and lacking in perception. Nothing like our Masque had ever been done anywhere. But after this rebuff it seemed unlikely that the Masque would ever reach the stage, and Ralph, assuming that his music would probably be performed as a concert piece, orchestrated it for some eighty instruments. The piece was finished early in 1930 and was first performed on 23 October, by the Queen's Hall Orchestra conducted by the composer, at the thirty-third Norfolk and Norwich Triennial Music Festival.

I have never listened to the Vaughan Williams music without feeling the same thrill as when I first heard it. The most moving rendering for me was conducted by Sir Adrian Boult in Westminster Abbey for Ralph's memorial service in 1958. I was sitting in the choir stalls and while listening to the music in praise, as it were, of William Blake, was gazing over to Poets' Corner where I could see Epstein's bronze head of Blake. I had unveiled this in 1957, as deputy for Ralph when he happened to be too unwell to officiate himself, and went afterwards to the artist's studio where I saw plaster casts of a multitude of his creations, including the huge figure of Lucifer now fixed on the outside of Coventry Cathedral. Epstein's conception of Blake was based on the life mask now in the National Portrait Gallery. He chose, with some justification, to exaggerate Blake's visionary faculties so that his eyes seem to be popping out of his head as if in astonishment at what he was able to see—nevertheless a worthwhile image of the artist.

Vaughan Williams's piece, when first performed in 1930, had been received with enthusiasm by *The Times* critic, who demanded that it should be heard in conjunction with the Masque for which it was intended. A second performance of the piece, which was broadcast from Savoy Hill on 13 February 1931, revived our hopes of staging the Masque. Before this date the settings on the toy stage had been shewn to Ninette de Valois and Lilian Baylis, who came together to our house to see them, and had won their approval. Ninette agreed to do the choreography, and I provided her with all the available reproductions of the whole range of Blake's designs so that she could steep herself in Blake's own atmosphere. Diaghilev having died in 1928, it was feared that the art of ballet might decay in Great Britain and disappear. To prevent this the Camargo Society had been formed in 1930, and it was under its auspices that the Job Masque was finally produced the next year at the Cambridge Theatre in London. With the help of my father and Sir Thomas Dunhill I made myself responsible for the initial expenses. Gwen Raverat herself painted most of the scenery in the rat-infested vaults of Sadler's Wells Theatre.

Our plan in the Masque had been to preserve the essential characters and situations of Blake's *Vision of the Book of Job*, as Wicksteed called it. The symmetry, so characteristic a feature of Blake's designs, was there. Job is seen at the beginning seated in the sunset of material prosperity; he is tried and tormented and descends into the pit of affliction; the truth is revealed to him and he repents; he is seen at the end in the sunrise of a new spiritual life. A dramatic climax is provided in the centre of the performance when Job summons his vision of the Godhead, and, to his horror, Satan is revealed upon the throne. The ending startles the audience when Satan, his claims rejected by Jehovah, rolls down the flight of steps, apparently unaware of any pain he may suffer.

An effective contrast is made between the static characters of Job and Jehovah, his spiritual self, and the volcanic exuberance of Satan, Job's material and physical counterpart; another contrast is made between the double-faced contortions of the Comforters and the purity of the young and beautiful Elihu, with a broader one between the dark horror of Satan's enthronement and the severe beauty of the scene when the Godhead is restored to His place by Job's enlightenment. Variety in the stage effects is introduced by the use of two levels, Jehovah's throne being set on a platform with steps leading up to it. The earthly characters move only on the stage level, while movements can be carried out by the heavenly beings around the throne and on the steps.

We were at first uneasy lest there might be trouble over introducing a representation of the Deity on to the stage, but were reassured by finding out that the Lord Chamberlain's licence

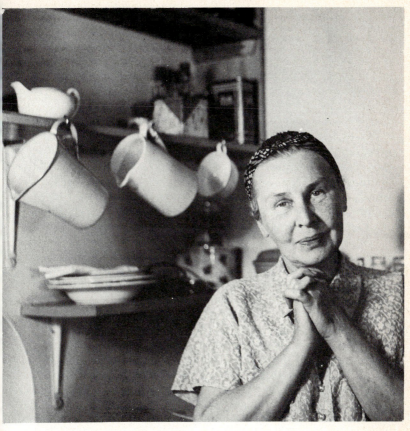

Lydia Lopokova at Gordon Square, 1956. Photograph by Cecil Beaton

did not have to be sought since no words were used in the performance. The only risk was that of prosecution by the police under the blasphemy laws. We thought this risk might be taken if we provided a mask for Jehovah, so as to make the presentation quite impersonal. The mask, rather larger than life-size, was made by Hedley Briggs after a large drawing by Blake of a 'Head of Job', which I had bought in 1918 after the great Linnell collection sale.

The first performances of 'Job: A Masque for Dancing' were given on 5 and 6 July 1931 with the Vaughan Williams music re-scored for a smaller orchestra by Constant Lambert, who conducted. Satan and Elihu were created by Anton Dolin and Stanley Judson, neither of whom has ever been surpassed in the parts. According to historians of the ballet the Job Masque helped to save British ballet by providing Ninette de Valois with her first major success in choreography. (In addition, it led her to using another pictured series on a moral subject in 'The Rake's Progress', from Hogarth's paintings.)

The further history of 'Job' has been one of continual success. It has been performed sixty-five times, mainly at the Opera House, Covent Garden. I watched the performances myself as often as I could, but missed a great many. One I can never forget was, I think, at the Cambridge Theatre during the Second World War, when German bombers were over London. A large bomb fell near by and the whole building seemed to jump, but the Job Masque went on as if nothing had happened.

In the 1930s Maynard prevailed upon Sir David Webster, the Director of the Opera House, to allow me free use of the royal box whenever it was not engaged, an opportunity of which I often took advantage with my friends. Some of my dressers at Bart's will probably not have forgotten the occasion when I took the whole firm to see 'Job' from this box, with supper in the annexe.

During the 1930s too I was frequently a member of the audience at the small Mercury Theatre in Notting Hill Gate, where the Ballet Rambert acted as nursery for so many dancers and choreographers who later served the Royal Ballet at Covent Garden. Marie Rambert became a firm friend, of irrepressible vitality and fun, and I got to know all her dancers,

Stanley Judson as Elihu in *Job: A Masque for Dancing*, 1932

from Freddie Ashton and Maude Lloyd to the youngest stars such as Sally Gilmour and Baronova. After one performance of 'Job' we invited the entire company to a midnight garden party at our house in Hampstead. A coachload was delivered at the house and they enjoyed themselves into the small hours, with Marie Rambert doing cartwheels on the tennis lawn. In March 1978, when I had just turned ninety and she was nearing the same age, she wrote to me:

Dearest Geoffrey,

How happy I was to read your letter, thank you very much for troubling to write. I always thought that you were much younger than I.

I go on practising my ballet exercises—even on Sunday I cannot resist the desire to move, to try and attain the best line and do the best movement I can. I am so happy to know that you too are feeling well.

Come and dance with me.

Much love,
MIM

17

BREAST CANCER

In the 1920s assistants in the professorial surgical unit at Bart's were expected to undertake some original research on surgical problems presented by our patients. For me my Professor, George Gask, suggested a careful investigation of the condition, very commonly seen in women's breasts, known as chronic mastitis. There was nothing spectacular about this minor discomfort experienced by so many women, and no determined effort seemed to have been made to find out its cause and possible relation to cancer of the breast. Its chief clinical importance lay in the fact that the most frequent symptom was intermittent pain of slight degree leading the patient to wonder uneasily whether she might not be developing what she most dreaded, namely a cancer.

The results of my research, begun in 1920, were presented to the world in May 1923, as a Hunterian Lecture at the Royal College of Surgeons, and afterwards published with numerous illustrations in the *British Journal of Surgery*. Rereading the lecture today I am astonished at the amount of painstaking work that had gone into it and how little renown it was likely to have brought to its author. But I was delighted to find that the solution of the problem could be summed up in two lines from *As You Like It*, supporting the conviction that Shakespeare can never be caught out in providing an apposite comment on anything in Life or Death. The normal physiology of the mammary gland determines that it is subjected to alternate periods of stimulation and inactivity; in the first phase there is active secretion, in the second the secretions, unable to escape, stagnate and irritate the ducts containing them by the decay of the chemical constituents. As expressed by the melancholy Jaques:

> And so from hour to hour, we ripe, and ripe,
> And then from hour to hour, we rot, and rot,
> And thereby hangs a tale.
>
> (*As You Like It*, ii. vii)

I do not remember if I quoted these lines at the Royal College. I cannot forget that just before I was to deliver this, my maiden oration, to a distinguished gathering of professional colleagues, one of them, a Grand Old Man of the profession in our eyes, famous for his blunt approach to his fellows, remarked to me, 'It will be a miracle, Keynes, if you make the subject interesting.' To do him justice I must add that he came up to me afterwards to tell me that I had made it interesting, and the printed version has been called by a respected colleague a classic contribution to the subject.

Meanwhile, in 1922, following the completion of my laboratory investigation of chronic mastitis, I was to be entrusted with the far more important clinical trial of treating cancer (carcinoma) of the breast with the intense irradiation given off by radium chloride. Treatment of the disease using the X-ray tubes mainly for diagnosis had not proved very successful, and the principle of applying the much more intense irradiation given out by a radium compound, put in actual contact with the diseased tissues, gave us a new and more powerful tool. This entailed obvious dangers to both patient and operator—the patient might suffer an overdose of irradiation with damage to normal tissues; the operator might be exposed to enough irradiation to cause physical damage, such as sterilization of the generative organs, or even induced cancer of his own fingers by handling the radium. Accordingly I placed myself under the guidance of the physicists in the scientific department of the Medical College; they would monitor the dosage I was using for this important clinical experiment so that it should not exceed a safe level. Accurately known quantities of radium were contained in hollow platinum needles and I could avoid touching these with my fingers by grasping them with long forceps, while wearing an apron impregnated with lead to protect my genitals.

This was venturing into unknown regions of therapy, and it would be unethical to use radium on patients who could be treated by well-known surgical means. Therefore the patients given to me to treat were only those suffering from 'inoperable' cancer—that is, those who had delayed going to see their doctor until it was too late for surgery to be of any service, and who were sure to die of the disease anyway. Local treatment by radium might improve the quality of their life even though it could not be prolonged, and valuable knowledge would be gained. The only operation needed was to take a tiny piece of the diseased tissue to provide a proof under the microscope that the diagnosis was correct. The implantation of the radium-filled needles could be done in a short time under a general anaesthetic, and they could be removed without pain after about seven days. Whatever suffering was entailed could be described as discomfort rather than pain. There would be no mutilation at all. I devised a method of implantation of the needles in a pattern which would give a definite dosage of irradiation (calculated by the physicists) covering the whole of the diseased area and those other areas immediately concerned in the lymphatic drainage of the breast, such as the lymph nodes in the armpit (axilla). The investigation would have to spread over several years while the patients were kept under careful observation and the results recorded.

In 1927, after five years' experience of the use of radium for cancer of the breast, I began to publish cautious reports on the results I was obtaining. Those results were quite astonishingly good. Inevitably some of my patients had died from dissemination of the cancer to other parts of the body, this having happened long before I had started the radium treatment. It had to be remembered that the victims never died from the primary disease in the breast, but always from the secondary disease elsewhere, sometimes lying dormant for several years in various parts of the skeleton. Yet I had many patients who were apparently cured—though that word was hardly ever used by anyone experienced in the treatment of cancer; I never used it myself, though I could present a number of patients in whom the local disease appeared to have been completely arrested and who were in good health for periods of up to five years. It seemed that perhaps a real advance had been made in the great cancer problem.

Having satisfied myself that radium could be used successfully when the disease was beyond surgery, I began to wonder whether it might not be used, perhaps in combination with conservative surgery, for treating cancer of the breast in its earlier stages. My thoughts turned to an examination of the whole theoretical foundation on which the accepted treatment was based. The so-called 'radical' operation then in accepted use had been first advocated by an American surgeon, Halsted, working in the Johns Hopkins Hospital, Baltimore. By 1898 he had carried the operation to its logical extreme. This entailed a gross mutilation of the patient's body in order to remove every scrap of tissue that might be infected by the spread of the disease through the lymphatic channels supposed to drain the breast. In 1906 a book by the London surgeon Sampson Handley had fortified the general belief in the absolute necessity for radical mastectomy by claiming to demonstrate that the disease spread by what Handley chose to call 'centrifugal permeation', i.e., that it proceeded from the outset to permeate lymphatic channels in all directions, thus reaching distant organs, such as the liver and the bones of the vertebral column. I had been taught to accept this and for a time advocated the most radical operation for the earliest forms of the disease. But when it came to performing the operation myself I found that it filled me with the utmost loathing and I soon became sceptical about its real efficiency.

I read Handley's book carefully and found that, although written in good faith by an honest surgeon who believed he was using scientific principles, it was based on fallacies. Handley had been insufficiently aware of what was now a growing realization, that cancerous growths quite early in their history begin to invade blood vessels, both arteries and veins, and so are distributed as separate cancerous cells or in small clumps of cells to all parts of the body. Not every cell thus circulating succeeds in starting a new colony of growth, but the invaders are almost certain to gain the upper hand in the end. This fact alone seemed to me to invalidate the efficacy of the radical operation, for if the circulating cancer cells had already obtained a hold it was too late, and if they had not done so, the operation was not necessary. Belief in the radical operation had become a dogma. Every patient had become a 'case', not an individual, whereas in fact there was good reason for regarding each patient as a separate problem for careful consideration according to the individual circumstances. I have ever since that time tried to eliminate the word 'case' from my writings. It had become a universal curse in medical thinking and still is.

Another serious flaw I detected in Handley's reasoning was that it was all based on evidence derived from the bodies of patients who had died of the disease, that is, in whom the normal channels of drainage had been completely blocked by the cancerous growth. He had assumed that lymphatic drainage could take place freely in all directions, but had never tried to find out if this was true. In fact, as others were to shew, hardly any of these channels were operative. The normal lymphatic drainage of the breast is almost wholly by one main vessel passing to the axilla, where the stream is interrupted by a group of lymph nodes which act as sieves to eliminate any foreign substances, such as bacteria or cancer cells, from the circulation. When these nodes and the channel leading to them became blocked, new channels had to be developed to relieve the pressure, and cancerous permeation could proceed along these; but this was a terminal event and was no ground for postulating centrifugal permeation—the main justification for the radical mastectomy—in all stages of the disease.

The logic of the facts as I saw them led me to abandon the orthodox radical operation without hesitation, and I never performed it thereafter. I practised conservative surgery, adapted to the needs of each patient, taking into consideration all the relevant circumstances. Often I removed only a small segment of the breast for a small tumour; if it was larger, I might do a simple mastectomy, removing the breast only, without any further dissection. I was convinced that nothing I or anyone else did could affect more than marginally the ultimate survival rate (all my cancer patients were kept on a systematic follow-up scheme, for an indefinite time), since mortality must depend on how early the disease had been diagnosed and treated. The patient could be permanently free from the threat of recurrence somewhere in the body only if the primary tumour had been removed before any cancer cells had been dispersed into the blood stream. If a patient survived for twenty years in good health the surgeon might be allowed to claim a 'cure'. But at least all my patients had avoided serious mutilation, none suffered the complication, produced by the great majority of radical mastectomies, of swelling of the arm following removal of the lymphatic channels, and I could claim a significant improvement in the quality of their lives, even though the prolongation may not have been great. In the present state of knowledge, as I have said, the main hope of improved survival lies in early diagnosis, so that the primary growth may be removed before dissemination has happened. Many women delay going to their doctor out of fear of what surgical treatment will mean for them; if they come to realize that radical mastectomy is a thing of the past they will respond by seeking advice much sooner.

From 1929 onwards I was publicly advocating conservative treatment for cancer of the breast. It was to be many years before I could produce significant statistical results, but my careful follow-up system would, I felt sure, influence surgical practice in the end. Any statistical evidence I published in the interim was prepared by a trained statistician, to avoid any suspicion of bias. Gradually I was treating more and more patients with breast cancer, both in hospital and in private practice, although I was frequently criticized for my unorthodox views. A built-in dogma of thirty years' standing dies hard, and I was regarded with grave disapproval and shaking of heads by the older surgeons of my own hospital.

My initial work with radium was regarded with some interest by American surgeons, and in due course I was invited to give an address on the subject to the American Association of Surgeons in New York. My views were received with gratifying respect, and I had my first experience of shaking more than three hundred hands of guests at the annual banquet of the Association, of which I was made an Honorary Fellow. I had not at that time fully developed my plan of practising only conservative surgery for cancer of the breast, but occasionally I became involved in transatlantic telegraphic altercations. An

American lady visiting London became aware that she had a small lump in one breast, and a general practitioner advised her to seek my advice. I was able to diagnose an early stage of malignancy with a very good prognosis. The tumour was removed by a trivial operation and the area given irradiation with radium needles. She returned home feeling quite confident and armed with a section of the tumour so that her doctor could see under the microscope that the diagnosis had been correct. But she was advised that she had been given quite inadequate treatment and must have an immediate Halsted's operation. She refused to submit to this, and I had to try to justify my action in telegraphic terms. Indignation on the other side subsided and some time later the surgeon concerned wrote to say that he was convinced I was right.

I was sure that I had initiated an important advance in practice by trying to eliminate what I regarded as surgical malpractice—the performance of a grossly mutilating and illogical operation, when similar or slightly better statistical results could be obtained by conservative surgery supplemented by radiotherapy. In various publications I suggested this new attitude as one of the most pressing problems in surgical treatment—*pressing* because of the very large number of patients suffering from the disease. I knew that other surgeons would not be satisfied with my reasoning until I could provide convincing statistical results and was therefore careful not to make what would be regarded as exaggerated claims until at least five years', or even as much as ten years', experience could be reported and analysed. At the same time I emphasized the necessity for earlier diagnosis as the best way to achieve improved results until such time as effective systemic treatment had been discovered. This position is still valid in spite of world-wide efforts to improve treatment by radiotherapy or by injection of chemical reagents into the bloodstream.

While teaching students I warned them not to press my unpopular views on their examiners and emphasized the importance of a minutely careful clinical examination of every patient complaining of a 'lump' in the breast. At the same time this had to be done with the utmost gentleness, demonstrated by me rather than by allowing a series of students to examine any patient with inexperienced and possibly rough hands by which the disease might be spread. There are now several scientific methods of examination which may help to eliminate the danger of dissemination by pressure of examining fingers.

As the years passed I was accumulating a considerable body of evidence in support of my convictions, but the possibility of reaching the climax of the clinical research was prevented by my spending six years as Consulting Surgeon to the Royal Air Force. I had to abandon both hospital and private practice and my follow-up system collapsed. I lost touch with my patients and never succeeded in recovering the lost ground.

Nevertheless the seed that I had sown did slowly germinate. The possible use of conservative surgery gradually attracted attention in other centres such as Edinburgh and one by one the younger surgeons on the staff at Bart's began to reject the radical operation. In spite of my various publications my initiative in the movement was usually ignored until in 1953 Reginald Murley, a former pupil (now Sir Reginald and President of the Royal College of Surgeons of England), investigated the results achieved in the treatment of a very large number of patients admitted to Bart's over a long period, giving special notice to the group treated in my wards. This demonstrated that conservative methods gave, as expected, only slight improvement in survival, but a significant gain in the quality of life. Murley's investigation did not include the large number of patients treated privately. If they had been added the results would have been proved better in both survival and quality of life, because, being derived from the more educated classes, they tended to come earlier for diagnosis and treatment.

A gratifying incident took place in 1967 when an American surgeon, George Crile, of Cleveland, Ohio, while writing a book on conservative treatment of cancer of the breast, discovered before finishing his book that I had said most of it thirty years before. He then generously dedicated his book to me.

At the present time the radical operation is seldom done in Great Britain. It is disappearing more slowly in the United States of America. Sometimes I am being rediscovered in my retirement by young researchers, who come to me to find out how I came to have such advanced views fifty years ago.

18

ASSISTANT SURGEON AT BART'S

IN 1928, after nine years in the position of chief assistant (or registrar, as it would now be called) in the professorial surgical unit at Bart's I was at length appointed Assistant Surgeon on the staff of the hospital. There had been no certainty about my achieving this much coveted position, for which there was fierce competition. For years my wife and I had teased ourselves with the grim possibility that I might end up as a practitioner in Wigan, a place we had never seen but which somehow represented the extreme of provincial obscurity. Now a satisfactory future seemed to be assured by my having achieved my life's ambition to be on the surgical staff of the greatest hospital in the world.

My beloved Chief, George Gask, I believe had formerly hoped that I would wish to follow him in an academic career, but I had decided not to attempt this, the main consideration being that the practice of surgery was the central passion of my life. I was a craftsman by instinct, not a teacher, an administrator, a committee man, or a medical politician, as I had noticed a professor had to be. I did not dislike teaching and enjoyed the company of students but I had many outside interests, among them a strong desire to acquire as many works by Blake as possible and to form a library of original editions of English literature, science, and medical history. In addition I had a growing family of sons who had to be educated. All these things required a larger income than was awarded to a professor, and could only be provided by private practice; this had the additional advantage of fulfilling my desire to have human relations with a proportion of my patients, which one loses if they are all confined in hospital beds as 'cases'.

I had been serving for some years as private assistant to the

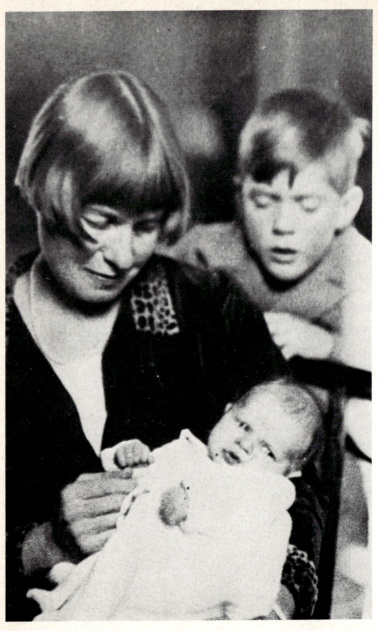

Margaret Keynes with her eldest and youngest sons, Richard (8) and Stephen (three weeks), 1927

great surgeon Sir Berkeley Moynihan, of Leeds, who in 1926 had opened a surgical practice in London. I have paid tribute elsewhere in this book (see below, p. 362) to Sir Berkeley, later Lord Moynihan, whose friendship and distinguished example had influenced my decision to devote myself to surgery rather than teaching.

I wanted to advance British surgery if it were possible and to have a full life, intellectually, aesthetically, and humanly, no matter how hard I had to work. Above all, I wanted the understanding and affection of friends and family. It was asking a great deal of life, but not too much. I had found Blake and his conviction that Imagination was the divine gift to the human race and believed that he was right. The gift must therefore be exercised and appreciated in others to the utmost of one's ability.

Not long after I had been appointed to the hospital staff I had the adventure I later recorded in a somewhat dramatized form as 'Lena's Crab, or, The Old Lady Who Knew'.[1] It might teach a lesson to students concerning the instinctive knowledge possessed by some patients, transcending all the acquired knowledge of the experts:

On November 9th, 1929, Mrs. Lena C——, already in her sixty-third year, presented herself in the Out-Patient Department at St. Bartholomew's Hospital. She lived in Barking, and on her way to the City passed near another famous hospital where she had been operated upon several years before. But she kept steadfastly upon her way. She had heard about Bart's, and she felt that she *knew* something, and Bart's it was to be.

Lena was examined by a sympathetic clerk, to whom she confided that she was suffering from 'pains in the chest and body, and a lump in the stomach'. The pains might have been functional, but there was no doubt about the lump. It stuck out for three inches or more below her left ribs, and could not escape the most inexperienced fingers, hardly, even, the most unobservant eye, for Lena was terribly thin.

[1] Published in *Bart's Hospital Journal*, vol. 38, November 1930, pp. 28–30.

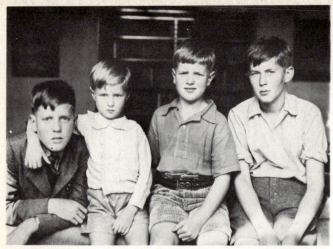

A Family of Four, 1932: Richard, Stephen, Milo, Quentin

The male Keynes Family, 1952: as above,
with Adrian, Roger, and Randal

She had 'gone off her food' seven months before, after breaking her leg; for four months she had the aching pain in her stomach, which was made worse by food, and recently she had vomited her food occasionally. Altogether, she could find many reasons for not having any food at all, and only one, her determination to live, for swallowing it. Seven years or more ago she had had pain and vomited blood, and her first operation was done at the other hospital, so that the clinical picture was complete, and not even the most obtuse clinician could doubt that Lena had a cancer of the stomach. It was indeed a very large cancer, and being so easily felt might have been pronounced, by those of the dogmatic school, inoperable ('All palpable cancers of the stomach are inoperable'). It was indeed an uncertain prospect, and the assistant surgeon put her name without enthusiasm on the admission list.

A month later Lena found herself in bed in Bart's. She felt herself secure. She had reached the goal of her desires, and Something (so Lena thought) was going to be Done. Her faith in the hospital of her choice—her second choice—was unbounded, and this crab that was gnawing so relentlessly at her vitals was going to be taken right away, and she was going to live for another twenty years contentedly and painlessly in Barking, gossiping about Bart's, and helping others to decide to try the healing waters of the Fountain. But, alas! Lena's luck was out. It was the 13th of December. She weighed only 76 lb. She coughed, and her lungs were full of crackles. True, she had not vomited for a month, but the crab had grown larger than ever, and Lena could almost feel his separate claws. The dresser, the house surgeon, the assistant surgeon looked at her with lack-lustre eyes. Death from acute bronchitis after a probably useless operation would not be euthanasia. Even a Christmas dinner would be no use to her. Lena was sent back to Barking on 18 December, and her end was confidently stated to be near. They knew— or thought they did; but so did she, and knew she did.

Lena, in the face of Expert Opinion, could but accept their ruling, and for six miserable months she lived with her crab and tried to believe that they were right. More and more she vomited, less and less could she get anything to keep company with her crab. Even fluid took fright at the monster within her, and fled upwards with greater regularity than ever. But as she became thinner and feebler, yet the spirit within her remained undimmed. Suddenly, one day in the flaming month of July, she realized that for some time she had not coughed. Her lungs seemed to have dried up. Wonder indeed that she had not dried completely up, lungs and everything else! But at any rate the Experts had said they would do nothing because of her cough, and now she had no cough, so they couldn't refuse any longer. Lena pulled herself up into a chair at the table and proceeded to write a letter, a personal appeal, to the assistant surgeon. She was so feeble that she could hardly hold the pen, but she wrote, 'I am *much better* than when I was in hospital in December. I have no cough, and I am quite sure that something can be done to help me at the hospital.' She had to add, 'I am vomiting so much that I have had practically no food or drink for more than three weeks, and I can't go on for long like this.' When the surgeon read this appeal from someone who, according to all the rules of the game, ought to have been dead several months before, he felt that she must at any rate be seen, though of course it couldn't be of any real use, and he wondered what he should say to her. A few days later Lena dragged herself to the hospital. She didn't know, she said, how she got there. She lay upon a couch in the surgery, a little desiccated object, the skin hanging in folds round her small bones. She weighed scarcely more than 4 stone, but still she was able to make an appeal that was almost fierce in its confident intensity. 'I feel,' she said, 'that if only this lump were gone, I should be quite well,' and as she spoke she made a movement with her hands as of tearing something from her stomach. 'It's only my own spirit,' she added, 'that is keeping me alive.' No refusal was any longer possible. The surgeon became filled with something of Lena's own confidence. There was no bed vacant at the moment, but no time was to be lost. She was sent home in a taxi, brightly assuring the surgeon that she would get to the hospital somehow as soon as she was sent for.

A few days later, on 16 July, she was back again in the ward, and she seemed to irradiate confidence from her exhausted frame. She was put immediately on continuous rectal saline with 10 per cent glucose, and her mucous membranes sucked it up like blotting paper. In thirty-six hours she had absorbed 150 oz., but had taken nothing by the mouth. The operation was arranged to take place on 18 July. Anaesthesia was obtained with an injection of hyoscine-A mixture, a mid-line and subcostal infiltration with 0·5 per cent novocaine, and a minimal amount of gas and oxygen. The abdomen was then opened through a mid-line incision above the navel. The lower half of the stomach was found to be filled with a massive cancer, but in spite of its size, it was not adherent to surrounding viscera. Certainly it could be removed, but there must surely be secondary growths. Almost incredulously the surgeon searched Lena's inside, but her crab was clearly celibate; there was no offspring anywhere. Without waste of time it must be taken out, and the work immediately began. When the greater curvature of the stomach came to be freed it was found that the transverse mesocolon was caught up in the growth, and though the colon itself was free, the middle colic artery was deeply involved for a considerable distance. There was no time for regrets or timidities. The middle colic artery was clamped and divided, and the transverse colon was invited to turn blue. Two-thirds of the stomach was removed, and the stump joined to a short loop of the jejunum. The transverse colon remained a smiling pink.

Lena was back in bed again, still too drowsy to be able to enjoy her triumph properly, but with an unmistakable air of complacency. During the stress of the operation she had allowed her pulse rate to rise from 70 to 80, but she soon brought it down again to 70. Her crab was gone, and now she was well. No more vomiting for her. She dismissed the pewter with a gesture of contempt. Six days later she announced that she felt hungrier than she had done for years, and on the 28th day after her operation she walked firmly out of the hospital, undeniably weighing more than 5 stone, and looking forward to a prolonged and triumphant convalescence. Two months later she had not completed her round of the available convalescent homes, and evidently Sister was being boundlessly indulgent. But by now she has tripped back to Barking, and the story that she has to tell is providing an endless source of satisfaction to the circles of her acquaintance.

Lena's brief history provides much material for reflection, but the outstanding question remains—how did she know? Apparently she knew quite positively—(1) that her crab could be removed; (2) that it was childless; (3) that her transverse colon didn't need a middle colic artery; (4) that whatever else happened she was going to get well. Probably the explanation is that she knew none of these things, but that she did know two others: (1) her own indomitable spirit; (2) the reputation of Bart's.

Lena lived happily for many years after losing her crab. I sent her a packet of tea each Christmas with a message, and eventually I heard from her son John that she had died of old age.

John became a firm friend. He had worked all his life as an engineer for the Gas Board. Now, in his retirement, he and his wife come to see me once or twice every year, bringing with him his latest paintings. He does not like painting out of doors, and instead chooses an idea from some photograph he has seen in a newspaper (preferably *The Times*) and turns it into a painting, supplying the colouring as he imagines it ought to be. Occasionally he goes to verify what he has done, as when recently he painted a scene in the Shetland Islands and afterwards went to look, returning quite satisfied. As a child he enjoyed drawing, but has never had any training. His pictures—ranging from portraits to landscapes or seascapes—are works of art and imagination though the newsprint source is often little more than a blur. He does not like parting with these extraordinarily skilful and attractive pictures, and keeps most of them under his bed (or beds). When he comes to see me and is in good spirits he quotes a good deal of poetry and I suspect that he writes some himself.

When I was appointed Assistant Surgeon to Bart's it was customary, when the firm was on duty for the admission of emergencies, to call on the Senior Surgeon to do any necessary operations during the daytime, but to call up the assistant at night. This was supposed to be an unpopular duty, but for me it was the high spot of professional life. The telephone would wake me from my deepest sleep and the House Surgeon's voice would request me to come at once to provide a solution for some urgent problem in which the patient's life was in danger. Often it would be an acute appendicitis, regarded at some hospitals as a condition in which the decision about operating could safely be left until the next day. With this attitude I profoundly disagreed, having learnt by experience that delay was always more dangerous than quick action, and had never had reason to regret it. Apart from appendicitis, there were many other possibilities embracing a great variety of abdominal catastrophes endangering life unless dealt with at once, and often a decision had to be taken before a definite diagnosis could be made—a situation which appealed to my instinct for accepting responsibility in difficult circumstances. On such occasions, when the whole of our great hospital was in darkness and at peace except for the one small area where a patient's life or death might be in question, it gave me immense satisfaction to be there. A really productive night duty might bring two or even three emergencies in succession. We would go on working through the night until the hospital had resumed its daytime activities and our nocturnal excitements would end with breakfast in the residents' quarters.

One of these nocturnal sessions in about 1932 resulted in my doing what I have regarded as being the best night's work I ever achieved. Before the incident I had occasionally noticed a student who attracted attention by his exceptionally distinguished appearance; he was working as a beginner in the preliminary sciences and I did not know his name. My telephone rang about 3 a.m. and I was told that a student, lying in a medical ward, was dying, and there was extreme urgency. He was presumably suffering from a surgical condition since I had been called up instead of a physician. The drive through the empty streets at night from Hampstead to Bart's took barely twenty minutes, and I was shewn the patient, whom I recognized as the pre-clinical student I had previously noticed. He was completely exsanguinated and about to die from sheer loss of blood.

It was hard to understand how he could have been allowed to reach this state without something having been done somehow to avoid it. I was told that he had been admitted to hospital two or three days before on account of passing a trace of blood in his urine, the cause unknown. Any connexion with a game of football had been discounted, but it was now suggested that there might have been a collision during a game resulting in injury to one or other kidney. The history was vague. Clearly the bleeding had suddenly become far worse. He was in extreme agony from distension of his bladder with blood—it could be felt as a mass the size of a football, but owing to clotting of the blood it could not be passed.

Clearly the first need was a transfusion of blood into his veins to save his life. There was so little time to spare that Oliver's London Transfusion Service would not be any use. Somehow a donor was found—I suppose one of the night staff of the hospital —and the immediate danger was averted by giving him a pint of fresh blood. The next step was to get rid of the mass of blood clot from the bladder and this had to be done with a Bigelow's evacuator, an instrument used for removing urinary stones by breaking them up and washing out the fragments with water. This took a very long time. Removal of the presumably injured kidney was the next logical step, but which one? The evidence had been equivocal, but pointed on the whole to the one on the left. When exposed this appeared to be normal, but the situation did not allow of hesitation and it was removed.

The first transfusion had been effective for the moment, but the patient's condition being still serious, a second transfusion from another donor was necessary to restore the balance, and the patient, after four hours in the operating theatre, was sent back to bed—in a surgical ward. Being young and healthy he made a good recovery, and it was reassuring to find that the kidney responsible for the bleeding had been removed. Although it had looked outwardly normal, it was in fact in an early stage of abnormality rendering it liable to injury by slight violence, and the bleeding blood vessel was identified.

The night's work had been rewarding and gave me a friend

Dr. Brian Bamford, High Sheriff of Cambridgeshire and the Isle of Ely, 1960, Mr. Justice Thesiger behind

who stood in a rather special relationship. Brian Bamford in due course became my house surgeon at Bart's, one of the ablest who ever worked for me. Later he practised with a group of doctors in the city of Ely and proved that my first impression of unusual distinction was justified. As a student he did not shine academically, but as a general practitioner he was outstanding. His general good sense, sympathy, and humanity gave him a flair for healing. He *cared* for his patients in a way that won their devotion and trust, with the almost inevitable result that he worked too hard and paid the price in a serious coronary heart attack.

During the Second World War he served in the R.A.M.C. in a field unit attached to Montgomery's army in the Middle East. In North Africa during the battle of Alamein his unit was overrun by a detachment of Rommel's tanks and Brian became so much annoyed by the noise they made that he ordered them to move away—and they immediately obeyed. He was pricked by the Queen in 1964–5 as High Sheriff for the County of Cambridge and the Isle of Ely, an official tribute to a most distinguished citizen and one of the finest human beings I have ever known.

Brian had generously accepted my wife and myself on his panel, although my residence was only just within the twenty-mile limit of distance, and on more than one occasion he hurried over from Ely in the middle of the night to attend my summons. Now, alas, his defective coronary artery has claimed its victim (1979). The worst penalty for living an abnormally long time is losing so many younger, sometimes much younger, friends.

—◆◆◆◆—

19

SIEGFRIED SASSOON

Siegfried Sassoon had published his *Memoirs of a Fox-hunting Man* in 1928. I had read the book more than once with intense enjoyment and felt a longing to know the author, though without any conscious plan of trying to find my way into his orbit. I knew and admired some of his hard-hitting and satirical war poetry, but this gentle evocation of a vanished Victorian and pre-War world and of the Kentish countryside, in simple luminous prose that was affectionate but not sentimental, seemed to have little in common with the poems. Sassoon was almost the same age as myself and had been at Cambridge at the same time, though he had never come into contact with any members of our group. If he had done so, I am not sure that our company, none of us having any interest in cricket or horsemanship, would have prevented his leaving Cambridge as he did without a degree owing to sheer boredom. I knew vaguely that he had been acquainted with my friend Theo Bartholomew, who had helped 'SS' (as he so often signed himself) by designing the typography and layout of several of his volumes of verse. When Theo died in 1933 it was natural, therefore, to send Sassoon a copy of the obituary I had written.

The reply came quickly, dated 14 June 1933, from Fitz House, Teffont: 'Many thanks for "A.T.B." which is a model of what a miniature biography should be & does not contain a redundant word. I wish you could come down here for a weekend. This place is perfection now, & I should like to show you my desultory accumulation of books. Also I should like to discuss the problem of a limited edition of my new poems which I am assured are "few but roses".'

So, without making a further move, I had been given the opportunity of becoming Siegfried's friend before I had even

Siegfried Sassoon at Lammas House, 1951

seen him, and appeared to be already installed in Theo's place as designer of his books. I accepted his invitation, and at the first opportunity drove down to Wiltshire to find him in the delightful stone-built house he was renting in Teffont. To reach his front door one had to cross a clear chalk stream and pause to watch a few large trout dawdling below before being welcomed by the solitary poet and asked to enter his very beautiful and peaceful retreat. It could be felt at once that he was a very private and indeed withdrawn person, but he accepted me at sight as a friend from whom he had no secrets or reservations. We were soon discussing the production of his volume of poems to be called *Vigils*, and I carried away the manuscripts for further planning.

Sassoon had ambivalent feelings about publishing his poems. While publication seemed to be an invasion of his privacy, he disliked being ignored. He knew that his poems were old-fashioned in form, at a time when Eliot (whom SS always referred to as 'Towering Tom') held the favour of the critics, but he believed in his own quiet Muse and was very sensitive to criticism. Any publication was therefore an ordeal, which could be mitigated by the preliminary issue of an inconspicuous private edition. I formed the notion of presenting these serious and reflective poems in a novel and attractive form by having the entire book engraved on copperplates, and appealed to Stephen Gooden for advice. He offered to design and engrave the title-page himself and to introduce me to a journeyman engraver, Charles Sigrist, who would engrave the text. SS liked the idea, and I sought to make the book even more personal by asking the engraver to base his script on the poet's own hand, a very beautiful and individual one with perfect legibility. Every manuscript of Sassoon's was a visual as well as a literary work of art. The whole of *A Fox-hunting Man*, his first prose work, had been written out by hand. The work was published anonymously because Sassoon, as a poet writing for the first time in prose, had feared his unexpected venture might be damned on that account. When the book was instantly recognized as a work of art in its own right, the anonymity was quickly lifted.

We both felt that *Vigils* was entirely successful as a book, and it contained what were to me some of his best poems. Douglas Cleverdon was the publisher and distributor of the 212 copies sold to subscribers, with a few more on large paper or on vellum.

Other visits both ways followed that first meeting, so that Margaret came to know and appreciate Sassoon as I did. Then a letter reached me dated 24 October 1934, announcing his engagement. 'Now Geoffrey,' he wrote,

> I have something to tell you which will give you a terrific surprise. It is difficult to know how to tell you. All I ask is that you *believe* that it is the best thing that could possibly have happened, and continue to be the glorious friend you have been in 1933. At the Wilton Pageant I met Hester Gatty (whose father was a younger brother of Juliana Horatia Ewing). I saw her several times in September, and the end of it was that I realised (I can't describe how strongly and inevitably) that we were 'made for one another', as the saying is.

The news certainly came as a surprise, though I was taken aback by his fear of how it might affect me. Our friendship had been a sober affair, not passionate in any sense. I was a good listener and enjoyed his conversation, largely an analysis of the person, SS, about whom he was writing and whom he viewed as through an independent observer. This distinguished it from egotism. He shewed no lack of interest in other people and was endlessly generous to friends in need. In his letter he stressed his loneliness, but in fact as a literary artist he demanded a great deal of solitude.

For myself, as a friend, I was not at all dismayed by this 'defection'. I was always delighted when any of my closest friends indulged in matrimony. It invariably meant that one friend turned into two. The wedding took place quietly at Christchurch near Bournemouth. Of his friends SS had invited only four: Rex Whistler, the artist, Glen Byam Shaw, the theatrical producer, Aircraftman T. E. Shaw, and myself.

For me it was a heaven-sent opportunity to meet at last with Lawrence of Arabia, who had long been one of my top heroes. I was fascinated by his extraordinary and complicated personality and by his achievements, in spite of efforts by jealous regular soldiers to belittle them. David (Bunny) Garnett had generously given me one of his two copies of *The Seven Pillars of Wisdom* in its original form together with several columns of the linotype edition containing unpublished passages. I had read the book three times, making a comparison of the authorized version with the whole of the linotype printing, and beyond this had read everything else about Lawrence that I could find. In the church I was placed opposite him and could gaze my fill at the small but strongly built man, with a pink face and a shock of yellow hair, so that I can see him still. After the wedding I held a long conversation with him, leaning on opposite sides of his motor bicycle, Boanerges. This was followed by an interesting correspondence, abruptly cut off by his lamented death in 1935 in a motor-bicycle crash.

Siegfried's marriage had the expected result, in that Margaret and I became very much attached to Hester, and she was an added attraction for my frequent visits to Heytesbury House near Warminster where they chose to settle. The plain, dignified eighteenth-century building of Bath stone, set in a spacious park well found with ancient trees, made a perfect setting for a writer who valued solitude but could no longer complain that he was lonely. Sassoon's mind had been so deeply seared by his experiences in the First World War that he could never forget it. Writing *A Fox-hunting Man* had been an escape into a happier life lived before 1914. His later books, centred on life (and death) in the trenches, enabled him in a way to sweat those memories out of his system, but the underlying melancholy was never far away. He could be a most entertaining companion, however, and there was much laughter in our converse, sometimes concerning other friends such as the Sitwell family, of whom he would often draw crude caricatures. He would also tell of his visits to Thomas Hardy at Max Gate, or to Max Beerbohm at Rapallo, both being to him figures inspiring the utmost reverence and affection.[1]

---

[1] Hardy I never saw myself; Max I met but once at the house of the artist Thomas Lowinsky, and I can recall only a vision of a very old man with a

Siegfried took me one day to call on Lord Pembroke at Wilton House. Lady Juliet Duff, the distinguished patron of the Russian ballet and friend of Diaghilev, was there with Somerset Maugham, whose sardonic visage frightened me into complete silence, though I cannot remember that he contributed anything to the conversation himself.

Often we would drive out into the surrounding country, visiting bookshops, cathedrals, and country churches. Siegfried was a dangerous driver. A neighbour happened to have a pond near the roadside, and after SS had driven his car into it twice, the owner was constrained to put up a notice-board: THIS POND IS PRIVATE, to remind SS to keep to the road. Fortunately he did not mind being driven in my car.

On one of our expeditions to Exeter we called in at a bookshop where I was shewn the galley proofs of a catalogue in which I noticed what seemed to be an unusually attractive copy of Somerville's *The Chase* (1796), with woodcut illustrations by the Bewicks. I was told the copy was in the warehouse and not available, but by great good fortune we called again in the afternoon and found the book had been brought to the shop. It proved to be a fine edition, printed on vellum leaves of exquisite quality in a magnificent contemporary tooled morocco binding by Walther. Inside was a letter from the printer, Bulmer, to the original owner, Charles Hoar. It was offered at the ludicrous price of twelve guineas, truly a bibliophilic prize.

In the course of time I designed three more books for SS: *Rhymed Ruminations* (1939), with a title-page designed by Laurence Whistler, printed in a small format at the Chiswick Press; *Emblems of Experience* (1951), printed by Will Carter in Cambridge at the Rampant Lions Press; and *The Tasking*

---

large round head to whom we listened with proper reverence. I have a copy of his early book, *Caricatures of Twenty-five Gentlemen* (1896), on the fly-leaf of which he has drawn a vision of himself as a young man kneeling before the bloated figure of the critic, G. S. Street, seated on a pedestal. I have also his drawing of 'Everyman', the typical smarty of the 1890s. Neither has been reproduced.

(1954), printed at the Cambridge University Press. After his conversion to the Roman faith, I helped to design *Lenten Illuminations* (1958), in collaboration with the Cambridge printers at the University Press. His later books were mostly printed by the Stanbrook Abbey Press.

In 1958, believing that I was better equipped than anyone else for the task, I suggested compiling a bibliography of Siegfried's books. He seemed not to like the idea and my saying that it might serve to establish his fame as a writer probably prompted him to write a poem of negation:

> I saw that smiling conjuror Success—
> An impresario in full evening dress—
> Advancing toward me from some floodlit place
> Where Fame resides. I did not like his face.
>
> I did not like this too forthcoming chap
> Whose programme was 'to put me on the map'.
> Therefore I left his blandishments unheeded,
> And told him he was not the man I needed.

This was his usual ambivalence, for there was nothing he liked better than praise and recognition. He soon agreed to help me in my work, for I needed his memory to recall facts I could not otherwise discover. The book was published by Rupert Hart-Davis in 1962, as one of the Soho Bibliographies. I had taken immense trouble to get it all right and thought it deserved to be given some praise. But bibliography seems to arouse in its devotees a specially malignant form of *odium scholasticum*, which was illustrated by a malicious review of my book in the *Times Literary Supplement*. The writer allowed himself to indulge in several offensive personal remarks and then to exhibit his own superior knowledge by listing a number of supposed omissions —none of which in fact qualified for inclusion under the principles I had made quite plain in a preface to the relevant section.

The birth of their son George in 1935 was a happy event for the Sassoons and might have been expected to help in ensuring that

Heytesbury House and Park; Siegfried Sassoon and George at
Heytesbury, 22 April 1944

the marriage would prove permanently happy; but it was unfortunately a factor in producing division and estrangement, each of the parents trying to outdo the other in winning the boy's affection. In addition, a too-possessive wife came to irritate a rather neurotic poet and creative writer who needed much solitude and tactful, not fussy, affection. Gradually they drifted apart, Hester living mainly in her country home in the island of Mull, while Siegfried remained alone at Heytesbury. Margaret and I remained close friends of both of them, frequently staying in their houses. Hester kept in touch with Siegfried by long telephone conversations several times a week, usually, as SS rather ruefully told me, reversing the charges. He once came with us for a family holiday in Northumberland, shewing how well he could, on occasion, stand the company of our four small boys without getting fussed.

Our friendship remained unclouded except for two brief periods, firstly when he gave his faith to the Church of Rome, thereby setting up a subtle spiritual barrier, though I fully accepted the necessity he felt of being enclosed within a fellowship of moral security from which I was excluded. He did take us to meet the Mother Superior of the convent school at Hengrave Hall, and we could only agree that Mother Margaret, who had played some part in Siegfried's conversion, was the loveliest and holiest—there is no other word for it—personality we had ever encountered. I corresponded with her for a time and pleased SS by recognizing her almost irresistible influence, which had given him so much trust and affection.

The other cloud was when I was preparing to publish *The Letters of Rupert Brooke*. Siegfried regarded it as unjustifiable and a misuse of my responsibilities as Literary Trustee to expose to the public gaze all Rupert's most intimate affairs and emotional contortions. It was useless to point out that Rupert had himself hoped that this would be done and that it was necessary in order to establish a more human image of him in the public eye, to replace the lay figure so widely accepted. SS clearly felt that Rupert's ghost would resent the exposure as deeply as he would himself have felt it if stripped naked. Another beloved friend, Dover Wilson, the great understander of Shakespeare and his works, sought to mitigate Siegfried's displeasure at my action. And gradually the cloud lifted after Brooke's *Letters* were published in 1968.

In June 1965 I had the uncommon satisfaction of receiving the Honorary Degree of Doctor of Letters within five days from both the Universities of Oxford and Cambridge. Perhaps this deserves a place in *The Guinness Book of Records*; in any case it gave me great pleasure. The authorities at Oxford, knowing how difficult it might be to prise SS out of his shell, believed it might be made easier if they invited him to receive the honour at the same time as myself, and so it came about that he and I proceeded as Hon. D.Litt. Oxon. in company with the distinguished Russian poetess Anna Akhmatova. The investiture took place on the day before Encaenia, when most of the degrees were bestowed, perhaps because neither the splendid old lady nor SS (already much weakened by the disease from which he died two years later) was physically able to climb the steep steps to the Vice-Chancellor's perch in the Sheldonian. Language difficulties made the luncheon at the Vice-Chancellor's table still more embarrassing, but we could admire the courage of the indomitable poetess in coming all the way from Moscow, disapproved by her own government, to receive the homage of the West.

Siegfried died on 1 September 1967 at Heytesbury, a place which in its beauty chimed so perfectly with the personality of its owner that I can never visualize the one without the other. He loved in particular a wide drive he had created in the woodland above the house, giving a splendid view over the surrounding Wiltshire country. It was attractively steep and dear George, SS's son, noticing this, told me he would like to convert it into a 'motorcycle scramble'.

George became Siegfried's executor, with Sir Rupert Hart-Davis as literary adviser, and we hoped that some of his father's manuscripts might become the property of the nation, for the sake both of their beauty and of their literary importance. But unfortunately George, except for his charm and his remarkable physical resemblance to SS, had nothing in common with his father. His interests lay in electronics, not in literature. One day, needing some substantial augmenting of his bank account, he summoned a van from Christie's which carried off the whole Sassoon archive remaining at Heytesbury House, to be thrown to the wolves at auction. No advice had been sought from anyone, so that everything—juvenilia, manuscript drafts of poems and prose, final versions in the beautiful Sassoon script, autobiographical notes, letters from his friends, Edmund Blunden, T. E. Lawrence, Sir Max Beerbohm, and the rest, together with many of his own letters and books—was sold to the highest bidder. One enterprising New York bookseller, Lew David Feldman (House of El Dieff Inc.), had come to London determined to grab the lion's share and this he proceeded ruthlessly to do.

There was one lot (No. 327) of special interest to me. While I was designing for him that first volume of poems, *Vigils*, I had no doubt talked to SS about Blake's Illuminated Books, *Songs of Innocence and of Experience* and *Prophetic Poems* with coloured designs executed by his own peculiar methods. One day SS told me that he intended to do the same thing, on a smaller scale, with *Vigils*; he would write out each poem and surround the manuscript with watercolour designs. When it was finished he would give it to me. I never heard anything more of it and supposed that the task had not been even begun, having gone the way of so many good intentions. Yet there, in Christie's lot 327, was at least a good part of it, with a title-page and fourteen of the poems decorated in watercolours, most with abstract designs, some with delicate landscape drawings. His hand was untrained, but often succeeded in getting a lovely effect.

I listened glumly to the bidding, with El Dieff as usual in the lead, when he suddenly turned round to tell Quaritch, the underbidder, 'I'll let you have this one,' and it was duly knocked down to Quaritch at the auctioneer's valuation of £1,500. The slim volume in decorated boards then appeared in Quaritch's next catalogue at £2,000, and I felt it to be my natural, if expensive, duty to carry out Siegfried's original intention. The volume is now safely on my shelf awaiting its final removal to the Cambridge University Library. Fortunately, at the time of the Rape of Heytesbury, Sassoon's massive diary (more than a million words) was in the keeping of Sir

Rupert in Yorkshire for transcription and ultimate publication.

Almost everything else in that sale has now been dispersed among libraries and collectors in the United States. I had implored George Sassoon to withdraw one lot (No. 337) because it was of special biographical value in relation to the writing of *Memoirs of a Fox-hunting Man*, but his efforts to do so were half-hearted. The lot (valued at £2,300) was duly sold, though a photocopy was made which I was able to use when writing an Introduction for an American edition of the book published by the Limited Editions Club in 1977. The 413 lots realized about £120,000 under the hammer, a price which gives some idea of the importance of this literary archive so hastily dispersed and lost to the nation. My relatively small collection of manuscripts, with some three hundred letters, remains and this will go to the Cambridge University Library in due course, a poor recompense for what has gone abroad.

Siegfried directed me by his will to make a choice of one picture and one book from Heytesbury. There was a wide field to choose from, but I had no hesitation in taking what attracted me and had given continual pleasure to him; he had, indeed, written one of his favourite poems around it—'A View of Old Exeter', an oblong canvas by J. B. Pyne of about 1840, giving a panorama of the country from the north-east outskirts of the city, with the cathedral in the middle distance:

> For J. B. Pyne Old Exeter was good;
> Cows in his foreground grazed and strolled and stood:
> For J. B. Pyne Victorian clumps of trees
> Were golden in a bland October breeze:
> Large clouds, like safe investments, loitered by;
> And distant Dartmoor loomed in sombre blue.
> Perpetuator of that shifting sky,
> It never crossed his mind that he might do
> From death such things as make me stare and sigh,—
> Sigh for that afternoon he thus depicted,—
> That simpler world from which we've been evicted.[1]

Nor did I have any hesitation about which book to choose. When Siegfried was married I had given him a *real* gift, that is

[1] *Rhymed Ruminations* (1939), p. 17.

to say, something which I would have very much liked to keep —a small but lovely humanistic manuscript, written on vellum in Italy about 1530. I was glad to have it back, with the added attraction of its associations.

It might well have been through Siegfried that I first came to know another poet, Edmund Blunden, though in fact I had first met him in 1923 in the Church of St. Bartholomew the Great in Smithfield after we had both witnessed the very beautiful pageant performed there in celebration of the octo-centenary of the foundation in 1123 of the neighbouring Hospital of St. Bartholomew by the monk, Rahere. We had both been much moved by what we had seen and heard and I was attracted by Blunden's shy and sensitive personality but was unable immediately to follow up this brief encounter; in 1924 he went to the Far East to take up an academic post in Japan, and it was not until after 1933, when I had again met him at Heytesbury, that I was able to find in him a very dear friend. He and Siegfried had coalesced in their addiction to village cricket, which was not at all my 'thing'. Edmund and I, however, came together in the hunt for books and shared literary heroes. While Edmund was at Merton College, Oxford, I did not often see him, but I have a packet of interesting and affectionate letters from 1937 onwards. I would give him copies of my books as they came out and he would retaliate by handing me books that he knew would appeal to my bibliophilic instincts, such as a volume of Swift's *Miscellanies*, 1727, with the signature of Christopher Smart, one of Edmund's favourite poets, inside the cover. On another occasion he gave me the three tiny volumes of Cary's translation of *Dante's Vision*, 1814, inscribed on the fly-leaf in his beautiful hand, 'A proud achievement on the part of Edmund Blunden—to have installed an Item on the shelves of Geoffrey Keynes. By accident as well as design. 22 Octr. 1950'. I already possessed a copy of his prose masterpiece, *Undertones of War*, 1928; when I asked him to inscribe it for me, he paused for a few moments in thought, and then quickly wrote on the fly-leaf the following lines, shewing how naturally his mind seemed to flow in easy verse:

Edmund Blunden, *c.* 1925, by William Rothenstein

Geoffrey, whose coming to our doors so pleases
And whose delightful gifts adorn our shelves,
That you were in 'that war' 's a thing that seizes
My quiet thought, and seems to show two selves
Profoundly sympathied; all in my book
Was in your early life, the map then drawn
For your endurance as you undertook
Things beyond dreams was yours those years, each dawn
For yet one more enigma of a day.
But when you speak of that bewildering time
Which even in calms could almost shatter meaning
You leave me thinking of the quiet way
Which Browne (Sir T.) in our pains intervening
Would bring to miles of mud, nitre and lime.

This referred to my contribution (here reprinted), entitled
'A Doctor's War', in a book of essays for which he had also
written (*Promise of Greatness*, New York, 1960). When he and
his wife, Claire, had moved to the house in Long Melford,
Suffolk, given to Edmund by Siegfried Sassoon, not far from
our Brinkley home, Margaret and I could pay them frequent
visits, latterly to witness the slow decay of his mind until he
could barely recognize our presence. He died in January 1974
and was buried just outside the Great Church of the Holy
Trinity, Long Melford; in 1966 he had tried to help the work of
restoration of the Church by putting on sale there a selection of
his shorter poems. So passed one of the most beautiful
personalities I had ever known.

20

A GIBBONIAN ADVENTURE

THROUGH the 1930s I kept up my collecting, not just of Blake but of other important books and manuscripts in English literature, still possible in those years for people of modest means and even of modest knowledge. In 1916, when I had come home on leave from France, I had decided to be kind to myself and bought at Quaritch's a superb copy of Fuchs's Herbal (1543), in a binding of stamped vellum dated 1568; this, the loveliest illustrated herbal ever published and one of the finest printed books ever to come from the press, seemed to me to be a bargain at £40. In 1931 I had bought at the published price of £15 the Golden Cockerel Press edition of the Four Gospels, illustrated by Eric Gill, now regarded as one of the handsomest books printed in modern times and in great demand.

Donne remained a great interest with me. In 1928 I had bought for £100 the Leconfield Manuscript of his poems, the most beautiful of all the contemporary collections, and one of the earliest, dating from about 1620. It had belonged to the ninth Earl of Northumberland, called the 'Wizard Earl' because of his knowledge of chemistry; a close friend of Donne, he could have been the person who wrote out the poems in their beautiful Italianate script during the eighteen years he spent in the Tower of London. King James had put him there on suspicion of complicity in the Gunpowder Plot. Through the line of descent the book came to be at Petworth House in 1928. By rights this book, one of the most desirable poetical manuscripts in existence, should still be either at Alnwick Castle or at Petworth House, had not the then Lord Leconfield believed (quite wrongly, as he was told by his advisers) that he needed more cash for the maintenance of his pack of foxhounds, and so sold a number of 'old books' from his library. The present

Duke of Northumberland (an old friend) has tried to identify for me the hand that wrote out the poems among the documents preserved in the Muniment Room at Alnwick, and the present Lord Egremont (a young friend) has gazed wistfully at what should rightfully still be his, and both of them are still my friends.[1]

About 1930 I was able to buy the Luttrell Manuscript of Donne's poems, which had belonged to Narcissus Luttrell, the seventeenth-century historian, and had obviously been made by someone with a view to publication. And later, in 1941, I acquired a third, smaller collection made by 'Edward Hyde', to be identified, I believe, with the great Lord Clarendon, written in his own hand when he was a boy of fourteen while being educated at Oxford. The manuscript is of much less importance than the other two, but the original compilers of these poetical manuscripts are seldom known, and Clarendon is at least an interesting provenance.[2]

The possession of these precious manuscripts has brought me the friendship of some great modern scholars, such as Dame Helen Gardner, by the mere fact that I am able to put the manuscripts at their disposal for their scholarly purposes. I have myself been put under similar obligations by other collectors, such as the late W. A. White of New York and his daughter, Frances White Emerson of Cambridge, Massachusetts, both of whom, at different times, put at my disposal Blake's Notebook, a priceless manuscript and an essential tool for my editorial work.

IN December 1934 Sotheby's catalogued a sale of a considerable proportion of the books in Edward Gibbon's library: books left in Lausanne when he came on his last visit to England, during which he so unexpectedly died. I had for some time been interested in Gibbon and his great work, *The Decline and Fall of the Roman Empire*, and was collecting his books. I already had

---

[1] It will, I hope, appease them both to know that the book will pass, at my death, to the Cambridge University Library.

[2] After the war, in 1948, I bought at Sotheby's one of two existing copies of Donne's *Anatomy of the World* (1611), his first published poem in book form—the other copy being in the Huntington Library in California.

the six quarto volumes of *The Decline and Fall*, all first editions except the first volume, and some of the lesser works. It would be wonderful to see part of his own library on the shelves, and I arranged to go with my brother Maynard to see the books. Looking through the catalogue I had noticed that not a single volume had been listed as containing annotations of any consequence by the owner, and very few with presentation inscriptions, so that little in the way of 'association interest' was to be expected.

It was a joy to see how well Gibbon's books had been cared for since his death, though they had been through the hands of various people since 1794. Maynard and I looked round the shelves and wondered how to get an idea of what any of them might be worth to us. Idly I pulled two or three off the shelves, naturally choosing the smaller ones as being easier to handle than any of the large folios, of which there were a good many. Yet my hand strayed on to a huge folio, lot 107, 'Herodotus, *Historiarum lib IX* gr. et lat., stamped vellum with bookplate, folio Amsterdam 1763'. Nearly all the books in the sale contained Gibbon's ticket or bookplate, or both, so the volume had at first sight no special interest; but when I opened it and turned over the leaves I saw to my astonishment numerous annotations written in ink in the margins unmistakably in Gibbon's hand, with which I was familiar. These had been overlooked by Sotheby's cataloguer; this Herodotus was likely to be the most interesting lot of the whole sale if the fact became generally known. I hastily closed the volume and put it back on the shelf, hoping that no one had noticed my excitement.

An auction-room situation of this kind is often difficult to deal with, but I decided at once to assume that no one else would notice the annotations and sent in a bid of £10, a sum which might be the intrinsic value of the book unannotated, and to attend the sale myself. When the sale began the prices in general were not high, though when lot 107 came up the bids quickly rose to over £10 and I could only take up the bidding myself. When book collectors bid in person and are known to the dealers they may find persistent opposition. On this occasion Bernard Quaritch's agent was bidding against me, but when he had bid £25 and I had signalled £26, he turned round to identify his opponent and stopped, making it plain that he did not know about the special attractions of this folio and had given in simply out of kindness. So I became its owner.

My obvious keenness to acquire the book aroused the curiosity of some of the other dealers, and presently Lionel Robinson of the well-known firm operating in Pall Mall came round behind me and whispered into my ear, 'That is a very nice book you have just bought—will you take a hundred pounds for it?' I replied, 'Certainly not—I have hardly looked at it yet.'

When I was able to examine the Herodotus at leisure I found that Gibbon's annotations amounted to more than 3,000 words, including a long note on page 298 in which he discussed the circumnavigation of Africa in ancient times. The note concluded:

> The Portuguese, inspired by the genius of Prince Henry, directed by the Compass, and impelled by a strong commercial interest, sailed round the Cape of Good Hope, after the laborious perseverance of fourscore years. Does their success render it more probable, that the Phoenicians, to gratify the curiosity of a King of Egypt, atchieved the same discovery in the term of about eighteen months, which was all they spent in actual navigation?
>
> Listen to the Spirit of the Cape, the dark sublime phantom created by the fancy of Camoens (Lusiad Lv p. 211 Mickle's translation).
>
> Nor Roman prow, nor daring Tyrian oar
> Ere dash'd the white wave foaming to my shore;
> Nor Greece nor Carthage ever spread the sail
> On these my seas to catch the trading gale.
> You, you alone have dared to plough my Main;
> And with the human voice disturb my lonesome reign.
>
> I would take the Ghost's word for a thousand pounds.

I allowed myself to enjoy this unique addition to my Gibbon collection—which, however, could not easily swallow it, since I had no shelf tall enough to take so large a book. In addition, I was then faced with having to furnish a consulting room I had leased in Weymouth Street, off Harley Street, to chime with my status as a struggling medical consultant. To meet this I offered the Herodotus as a sacrifice to Lionel Robinson (knowing that his client, Lord Rothschild, was eager to acquire it) for £200. The book has now found its final resting place with the Rothschild Library in Trinity College, Cambridge.

This Gibbonian adventure, due entirely to good fortune, strengthened a resolve I was forming to compile a catalogue, as nearly complete as possible, of Gibbon's library—surely a worthwhile objective to assemble the foundation on which one of the greatest intellectual efforts of any human mind had been based. I was familiar with the very extensive catalogue written largely in Gibbon's hand on the plain backs of playing cards kept in the British Museum. In addition I had been given the indefinite loan of Gibbon's main catalogue of the books kept in his house in Bentinck Street, London, and had assembled photocopies of various catalogues made for successive custodians of the books left in Lausanne after the historian's death. I composed as Preface a study of Gibbon the bibliophile and scholar, written in a somewhat Gibbonian style, and began to organize a method of publication. The Bibliographical Society of London would consider publication if the cost was subsidized; I remember getting the interest of at least two supporters, my brother and Victor Rothschild. Fortunately my Preface came to be read by David Garnett, and he liked it so much that he recommended the project to the firm of Jonathan Cape. Cape accepted it for publication, and so I came to form a very happy friendship with Rupert Hart-Davis, then a member of the firm, who was put in charge of me and my editorial efforts. My friendship with Sir Rupert has ripened through fifty years of association with him in various capacities. For some of them I served as unpaid director of his publishing firm, Rupert Hart-Davis Ltd., and had the interest of attending the board's meetings. The firm's first publication was my edition of Rupert Brooke's essay, *Democracy and the Arts* (1946), and in 1949 it published the first edition of my *Blake Studies*.

The actual compilation of the catalogue from the material I had accumulated needed the skills of a professional librarian, and the late R. A. Skelton, on the staff of the British Museum, was engaged to supply them.

In this way a team produced an attractive volume, well illustrated, for publication in 1940. By that date, however, everyone, including historians, was too fully occupied with other
matters to be able to take much interest in Gibbon's library,
and very few copies were sold. A few months later most of the
stock was destroyed by German bombs. I did not know of this
until several years later, when it appeared that fewer than 100
sets of sheets of the book had been salvaged. These I offered
to the Bibliographical Society for sale to its members, and they
were soon taken up, while Cape's bound volume became much
sought after and had the status and price of a rare book. I had
the copy given to me by the firm on publication and never
found another one.

In 1979 Robert Cross, an enterprising publisher of bibliographies and catalogues, undertook to reprint the volume. But
while the second edition was in preparation yet another manuscript catalogue of Gibbon's library, hitherto unused, came to
light in the Pierpont Morgan Library in New York. Professor
Charles Ryskamp, the Director of the Library, of which I am
an Honorary Fellow, and a close friend of many years' standing,
provided me with photocopies of this catalogue, which proved
to be a classified list of over 1,000 titles, many of them very
difficult to identify. From it, after many hours of work, I sorted
out 140 titles which I thought might be unrecorded. At this
point it again became necessary to seek professional help, and
David McKitterick of the Cambridge University Library vol-
unteered. He found that 61 of my suggested 140 titles were
genuinely new entries, and the second edition of my Gibbon
catalogue will have an appendix containing these additions,
bringing the list more nearly to completion. Among the illustrations in the first edition had been reproductions of both sides of
six of the playing cards from the catalogue in the British
Library; these will now be replaced by six others from my own
collection. These had been given to visitors to Lausanne during
the nineteenth century by a custodian of the library there and
had drifted into the sale rooms, where I was able to acquire
them.

21

LIFE IN THE THIRTIES

DURING the early 1930s there was little thought of a second World War, or perhaps we tried not to believe in the likelihood of such another disaster in our lives. It couldn't happen to anybody *twice*.

In 1932 we had become tenants in Suffolk of Justin Brooke, many years before founder of the Marlowe Dramatic Society in Cambridge, now a large-scale fruit farmer. For some years after leaving Cambridge Justin had worked in the family's Brooke Bond tea business, as branch manager in the west of England. He had married during the Great War and fathered a family, but some years later was divorced by his wife and married again, and this was so much disapproved by his brothers that they evicted him from the firm. He then turned to fruit farming in Somerset. A few years later, in Suffolk, he bought a farm with a milk round, and started converting the land to apple growing. The milk round helped him to distribute his farm produce until the dairying could be given up and he could give his whole attention to fruit farming. This he did on a larger and still larger scale, as he acquired ever more land, in the end almost 2,000 acres. The farm has been carried on and even enlarged by his widow since his death.

We had taken one of Justin's redundant farmhouses, at a nominal rent, outside the village of Stradishall, a few miles from Clopton Hall, his farm headquarters in the parish of Wickhambrook, West Suffolk. The Home Farm, as our house was called, was a plain mid-sixteenth-century house with a huge central chimney stack. It gave promise of being an ideal rural retreat for perfect week-end peace and quiet. Almost immediately after we had settled in, news came that a very large R.A.F. bomber station was to be established about a mile away

—a permanent reminder, if any was needed, of imminent possibilities, but again we tried to hide even that away in the back of our minds and we proceeded to adapt the place to our liking as if for permanence.

Week-ends were very short, Saturday afternoon to Sunday evening, but we enjoyed them to the full. In a neighbouring field there was a small pond which over the next two years we enlarged to make a bathing pool sixty feet by forty by means of 'slave labour', that is, my students from Bart's. We planted sweet-brier and mirabelle plum bushes round it, and had the floor and sides cemented by a local builder, who supplied a properly tapered diving board of pine wood from which one of the students, Gordon Evans, a true Welshman innocent of English until he was six years old and an exhibition diver, could shew off his skills. The pool was filled with water, at one end nine feet deep, by a windmill on a near-by hillock, drawing water from a well sunk by Justin, and was drained at the year's end by syphoning the water into a ditch below. There all our four sons learnt to swim like fishes. The youngest one scorned any teaching, jumped straight into the deep end without hesitation, and swam.

In a barn close to the house I fitted out a workshop, and started on my career as maker of furniture and other wooden objects, seldom using any wood but oak. I made fences, gates, and carved gateposts in the form of guardian owls, or as Mr. and Mrs. Job: Steve Gooden undertook the lady and left the easier bearded head to me. I had some instruction in woodwork from a professional friend, David Haes, who himself made for me a magnificent refectory table of heavy oak, two great slabs of timber forming the top and the whole fashioned with fault-less workmanship. He charged £12 for it and I have always believed there must have been something wrong in his reckoning of the costings. Like all good craftsmen, David is fully aware of his worth because he knows his standards, but is always modest and anxious to do his best because he enjoys it. His table should last for a thousand years. It has never been soiled with 'furniture polish', only rubbed with bees-wax to make a lovely surface (vulnerable to heat).

The workshop at Stradishall

An owl gatepost of oak

The Job gatepost and gates of oak

Though Stradishall was a week-end haven, Margaret and I continued our busy week-day lives in London and all the literary and social interests we shared. Our shared enjoyment of Housman's poetry had survived the passage of time and I can still derive almost as much pleasure from rereading it as when the experience was fresh. In July 1928 I wrote to him to tell him that I had detected a serious misprint in a recent edition of *A Shropshire Lad* and received a letter of thanks, adding that he had been through the text and had found another fourteen errors. In June 1933, having heard his lecture on 'The Name and Nature of Poetry', in which he had quoted Blake's poem 'In a Myrtle Shade', I sent him my latest text of Blake, pointing out that he might be interested to see the manuscript versions of the poem. He wrote in reply: 'I write hastily and inadequately lest I should omit writing, as I am just leaving Cambridge for some weeks, to thank you for your valuable gift of the most correct text of Blake. But the old eight-line text of the Myrtle, however ill authenticated, is one of the most beautiful of all the poems.' Evidently he had used the edition edited by W. B. Yeats in 1893, where the lines were correctly given, but rearranged according to the editor's taste.

Margaret and I did not meet Housman until January 1934. We knew that he always accepted invitations from Margaret's mother, Lady Maud Darwin, because he enjoyed the food provided by her kitchen, and we therefore asked her to invite him as well as ourselves. His reputation was that he seldom spoke a word on these occasions, but Margaret recorded in her book, *A House by the River*: 'He accepted and to our gratification talked a good deal at dinner, and afterwards I remember sitting by him on the sofa in the drawing-room having an agreeable psychological discussion with him, he agreeing with me that we did *not* forget the horrid things that had happened to us, as psychologists said we do. I took great care not to mention the *Shropshire Lad*, having been warned that he disliked allusions to his poetry' (p. 217).

So the pre-Second-World-War years passed all too quickly, while the shadow of Hitler deepened and lengthened over our lives whether we chose to recognize it or not. Then came the

The Sun Worshipper: my only creation in stone, *c.* 1935

late summer of 1938 with the Münich crisis and the almost comic figure of our Prime Minister, Neville Chamberlain, in bowler hat and with rolled umbrella, waving a bit of paper with his bogus assurance of 'Peace in our time' and trust in Hitler. It so happened that at this time we were staying with a well-known artist and portrait painter, John Wells, who had an enchanting villa near Grasse on the Riviera, but without a telephone. News came that our second son, Quentin, was seriously ill in Zurich. Quentin was no ordinary boy. At the age of fourteen he had decided that he was grown up and was not going to accept any more serious education, or to be moulded into the shape of an English public schoolboy. With great difficulty we managed to keep him at a day school in London for a year and then for nearly two years at Blundell's School in Devonshire. After that we gave up the struggle and had taken him to Zurich to live with a Swiss family in the hope that at least he might learn to speak a foreign language. Now this plan had been wrecked by his illness.

From the information I had received by letter I felt sure he had contracted poliomyelitis, though the Swiss doctor refused to confirm this. He could not be moved until the acute stage of his illness had subsided, but as soon as possible he was flown back to London. Even then my medical colleague from Bart's would not diagnose polio, although in the end I was proved right. Quentin had been very ill and was lucky to escape with nothing worse than permanent paralysis of the muscles controlling his right thumb. His back remained weak for a time, which was serious because his height was two or three inches over six feet, but he finally made a good recovery.

In 1939 it was thought it might help his convalescence to go to the United States, where he could visit relations of his American grandmother, Lady Maud Darwin, and there he stayed for the next eight years. He was unfit for military service, so there was no good reason for him to return while the country was at war. His secret ambition all the time had been to get to Hollywood and somehow creep into the film business, but although he was provided with an introduction to the film producer, James Roosevelt, husband of one of the daughters of Harvey Cushing, the surgeon whom Milo had nearly killed in our garden some years before, this proved fruitless. He was left all but penniless in a Hollywood doss house where he had been able to find a bed whose other occupant worked by night and slept by day. Quentin had lost his money to a Negro performing the famous three-card trick under a railway arch somewhere. He was learning about life the hard way.

During the war years he was for a time press-cutting attaché to Lord Halifax, British Ambassador in Washington, and at another time landed on the doorstep of a surgical acquaintance of mine with an 'acute abdomen'. All I knew about this was a cable saying that Quentin had been operated on and was not expected to recover. This was a characteristic incident (just one of his available nine lives) in his very chequered career, because of course he recovered.

When after his eight years' absence I met him at the London airport I encountered a handsome young man, full of fun and enthusiasm with strong drives in odd directions. Though nominally visiting his parents, he was in fact on his way to join a retired lion-hunter, Cleland Scott, who was taking a party of American boys on a journey by truck from Juba, in southern Sudan, to the Cape. Quentin thought he might take some photographs, so bought a camera and took some hasty instruction from his elder brother, Richard, before setting off for Africa. He returned with a large number of excellent photographs, announcing that the next year he was going to take an expedition himself, having had enough of being led.

This was the beginning of his real career as traveller, leader of safaris, lecturer, and the maker of splendid films of animals, people, and places, mostly in Africa, with side-tracks to the islands of St. Helena, Ascension, Madagascar, the Seychelles, the Falklands, and so on. As I write these words (August 1979) he is somewhere in south-west Africa leading a safari of eleven boys and young men travelling in Land-Rovers. The animals in his films—from charging rhinoceroses to lemurs leaping about in trees—are genuinely wild, not posed in zoos or laboratories, and his lectures, immensely popular in the schools of America and Great Britain, are never read, coming spontaneously from his lips illuminated by his own enthusiasm. In the past it has been useful to let it be known that he is the great-grandson of

Charles Darwin, but propaganda is not now needed to advertise his wares.

Quentin thought he was grown up when he was fourteen; in fact he is not grown up now and clearly never will be—except as a book collector. In this field he is very shrewd and knowledgeable, owning an impressive library of books on travel and natural history, and large colour-plate volumes.

22

THE R.A.F. IN
THE SECOND WORLD WAR

AT some point in 1938, when war clouds seemed to be gathering, I was asked by one of the Senior Surgeons at Bart's if I would like to be nominated as Consulting Surgeon to the Royal Air Force in the event of war. I had little hesitation in accepting the offer. I had always admired the R.A.F. since the days of the First World War, and would be proud to wear the blue uniform in the next war if it came about. I had seen in France in 1914–18 that the consultants had an interesting task and hoped I might be of real service.

When war was declared in 1939 I was notified that I was to be gazetted as Consultant in Surgery in the R.A.F. with the rank of group captain, though there was a long delay before I was actually called up and given my uniform. I was to be stationed at Halton in Buckinghamshire, where the central hospital for the Service was, and I arranged to live at Boswells, the home near Wendover, not far from Halton, of Sir Alan Barlow, head of the Treasury. Lady Barlow was the daughter of Sir Horace Darwin and a cousin of my wife.

Sir Thomas Barlow, Bart., former physician to Queen Victoria and President of the Royal College of Physicians, was a member of the household. He was then in his late nineties, very hard of hearing and almost blind, but still taking some exercise by chopping up small logs of wood carefully balanced for him on a block by his chauffeur. He quite often succeeded in hitting them. I sometimes succeeded in having medical conversations with him, but communication was very difficult. The younger members of the Barlow family were a lively crew and on 1 April 1940 I received at breakfast a letter from the famous physician and friend of mine, Lord Horder, asking me to

G.L.K., Group Captain R.A.F.V.R., 1939, later
Acting Air Vice-Marshal

arrange for a thyroid operation on Winston Churchill. I was momentarily deceived, but Sir Alan, understanding the cruelty of the joke, quickly came to the rescue.

Soon after joining the R.A.F. I had a long conversation with a former Director General (DG) of the Medical Service, who explained to me how difficult it was for the Medical Officers to acquire any real competence in medicine or surgery—particularly the latter—while they were in charge of so healthy a body of young men. Their chief interest was in climbing the ladder of promotion as administrators; if any difficult problem arose they sought the advice of a civilian consultant. Now, in wartime, I had been put in over their heads, as an expert with a senior rank, and they seemed to dislike me on sight. I was, after all, only assistant surgeon at Bart's and had always looked much younger than I really was, and my presence was clearly resented. I was never asked to see the DG and was not given any satisfying employment, or, indeed, any employment at all. I was in the position of being a Consulting Surgeon who was never consulted and feeling very unhappy.

It was the time of the 'Phoney War', but at least, I thought, I should be given a chance of finding out how the Service worked and what I could do to help. I therefore decided to demand that I be allowed to visit every R.A.F. station or unit from Land's End to the Shetlands. Each one of these had attached to it a young Medical Officer who was almost completely isolated and inexperienced, whom I could perhaps help with advice and in getting equipment he would need. The Air Ministry gave me permission to do this, though they seemed mystified as to why I wanted to. 'But you won't *learn* anything,' they said. I felt sure I could learn a great deal and persisted in my request.

My plan meant putting the higher authorities to some trouble. Every tour had to be arranged and each one of several R.A.F. stations notified of the day and time of my visit. I also had to find somewhere to sleep, as the expeditions might spread over three or more days. Sometimes I spent the night in R.A.F. quarters, or in a hotel, but if possible I made arrangements to stay with friends in various parts of the country: with Mona Wilson, who lived with G. M. Young, the historian, at Oare in

Wiltshire; with George Spencer Churchill, a Roxburghe Club[1] friend, and Winston Churchill's cousin, at Northwick Park in the Cotswolds; or with Serge Freeman, who had been my House Surgeon at Bart's and was practising as an orthopaedic surgeon in Wolverhampton, and so on. Serge was so named in our family because he had a remarkably close resemblance to Serge Lifar of the Ballets Russes; during a summer holiday some years earlier we had deceived John Sparrow for two days into believing that he really was the famous dancer. Often I travelled alone in the small Rover car I had bought in 1939, or I would take with me a youth I had engaged to act as my batman, and he could share the driving. In this way I covered many thousands of miles and in the end wore out my first Rover in the service of the R.A.F. To reach the Shetlands I had to be flown from the R.A.F. station at Lossiemouth and on the return journey the pilot gave me the exciting experience of flying through the mountains of Orkney rather than over them; perhaps this was quite an ordinary thing to do, though it seemed very extraordinary to me, an inexperienced passenger in an open two-seater plane.

Having fulfilled my original plan of covering the whole of the country, I felt I had learnt a great deal about the Service, and the young Medical Officers were grateful for my visits. During the 'Phoney War' there had been little opportunity for them to see the results of crashed aeroplanes, yet it was obvious that when hostilities began in earnest, the pilots who 'ditched' or 'pranged' would be killed, burned, or broken. I had no particular views about the treatment of burns; the solution to that problem lay in future experience by trial and error. But it was obvious to me that the Service would be sadly deficient in the proper treatment of the many complicated fractures with which it would be faced. Orthopaedic surgery in civil practice had been rapidly developing before 1939 and had tended to become a recognized speciality beyond the range of most general surgeons. I had some experience of most forms of fracture since they were treated in the general wards of the hospitals, but I was far from being an expert in the art. I knew enough, how-

[1] See below, p. 311.

ever, to see that the R.A.F. Service had not a single Medical Officer with the necessary knowledge. I therefore drew up a scheme for an orthopaedic organization which would give our broken pilots the best possible chance of making a good recovery from their injuries. It would have to be under the direction of the most expert and imaginative orthopaedic surgeon available. During the years when I was chief assistant to Professor Gask at Bart's he had systematically taken his staff to visit other clinics in Great Britain and abroad, to widen our views; I had never forgotten our visit to Liverpool, where we saw a brilliant young surgeon, Reginald Watson-Jones, at work in his orthopaedic unit. I thought we must certainly try to get this man's services for the R.A.F.

I sent up my completed scheme to the D.G. at the Air Ministry and awaited results. It was not acknowledged. I then demanded an interview with the D.G., whom I had never seen in my several months of service. The interview was brief. The D.G. said he was sorry to disappoint me, but that no such organization as I proposed was necessary, and I was dismissed. I was in despair, for I was quite certain of the urgent necessity for action in the matter. Perhaps, I thought, a question might be asked in Parliament regarding this gap in the Service, and I approached two or three Members, including my brother-in-law, the scientist A. V. Hill (winner of the Nobel Prize for his work on the physiology of the muscle), who represented Cambridge University, but they all declined.

Finally I appealed to my brother Maynard, and he, seeing that I felt very strongly about the matter, arranged that I should meet the Minister for Air, Archie Sinclair (afterwards 1st Viscount Thurso), at luncheon in the Athenaeum Club. The Minister took the point at once and was entirely sympathetic. Evidently he gave the D.G. a strong hint, or, to put it in more vulgar terms, 'a kick in the pants', for the construction of an orthopaedic service was soon initiated on exactly the lines I had suggested. The establishment of four R.A.F. orthopaedic centres was announced on 12 August 1940, and the service worked well throughout the war under the direction of Watson-Jones (later Sir Reginald), who became the most eminent orthopaedist of his time. He had wisely refused to put on the blue uniform, preferring to remain a civilian, enjoying more respect and less interference.

In the middle of May 1940 France had given up the struggle against the German invaders, and on 12 August the so-called 'Battle of Britain' began. I had never given a serious thought to an effective invasion of England by Hitler's troops, believing it was impossible; but driving about the country that summer it was sometimes very difficult to find the way, particularly in the dark, all the signposts having been removed from the roads. Occasionally there would be a strange reminder of the dreaded invasion when an appeal to a passing countryman for help over directions was met by absolute refusal to give any. The man had been instructed that any stranger on the road, whether he was in uniform or not, might be an enemy spy sent in advance of the troops.

From that day in August our pilots were falling from the sky in ever increasing numbers. Those that survived, usually with terrible injuries, were taken to the medical institution nearest the place where they had fallen, and I was sent out to see if they were being properly treated. Soon this led to the formation of a tiny organization at the Air Ministry in Whitehall. Every R.A.F. casualty was reported by the police to an officer in the Ministry, who then arranged for me to carry out a round journey to several places where there was a casualty to be visited and usually to be transferred to the appropriate R.A.F. hospital. For many months I was continually on the road on these sad missions. Occasionally I was content to leave an injured airman where I had found him—if, for example, he was lying with a fractured femur in a hospital in Penzance, where he was clearly being treated efficiently; but usually I transferred the casualties to one of the orthopaedic centres or to East Grinstead.

Travelling widely as I did, I had some odd experiences. In the early days we were encouraged to travel by air, and on one occasion I was flown from Weston-super-Mare to St. Athan in South Wales. I was thanking the very youthful pilot for bringing me across, when I noticed some other young pilots were giggling as I did so. I was then told that I had been brought through a balloon barrage and was lucky to be alive. Another time I had to fly from Cranwell to Hull for an urgent consultation, travelling in an open two-seater machine, guided by the Commandant's presumably trustworthy pilot. We flew through a fog so thick that we hardly ever saw the ground after having encircled the tower of Lincoln Cathedral. I think the pilot must have sometimes glimpsed the Great North Road, for we arrived intact, though I was so chilled that I could hardly speak and have often wondered how I managed the consultation. On another occasion I was flying from Halton in a small machine with a cabin, closed by a hinged top; this had not been properly secured and it was blown open by the slipstream of air, seriously upsetting the aerodynamics of the machine. The pilot tilted the plane so as to reduce the drag on the open top, while I had to 'stand up' and pull it down into position and fix it. It was an interesting moment, but fortunately my 'nerves' are good.

My organization at the Ministry continued to function usefully for some time after the crisis of the air battles was past, since many crashes still happened. By the time it was given up I found I had visited over 360 cottage hospitals, maternity homes, military hospitals, main district hospitals, and private hospitals, some of them several times. Every R.A.F. pilot was inevitably the darling of the institution he had landed in, yet I never had any kind of argument or obstruction when I said I wished to take an airman away. Those who had cared for him always knew the transfer was for his good, even though it might result in his being returned to active duty in the air.

The transfer to a centre for specialist treatment was particularly urgent for those pilots who had suffered burns. In 1939 the conventional treatment was to apply a dressing of tannic acid, which coagulated the exudate from the burnt area and formed a tough covering beneath which healing was supposed to take place. It was soon found that this treatment was disastrous for third-degree burns, leading to prolonged suppuration and fearful scarring with consequent disfigurement, particularly serious in facial burns. Tannic acid was therefore abandoned. John Bunyan, a Medical Officer in the R.A.F., introduced the bath of mildly disinfective fluid in which patients with extensive burns were made to float, and plastic surgery was developed by two Bart's surgeons, Archie McIndoe at East Grinstead and Sir Harold Gillies at Park Prewit, near Basingstoke.

I had myself employed an unusual method of treatment for very extensive burns before the war. The patient was a youth who had suffered widespread petrol burns of his body and had lain in bed for many weeks without any healing of the burnt areas. I removed from his thigh, with the help of a local an-aesthetic, a piece of healthy skin the size of a postage stamp, cut it up into tiny fragments and implanted these into the soft granulations covering the unhealed areas. Each of these sprouted to the surface and formed a small centre of new-grown skin until the numerous areas coalesced to form a continuous covering for the unhealed parts. Hope for the boy's life had been abandoned, yet he made a good recovery once the process of healing had been started in this simple way.

My method was a primitive affair compared with the in-genious and complicated methods developed by plastic sur-geons during the war, who would reconstruct noses, eyelids, or almost complete faces, and restore movement to limbs with joints fixed by contracting scars. Newly admitted casualties who watched the slow progress were given hope of recovery. McIndoe inspired his patients with the morale needed to reinforce the surgery, and some of them afterwards formed the well-known Guinea Pig Club, described as 'the most exclusive club in the world, the club that nobody wants to belong to'. One of the first members was a pilot named Tom Gleave, still known as the Chief Guinea Pig, though afterwards a group captain in the R.A.F. I first saw Gleave on 31 August 1940 after he had been shot down and his face almost destroyed. We met again thirty-one years later and recalled how I had plucked him from a maternity home, which happened to be the hospital nearest to where he had crashed his plane, and despatched him urgently to East Grinstead to undergo Archie McIndoe's ex-perimental wizardry, with ultimate success.

I was a frequent visitor to East Grinstead. Among the airmen I came to know there was Richard Hillary, who had been shot down on 3 September 1940, and fallen, very badly burnt, into the sea fifteen miles from the coast. He was rescued by the

Margate Lifeboat, and somehow escaped being reported to my small organization; he landed in the Royal Masonic Hospital, which he regarded as 'the best hospital in England'. His burns were treated with tannic acid and his face was very badly scarred before McIndoe was called to see him. Hillary was transferred to East Grinstead for prolonged plastic surgery and in 1942 published his remarkable book, *The Last Enemy*, an account of his experiences in the R.A.F. and afterwards in hospitals. He seemed to make a good recovery and became eager to return to flying. Referred to the consulting surgeons for an opinion, he was so persuasive that we rather reluctantly gave our approval to his request, with a tragic result. He crashed on a training flight with a pupil, and they were both killed. Probably he should have been seen by a psychiatrist instead of by the surgeons. The Last Enemy claimed him in the end.

Several times, on my journeys around England, I stayed for a night with Group Commander Trafford Leigh-Mallory at his headquarters near Nottingham. He was the younger brother of George Mallory, my climbing companion of former days, and I had known him as a youth. He had not been a climber, but had some of his brother's qualities, including a fearlessness which had made him a notable airman in the First World War, and now a leading member of the R.A.F. High Command in the Second. I greatly admired his impressive personality and it was wonderful to be given the background on the critical battles that were in progress.

At this time there was a serious disagreement between Hugh Dowding, the R.A.F. Commander-in-Chief, and Leigh-Mallory concerning tactics in the defence of the country from attacks by the Luftwaffe. Dowding believed that the Germans should be met as quickly as possible by a squadron of fighters before the bombers could reach their target; Leigh-Mallory—greatly influenced by Douglas Bader, the famous legless airman who served in the wing (Group 11) under Leigh-Mallory's command—insisted that a wing of fighters was more effective. Dowding believed that only a squadron, because of its small number, could get into the air quickly enough to counter the

German attack; assembling a whole wing took too much time. Leigh-Mallory was an obstinately opinionated man and he told me that he was trying to get the Prime Minister to support him in his view against the authority of Dowding. But on this point, crucial in our fighter pilots winning the Battle of Britain, as on so many others, Dowding was proved right.

In 1970 I came to know Robert Wright, Dowding's personal assistant, who published his authoritative book, *Dowding and the Battle of Britain*, in 1971. He told me that Dowding had not been aware of the lengths to which Leigh-Mallory had gone in insubordination, and he thought that Dowding should be told of this; Wright conveyed my message to the former C.-in-C. shortly before he died.

Later—some time after I had had the embarrassing duty of telling Trafford that I must discharge his only son from the R.A.F. owing to a chronic physical disability—Trafford's obstinacy led him to his death. When he was given the High Command in the Far East, he insisted on being flown out by his own crew, in the face of expert advice that he should have a crew with more experience of the route. His plane crashed in the Swiss Alps and everyone on board, including Trafford's wife, was killed; the remains of the machine with the bodies were not found until many years later. I could only mourn the death of two splendid friends from what seemed to be a defect in character.

As the war in the air continued I was more and more in the West Country, doing major surgery at R.A.F. hospitals where surgeons were usually junior Fellows of the Royal College and preferred to have me deal with some of their more serious problems, particularly if the patient was a senior officer, or even, as once happened, the Commanding Officer. The only R.A.F. hospital in East Anglia was at Ely, but there the surgeon was of my own standing and needed no help.

Our week-end house at Stradishall in Suffolk had become a noisy place because of the bomber station near by. When the war began in 1939 we had constructed a ramshackle air-raid shelter within the house; its protective strength was never tested, even when a land mine was dropped by the Germans in the next field, because the thing failed to explode—otherwise the whole house would have disappeared. One day Margaret narrowly escaped being machine-gunned by a German aircraft, but in the end we were unharmed.

Meanwhile our sons were growing up. The eldest, Richard, having taken an honours degree in Natural Sciences at Cambridge, was engaged in research on radar in an Admiralty laboratory. There, like me, he found himself working under a chief whose sights seemed to be set on the conditions of the past, not those of the present, war. Richard finally felt obliged to report to the authorities in London that he was wasting his time. He was summoned to attend a Board of Enquiry, after which the Lords of the Admiralty (with their tongues in their cheeks) reprimanded him for insubordination and transferred him to a laboratory with a higher standard of efficiency, where he was able to do valuable research during the remainder of the war.

I had continued to live mostly at Sir Alan Barlow's house in Buckinghamshire, to be near the base at Halton, but in 1942 we gave up Stradishall and rented a farmhouse at Great Hampden in the Chilterns so that Margaret could join me outside London, and where my sons could spend their holidays. The farmer at Pond House had moved to a smaller modern house near by, leaving us to enjoy the close proximity of the cows; we stepped straight out of our back door on to the straw and manure of their yard, but we liked this: it was *living* in the country.

Pond House had formerly been the home of the Poet Laureate, John Masefield, and I worked in the room in which he had written his poem, *The Everlasting Mercy*, which I had read many times with admiration. Rupert Brooke had been a friend of Masefield's and it was probably at a time when he was visiting him at Pond House that he wrote his doggerel verses, 'The Pink and Lily', this being the name of a neighbouring public house. I never met Masefield myself, though I heard him read, in a magnificent booming voice, his poem *Reynard the Fox* to the assembled apprentices at the Halton training centre.

Life in Buckinghamshire was very quiet compared with London where the inhabitants were constantly subjected to the bombing raids designed by Hermann Goering to terrorize the nation into capitulation. I often had to go to London on various duties and stayed for many nights in my Hampstead home. There too we had constructed an air-raid shelter in the garden as instructed by the authorities, but no one ever used it. On different occasions large bombs fell both behind and in front of the house with damage to windows only. The house was very strongly built and I felt safer in a room at the top of it than in the garden. On only one occasion did my visit coincide with Goering's fury. That night it was a full-scale blitz of terrible grandeur—as seen by a spectator on the top floor of a house high up on the Hampstead hills—a spectacle such as could not really have been staged for me to watch. It must have been devised by a latter-day Dante for the punishment of war profiteers.

In due course came the era of the buzz bomb, Hitler's secret weapon, which would surely bring the foolish British people to their knees. I had been called out one night to attend an emergency at the Uxbridge Hospital; it was a young man in his twenties who had been mutilated by a small railway engine, which had hit him from behind and sheared off one of his buttocks with a fracture of the pelvis. He was in a pitiful state of psychological shock, crying out incessantly 'Mother! Mother!', a style of reaction I had never encountered before. On my return about dawn to Pond House, I was just entering the garden gate when I heard a new sound, a rushing noise coming from directly overhead, accompanied by stuttering like that of a motor-bicycle engine. A moment later the engine cut out and there was a loud explosion in a field about two hundred yards away. It was one of the very first V-1 weapons to reach this country and had clearly been aimed at Chequers, barely half a mile away, where the Prime Minister was in residence. The only victim was a rabbit in a hedge near by, but the bomb was well aimed and had nearly reached its target. Winston Churchill walked over during the morning to look at the crater it had made, and a rustic hand soon afterwards picked up on the crater's margin the unburnt half of one of his large cigars. This was reverently preserved as a memento of the occasion.

As we worked through the year 1944 it was encouraging to see, as I drove around the country, increasing signs of the possibility of a move across the English Channel. Not only were the skies becoming darkened with huge flights of bombers setting out to attack the German submarine centres on the coast of France; I also noticed more and more often large numbers of aeroplanes without engines parked close together in the neighbourhood of airfields. Impossible to conceal, these were clear evidence of the approaching invasion of France by airborne troops carried in huge trailers pulled by aeroplanes.

As D-Day approached I had orders to go to Down Ampney in Gloucestershire, an Air Force station which was to be the receiving end for the casualties from Normandy. The wounded were all given first aid and dressings in the field before being despatched by air to Down Ampney, where they were examined and sent on by ambulance to the appropriate hospital. We seldom operated on the patients, though occasionally we would do an amputation if it was clearly a matter of urgency, or give a blood transfusion. Our main function was distribution of most patients to Army hospitals, a special category, those with head injuries, being sent to a neurological centre in Oxford. Most of the men reached their final destination within a few hours of being wounded. I was no longer serving only the Royal Air Force, but was speeding all that came, whatever the colour of their uniforms, on their way.

When it had become plain that the invasion of northern France had been successfully accomplished, service in the R.A.F. became a matter of routine consultations until such time as the declaration of peace should allow us to discard our blue uniforms, hats resplendent with gold braid, and titles such as Acting Air Vice-Marshal, and to return as soon as might be to civilian status.

23

MYASTHENIA GRAVIS

During the decade preceding the war my association with Sir Thomas Dunhill had helped me to build up a reputation as an expert in thyroid surgery, and I had operated on several thousands of patients with various forms of thyroid trouble, the majority of these with an overacting gland. The sufferers were often in a precarious state owing to the effect of the disease on their hearts and to the inadequacy of the available treatment by drugs. Their safety depended on a close collaboration between physician and surgeon, and frequently on the use of local analgesia rather than a general anaesthetic for the operation. My special experience also equipped me for dealing with the more unusual complications arising from extensions of the enlarged thyroid gland, or goitre, into the thoracic cavity.

Expert knowledge of the technical details was of very great importance in performing all thyroid operations. The particular risks were from haemorrhage after the operation or from damage to the nerves supplying the larynx, which might interfere seriously with the patient's voice or breathing. I was seldom troubled by a patient's post-operative bleeding and almost never by injury to the laryngeal nerves. Many surgeons gave such weight to the latter possibility that they believed it was necessary to expose the nerves by dissection in order to be assured of their safety. I regarded this procedure as in itself a danger to the nerves by handling, and in any case a waste of time. Dunhill had taught me a trick by which the nerves could be pushed into a position of safety very quickly and without being seen.

Because I had performed so many thyroid operations, I enjoyed the trust of the physicians from whom the patients came. Physicians vary in their attitude to surgery. Some regard the avoidance of an operation as an end in itself, and this may not be really in the patient's interest. An operation that can be done with safety while at the same time promising a quick return to normal life and health is surely better than condemning a patient to years of invalidism while under medical treatment: the position has to be weighed up for each individual set of circumstances. Treatment with radio-active drugs has been improved in recent years, however, and no doubt I should not now be doing so many thyroidectomies as I did thirty years ago.

On one occasion I was called upon to deal with much the largest goitre in East Anglia. The elderly woman who possessed it was a well-known figure in Newmarket. She had to wear a double-decker blouse to house the gigantic mass depending from her neck and had been dodging the doctors for many years, but now the gland had become toxic as well as obstructive. Her heart was seriously affected and it was plain that she could not live long unless some heroic operation was done for her relief, even though there might be some risk to her life. She was admitted to a medical ward at Bart's where she was nursed for several weeks until she had reached the optimum condition for facing the formidable adventure. The surgery was carried out in two stages. She was restored in a short time to good health and was able to pursue her occupation of upholsterer for many years afterwards, often paying professional visits to my house. A surgical *tour de force* of this kind gives great pleasure to all concerned, but is chiefly of value in demonstrating the importance of careful team work. Everyone—physician, radiologist, clinical pathologist, anaesthetist, surgeon, his assistant, and the nurses—each has to play his or her part, with a blood donor and a bottle of his blood ready to turn the balance in the patient's favour at a critical moment. I have often reflected that there cannot be any other profession in the world giving such intense 'job-satisfaction' as my own.

Patients from the Middle East had not yet begun to come to Britain in such numbers before the Second World War, though I did operate on one such visitor, the paramount Sheikh of Southern Iraq, who had a thyroid tumour the size of a cricket ball. There were no complications and the operation was a simple one, but the patient was accompanied by his own medical adviser, and a formidable armed bodyguard who slept on the mat outside the door of his room in the London Clinic. When I went to bid him farewell, I found him sitting cross-legged on his bed. He handed me a gift of eight pounds of stuffed dates and a heavy gold ring set with a half-sovereign dated 1913—no doubt from one of the bags of coins distributed to the Arabs by Lawrence of Arabia during the First World War. The Sheikh asked, through his doctor, 'How many sons have you got?' I answered, 'Four.' He replied, 'God bless them all.' I could not help asking him the more interesting question, 'How many sons have *you* got?' He instantly replied, 'Eighteen.' I could only bow my head and say, 'God bless them ALL,' and so we parted in mutual goodwill.

It was my reputation for thyroid surgery that led in 1942 to the most interesting development in surgical practice in which I took part. A year or two earlier I had happened to operate on a young woman for a mildly toxic goitre. The operation had been done in the Endocrine Clinic recently started at New End Hospital in Hampstead by Sir Thomas Dunhill, whom I had been appointed to follow in doing special work in the treatment of the so-called endocrine glands—that is, the organs supplying the special secretions needed by the bodies of mammals for their proper functioning. Chief among these is the thyroid gland, since it is more often affected by malfunction than any other of the 'endocrine orchestra' (a term invented by my uncle Sir Walter Langdon-Brown, physician at Bart's); others include the parathyroid glands, the pituitary, the adrenals, and so on. My former thyroid patient had subsequently come under the care of Dr. E. A. Carmichael, physician to the National Hospital for Nervous Diseases in Queen Square, Bloomsbury, who had found her to be suffering from a paralytic condition known as myasthenia gravis, in which, it is believed, the proper functioning of the neuro-muscular mechanism is prevented by the failure of the nervous impulse to pass from the nerve to the muscle. The failure may start in one small group of muscles such as those controlling the upper eyelids, and then become gradually more widespread until the victim dies from failure of the muscles responsible for breathing. At the same time there may be no recognizable signs of disease except an apparently inexplicable weakness, the cause of which remains undiagnosed.

The condition had been clearly described in the latter part of the seventeenth century, but then was completely forgotten for more than two centuries. Even Sir William Osler, in his famous textbook of medicine published in 1892, did not mention it. After 1900 the disease was being more often described, but the cause remained a mystery and there was no effective treatment. It was then discovered almost accidentally that a striking temporary improvement could be obtained by injection of a drug called physostigmine, which was also effective in treating poisoning by curare, the lethal drug used by the South American Indians on their poisoned arrowheads. This was an important discovery for patients in whom myasthenia gravis was diagnosed, since their miseries could now be for a time alleviated by giving the injection several times a day; but it still left them without any cure.

Meanwhile it had come to light that myasthenia gravis was sometimes associated with the presence of a tumour, that is a growth of some kind, in the thymus gland. This too was mysterious, since the thymus gland was not known to have any function whatever in the physiology of the human body; but removal of the tumour from a myasthenic patient could sometimes produce a striking temporary improvement—though the patient was usually so ill that he did not long survive the operation. Then in 1939 an American surgeon, Alfred Blalock, working at the Johns Hopkins Hospital in Baltimore, took a step forward by removing a thymus gland not shewing any outward abnormality, again with a remarkable effect on the patient; he repeated the experiment several times with the same effect, and reported his results that same year in a medical journal. This was seen by Dr. Carmichael, who believed that the operation should be tried on our patient, who was certainly going to die very soon if nothing was done for her. He asked me if I would do the operation. I of course agreed to try.

This was an exciting surgical challenge. Blalock meanwhile had lost interest in the problem and no one else had taken it up. The operation had never before been done in this country— indeed, I had never in my life even seen the thymus gland. It was very difficult to demonstrate to students of anatomy, being always much shrivelled in the cadavers used for teaching; and because it had no known function or importance, was completely overlooked. Moreover the gland lay deep in the chest, in a position over the heart to which one could only gain access by splitting down the midline the bone known as the sternum. This manoeuvre I had sometimes carried out when removing a thyroid gland which had extended far into the thorax, but identifying the thymus once I had exposed it would be a surgical novelty.

Notwithstanding all this—and with the added hazard that we had no experience of how best to use the relevant drugs for a patient so ill as ours—the first thymectomy done in Great Britain was performed at New End Hospital in February 1942. I was of course at that time wearing the uniform of the R.A.F., which did not prevent my doing an occasional operation as a member of the hospital staff. My assistant was J. E. Piercy, Superintendent of the hospital, who as it happened had himself been a pilot in the Canadian Royal Flying Corps of the First World War. It was Piercy who, without any previous experience of the clinical situation, had to steer the patient through the sometimes stormy post-operative days.

Fortune favoured our efforts. The patient, aged thirty-seven, was helped by her courage and will to live. She made a good recovery and in a short time lost all her symptoms. Soon there was no need for injections of drugs. After a normal convalescence she appeared to be cured and for a year worked ten hours a day as a land-girl.

Although myasthenia gravis was generally supposed to be a rare disease—many practitioners would say that they had never seen the condition during a lifetime of experience—later events proved that it was not quite so uncommon as had been thought. The absence of any clinical signs, apart from a rather vague muscular weakness, had frequently kept it from being diagnosed. Further experience with the disease made me understand what misery the sufferers had to endure. Their weakness was real enough to them, but many of them told me how they had been accused of 'putting on an act' or, in a word, malingering. Sometimes there would be a spontaneous remission of the symptoms, which was held to confirm that the patient had been shamming, although these remissions were usually followed by a return of the weakness. It was pitiful to hear how the patients had appealed for belief in their complaints—appeals to which we were now very ready to respond.

Our initial success with the thymectomy naturally brought more patients, chiefly from the clinic at Queen Square. Yet that one resounding success did not mean that all who came to us were cured. Indeed the sad fact was that of the first twenty-one patients on whom we operated, eight died soon after the operation. This would have been an unacceptable rate of mortality had it remained at that level; but it was clear that these deaths were due in large part to a late stage of the disease having already been reached before the patients were presented to us for treatment. Too many of them came to us too ill and debilitated, when the operation was a last hope for survival; we concluded that they must come much sooner for surgical treatment, when the operation could be done with comparative safety. Also we were quickly learning how to use the drugs in the preparatory period and afterwards, and the nursing staff were becoming more experienced in managing their patients.

I was naturally cautious in publishing our results, being anxious not to make claims which might later prove to be unjustified. The treatment was what is known as 'empirical', in that we did not have scientific grounds for doing the operation, because the true function of the thymus was not known. The only reason we could give for removing the gland was that its removal did, on the whole, produce very good results. One important reservation, however, did force itself on our minds. As the number of our patients increased, we found that 15 per cent of them had a tumour, a form of new growth (perhaps a kind of cancer) in the thymus, and when this was present the results of the operation were very bad indeed. Sometimes a patient would seem to make a spectacular recovery, yet would quickly relapse and die from respiratory failure. It was plainly important to detect these tumours before operation, and we would invite the radiologists to come to the operating theatre to see the tumours they had failed to find on their films. They learned in this way to modify their technique until they could nearly always identify the tumours; we could then be fore-warned and get the radiologists to apply radiotherapy before operation—though this proved to have little or no effect on the result.

The most tragic example of misunderstanding of the condition was that of a colleague—a distinguished surgeon who had, over many years, been seen by a number of physicians, none of whom had made the diagnosis. The unfortunate man had consequently been regarded as a notorious malingerer or psychopath. When he finally reached my consulting room, the diagnosis of myasthenia gravis was only too obvious. An X-ray film shewed a very large tumour and the patient died a few days later before any treatment could be attempted.

From a scientific point of view it was a great satisfaction to be able to provide a full description of the thymus, an organ hitherto almost unknown and evidently destined to become of great interest and importance in the physiology and pathology of the animal body. For this enigmatic gland is present in every kind of chordate animal, that is, in every kind sufficiently advanced in evolution to have a backbone. Complete removal of the thymus, moreover, meant acquiring detailed knowledge of its anatomy, never before fully described. The small arteries supplying the gland were known, but the venous drainage was not. I demonstrated that each of the two lobes had a vein draining it and that these united to form a fairly large single vein discharging into the Great Innominate Vein on its way to the heart. It was obviously of great importance to identify and tie off this vein securely if serious secondary haemorrhage was to be avoided. My assistants promptly dubbed this structure 'the Great Vein of Keynes', though this historical eponym has not been adopted by the anatomists. Perhaps they have felt some annoyance that it should have fallen to a mere surgeon to describe for the first time an important structure which they had failed to find.

When I was able to base my evidence on the removal of the thymus gland from fifty-one myasthenic patients, I judged that the time had come to describe and publicize the whole problem and its probable solution by surgery, so that the operation might be more widely practised and more sufferers relieved from a truly terrible disease. All the operations had been done at New End Hospital under the care of J. E. Piercy, who had borne the brunt of the post-operative difficulties. My own exposition of the philosophy and practice of thymectomy was delivered on 13 June 1945 at the Royal College of Surgeons of England as a Hunterian Lecture, so named in honour of the great surgeon and biologist John Hunter, founder of the Hunterian Museum. In summing up the results of our work I emphasized that, although as I have said eight of the first twenty-one patients had died, all except one of the next thirty had survived, thus justifying our determination not to be discouraged by our early results.

By the time the Hunterian Lecture was published, in 1946, it had become clear to J. E. Piercy and myself, and to many of our medical colleagues, that the operation was an acceptable form of treatment for an otherwise incurable disease. Meanwhile, however, a different view was gaining ground on the other side of the Atlantic. A medical team at the Mayo Clinic in Rochester, Minnesota, one of the most famous medical centres in the world, had been doing similar operations and had arrived at the conclusion that thymectomy did not influence beneficially the course of myasthenia gravis. They therefore advised operation only for removal of thymic tumours because these were potentially malignant. This was exactly the opposite of the opinion we had come to. We had found the performance of a simple thymectomy highly rewarding, 80 per cent of the patients being either cured or greatly improved. This result had been attested to by an independent observer at the clinic in Queen Square, who had carefully and without bias examined our first hundred patients. Our experience of tumours, on the other hand, had been so unsatisfactory that we had placed these patients in a different category from the others, omitting them from the statistical record. The removal of a thymic tumour could, moreover, be both difficult and dangerous. (On one occasion, when I was engaged in such an operation, I heard an American visitor, who could see that I was in difficulties, remark in a loud whisper: 'He can't possibly remove it.'

This was a serious breach of international good manners, but I pretended not to hear and went on to complete the removal of the tumour with, I am glad to say, an unusually good result.)

The adverse opinion emanating from so authoritative a source as the Mayo Clinic soon spread all over the world and put me in a somewhat difficult position. I had to become accustomed to being told, 'Why do you go on doing this operation? The Mayo Clinic says it is no good.' I found myself again shewing signs of suffering from Lord Taylor's 'salmon syndrome',[1] swimming against the stream. But as I enjoyed the support of the physicians at Queen Square, I felt I could ignore the criticism and pursue my own path. Patients came from all over the world and I was operating at New End, Bart's, and sometimes at Queen Square.

A girl of sixteen, sent to Bart's from Australia, was met by a cousin who was a reporter on a London daily paper. As a relative he obtained access to the patient's notes and set to work to tell her story. Before long she became known to the press everywhere as 'The Girl with the Frozen Smile', the muscles of her face being affected by the paralysis so that she could not form a smile, and her fortunes were followed by thousands of sympathetic readers. Her progress was slow, but recovery was ultimately complete. Her smile unfroze, and the young man who welcomed her home became her husband, with the happiest results. I still sometimes hear from her forty years later, with news of her large family.

It might be said that I had a monopoly on surgery in this area, and occasionally an acquaintance would remark almost enviously, 'You must be doing very well out of your new operation.' But in fact, though by the time I had completely retired from surgery I had operated on 281 myasthenic patients, all except 2 of these were treated in hospital, because of the complexity of the condition, and the financial reward to me was almost nothing.

While this was going on scientific examination of the biology of the enigmatic thymus was proceeding. I collaborated with Professor Andrew Wilson of Liverpool University, who was

[1] See Professor Lord Taylor, M.D., F.R.C.P., 'Psychiatry and natural history', *British Medical Journal*, December 1978, 2, pp. 1754–8.

trying to find out whether the glands taken from my patients contained a substance which could be extracted and tested on small animals. It had been found that an extract from the thymus gland of foetal animals did shew evidence of having in it a substance with the capability of causing signs of paralysis, and that the gland tends to be very large in most mammals before birth. Andrew Wilson therefore sent one of his assistants on a whaling expedition to collect the relatively enormous glands of foetal whales, thus providing him with a very large amount of active tissue for extraction. Eventually he was able in this way to produce in the laboratory a temporary myasthenic condition in animals resembling the disease in human patients. It was also found that the thymus glands taken at operations were usually abnormal under the microscope, suggesting that they were in a state of inflammation.

In 1954 I was invited to give the annual Oration to the Medical Society of London and took the opportunity to present a full account of my position with regard to the much criticized operation for the treatment of myasthenia gravis. The large audience was obviously expecting to hear an apologia and withdrawal of the claims I had been making, but this was not at all my intention. I had carefully examined the statements made by the surgeons of the Mayo Clinic and had discovered the origin of the difference in our positions. They had been concentrating almost exclusively on tumour patients and any results obtained from simple thymectomies had been overwhelmed and lost among the extremely bad results given by the large number of tumours. This misuse of statistics had gravely misled the investigators. Our results and theirs were derived from entirely different kinds of patients and could not be compared. I was able in pointing out this discrepancy to drive home the soundness of our conclusions, and also to tell the audience that the Mayo Clinic had suddenly completely reversed its stand on the value of thymectomy, in a paper which now confirmed the results I had put forward nine years before, but which had been damned with fainter and fainter praise, even as the results as seen in the actual patients got better. The revised opinion had been expressed almost *sotto voce*, in a highly specialized journal which would be read by no one except a few neurologists; in the Oration I expressed my gratitude to Dr. J. A. Simpson of Queen Square Hospital who had drawn my attention to the paper. The whole affair, I said, was an interesting study in the formation of medical opinion, shewing the way in which truth gets overlaid by muddled thinking, and how exaggerated deference is paid to a given opinion because it emanates from a large American clinic rather than from a smaller London one.

It was not until 1976 that the Mayo Clinic really came clean, with a full-dress article published in *Annals of Surgery* under the grandiose title 'The Value of Thymectomy in Myasthenia Gravis. A Computer-Assisted Matched Study'. Referring to my paper, 'The Surgery of the Thymus Gland', published exactly thirty years earlier, they now gave a considered opinion exactly the same as mine: 'Until more effective treatment is available for myasthenia gravis, thymectomy deserves consideration for both sexes.' (Previously they had said that the operation was useless in male patients.) Untold harm had been done to the victims of one of the most distressing and humiliating diseases to which human beings are prone by the Mayo Clinic's attempts to belittle the value of surgery.

I had been given living proof of this value in 1961, when I was invited to deliver the Grey Turner Memorial Lecture at Durham University. I had first met George Grey Turner when George Gask had taken his professorial surgical unit at Bart's to visit Grey Turner's corresponding unit in Newcastle, and later we had served together on the Council of the Royal College of Surgeons. In the 1940s I had travelled to Newcastle in order to perform a demonstration thymectomy on a myasthenic patient. There can be no more severe test of self-confidence than to operate under these conditions in strange surroundings. Luckily nothing took place to upset my equanimity and the episode passed over without any loss of face by the demonstrator. Soon afterwards Grey Turner had asked me to contribute a section on the surgery of my favourite glands for a new edition of his textbook on *Modern Operative Surgery*, so on all accounts it seemed to be right that the subject of my lecture should be 'The History of Myasthenia Gravis' from the first description of the symptoms in 1672 to the first successful treatment by thymectomy at New End Hospital in 1942. But what I had not anticipated was that my hosts at Durham had asked my former patient to come forward and present herself as a proof of the efficacy of the operation she had undergone at my hands.

In 1961 the secrets of thymic function were still unresolved. But the operation had served to focus the attention of several research centres on the status in human physiology of the thymus gland and its function in organizing the immunities by which we are enabled to survive the dangers of being alive. It has proved the key to a whole new science of immunology; and investigation of the structure of the neuro-muscular junction by means of the electron microscope has thrown much light on the pathology of myasthenia gravis. But all that is another story. My own status is still often being raised in my own eyes by the letters I receive from patients with touching expressions of their gratitude. The last one, received in 1978, was from a patient first seen in 1944 when she 'was a very frightened little girl, unable to speak or smile for two years', and 'with many other weaknesses'.

Many years ago the patients who had undergone thymectomy formed the British Association of Myasthenics, with Her Grace the Duchess of Devonshire as Patron, in order to draw attention to the continuing need for investigation of their mysterious disease. Their letter-form bears the slogan: HELP CONQUER MYASTHENIA GRAVIS 'THE DISEASE NOBODY KNOWS'. At a recent Annual Meeting, the members present, many of whom had been my patients, wished to place on record their 'total and sincere appreciation' of my life's work, in particular my 'dedication and service in the treatment of all those who suffer from the disease of myasthenia gravis'—a most touching tribute to a surgeon who has been on the retired list for nearly thirty years. There were few people who understood how much these unfortunates suffered when, in 1942, Jack Piercy and I resolved to find out what surgery could do to help them.

24

THE NATIONAL PORTRAIT GALLERY
AND WILLIAM HARVEY

An unexpected pleasure and an alleviation of the war years was my being chosen in 1942 to serve as a Trustee of the National Portrait Gallery. A special feature of this trusteeship lies in the fact that every decision to add a portrait to the Gallery, whether by gift or by purchase, is made by the Trustees; they are able in every case to have the advice of the Gallery's Director, but are not bound by the views of expert Keepers of the special departments, and are free to exercise their own judgement. In former times the Trustees were appointed for life, which was obviously undesirable; by 1942 this had been changed, and when the Prime Minister's Office decided that any Trustee had reached an age when he or she was suitable for retirement a polite notice of this fact was given to the victim.

Nobody ever wanted to retire. At the time of my appointment the Chairman was Lord Ilchester, one of the last of the lifers, and a most lovable old man. Yet he was, as it seemed to me, getting rather too lax in gathering an agreed decision from the Board. On one occasion the claims of the late Dylan Thomas were being considered—or, as I thought, insufficiently considered. Few Trustees had spoken and acceptance was being reached rather by default. I was not myself familiar with the poet's work, but fancied that he was being overvalued by popular opinion, which attached more importance to his consumption of large quantities of alcohol than to the literary quality of his poems. I therefore asked the Chairman whether he would obtain a more definite opinion from the Board. It then emerged that many of the other Trustees were as doubtful as I was. When the question was put to the vote the portrait (a good one by Augustus John, R.A.) was rejected. In fact we were mistaken and it fell to me as Chairman a few years later to accept another, somewhat inferior, picture.

I served on the Board with great enjoyment for twenty-four years and for the last eight years was Chairman, having succeeded Lord Ilchester. There were four Directors during those twenty-four years: Sir Henry Hake, Kingsley Adams, David Piper, and finally Roy Strong, all of whom I numbered among my best friends. My method as Chairman was to make every Trustee pull his weight. When the Director had stated the pros and cons of a picture I asked every Trustee round the table to give an opinion, no time being wasted in three-cornered wrangles. This done, a vote was taken by counting a show of hands and the Director had a definite decision upon which to act. The business went briskly and the Trustees liked it. When I reached the age of seventy-five the Prime Minister's Office indicated I must go, but the Trustees protested so loudly that I was given two more years. At the end of the two years the same thing happened, and I was given one more year. I then received an official note, signed by Mr. Harold Wilson, thanking me for my services.

I was still serving at the National Portrait Gallery when (I forget the year) I was astonished to receive from Lord Fisher, Archbishop of Canterbury, an invitation to be appointed a Trustee of the British Museum. I knew how great an honour this must be and how much I should enjoy it, but all meetings of that board were held on Saturdays. I had been taking Saturday morning duties at Bart's for many years and still depended on week-ends at our country home for rest and variety in my strenuous professional life. Also I was surprised that, being already on the board of one public gallery (at the N.P.G. we always met on Thursdays), I was now asked to serve on a second. I therefore felt that I must ask to be excused, though with a feeling of shame. I had met Lord Fisher when I was one of the speakers at an annual meeting of the National Art-Collections Fund at Bart's, and knowing that he liked a joke, added in my letter that if the Trustees would be willing to change their day to a Thursday I would be happy to accept the duty. He replied that he feared the Lord Chancellor (an *ex officio* member of the board who never attended) would not agree to this. Some of my friends who were on the Museum board were much shocked by my refusal; it was all most embarrassing.

In 1944 I was thinking of whether I should make an attempt to achieve election to the Council of the Royal College of Surgeons of England. A Russian-born colleague whose assistance I had requested as consulting surgeon to the R.A.F. had the same ambition and we held a long discussion about whether we should offer ourselves for the much desired distinction. We concluded that it would be unsuitable for either of us to try as long as we were in uniform—but when the list of candidates appeared his name was on it and mine was not. Council members are elected by a vote of the whole body of Fellows of the College, and my colleague was unfortunate; receiving very few votes he was not elected. I then felt free to try my own luck and both our names appeared as candidates. My colleague suffered the same misfortune as before, but I was luckier, receiving a large number of votes which carried me easily into the Council. This was the beginning of eight years of deep satisfaction in my professional life. I was given the friendship of many of the leading surgeons in Great Britain, particularly of Lord Webb-Johnson, President of the College; George Grey Turner of Newcastle upon Tyne, whom I have already mentioned and who shared my interest in medical history; Sir Harry Platt, doyen of the orthopaedic fraternity; Lord Brock, pioneer in the surgery of the heart—but I cannot name them all.

While a member of the Council I was given the title of Honorary Librarian and Curator of Pictures. After my retirement from professional surgery I was allowed to keep the title of Honorary Librarian and attended meetings of the Library Committee. Later I gave the College the whole of my collection of books concerned with the history of blood transfusion. In the Library I was associated with William Le Fanu, librarian and classical scholar, to whom I could turn for translations from Latin texts when I was working on Sir Thomas Browne, William Harvey, and others. The College owns a large collection of important pictures and as Curator I had to call upon an expert, Dr. Johann Hell, for help in caring for Reynolds's portrait of

John Hunter and for some of George Stubbs's animal pictures. Most interesting of all was the investigation of the great painting by Holbein of Henry VIII giving a Charter to the Barber Surgeons. The Company of Barber-Surgeons have long had a replica of the Holbein canvas, which has been claimed to be the original painting, though damaged in the Great Fire of 1666 and later extensively repainted. X-ray examination of the College canvas had proved that parts of Holbein's original cartoon still lay beneath the paint, so that this picture had to be regarded as of far greater importance than the other one. It was fascinating to watch at the Courtauld Institute the task, lasting some two years, of careful cleaning with minimal restoration.

I spent so much time at the College in Lincoln's Inn Fields that it became in effect my 'club'; some years earlier I had been elected to the Athenaeum Club, but now I resigned my membership because I hardly ever went there. When I felt that it was my turn to entertain the members of the Roxburghe Club, the bibliophilic society to which I belonged, I was allowed to invite them to dine in the beautiful Council Room of the College, which could also provide an interesting display of books in the library.

While a member of the Council I was called upon to give two of the commemorative lectures sponsored by the College. One, commemorating Cecil Joll, a great thyroid surgeon, gave me an opportunity to discourse on tumours of the thymus, my special interest. The other lecture, sponsored jointly by the College and the Company of Barber-Surgeons, commemorated Thomas Vicary, a Bart's surgeon during the sixteenth century. I was greatly interested in portraits, partly through my long service as Trustee of the National Portrait Gallery, and I chose as my subject for the Vicary lecture, 'The Portraiture of William Harvey, 1578–1657'.

In 1928, when the Royal College of Physicians was celebrating the tercentenary of the publication of Harvey's book *De Motu Cordis*, announcing his demonstration of the circulation of the blood, one of the events had been a visit to the church at Hempstead in Essex where Harvey's remains lie. The massive marble sarcophagus in the Harvey Chapel there is watched over by a life-like bust of Harvey, in my opinion done from the life. Underneath the chapel is the Harvey vault, where the family lie in serried rows, all lapped in lead, only William having been taken upstairs to do him greater honour. I had taken with me to Hempstead in my motor car my dear friend, Sir D'Arcy Power, one of the senior surgeons at Bart's and author of a short biography of Harvey published in 1897. On our way home we called at Rolls Park, near Chigwell in Essex, to visit Lady Lloyd, whose late husband was descended in direct line from William Harvey's younger brother Eliab. William had been childless, so Eliab's line had seniority. While we had tea in Lady Lloyd's drawing room I found my-self looking at eight portraits fixed on one wall in plaster surrounds. Sir D'Arcy told me that these were only copies of portraits of the Harvey family and of no special interest. I found out some years later that soon afterwards he had changed his mind and written about the portraits. They were in fact portraits of Thomas Harvey and his seven sons, but because of what I had been told about them I gave them no further thought.

When in November 1948 I was composing my Vicary lecture I did not think of going again to look at these pictures, supposing them to be of little or no importance, until it was already almost too late. I then wrote to Andrew Lloyd, by that time the owner of Rolls Park, asking his permission to see them. He said I might do so, though the house was derelict, having suffered from bombing during the war. My first visit was made too late in the day to see the pictures clearly, as the great shutters in the lofty room could not be opened, but I now felt sure that they were of great interest. A week later I visited the house again and found that the two portraits in the lowest positions had been cut out by intruders and were lost. With the help of a ladder brought by the caretaker and a candle I then found to my astonishment that the portrait in the highest position on the right was undoubtedly a contemporary painting, and was in-scribed *Doctor William Harvey*. I arranged for all the remaining portraits to be taken down and transferred to the National Portrait Gallery to be cleaned and framed. So I was, after all, able to exhibit William at my lecture and to announce the recovery of the only surviving portrait of him as a young man.

It was only just in time, for no one was doing anything about saving these pictures fixed in their plaster frames and not long afterwards the house was demolished.

Andrew Lloyd then agreed to loan the whole set of portraits, of Thomas Harvey with five of his seven sons, to the Royal College of Physicians for ten years, and there they hung for the allotted time as objects of great interest. We had been promised that if ever the portrait of William were to be sold the College of Physicians should have the first chance of buying it. Not long afterwards I was alarmed at hearing rumours that the portrait of William might be going to the United States. At my suggestion the then Director of the National Portrait Gallery, Kingsley Adams, made an offer to the owner of a sum large enough to ensure that the picture would have to be submitted to the Reviewing Committee before it could be licensed for export. We hoped that this would make it secure as an object of national importance; yet presently I was told by an American friend that it had in fact reached California, and was in the possession of an eminent cardiologist, Dr. Prinzmetal.

From the Portrait Gallery we insisted that the officials of the Board of Trade find out how the picture had escaped the net. Examination of the papers submitted before export revealed false statements as to the identity of the subject (an 'unknown gentleman' and so forth) incriminating both the picture dealer concerned in the fraud and the shipping agent. Both were called for trial in the Magistrates' Court in the City of London, and I went with Kingsley Adams to see the fun. Andrew Lloyd was there, but did not give evidence and we did not speak to him. When the official Prosecutor had given his evidence two solicitors rose in turn to make eloquent speeches telling us how the accused were entirely innocent of any bad intent. The magistrate listened with poker face to their pleas and then told the accused men, 'You have clearly been guilty of a bare-faced attempt to effect a fraudulent export of the portrait of Dr. William Harvey, but I will tell you at once that I am not going to send you to prison.' As their highly respectable backs were turned to the rest of the Court we could not see how they received this news. The magistrate then proceeded to fine each of them a large sum of money and that was the end of the matter.

We had no means of enforcing the return of the portrait to its proper home. Dr. Prinzmetal stated that he was entirely unaware of any illegality in the transaction and resisted pressure by his colleagues and by his government to send the picture back to England. He no doubt enjoyed his triumphant 'collector's pride' in keeping his prize. Many years passed and he never changed his mind, but finally he had the misfortune to lose it. His family then took power of attorney and offered to sell the picture to the National Portrait Gallery for £20,000, a sum enormously greater than had been paid for it. The Gallery took the responsibility for half the ransom demanded and Dr. William Gibson, a physician of Toronto, organized an appeal to raise the rest of the money by subscription from the medical profession in America. He was helped in this by Jacob Zeitlin, the Los Angeles bookseller, who had tried many times to persuade his customer and friend Dr. Prinzmetal to change his mind. So, in the end, Harvey came home again and was put on show in the Portrait Gallery with, to my embarrassment, a photograph of myself alongside.

My interest in William Harvey continued to grow and in 1949 I was called upon to deliver the Linacre Lecture at St. John's College, Cambridge, commemorating Thomas Linacre, the famous fifteenth-century physician and alumnus of the College. I called my address 'The Personality of William Harvey', and included a brief survey of his appearance in his portraits. This involved me in the unpleasant duty of stating my belief that the portrait, which had hung in Caius College for many years as a portrait of Harvey, was in fact an image of an unknown and irrelevant individual. It bears no resemblance to Harvey and has no known history connecting it with him.

In 1958, I was invited to deliver the Harveian Oration at the Royal College of Physicians of London, then an unusual honour for a surgeon. The memorial had been founded by Harvey himself in his will and an Oration had been delivered annually with very few intermissions since 1658; mine was the 254th in the series. Most lecturers had chosen medical or scientific subjects, some having little or no connexion with Harvey. Not being a physician I chose to make my lecture biographical, and called it 'Harvey through John Aubrey's Eyes'. I believed it would be of interest to study in detail the relations of these two dissimilar men, Harvey's younger contemporary and admiring friend, Aubrey having left among his writings a gossipy account of Harvey's life.

I had first published a *Bibliography* of Harvey in 1928 under the imprint of the Cambridge University Press; a second revised edition appeared in 1953. I had also formed an almost complete collection of his works, lacking only the first edition of *De Motu Cordis*; the book is not especially uncommon (I have a register of between fifty and sixty copies in Europe and the United States), but always too costly for my means. I also had a great many of the Harvey source books, some gathered from the library of Sir D'Arcy Power, thrown on the market by his son after his death. I was in fact well equipped, by 1960, for writing a full-scale biography of my hero. About that time I was talking to Russell Brain about the project and was, I suppose, expressing a foolish diffidence. It was indeed a formidable undertaking, but Brain had replied somewhat roughly, 'If you can't do it, nobody can.' I saw that I must confront the task. By then I had retired from my professional duties and so had the time needed for research. I spent the next three years concentrating on Harvey and his times, using mainly my own library and the Cambridge University Library, supplemented by visits to the British Museum, the Bodleian Library in Oxford, the Public Record Office, and other repositories of documents in London. I also searched for material in Harvey's native county of Kent, visiting Canterbury and his birthplace, Folkestone, and re-visiting his mortal remains in Hempstead in Essex. In addition I made use of two invaluable sources of information: the *Annals of the College of Physicians*, seemingly not used by any previous biographer, and Dr. Gweneth Whitteridge's recent transcription of Harvey's lecture notes. Harvey's hand is just about the worst of all the notoriously bad medical scripts, and the patient ingenuity of Dr. Whitteridge was needed to make his message intelligible. Dr. Whitteridge had been a valued friend since the days when she was Archivist at Bart's, and her matchless Harvey scholarship was always at my disposal.

The *Life of William Harvey*, well illustrated, was published by

Oxford University Press in 1966. It had favourable reviews and was awarded the James Tait Black Memorial Prize as the best biography published in that year. It was, however, of somewhat specialized appeal, and though it had no rival, the edition of 3,000 copies was not sold out for several years. A second corrected edition was published in the quatercentenary year of Harvey's birth, 1978, but again sold slowly.

While writing the *Life of Harvey*, I could not help being impressed by his contribution to the scientific life of seventeenth-century England. When the President of the Royal Society called on me the following year to give the lecture named after John Wilkins, one of the founders of the Society in 1662, it was inevitable that I should focus my attention on Sir Francis Bacon, for three centuries generally accepted as the prime mover in the formation of the Royal Society. One of the great prizes in my library was Blake's copy of *Bacon's Essays* (1798), on the title-page of which he had written, 'Good Advice for Satan's Kingdom'. His annotations pencilled in the margins were in his most caustic manner, for he regarded Bacon as the arch-materialist and enemy of the imagination and of all art. Prejudiced by Blake, I began to wonder whether Bacon was really all he was cracked up to be and whether Harvey and his predecessor Gilbert, the authority on magnetism, might not have been the real inspiration of the Royal Society's founders, the great majority of whom had been medical men. The result of these speculations was the lecture, 'Bacon, Harvey and the Foundation of the Royal Society', delivered on 8 June 1967.

When I came to examine the evidence in detail I found that all of it favoured Harvey as the true author of experimental science, whereas Bacon had no claims whatever. He had written impressive books on the philosophical aspects of the idea of science, yet his knowledge of the meaning of the experimental method, to which the Royal Society Fellows had pinned their faith, was less than none. Bacon's celebrated book, *Sylva Sylvarum* (1627), a folio volume which had passed through eleven editions in the seventeenth century, was nothing but a bundle of rubbish. Bacon sitting in his armchair had collected out of books by others all the folklore and popular superstitions he could find and tried to pass them off as the foundation of 'science', and all as being of value as knowledge because he said they were. He had also proved his ignorance of real science by writing of how much he despised the modern 'men of science', in particular Gilbert, the chief exponent of experimental science before Harvey. Bacon did not mention Harvey, though he knew him well, having been his patient. Harvey had told John Aubrey that Bacon wrote of philosophy 'like a Lord Chancellor'. From the opinions of Harvey voiced by the Fellows of the Royal Society it became plain that they had almost worshipped him, while ignoring Bacon. My case seemed to be watertight and no dissenting voice has been raised against it. I learned several years later that Peter Laslett, the social historian of Trinity College, Cambridge, had published in 1960 a paper entitled 'The Foundation of the Royal Society and the Medical Profession' (*British Medical Journal*, 16 June 1960), which I had somehow failed to read and which contained the essence of my theme. Soon after the publication of my lecture another paper on the same theme, by Dr. Charles Webster of the University of Leeds, was published in *Medical History* (vol. XLI, 1967). We were all thinking quite independently on the same lines.

———————•◆•———————

25

BIBLIOMANIA

In 1942, while I was living at Great Hampden as surgical consultant to the R.A.F., a message came from a book auctioneer in London asking me to call as soon as possible at his rooms. I responded to the call not knowing with what I was to be confronted, and was amazed to find that I was to be offered a Blake collection at a knock-down price. The auctioneer told me that he had been sent the collection to sell, but since it consisted chiefly of prints and pictures of which as a book man he had no knowledge, he wished to dispose of it privately. He had been offered £350 by a furniture dealer and any offer over that would be accepted. Evidently he was in fear of German bombs and anxious to be rid of the property at any price. I had no hesitation in naming the round sum of £500 and so became the owner of eleven important Blakes at one blow.

It was an event beyond my wildest dreams—I had once had a dream of just such a find, but not on the scale of this real treasure trove. I had acquired one of Blake's finest tempera paintings, his illustration of Dante's episode of 'Count Ugolino with his sons and grandsons imprisoned in the Tower of Pisa', together with two early watercolours illustrating the poem *Tiriel*; a unique proof of the frontispiece to *Jerusalem*, carrying text afterwards erased; a watercolour painting for the frontispiece to *Europe* shewing an earlier state of 'The Ancient of Days'; a magnificent pencil drawing of Blake's version of the 'Laocöon'; and other interesting prints. The 'Ugolino' had a coat of yellow varnish, which was easily removed by my friend Dr. Johann Hell. One of the greatest experts in Europe, Dr. Hell was generous with his help and dealt with several of my pictures, usually without charge. The 'Ugolino' afterwards became so valuable that I could no longer afford to insure it and I gave it to the Fitzwilliam Museum, Cambridge.

Another great Blake treasure came to me only a few years ago in an equally fortuitous way, through my friend Edwin Kersley, whom I had known since the 1930s. 'Puff', as his son Leo, a ballet dancer, called him, had had a chequered career, starting life in an orphanage. At the age of nine he distinguished himself by springing to defend another boy who was being flogged by the matron of the institution with a metal-studded leather belt. He butted the ferocious female with his head in her abdomen and forced her to desist. At the subsequent enquiry held by the governors of the orphanage he produced the weapon she had used, which he had wisely taken and hidden in his blouse, and so justified his action.

As Puff grew up he remained of diminutive stature but became immensely strong—so strong indeed that when as a young man he became for a time a professional pugilist he soon gave it up, realizing that his strength was too dangerous since it might result in the death of an opponent. He had been a footloose adventurer in Canada and the United States, later working as a lumber-jack, and cook in a Canadian lumber camp; back in London in 1915 he worked as a milkman, and stevedore in the docks. When he was conscripted in 1916, he registered as a conscientious objector and was sent to France as cook to the Suffolk Regiment. After the war ended he was for some time on the dole, but in 1925 took to tramping round the villages with a suitcase, selling socks and stockings. This somehow led to his becoming a dealer in second-hand furniture in Croxley Green. By 1929, he was buying miscellaneous objects in the sale rooms for resale 'on the stones' in the Caledonian Market, having acquired along the way a wide knowledge of art in all its aspects.

Puff came into my life by sending me a letter in April 1937 offering a supposed portrait of William Blake. I have no memory of this, but it was rejected. Nevertheless from that moment I became one of Puff's most favoured 'customers', though he would often give me things in which he knew I was interested rather than sell them to me. On this peculiar principle he actually made me pay £4 for a beautiful self-portrait drawing by George Richmond, though he gave me a number of

watercolour drawings and prints by the same artist. Again I
had to pay him £4 for a copy of the *Life of Calvert* by the
artist's son with prints of all Calvert's small wood engravings,
lithographs, and copperplates; the present market value of the
book is £1,000 or more. Sometimes Puff would tell me of
Blake prints to be sold in some obscure sale room where competition would be slight; it was in this way that I acquired my
set of early states of Blake's *Illustrations of the Book of Job*.

For all these years Puff had been working as professional
'runner' for the Bond Street dealers, Colnaghi's and the rest.
He enjoyed the fun of the hunt while leaving the fashionable
West End dealers to make the profits out of his skill and knowledge. He had indeed become a notable expert and could himself have operated successfully as a dealer if he had cared to be
bothered with a shop or office. All his life his widely receptive
mind had been gathering knowledge of books and pictures for
the instruction of others. He would sometimes take a party of
children to the National Gallery and lecture to them so effectively that the officials would stop to listen to him.

The climax of my dealings with my generous friend came
about eight years ago. Some fifteen years before that I had
heard that someone living in Hampstead possessed a coloured
copy of Blake's splendid engraving of 'The Canterbury Pilgrims'. This was most exciting news which had to be explored.
I obtained the address of the kindly owner, who invited me to
come and see the picture in his house. He was an elderly
solicitor, who told me that he had acquired the picture in connexion with some documents pertaining to an estate in Golden
Square, Soho, which suggested that the picture originated
somewhere close to Blake's birthplace. It was an example of the
rare first state of Blake's celebrated engraving, painted with
watercolours applied with such perfect judgement and effect
that the picture proclaimed the master's hand though there
was no documentary confirmation. Before leaving the house I
asked the owner if he had ever thought of selling the picture.
He replied that he intended to leave it to the Ashmolean
Museum in Oxford. I thought no more about it until, a year
or two later, it occurred to me that I should go to see it again.
I wrote to the Museum, who replied that the picture was not

there and that they knew nothing about it. I then recalled that when I had talked to the kind old man I had recognized that he was in the last stages of chronic bronchial trouble. I could not be surprised that he had failed to carry out his intention.

There was nothing more to be done—until one day some months later Puff Kersley kindly asked me to visit him at the basement in Maida Vale where he lived. There I was amazed to see on the wall the missing 'Pilgrims' in all their beauty. Puff had bought the picture, unrecognized by anyone except himself, for a small sum at a sale of furniture in London. He did not offer to sell it, or even to give it, to me. I well knew that he liked Blake as much as I did and did not have the heart to test his generosity by making an offer. I knew that the picture was safe in Puff's dark basement from any risk of fading by overexposure to light, and there it remained for the next ten years. Then I became engaged, with the expert help of Iain Bain of the Tate Gallery, in an investigation of how Blake had made prints from this very large plate, and needed to examine the print more closely out of its frame. Puff's son Leo, now the owner of a successful Ballet School in Harlow, brought the picture to my Brinkley home so that we could make our examination. It was now in my house and I began to feel that perhaps this was a fit moment to ensure that it remained there until it went to its ultimate destination, the Fitzwilliam Museum. I accordingly offered Puff a good round sum, which he immediately accepted.

The beauty of Blake's vision was soon enhanced by giving it a handsome frame, and it was exhibited for the first time in Edinburgh, close to the original large tempera painting lent from Pollok House, Glasgow, at a Blake exhibition which I had been called upon to open. It was interesting to find that Blake's watercolour brush had followed the tempera fairly closely. The engraving was exhibited again in the great exhibition held at the Tate Gallery in 1978 in association with the William Blake Trust, where it shone, well hung and lighted, in all its glory.

Though I have acquired some rare Blake pictures, I knew I

should never be wealthy enough to own a complete copy of one of his illuminated books, which are reserved for millionaires. In 1952, however, I 'picked up' (as book collectors are always said by non-collectors to be doing, as if it were through casual good fortune and not the result of special knowledge acquired in the hard way) at Sotheby's auction rooms nine leaves of a most lovely copy of the *Songs of Innocence*. The book had been bought from Blake himself by Baron Dimsdale (1712–1800), given his title by the Empress of Russia for having inoculated herself and various members of the royal family against small pox. The apparently insignificant volume had descended in the family until at some time in the 1890s it had been thrown on a bonfire together with the other contents of a nursery cupboard. Its value had been realized too late and only nine of the twenty-seven leaves were rescued from the flames. Some of these shew singeing at their edges as evidence of the truth of this sad story. My first cousin, Neville Brown, had married into the Dimsdale family, so that they knew of my interest in Blake and had let me keep for some years a copy of Blake's *Book of Urizen*, also bought from Blake by the Baron. I therefore regarded this fragmentary example of the *Songs*—in my eyes one of the most wonderful books in the world—as 'the family copy' and I was determined to add it to my collection. Its exceptional quality was not recognized by anyone else and I bought it for a quite ridiculous price compared with present valuations.

Stories of this kind savour perhaps too much of the acquisition of 'high spots', a pursuit possible only for collectors whose purses are deep enough and who are therefore rather despised by the penniless scholars whose successes depend on knowledge and judgement. The interest of my own collections depends rather on a principle already mentioned, of choosing to study in depth the works of an author whom I found interesting though unfashionable. Market values were determined largely by fashion in the years when the books were plentiful and so my method avoided competition and high prices—until I had compiled my bibliography. Then everyone took notice and the prices rose rapidly, but by that time I had acquired good copies of all the books and could view with complacency the change in market values. The principle is no longer applicable since the supply of the right kind of books has dried up and all books have become expensive.

I do not pretend that I neglected opportunities that came my way of buying high spots at bargain prices—as when, during a surgical conference at Manchester, I stole out between meetings to visit a suburban bookshop and found a fine copy of the true first edition of Pope's *Dunciad*, bound up with other rarities for five shillings; or when, dropping in idly to Hodgson's auction rooms, I saw an attractive-looking item about to be sold for £24. I hastily said 'Twenty-five'—and found that I had bought a lovely humanistic manuscript of about 1530 written in Italy by a scribe named Niccolo Pollini. But such anecdotes become tedious; it would perhaps be of greater interest to relate how I acquired a group of books all of special value, such as those from Blake's own collection.

Blake is often regarded as 'uneducated', having left school at the age of ten to go to a drawing master. Yet we know from his own statements that he was reading widely from an early age and it is clear from his own writings that he became extremely well read, though it seems unlikely that he ever had a large library of his own. About 1808 he wrote in his copy of Reynolds's *Discourses*, 'I read Burke's Treatise [*On the Sublime*] when very young; at the same time I read Locke on Human Understanding & Bacon's Advancement of Learning; on Every one of these Books I wrote my Opinions.' This remark about his habit of annotating his books suggests that it is particularly important to find those that Blake owned. It is less likely that he would have written his opinions in borrowed books, though he is known sometimes to have done so. At the present time there are seventeen books definitely known to have been in his possession, and eight of them are now in my library.

The earliest of these, Fuseli's translation of Winckelmann's *Reflections on the Painting and Sculpture of the Greeks* (1765), was offered to me in 1914 by the London bookseller Percy Dobell, with whom I had many dealings. He pointed out that the book was conspicuously signed on the fly-leaf 'William Blake Lincolns Inn', though he clearly did not believe that this was the right Blake. He said, 'You can have this as a speculation for 3/6.' I accepted the offer, not really believing in its authenticity, but realized on later reflection that Blake might well have possessed the book when living as an apprentice with the master engraver James Basire in Queen Street, Lincoln's Inn Fields. The subject too would have been of great interest to him. Comparison with other examples shewed that the signature was indeed authentic, written by a boy who was amusing himself by giving a grander address than he was entitled to. I had stumbled on a book of great importance to its former owner, since he had found in it many ideas influencing his views on painting. It had no annotations.

The next chance came in 1938. The London bookseller Lionel Robinson, whom I had known since he was a boy serving in his uncle's shop in Newcastle upon Tyne, had told me that, if he ever bought at auction anything connected with Blake which I coveted, he would let me have it for what he gave for it. On 27 July 1938 Swedenborg's *Wisdom of Angels concerning the Divine Providence* (1788), containing annotations by Blake and his signature on the half-title, was offered at Sotheby's and bought by Robinson. I reminded him of his promise and he generously let me have the book at its sale price.

In 1947 I was visiting the United States and called in at Goodspeed's bookshop in Boston. I asked the friendly proprietor if he had recently had anything by Blake. He said No, he could not recall anything. Then, after a few moments' thought, he added that he had sold a very interesting book eighteen years before, which he believed was annotated by Blake. For thirty years I had been searching for a copy of Bacon's *Essays*, which I knew from Gilchrist's *Life of Blake* contained annotations by him. Some had been quoted by Gilchrist, but by no means all, and it was therefore of great importance for the new edition of Blake's writings I was then contemplating. This came to my mind at the right moment and I rather breathlessly asked Goodspeed if the book could have been a copy of Bacon's *Essays*. Yes, he believed it was, and he could reveal the owner's name if he was allowed to do so. Later the message came that the book was owned by J. K. Lilly, Jr., the pharmaceutical millionaire of Indianapolis.

A letter to Lilly asking for photographs of the annotated pages brought a courteous reply saying that the book was in a

fragile state and that there was no photographer in Indianapolis who could do the work, but, since it would be in the
interests of scholarship, he would let me have the book for
what he had paid for it. I was asked to pay $1,000 (in fact much
less than had been given eighteen years before) and I gratefully
agreed to the proposal. In 1947 it was still forbidden to export
cash and I applied for permission to send the paltry sum of
£250 to the United States, explaining that it was in order to
bring back to England a book of national importance. This was
refused and the refusal was finally confirmed by the head of the
Treasury. The problem was easily solved by my friend Dr.
John Fulton of Yale University paying the generous owner and
I reimbursing Fulton by meeting his hotel bills in London. The
book was an attractive edition of the *Essays* dated 1798. The
unpublished annotations were of great interest, as I have noted
elsewhere, and I published them in full in the *Times Literary
Supplement* soon afterwards.

In 1927 A. H. Palmer, son of Samuel Palmer, Blake's
follower and friend, held an exhibition of his father's works in
London with a few prints by Blake. In this connexion I had
heard that A. H. Palmer possessed a volume annotated by
Blake, but its identity was not known. In 1928 Palmer sent the
whole collection to Christie's for sale, but the book was not included. I then wrote to him asking for information about the
book if it existed. I received in reply two long, rambling letters
written in different coloured inks telling me that he had the
book, but could not reveal its title because it was connected
with an important event in Blake's life wrongly reported by his
grandfather, John Linnell, whose *Life* he was rewriting with
corrections. This was all I could glean and Palmer died in the
following year. I attempted repeatedly to make contact with
his family in Vancouver, B.C., but failed to get any answer, and
finally gave up trying.

Then in 1956, when I was to visit Vancouver on my tour, as
Sims Commonwealth Professor, of Canadian medical schools,[1]
I decided that now or never Blake's book must be found.
Having learnt the address of a son of the late A. H. Palmer, I
was soon knocking on the door of a small house on the outskirts

[1] See below, p. 331.

of Vancouver. When the son, Bryan Palmer, an elderly engineer, opened the door he said at once, 'I know what you have
come for, but I have nothing of any interest except perhaps
these,' pointing to a pile of exercise books containing his father's
notes on the projected life of Linnell, adding that I could take
them if I wished. I accepted the offer with gratitude and then
asked if he knew anything about the books his father might have
owned. He said that he believed there were some stored in the
attic, but he was certain there was nothing of value. I had to
insist that I must have a look at them, and he climbed the stairs
unwillingly and brought down an armful of volumes. A quick
inspection told me that my quarry was not among them, and I
asked again if that was all. The poor old man grumblingly said
that there might be some more, and made two more ascents.

The third armful was for the most part as dull as the others,
but my heart gave a jump when I caught sight of a book bound
in rough cloth with a gold-leaf label on the spine similar to that
on the Bacon *Essays*. But I was surprised to read on it the name
Dante. It was Henry Boyd's translation of the *Inferno* (1785); the
list of subscribers shewed that William Hayley had taken seven
copies, and this suggested that it was Hayley who had first introduced Dante to Blake and not John Linnell, as Linnell had
claimed. A. H. Palmer had hated Linnell for his cruelty to
Samuel Palmer and delighted to find him guilty of false claims.
Fifteen pages of the introduction to the Dante volume bore
annotations in Blake's hand, and laid in was a receipt for
money paid by Linnell to Blake. A long note by A. H. Palmer
authenticated the volume as having been Blake's property.
When I asked Bryan Palmer about the destiny of the book,
which he evidently had not known he owned, he replied on the
spur of the moment that he would give it to the University of
Vancouver. However he could not resist an offer of £50 down
and it passed into my keeping.

This was not quite the end of the story. As I was saying
farewell I reminded Bryan Palmer that he or his brother, living
in Victoria Island, still possessed the large Linnell archive
loaned by the family many years ago to A. H. Palmer to help
him with his life of Linnell. Linnell's great-grand-daughter,
Joan Linnell Ivimy, Bryan Palmer's cousin, had been a friend

of mine for many years. She would like to have the documents sent back to their owners. Palmer denied all knowledge of the archive, but promised to look into it. Eighteen months later a trunkful of papers, so huge that it was admitted with difficulty, arrived at the Ivimys' front door. I had the satisfaction of going through the contents with Joan Ivimy and we found among them Samuel Palmer's sketchbook of 1824, a priceless relic of his most creative period. This was probably given by Palmer to George Richmond and so came to rest among the Linnell papers. Otherwise it would have been sacrificed through the crazy prejudices of A. H. Palmer, who burnt twenty-four other sketchbooks of his father's on the ground of their being too 'unmanly' to suit his taste. It will never be known what we have lost of a great artist's work through his son's action. The surviving sketchbook was later reproduced in facsimile for the William Blake Trust; the original is preserved in the Print Room of the British Museum. Linnell's journal was not found among the papers (the original turned up afterwards in a London solicitor's office), but it had been copied in one of the exercise books I had brought from Vancouver. It gave a valuable record of Linnell's association with Blake, which I was able to use in my own researches.

Blake's copy of John Wesley's *Hymns for the Nation* I first saw in Dublin in the library of Seumas O'Sullivan (pen-name of Dr. James Starkey), a friend of the Goodens. After his death his books were sent to Christie's for sale. Luckily for me the cataloguer had not thought much of the somewhat cropped signature and had hidden the thin volume in a parcel of rubbish, so that it was easy for me to acquire it on 8 December 1958.

In 1908 Blake's copy of Chatterton's *Poems* (third edition, 1778), with his signature on the title-page, was bought by Sydney Cockerell, Director of the Fitzwilliam Museum, Cambridge, when I was an undergraduate at Pembroke College. Cockerell had been a kind friend over many years. I used to visit him after his retirement and paid my last visit when he was very near his end. When at Cambridge he had been very persuasive in getting owners of beautiful things to give or bequeath their possessions to the Museum. It was unkindly said that he specialized in squeezing wealthy donors when they lay on their deathbeds. I had no thought of this when I saw Uncle Sydney, as I called him, for the last time, in 1957, but I knew that he had been selling many of his manuscripts and, being himself blunt of speech, would not mind my asking if he would sell me the Chatterton. His immediate reaction was to say that he would like to give it to me. It had a gold-leaf label on the spine similar to the others. In 1952 Jacob Zeitlin, the Los Angeles bookseller, wrote saying that he would like me to have his copy of James Barry's *Account of a Series of Pictures in the Great Room of the Society of Arts* (1783). It was certified as having been Blake's copy and inserted in it was a drawing by him of 'Barry in Old Age'. The terms were easy and I accepted the book, though it did not have Blake's signature.

In 1971 an undergraduate of Jesus College told me that a friend of his living in Petersfield, Hampshire, had a book with Blake's signature dated 1799. I asked if I might see it and it proved to be a copy of Will Shenstone's *Poetical Works* (Cooke's edition), with an authentic signature. I told the owner that it would ultimately find its home in the Fitzwilliam Museum. She was satisfied with a cheque for £30 payable to the charity known as Oxfam, remarking that she found Shenstone rather a dull poet. I agreed with her and have a fancy that Blake felt the same. Petersfield is not too far from Felpham in Sussex where he lived from 1800 to 1803 under Hayley's patronage. He had taken the book with him to Felpham, but finding it of little interest had perhaps given it away, so that it had remained in the district to the present time.

26

RETIREMENT FROM SURGERY

My retirement from my profession as a consulting surgeon was a kind of anticlimax, being a rather long-drawn-out affair. When I entered the Royal Air Force in 1939 I was still an Assistant Surgeon at Bart's, and returned in 1945 to find myself Senior Surgeon to the hospital. The retiring age in our hospital had been fixed a few years before at the age of sixty; I was therefore due to retire in 1946. But by then the National Health Service had come into being, with a retiring age of sixty-five, so that I was caught in an equivocal position. My hospital colleagues solved the difficulty by giving me five more years on the senior staff as Emeritus Surgeon, with no further duties on the Medical Council or committee work, very little teaching, and no emergency work.

Retirement from the staff of a teaching hospital is by tradition a pleasantly affectionate and dramatic occasion, the last clinical lecture and the last teaching round in the wards usually being packed with an audience of friendly students. When in 1951 the time came for me to retire altogether from Bart's I had thought it might pass almost unnoticed, because as Emeritus Surgeon I had had only five beds at my disposal for my surgical patients, and my ward rounds attracted but few students. Yet I was touched to find the ward crowded to capacity on my last day and I was able to shew the appreciative audience a collection of patients such as had certainly never before been seen in any teaching hospital—that is, five beds occupied by patients all suffering from myasthenia gravis, two of them with thymic tumours. I delivered my last clinical lecture, a survey of the history of the treatment of breast cancer concluding with my own (as I hoped) historical contribution to the abolition of the dogma enshrined in the 'radical' operation, to another large audience, including several members of the staff.

My private surgical practice had almost evaporated in the six years I had been absent from London in the R.A.F., but I still had a reputation for thyroid surgery, and after my formal retirement from the surgical staff at Bart's I continued to operate occasionally at New End Hospital and saw some patients in my consulting room. After a few months of twilight existence as a surgeon, however, I recognized that a complete and clean ending to that phase of my life must be faced. It was a hard decision. Though my friends had often thought that literature and bibliography were my first loves, with surgery as a background, in reality it had been the other way round. My most intense interest had been in the science and practice of surgery, with a parallel delight in literature and in particular the life and work of William Blake to keep alive in my mind the value of imagination in a material world—an important background to a profession which might lead to a slight twist of inhumanity. I like to think that perhaps Blake had contributed something to my attempted humanization of the current fashion in the treatment of cancer of the breast. I wanted above all to have recognition as a creative contributor to British surgery, and with the conferring of an honour by the Queen in 1955 and my appointment by the Royal Colleges to the office of Sims Commonwealth Professor, I knew I had achieved what I had so much wanted.

When the severance from professional surgery was complete the centre of my life could still be the College of Surgeons, whose Honorary Librarian I remained. In 1958 the invitation to give the Harveian Oration to the Royal College of Physicians led to my being elected a Fellow of that body as well, a distinction which I greatly enjoyed and valued for the additional friendships it brought me among the members of 'the other half' of the medical profession. While serving on the Council of the Royal College of Surgeons from 1944 to 1952 I had sat as representative of that College on the Council of the Royal College of Obstetricians and Gynaecologists, and was afterwards elected a Fellow of this third Royal College, giving me the right to a formidable array of letters following my name. It also brought me the friendship of Sir John Stallworthy and his family, so much so that their house at Shotover Edge, Headington, near Oxford, became for me another 'second home' within easy reach of the other University, and my wife and I often stayed there when not imposing ourselves on the Warden of All Souls. What I owe to the son, Jon Stallworthy, Oxford poet and now Anderson Professor of English at Cornell University, Ithaca, New York, is more than I can tell.

After retiring from professional duties I was able to fill my newly found leisure with the many literary interests I had already acquired, and have never had a dull moment from that time to the present day. I had laid the foundation for what has been almost a second career as a 'writer', saving me from the lack of interest in life which has afflicted so many professional men of my generation—not thanks to any deliberate planning focused on my retirement, but to a natural mental attitude.

During the war years it had been difficult to carry on any bibliographical work while cut off from the larger libraries, yet I had managed to make good progress with a bibliography of John Ray, the great seventeenth-century naturalist. I had acquired copies of many of his works; others that I did not hold were sent to me by post from Cambridge by A. F. Scholfield, University Librarian. He was thereby breaking his own rules, but was an old friend who took pity on my situation isolated in the country wearing a blue uniform. The *Bibliography* of the modest and lovable John Ray was published in 1951 by Messrs. Faber and Faber, largely, I think, by the favour of Richard de la Mare, son of the poet and a senior member of the firm. It was very well produced and seemed to me to be one of the most satisfying of all my books. It failed to sell, however, only about seventy copies being disposed of. Two or three years later it was remaindered and quickly sold out, since when it has become an uncommon and expensive book, only 750 copies having been printed. A second edition, revised and enlarged, was published by a Dutch firm in 1976, but I have had word from the publisher that it has not sold well.

From the time I was an undergraduate at Cambridge I had been studying in depth the works of authors who interested me by making collections of their books, each of which in turn formed the basis of a 'bio-bibliography' of the kind that I enjoyed compiling. These followed a different pattern from that used by professional bibliographers, and when in 1952–4 I was President of the Bibliographical Society of London I felt that an amateur presiding over gatherings of professionals should offer some sort of apologia or justification for a partial rejection of the rules by which leading practitioners of bibliography worked. Under the leadership of Professor Fredson Bowers of the University of Virginia, bibliographers were insisting on a form of notation which was incomprehensible to most of the people who would use my books—book collectors, booksellers, and even many librarians. I preferred to give readers less pedantry and more humanity, so that they gained knowledge about the authors of the books as well as a perhaps old-fashioned, but easily understood, analysis of the constitution of their books. I chose to call my Presidential Address to the Society (reprinted as an appendix to this volume) '*Religio Bibliographici*' (The Religion of a Bibliographer), in imitation of Sir Thomas Browne's *Religio Medici* (The Religion of a Doctor); it contained what was intended to be a friendly attack on the Bowers school of analytical bibliographers who considered the work which had given me so much enjoyment 'impure bibliography' and therefore inadequate. It chanced that Professor Bowers was present at the occasion. I was glad that he accepted the address in the spirit in which it was meant, complaining only that he had not thought of the title himself.

In the intervening years my 'impure' productions have continued to be in demand. My *Bibliography of Jane Austen*, first published in 1929, has been pirated four times by American publishers owing to its scarcity (I fought the first culprit with acrimonious correspondence and recovered my royalties, but have not bothered to do this again); now an industrious Oxford scholar, David Gilson, has compiled a much more detailed bibliography of this author, several times as large, which I pray may relieve me of the pirating nuisance. A number of my other bibliographies—the *William Harvey* (1928), the *William Hazlitt* (1931), and the *John Evelyn* (1937)—have been reprinted, and my 1915 *Bibliography of Dr. John Donne* reached a fourth magnificent edition in 1974. Though a reviewer of my

Bibliography of Bishop Berkeley (1977) expressed the opinion that, 'that publications so fraught with error and misunderstandings should run to second or third editions is a matter not only of amazement but of concern',[1] the book sold out within two years.

In 1960 I started on a plan long contemplated of compiling a catalogue of my library, recording more than 4,000 titles. It was not to have bibliographical details because they would make the book too bulky and would duplicate much information already made available in my bibliographies of various authors; it would however provide lists of the works of these writers useful for reference and would emphasize the interest of the numerous 'association copies', for which I proposed to print a full 'Index of Owners and Donors', a feature not usually found in library catalogues. It was to be well illustrated and this was easy to do because my 'library catalogue' was as 'impure' as my bibliographies, and listed pictures, prints, and even sculptures. Thus a choice could be made from prints after Pieter Bruegel the Elder and Hieronymus Bosch, as well as by Stephen Gooden, R.A., and from watercolour paintings by Thomas Bewick and the American naturalist John James Audubon. These, with a variety of leaves from manuscripts, medieval to modern, fine bindings and title-pages of unusual books, gave a good effect among the forty-five plates printed in matchless collotype by Arnold Fawcus at the Trianon Press in Paris.

The catalogue was called *Bibliotheca Bibliographici*, to bring it into line with my Presidential Address, '*Religio Bibliographici*'; and I printed the latter as the Introduction—the pomposity being, I thought, justified by the fact that the books described were the tools with which all the bibliographies had been fashioned. I spent two years in the work of compilation and the proofs were checked and criticized by Cosmo Gordon and Nicolas Barker. The book, printed in accordance with my specifications by the Curwen Press, was a handsome volume and satisfied my pride of possession—I think, a harmless indulgence and giving pleasure to many other people. The 500

---

[1] J. D. Fleeman (*Notes & Queries*, May–June 1977, p. 286), whose views I record so that rash buyers of my books cannot say they have not been warned.

copies printed were distributed by Bernard Quaritch and in the course of ten years the cost was covered by the sales. The original price of £16 was never raised and before the edition, produced in 1964, was sold out the buyers, mostly booksellers, were getting an extremely good return for their (devalued) money. The only unsatisfactory feature was that the catalogue did not record the 500 other books added after 1964.

Over the years in which I was compiling the catalogue, and researching and writing my *Life of Harvey*, I was a constant visitor to the Cambridge University Library, where I could supplement the books in my own library with the many more needed for reference which I could not use at home. Most of the Library staff became my friends and their interest and help have been a delight for an imitation scholar which can never be forgotten.

In 1943 Sir Sydney Cockerell had proposed me as a member of the Roxburghe Club, regarded as the premier bibliophilic society in Great Britain, and I was delighted to be elected a member. The Club was founded by the action of the Revd. Thomas Dibdin, who organized a dinner party at the St. Albans Tavern on 17 June 1812 to commemorate the sale of the library formed by John, 3rd Duke of Roxburghe (1740–1804). The first President was Lord Spencer, who had formed the famous Althorp Library. Many of the original members were noblemen, owners of great libraries. There were at the start thirty-one members, later increased by stages to the present number of forty. As Sir Sydney told me, the members were owners, inheritors, and curators of libraries, with the addition of several humbler book collectors and scholars. The Club has retained its general character to the present time and is still in an active state, giving great enjoyment to its members. I was elected together with Hughie, the present Duke of Northumberland, now President of the Club, and membership brought me several other new friends. The members tend to be rather elderly, with the result that the 'turnover' (to put it bluntly) is all too rapid.

My greatest grief has been the loss in 1975 of David, 28th Earl of Crawford and Balcarres. I had been rather in awe of him—he was so distinguished, chairman of almost every important voluntary organization, beginning with the National Trust and the National Art-Collections Fund—but I soon came to love him with undiminished admiration and enjoyment of his company. On my first visit to Balcarres soon after the war I had not appreciated how things had changed for the owners of great houses. I imagined they still had servants and I put my shoes outside my bedroom door for cleaning. In the morning the shoes had indeed been cleaned, but the 'servant' was the 28th Earl of Crawford and Balcarres without a word of complaint.

We had many tastes in common, though his knowledge was far greater than mine. He was the most stalwart looker-at-books I have ever known. His appetite was insatiable. He had inherited from his grandfather, Ludovic, the nucleus of the greatest library ever formed by a private individual, yet he enjoyed turning over the comparatively humble occupants of my shelves. At his first visit to my house he went to bed at 3 a.m. still wanting more. In the course of time I came to know Balcarres almost as well as my own house, though a guided tour from attic to basement to see the pictures took all of three hours. Lord Crawford organized all his public duties without a secretary and communicated chiefly on postcards in handwriting which was almost illegible. It was a frequent breakfast exercise for Margaret and myself to read a message from him as if it was in a secret code for which we held no key, though we always got the meaning in the end. He was surprised if we mentioned the difficulty. One might have expected that his conversation, coming from so nobly aristocratic a face and form, would be overbearing, yet it never was. It was always modest and interesting while usually witty and amusing.

He commuted perpetually between Fife and London, using railway sleeping coaches, and some years before his death suffered a broken spine in a fearful railway crash. After this he was seldom free from pain and with coronary heart trouble in addition, would have bouts of exhaustion, disappearing suddenly in the middle of a meal; yet he carried on without complaint. One day he was found lying dead in the garden at Balcarres. I was proud that he returned my affection.

Cowell's, the approach

When the war ended we had left Pond House in Buckingham-shire and returned to Hampstead, but began looking for a country home near Cambridge, where Margaret and I really belonged by birth. Soon we found in Essex, near the border with Cambridgeshire, a small moated farmstead, called Cowell's, built about 1550. The greater part of the moat had been filled in, but one arm remained, the haunt of dragonflies and nymphs, not to mention mosquitoes. The house itself was in excellent condition, whitewashed lath-and-plaster with oak timbers at fairly wide intervals indicating the reign of Henry rather than Elizabeth. The original thatch on the roof had been replaced by tiles, though a large outhouse was still thatched and this was renewed for us by an elderly expert, whom it was a pleasure to watch as he worked. A garden shed provided an unusual feature in the form of a large hornets' nest in one wall. This beautiful and splendid insect is usually regarded with loathing born of unreasoning fear, but it is quite harmless and friendly if left undisturbed, and it gave me great pleasure to watch the lovely creatures flying round the house. Unfortunately I was foolish enough to change my mind when I found that the large hungry insects were devouring the green-gages all night as well as all day, and had the nest destroyed by cyanide of potassium—a silly piece of greedy vengeance which has shamed me ever since. The twenty-three acres of open arable land that went with the house were let to a neighbouring farmer, who grew flourishing crops of wheat right up to the garden's edge. As we looked out of our living-room windows in late July we saw a sea of heavy ears of corn rippled by the wind as far as the eye could see.

Cowell's was a lovely place, but proved to be too small a house for final retirement to a country life, for the owner of several thousand valuable books. It was also too far from the Cambridge University Library, access to which would make the books I owned far more valuable for the work I intended to do; and I wanted to feel that I was again almost part of the University, having been made an Honorary Fellow of Pem-broke, my former College.

In the autumn of 1949, when Margaret and I were attending a surgical conference in Ireland, my mother, still active in her

Lammas House, 1980

eighty-eighth year, found a notice of a house for sale in the village of Brinkley, about fourteen miles southeast of Cambridge. It was of exactly the right size, set in fifteen acres of land. Finally my mother's eye was caught by an extensive fixed bookcase in the big living room, which was obviously destined to hold many of my larger folios. So, aided and abetted by my eldest son, Richard, she boldly bought the estate in our names. When we arrived home from Ireland and had examined the position we heartily agreed.

The Brinkley house broke the sequence of three sixteenth-century houses we had lived in; its four front rooms had been built about 1790, and made a most attractive impression at first sight. It had been enlarged at the back by various additions built at different times, but it still had a pleasant old-fashioned aspect. It had been named Herdstown by the former owner, who came from a place of that name in Natal, but that seemed to us irrelevant and we changed it to Lammas House. Margaret had discovered from examination of maps made before the Enclosure Act of 1816 that one of the fields had been Lammas Land and that the track to it through the adjoining field, still a right-of-way, had been known as Lammas Lane, which seemed to give us ample justification for making the change.

An adjoining piece of woodland has been a source of interest and joy. A number of trees, chiefly larches, have been uprooted by storms, but I have planted many replacements, including the now well-known 'fossil tree' from Central China, named *Metasequoia glyptostroboides* or Dawn Redwood. This was sent from Kew Gardens by Sir Edward Salisbury, then Director, about twenty-six years ago as part of the experimental distribution of specimens grown from seeds to a variety of places to test their hardiness. The tree is now more than seventy feet high and of perfect shape, and belies the saying that one 'only plants trees for posterity'.

G.L.K. *aet.* 86 in the copse at Lammas House, 1973

27

THE WILLIAM BLAKE TRUST

Soon after the end of the Second World War, I had become worried about the unique coloured copy of Blake's *Jerusalem* which in 1920 I had borrowed from its owner, General Archibald Stirling of Keir, so that Sir Emery Walker could make lithographic facsimiles of two pages for my Blake *Bibliography* (1921). This magnificent book, whose one hundred etched plates constituted Blake's masterpiece among the whole range of the illuminated books, had come safely through the war, but in 1946 it had passed to Lieutenant-Colonel William Stirling, who I felt was much more likely than his father had been to sell the book to the first American collector who made an offer. I told the owner I felt the priceless copy should be reproduced by some means, and I was invited to stay at Keir to talk the matter over.

All owners of rare books fear that reproduction may result in the book's devaluation by making it as it were common property. Colonel Stirling immediately raised this question. I told him that if it was loaned to me for reproduction the *Jerusalem* would be insured for £10,000, and that its value would certainly be enhanced by becoming better known. When he seemed to accept this assurance I went on to explain that the book would have to be taken apart and each leaf put into a separate transparent envelope to protect it while the work was being done. I added that when the book was returned it would have been much improved by better binding. As it was, it did not open properly, because it had been too tightly sewn. When it was rebound, each leaf would be guarded and the whole properly sewn and re-backed so that each page could be enjoyed.

Colonel Stirling agreed to all this, and I felt encouraged to explore a means of reproduction and its probable cost. Estimates from the firm of Sir Emery Walker and from Oxford University Press were for £10,000, which seemed prohibitive. Soon afterwards I was visiting the United States when I happened to see in Boston a book containing facsimiles of watercolour designs by Cézanne such as might suit my purpose. I was told they had been done in Paris by a small firm, the Trianon Press.

A letter to Paris brought two young men, Arnold Fawcus and Patrick Macleod, to London to see Blake's *Jerusalem*, brought from Scotland for the purpose. Their estimate was £4,000 for 500 copies of a facsimile, to be made by printing a plain collotype reproduction of each page in the orange-coloured ink of the original, and then colouring these by hand through stencils made by a craftsman who analysed the colouring. The stencils could be cut as needed for each colour, the number for each page varying according to the complications of the colouring. The plan seemed reasonable and the partners took the book, duly insured as I had promised the owner, back to Paris with them. I had an anxious fortnight before hearing that it had arrived safely. It was then disbound and the bulk of the pages deposited in the Bibliothèque Nationale while the work of reproduction was done piecemeal, a few pages at a time.

The project had been rashly begun without means to pay for it. My first idea was to collect enough guarantors of £500 each, and I had actually found five before the supply seemed to be running out. I do not now recall all the guarantors' names, but three of them were my brother Maynard, Lord Rothschild, and Lady Sybil Cholmondeley. Victor Rothschild had previously shewn his goodwill by lending me his copy of Blake's *Songs of Innocence and of Experience*, allowing me to keep it for several years, and by offering to give me Blake's spectacles. This last was a kind offer, but I do not fancy personal relics of this sort (I had already burnt Rupert Brooke's khaki tie), and suggested he give them instead to the Fitzwilliam Museum, where David Piper, then Director of the Museum, had the plaster cast of Blake's head photographed with the glasses in position. An American dealer capped Lord Rothschild's gesture by giving me what was reputed to be Blake's palette, but this I diverted to the Victoria and Albert Museum.

Lady Cholmondeley had once been a patient of mine and became a much valued friend. (It seems that her husband the Marquis, who was interested in calligraphy, had first brought her to see me because he liked my writing—an encouragement, perhaps, to other medical practitioners whose handwriting is notoriously very bad indeed, to amend their ways.)

This was the state of affairs, with £1,500, or probably more, still to be raised, to pay for the *Jerusalem* facsimile, when my act of faith became fully justified. My old friend Graham Robertson had been ill for many months; he had suffered a stroke, and lay helpless in bed, unable to speak. Whenever I had an opportunity I would call at his house in Surrey to see him. As the butler opened the door, he would say, 'Oh yes—Mr. Blake', and take me up to Graham's room. I would then tell him all the latest Blake news and gossip and he would signal with his eyes that he had understood. In the natural course of things he died, in 1948, and I learnt from the newspapers that he, having no children or other natural heirs, had left his fortune of more than half a million pounds to charity at the discretion of his executor, Kerrison Preston, whom I knew very well. It occurred to me that Kerrison might possibly find a way of endowing the *Jerusalem* project with some of Graham's money, a plan which the ghost of this great Blake collector would surely applaud.

I then turned hopefully to another friend, George Goyder, whom I had come to know some years earlier because of a common interest in William Pickering and his books. George also placed a great value on Blake and had the means to acquire important pictures by him. As an experienced man of business he would be an important ally in solving financial problems. He entered with enthusiasm into my plans, procured the help of a competent lawyer, and within a few weeks had produced a deed for the constitution of a non-profit educational charity to be known as the William Blake Trust, administered by eight Trustees with myself as chairman. George and I each provided £10 as the initial endowment, Kerrison Preston undertaking to add £10,000 from the Graham Robertson estate. The project was now fairly launched, and in March

1949 the Trianon Press set to work on making 500 copies of the *Jerusalem* facsimile.

The original book was kept in Paris for two and a half years before it was returned to England for rebinding at Gray's bindery in Cambridge. Its return journey caused us some anxiety. Patrick Macleod was to bring it back in his car, but he had forgotten that the Trianon Press had omitted to obtain from the French authorities an official importation permit when they first brought it over from England. Macleod's car was searched by the Customs at the Belgian frontier and an intelligent official found the book. He somehow guessed its insurance value and it was impounded, thus causing an international incident. We had to call for help from the Government and the French Cultural Attaché managed to smooth things over so that the book could be released.

The *Jerusalem* facsimile was published in June 1951 — 500 copies at 33 guineas. I had contributed only a brief Introduction, as we had commissioned Joseph Wicksteed, then the most deeply versed Blake scholar in England, to write a full commentary, published as a separate volume in 1954. This was preceded in 1953 by a reproduction in photogravure of Blake's better-known version of *Jerusalem* in black and white, published at three guineas together with a typographical reprint of the text.

The coloured version may have seemed expensive, but the Trustees had aimed at producing a true facsimile of the finest quality that was technically possible, printed on fine paper resembling that used by the artist himself. The price at which it was offered was only a fraction of what it would have been if published in the ordinary way. It could be afforded by most museums and libraries, none of which would ever be able to acquire the original book, and the Trustees were satisfied that we had justified our status as an educational charity. We had also established an immediate reputation for accuracy in interpreting Blake's intentions. And we had found a perfectionist in Arnold Fawcus as producer and publisher.

Arnold was in many ways an unusual person. He had an English father whom he seldom saw and an American mother.

He was educated at an English public school and Trinity College, Cambridge, where he was awarded a scholarship in the History faculty; all that seems conventional enough. He held an American passport, and thus escaped conscription into the British Army in 1939. Although small in build he was a considerable athlete and had become an expert skier; when he returned to the States he became a U.S. Army instructor in Alpine warfare. After the Americans joined the war he was for some time uncertain what he should do. He had somehow learnt to speak idiomatic French—indeed, he told me that he felt happier talking French than English, though extremely voluble in both—and perhaps because he had this facility it was suggested that he should work with the American counter-intelligence service in detecting enemy agents in France. Based in London, he was entrusted by the British with the Ultra secret concerned with reading German codes, and succeeded in identifying many spies, a number of whom were persuaded to become double agents.

After the war Arnold chose to settle in Paris and use his small capital in founding a business for the production of fine books, using the collotype process for illustrations, combined with the skills of the practitioners of the *pochoir* method (that is, stencil work) for coloured facsimiles. He produced a variety of books, the most successful being a splendid work on the Romanesque sculpture in the cathedral at Autun in Burgundy. The book seemed to open the eyes of the French people to the glories of Gislebertus, the sculptor, before this largely unknown. We visited Autun with Arnold several times and I became familiar with the sculptor's style, which later enabled me to restore to the cathedral a sculptured capital from one of the side doors. Once when I was visiting my friend Puff Kersley, who was about to retire from his occupation in London and was disposing of his accumulated objects of art, he said he had a lump of stone outside which he did not know how to deal with. I asked to see it and recognized the unmistakable style of Gislebertus. I paid Puff the £4 he had given for the bit of stone at auction; it is now back in Burgundy.

Arnold Fawcus's life-style was unusual. He did not care to have money in stocks and shares, but preferred to collect various antiques. He had a vintage Bugatti motor car, a few valuable pictures, and two large châteaux. The first time we enjoyed his hospitality in the Jura we stayed in a massive medieval building, the Château de Boissia, Clairvaux les Lacs, with walls several feet thick and a lovely private chapel with no floor. On many later occasions we stayed in the enormous sixteenth-century Château de Villers in Burgundy. It had been built on medieval foundations with four huge towers, only two of which were still standing, with a great baronial hall and central courtyard with a stone-built fountain in the middle housing several large trout. The plentiful water supply was of Roman origin and supplied a large bathing pool behind the château. The top floors were infested with fruit **rats** and owls, and falcons nested in the walls outside, but they did not bother us below. All this grandeur sounds expensive, but Arnold was clever at getting government help in repairing roofs and other essentials, so that he was able to make the romantic building perfectly habitable. Among his other eccentricities he was known internationally as an expert breeder of magnificent blue delphiniums (and was experimenting to produce a pink variety) by a method of scientifically controlled selection of seed. All this was achieved during week-ends out of Paris where his real 'work' was carried on. In the winter he would take a holiday in a small house in the mountains of the Jura where he could ski.

Several of the colour-facsimile books Arnold had published were done for the Abbé Breuil, the leading authority on prehistoric cave paintings. The Abbé became so dependent on him for producing his books that he made Arnold his heir and adopted son, leaving him among other objects a remarkable collection of Chinese jade, which was kept in a secret place in the château.

Arnold's vitality and drive were rather exhausting for his friends, but his perfectionism was ideal for the objects of the William Blake Trust. When he began his work on Blake's *Jerusalem* he knew nothing about the artist or his techniques, but as he became familiar with Blake's work his interest and admiration grew, so that no trouble was too great in order to get everything right and just as Blake himself would have approved.

G.L.K. and Arnold Fawcus, *c.* 1970

A Meeting of the Blake Trust at the Travellers' Club, *c.* 1978.
G.L.K., Chairman, Lessing J. Rosenwald and Dr. Haven O'More,
Associate Trustees

When the *Jerusalem* project was initiated the object of the Trustees had been to produce the best possible facsimile of this one book. Its reception was so favourable, however, and its sales so rapid that it became clear we would soon have enough return on our investment to proceed with confidence to the production of another facsimile. The obvious choice was Blake's most popular book, *Songs of Innocence and of Experience*, with its fifty-four plates. One important factor in producing the best possible result was Arnold's insistence on allowing his craftsmen or -women to work with the original under their eyes. This entailed being able to borrow a copy whose owner did not mind having his book disbound and kept in Paris for a year or more. Such owners are rare, but we were very fortunate in the generous interest bestowed on us by the veteran Blake collector, the late Lessing J. Rosenwald of Jenkintown, Philadelphia. He possessed copies of nearly all the books, so that when one facsimile was finished Arnold could start without delay on the next. During thirty years' continuing effort, the whole range of Blake's Illuminated Books has passed through the workshops of the Trianon Press. Our benefactor's generosity extended far beyond lending his precious books; as the Trianon Press had no cash margin, Lessing Rosenwald also provided a loan to bridge the gap if there were any time-lag in the cash flow from one book to the financing of the next. Arnold made little or no profit for himself; he was content if his overheads were covered so that he could keep his craftsmen occupied.

In 1966 the William Blake Trust was fortunate in attracting the attention of a second major benefactor in the person of Paul Mellon, well known for his interest in British art and for his generosity in fostering its welfare. He had recently acquired the 1790 edition of Gray's *Poems* for which Blake had designed 116 large watercolours. John Flaxman had commissioned the work as a present for his wife; the volume later came to be in William Beckford's library and so to reach the Hamilton Palace library in Edinburgh. It was overlooked at the time of the Beckford sale in 1882, and was rediscovered in 1919. At that time I was consulted by Oxford University Press concerning the reproduction of the volume in monochrome, full-size or reduced, and I was invited to go to the Duke of Hamilton's London house to see the book. I was a shy young man unaccustomed to visiting in the homes of the great. So I put on an unnecessary tail coat and presented myself for the Duchess's inspection. She was very kind and a genuine admirer of Blake, eager to tell me of the splendours of the Gray water-colours, though we were rather alarmingly stood over by Admiral Jacky Fisher, hero of the war at sea and creator of the Dreadnought warships, who was always to be found at the side of the Duchess of Hamilton—a reincarnation of Nelson. The Admiral may have been interested in Blake, but my only memory is of his gruff naval tones asking, 'How much would it fetch at Sotheby's?'

I voted for full-size reproduction in 1919 and this was done. Now, in 1966, the volume had passed into the possession of Paul Mellon who was ready to subsidize its reproduction for the Blake Trust. It was a formidable undertaking, but Arnold Fawcus was of course enthusiastically in favour of accepting the challenge. The book was published in 1972, with an historical Introduction by myself and a commentary, descriptive and explanatory. I was careful not to provide too much 'interpreta-tion', so often overdone by eager Blake scholars, and tried mainly to shew how Blake added his own symbolic glosses to the themes of Gray's poems.

Arnold's staff in Paris had carried out his ambitious task with complete success. He organized an exhibition at the Tate Gallery, shewing the original watercolours side by side with the facsimiles, and it was generally agreed that, except for the slight difference in paper, they were virtually indistinguishable. Arnold produced for the exhibition a catalogue priced at £5 (the full-sized facsimile cost £640), with reduced reproductions of some of the illustrations. One eminent North American Blake scholar was apparently unable to distinguish between the large facsimile and the exhibition catalogue hastily produced by offset. Arnold, like any intelligent publisher, had made some slight changes in the title-page to make the cover of the catalogue more attractive to the passing customer. The Pro-fessor chose to review the catalogue as if it was the facsimile and, finding the deliberate alterations in the title-page, complained that the book was seriously inaccurate and that therefore *all* the facsimiles published by the Blake Trust must be regarded as unreliable! I found it very hard to forgive the crass stupidity of this damaging criticism disseminated in the widely read *Blake Newsletter*.

Arnold's talents were not limited to the technical skills expended on the production of his books. He was a skilful salesman on behalf of the Blake Trustees and had outstanding social qualities shewn in the delightful dinner parties with which he entertained our Associate Trustees from the United States, and in his powers of persuasion in organizing exhibitions in association with directors of public galleries. The superb Blake exhibition at the Tate Gallery in 1978 owed its success partly to his energetic co-operation with the Director and staff of the Gallery.

By 1978 all of Blake's illuminated books, together with several other related works such as Samuel Palmer's sketchbook of 1824, Blake's *Gates of Paradise*, his *Laocöon* and the *Complete Portraiture*, had been published from the Trianon Press. Aided by generous American benefactors—Lessing J. Rosenwald, Paul Mellon, and latterly Dr. Haven O'More, founder of the Institute of Traditional Science in Boston—it had been a unique experiment in noncommercial publishing. Arnold Fawcus, as its mainspring, had for thirty years devoted his matchless skill and energy to the service of Blake and the Blake Trust—partly motivated, it must be gratefully acknowledged, by a personal devotion to myself. As I was thirty years older than he, Arnold had come to regard me as an adopted father. Alas, in 1978 he was taken seriously ill with an uncommon form of cancer. He endured surgical and radiological treatment with great courage, but died, aged sixty-one, in June 1979, leaving four books still uncompleted. As I write this, his widow has bravely taken on the direction of the Trianon Press so that the Blake Trust's programme may be completed before the firm closes its doors. Responsibility for publication of one of these books, Martin Butlin's *catalogue raisonné* of Blake's complete output of paintings and drawings, has been taken over by the Yale University Press. Butlin, Keeper of British Watercolours in the Tate Gallery, had been commissioned by the Blake

Trustees some twelve years before Arnold's death but, as a work of reference, the book had become unsuitable for production in the usual Blake Trust style, depending for its value on being an ordinary printed book without facsimiles in colour. The financial burden had been undertaken by Paul Mellon, but much more financial support was needed owing to its greater size, far beyond the sources of the Trust. This difficulty was solved by Mellon's generous offer to transfer the burden to the Yale Centre, his own foundation, for publication by Yale University. The main benefactor for the remaining works has been Dr. Haven O'More through his Foundation in Boston.

In a recent book, *Blake and the New Age* (1979), Kathleen Raine has stated, 'The editorial and bibliographical labours of Sir Geoffrey Keynes over the last half-century have made Blake accessible, but not comprehensible.' This is, I trust, meant only as a statement and not a complaint. It has been a matter of priorities. My conviction of the value of Blake as poet, artist, and philosopher has been unwavering, but accessibility had to be established before explanation could be attempted. I have not regarded myself as being properly equipped for the role of literary critic or esoteric philosopher and so have never set myself up as Blake's interpreter. I have been content to work, by correspondence and through personal contact, with Blake scholars such as the late Foster Damon of Brown University, with whom I enjoyed a life-long friendship and whose first book, *William Blake, His Philosophy and Symbols* (1924), has never been superseded. I have also learnt much from the writings of Kathleen Raine herself, who has led the way—controversially but, in my view, correctly—in emphasizing Blake's debt to Thomas Taylor's Neo-Platonic studies.

28

KNIGHTHOOD AND
THE SIMS PROFESSORSHIP

ON 11 May 1955 I found on my consulting-room table a large envelope marked ON HER MAJESTY'S SERVICE/URGENT/PER-SONAL AND PRIVATE/PRIME MINISTER. Inside was a letter from No. 10 Downing Street asking if it would be agreeable to me that my name be submitted to the Queen for the honour of knighthood in the forthcoming list of Birthday Honours. It would have been a grotesque exhibition of mock modesty to say no. It would certainly be very agreeable indeed. I was to be given the honour for surgical distinction by recommendation of the Royal College of Surgeons of England. My various activities outside my profession caused some confusion, however—as when the secretary of the Medical Council of my own hospital wrote on behalf of the Council to congratulate me on receiving recognition for my services to literature, although the only citation had been 'Consulting Surgeon to St. Bartholomew's Hospital'. I knew that my colleagues had not approved of my views on the treatment of cancer of the breast, yet was a bit surprised at their apparently believing the Queen shared this view.

The ceremony at Buckingham Palace was delightfully simple and traditional. The Queen, having tapped my shoulder with the sword, said, as if she meant it, 'Pleased to meet you.' She could not possibly have been expected to remember the occasion some years before, when I had sat beside her through a dinner party at the Royal College of Obstetricians and Gynaecologists. I had felt slightly embarrassed at being given this favoured position at the R.C.O.G. dinner, which was to mark the birth of the Prince of Wales, when I was only present as a representative of the Royal College of Surgeons. But I felt a great affection for Sir William Gilliat, the royal obstetrician

G.L.K. with Her Majesty Queen Elizabeth and Lord Porritt,
P.R.C.S.,
7 November 1962, looking at *The Anatomy of the Horse* by
George Stubbs
in the Library of the Royal College of Surgeons

and President of the R.C.O.G. News of his death in a road accident reached me in Canada in 1956, when I was about to enter a lecture theatre to perform before a large medical audience—the worst possible moment to be given news of that kind. It would be improper to attempt to report everything that the then Princess Elizabeth said during our long conversation. She spoke of Prince Philip's unusual background and something of how they were planning to educate the young Prince of Wales. At one point I asked whether she was really serious in acquiring her stables at Newmarket. She instantly replied: '*Yes, deadly serious.*' Cold print cannot express the intensity of the conviction she put into her answer. I was delighted with her friendliness and sincerity. Moreover she has given me, through Sir Robin Mackworth-Young, her gracious permission to record this evidence of her youthful enthusiasm.

She had certainly forgotten the incident when, some years later, she paid a visit to the Royal College of Surgeons. I then found myself, as Honorary Librarian to the College, shewing the Queen the extraordinary volume by George Stubbs entitled *The Anatomy of the Horse*, published in 1766. A photograph taken at the time bears witness that her interest in the horse was unabated.

The honour conferred in May 1955 was perhaps the prelude to another honour that came to me later in that year, when I was appointed to the office of Sims Commonwealth Professor for 1956. This travelling professorship was founded and endowed by Sir Arthur Sims, a successful businessman from New Zealand, who believed that it would benefit the medical profession in all parts of the Commonwealth if its senior members visited one another as they worked in their various medical schools. The Royal College of Physicians and the Royal College of Surgeons each sent a representative annually to visit the medical schools in two parts of the Commonwealth. I was to spend periods visiting all the medical schools in the southern half of Africa and those in Canada. My wife was expected to go with me, all expenses covered. Margaret was of course eager to share the experience, and her companionship would certainly lighten the burden for me of a very strenuous assignment. Accordingly we set off in February 1956 with the intention of covering 'as much of Africa as I could reasonably manage'. We had visited Africa once before, in the winter of 1952, I to be present at and report to the Royal Colleges on the qualifying examinations at Khartoum. Several of the candidates who failed on that occasion complained that my presence at the oral examinations had caused them to give wrong answers—no doubt a customary plea.

On 13 February we landed at Kano in Northern Nigeria, spending a day in the ancient walled city before moving on. Northern Nigeria was at that time a wealthy country, with a herdsman society that was still feudal; there were ample food supplies, but the medical services were grossly inadequate. There were only two African general practitioners in the whole country, and the Kano Hospital, which we visited, had 400 beds for a population of 3 million. The half-dozen European specialists were trying to run the hospital without any trained medical assistants whatever; there were four European sisters, but no anaesthetists.

We had intended to go on to Ibadan, but we found that the Queen, who was paying a last visit to Nigeria before Independence, was to be there on the same day, so we went instead to Accra, capital of the Gold Coast (now Ghana), to stay with a niece, *née* Polly Hill, then married to a teacher at the attractive Achimoto School, the Eton of the Gold Coast. We visited the school and also the splendid University College, where we met the Vice-Chancellor, Alexander Kwapong, whom we had known when he was at King's College, Cambridge: the best classical scholar they had had there for many years. In Accra too, the hospital was quite inadequate: there were only 250 beds, but 460 patients, many lying on the floor under the beds. A former pupil of mine at Bart's, Dr. Michael Baddoo, M.B., B.Ch.Camb., came to see me from Tarkwa, 230 miles away in the gold fields, where he was in charge of a government hospital. He hoped to acquire the F.R.C.S.Eng., but became the Director of Medical Services in Ghana and was never to achieve his ambition. His eldest son, Henry, with an English mother, is now a qualified doctor and comes to see me when he visits England.

When the Queen had left Nigeria we moved on to Lagos and so to Ibadan, to stay for six crowded days with the Principal of the University. The situation and general atmosphere in Southern Nigeria were entirely different from that in the North; there was a flourishing medical school and a large well-organized hospital—though even this was quite inadequate for the growing needs of the country, and a large new one was being built. We visited the busy prenatal clinic, where 500 pregnant women were seen in one morning, and took part in a teaching round of visits with the Sister Tutor and two student nurses to see a few selected patients in some of the poorest houses in the city. I had luncheon in one of the University halls of residence, and was offered the choice of having the food supplied to the European staff or that to the students. Out of curiosity I chose the African variety and wished I hadn't. I then addressed 130 pre-clinical students on blood transfusion, and later lectured on William Blake, with slides, to a large mixed audience.

The Principal rewarded me for this by taking us to Ife to see the famous and quite astonishing portrait bronzes, the finest works of art in all Africa. In the museum I noticed a youthful African attendant sitting with his head buried in a book. I asked what he was reading, and he told me it was Shakespeare's Works, in order to learn English. I could but admire the intelligence shewn by his choice, and wondered how it would affect his manner of address in the new tongue.

During this visit, we were struck by the beauty of the African dress, with a preponderance of flowing garments dyed a lovely indigo blue.

On the way to Ife we saw two native shrines, one discreetly hidden among bushes, the other by the roadside. Both still shewed the remains of sacrificed dogs, offerings to one of their less attractive deities.

When we returned to Lagos I took the opportunity to visit the General Hospital, largely staffed by African doctors with British qualifications and a few European specialists. I saw all the surgical patients and found the work to be well organized, though the wards were overcrowded, mainly with road accidents. A very large part of the responsibility for the patients' welfare was shouldered by a single English Sister; she was grossly overworked and found the general system of demanding a 'dash' for every service rendered very difficult to overcome.

From Lagos we moved on by way of Kano again to Johannesburg, where we were to be the guests of Sarah Gertrude Millin, the South African historian and novelist, who had been a patient of mine in London some years before. She had been told in Johannesburg that she probably had a cancer of the breast and should submit to the radical operation; being a person of strong and independent mind, she set out to examine for herself the surgical literature on the subject, and in the *British Journal of Surgery* came across my unorthodox views on the operation. She sought my advice and I was able to prove, with a trivial exploratory operation, that she did not have cancer. Later the surgical situation repeated itself, and although I had by then retired from practice, she came to me, and again I saved her from an unnecessary operation—with the result that she conceived an exaggerated opinion of my skill and wisdom, and insisted that I and my wife should become her close friends. Mrs. Millin was a masterful woman of brilliant intellect and we greatly enjoyed her company with that of her charming, though somewhat subdued, husband, Judge Millin. She gave a large party in our honour where I had the immense satisfaction of having a long talk with Dame Sybil Thorndike and her husband, Lewis Casson, who happened also to be visiting South Africa. I had for long admired Dame Sybil as one of the greatest stage personalities of our time and she proved to be equally attractive as a private person.

Mrs. Millin knew everyone of importance in South African political circles, and had vociferous opinions on public questions, about which she used to write me long and interesting letters. In the years following our African tour she became more and more exercised over the treatment of Rhodesia by the British Government and her letters grew ever more bitter and even abusive owing to her assumption that my wife and I supported our politicians. I had given up trying to answer her letters when the news came that my admired but difficult friend had died from a heart attack. I believe her former hero,

Maynard Keynes with Field-Marshal Jan Smuts at a World
Economic Conference, 1933

Field-Marshal Smuts, about whom she had written a book, had also fallen from grace in her eyes. I had met this beautiful and charming man only once, on the occasion when we were giving him, rather inappropriately it might seem, the Honorary Fellowship of the Royal College of Obstetricians and Gynaecologists. When I was introduced he seized hold of the lapels of my jacket and talked with great kindness of his admiration for my brother, with whom he had been in sympathy over the discussions of the Peace Treaty terms after the First World War and at other international conferences. At a dinner party in Johannesburg in 1956 I met the sculptor Max Kottler, and was able to secure for the National Portrait Gallery his fine bronze bust of Smuts, which the latter's son Jani assured me was far the best image of him in existence.

In Johannesburg I was introduced to much of the experimental heart surgery then in progress; unfortunately the results achieved at that time were later shewn to have been deliberately falsified to make them seem more favourable than they actually had been, though the experiments did lead to valuable advances in technology. I gave several lectures to large audiences of students and teachers, though I could not tell them anything new about blood transfusion: their transfusion service was the most efficient I had ever seen. On the other hand I was surprised, as everywhere in Africa, by the entire lack of facilities for radiotherapy of malignant disease. I was told that this was of no importance owing to the small numbers of patients needing it, though this was always belied by the numerous patients with these conditions seen in the wards. The real reason was lack of trained technicians, and physicists to help in the use of the machines.

An exciting experience was seeing the rock faces a mile below the surface in the Durban Deep Gold Mine. We were told that occasionally the rocks enclosing the passages would explode without warning from the pressure of the stupendous weight of rocks above, with death for anyone who happened to be near; it was a relief to reach the surface again before this had happened to us. I was greatly impressed by the care taken for the health of the miners, which left nothing undone that could be done. The quantity of food consumed as a scientifically balanced diet was almost unbelievable. Modern methods of protecting the men from respiratory troubles and injuries were so effective that most of the 300 beds in the hospital had become redundant, and medical officers I met were clearly under-employed. In addition most of the miners were given a rela-tively short contract so that they did not have time to suffer the possible ill effects of their employment. The spirits of these men did not seem to be weighed down by confinement within a compound. They were in fact enjoying a form of slavery because it was so perfectly organized.

We spent one day in Pretoria, where the atmosphere in the medical school was unhappy, largely because a political element entered into the appointments. It was a strictly Afrikaans school, a particular stronghold of the Broderbond, a 'secret society' with fanatical nationalist, anti-British, and anti-Black aims. The members of the staff whom I met were most friendly, whatever their private feelings may have been, but when I lectured on myasthenia gravis it was significant that no students were present in the audience of about sixty people. I was told privately that they all came from hard-bitten Afrikaans homes, mostly farms, and were intent only on getting the necessary qualifications in order to cash in on the status of 'doctor'. The subject of my discourse was a disease they were not likely to encounter and so would not waste time hearing about it.

After Johannesburg, with its unquestioned acceptance of apartheid, the sensation in the Cape Province, four hours away by air, was entirely different. Cape Town must be one of the loveliest places on earth, but the moral atmosphere was quite agonizing and I do not wish to enlarge upon it. We had been invited to stay in Rondebosch with Mrs. Davie, widow of the recently deceased Principal of the University, Dr. Tom Davie, a strong and courageous man, whose loss would increase the political difficulties which bedevilled every field of activity in the Union. This had to be seen at close quarters to be believed.[1]

---

[1] This was no doubt the explanation of an incident which took place at a dinner at the Royal College of Surgeons in London soon after my return. I had been asked to speak about my experiences in Africa and my obvious

In Cape Town I made a close friend in the Professor of Surgery, Jani Louw. It has been a grief to me that it has been so difficult ever to see him again. He shewed me a great deal of the fruitful research work in physiology being done in the University, particularly into the variations of blood pressure in the neck of a giraffe during the normal movements for feeding and drinking. I gave a number of lectures to large audiences on such subjects as breast and thyroid surgery, William Harvey and William Blake, and was entertained by the Principal of Stellenbosch University, who, like so many other people, concealed his true feelings behind a mask of friendliness.

In the course of a five-day journey by coach to Durban, along the well-known 'garden route', I varied my experience by calling on one of the most powerful witch doctors, Dr. Godse, working in Kokstad on the edge of Pondoland. He allowed us to be present at a large gathering of his patients, who assembled in a wide semicircle outside his palace, an elaborate whitewashed building. When he emerged the patients began a slow hand-clapping to mark their respect, which continued as long as he was in sight. The only 'treatment' seemed to consist in handing round bowls of some unknown mixture to each seeker after health before they dispersed. In a room in the magician's palace we found tables spread with all manner of glittering objects interspersed with many loose bank notes to give an impression of wealth, the effect being somewhat spoiled because the only source of light was a hurricane lamp on the floor. The doctor's conversation was limited to asking my advice on the relative merits of the most expensive kinds of motor car. Although it was well known that this practitioner peddled the drug dagga to his clients, yet I signed his visitors' book; the Royal Colleges might not have approved of my giving him this recognition, but it seemed to me that his method of mass auto-suggestion probably did more good than harm.

At Durban—intolerably hot and humid—I found the medical services still in process of development. The students were not yet allowed to go into the wards of the largest hospital

---

interest in the Africans drew loud jeers from a few South African visitors. Seldom can guests on such an occasion have been seen to behave so offensively.

(where 2,000 patients were housed in a building intended for half that number), lest they should form wrong ideas as to how a hospital should be run. Back in Johannesburg I saw with great interest the plastic surgery being done for the rehabilitation of lepers, who had been cured by modern medicine, before we flew on to Rhodesia.

There we gathered an impression of a lovely and prosperous country, where everyone was happy. The whole situation in Rhodesia at that time seemed almost ideal, and I have grieved ever since over the crisis produced by Prime Minister Smith's intransigence. In Salisbury we met Dr. Walter Adams, who was about to begin his duties as head of a new college for both black and white students. At the moment he had only one student, a black girl, but he was planning a rapid recruitment. I failed to understand why, when he afterwards came to London University, Dr. Adams was attacked by the students as a racist, for he was obviously entirely without prejudice and eager to do the best for all under his charge. We had a most amusing interview with Lord Malvern, the incumbent Prime Minister. Obviously a very clever old man, he was too deaf for ordinary converse, but he gave us a brief history of his life with the reasons why he had adopted medicine as a career and ended as a politician.

The medical services in Rhodesia were excellent. In the Salisbury General Hospital I saw all the surgical patients and had a most instructive view of the terrible complications that can follow infection with the bilharzia parasite. In Salisbury and Bulawayo, as they had done in Johannesburg, my friends pleasured me by bringing forward people on whom I had operated in London for myasthenia gravis—I saw four such former patients, all of them in good health and grateful for having been cured of an 'incurable' disease.

After a visit to Livingstone and the Victoria Falls, designed as a four-day holiday away from hospitals, we flew on to Nairobi. Our visit there was far too short; only one full day to see the large hospital, one of the best in all Africa, before we moved on to our last and longest assignment—seventeen days—in Uganda. In Nairobi we had met the ex-Mayor and Minister of Finance, an extremely shrewd man, who told us that in his estimation the best hope for a multiracial society was in Kenya. So far he seems to have been right. After we had seen a great deal of the huge area called Uganda we hoped it might also be true of that country.

We arrived at Entebbe airport and were met by Professor Alexander Galloway, Dean of the Medical Faculty at Kampala's Makerere University, who had organized our African itinerary. The students at Makerere, a lively and progressive institution, were largely Kikuyus, an alert and intelligent tribe. I lectured to them about William Blake, which they seemed to enjoy, and they posed several questions which I found difficult to answer at short notice. I am afraid I gave a great many lectures—though all at their own request—to captive audiences at Makerere, and hope I did not overdo it. Later I was able to plead the University's cause at the highest levels; I do not know with what results.

We also stayed for two nights with Sir Andrew and Lady Cohen at Government House, which gave me the opportunity to talk with the highest authority about Uganda's medical services. They seemed to have found the key to the main problem, that of bringing the service to all the scattered population in that enormous country, in a system of medical aid posts, each with an African nursing orderly. I visited a centre where forty-eight Africans, from eighteen to twenty-five years old, were being given two years' training in simple diagnosis and treatment; some of them became familiar enough with surgical technique to be able to do an amputation of a limb in an emergency and could deal successfully with fractured bones. When I was shewn the surgical patients in the very efficient hospital I found that a not infrequent diagnosis written on their case-sheets was 'Bitten by a friend'; this could be serious, since a human bite is often very septic, so that the wounds can be grossly infected.

In Uganda I was provided with a comfortable motor car and an African driver so that I could range widely over the country and see every variety of medical organization. In this way we visited the south-west provinces, and spent two nights at Kabala, where we were taken in hand by the District Medical Officer, a man with wide experience of African problems. With a qualified African assistant he was performing surgical marvels under primitive conditions, and controlling the treatment of the large number of lepers in that area of 10,000 square miles. He took us to Kissoro, close to the Belgian Congo, where I spent a long time in the dispensary cross-examining the African medical assistant and seeing all his patients.

In the course of these travels, covering nearly 2,000 miles, we stayed for a few days in the Queen Elizabeth Game Reserve. The Reserve straddles the geographical Equator and wherever the track actually crosses it, a large brass hoop is seen fixed to a post. Our driver asked us anxiously whether we had any Equators in England and seemed relieved to know that we had nothing so distinguished. The driver gained great renown among his fellows because we were assigned the hut recently occupied by the Queen. She may have been acquainted with the bat which was flying around inside the hut all through the nights, but was probably not so rash as I was to risk having a bath. It was filled with river water bright green with hippopotamus dung and had a corresponding odour. She no doubt had the same pleasure as we had at seeing a notice board at the crossing of two tracks saying ELEPHANTS HAVE RIGHT OF WAY —and soon afterwards, the elephants themselves exercising their rights. I went quite elephant-mad, spending hours watching them at close quarters or through binoculars.

An expedition on the river gave us a sight of every species of the wonderful birds that could be seen, and from observing the huge reptiles basking on the banks we came to realize that crocodiles have an upper jaw that moves and can be raised at right angles to the lower, instead of the lower jaw movable in all other animals. One evening we had been having a drink at the house of the warden of the reserve when darkness fell in the sudden way it does in the tropics. We said we would walk back to our hut, but this was not allowed, as in the blackness of the night we might easily walk into an obstruction such as a hippopotamus. We had to be taken the short distance by car, and though all we saw in the light of the headlamps was a single hyena, we heard the hippos snuffling round our hut all through the night. On another occasion we went in a launch by night across Lake Albert, pushing through the reeds by the light of myriads of fire-flies to reach the Murchison Falls and a smaller game reserve.

I still remember the keen regret with which we left our friends in Uganda. It had been one of the greatest experiences of my life, never to be forgotten. I can now only sit and rage at the monstrous ogre, Idi Amin, who destroyed everything that was good in that lovely country in rivers of blood.

Arriving back in London, tired but happy, my wife and I came to realize that we had both fallen head-over-ears in love with Africa, and that we certainly had not seen it for the last time.

Later in 1956 we completed the Sims Professorial assignment by visiting the medical schools of Canada. Leaving London in October, I visited twelve medical schools and gave many lectures, chiefly on the unorthodox view of the treatment of cancer of the breast, probably leaving a trail of disapproval behind me, though making many new friends. The following year, 1957, at a conference at the Royal College of Surgeons, an American surgeon was pointed out to me as being specially interested in work on the breast. I introduced myself hoping for an exchange of views. He replied, 'Oh yes, I know about you. My patients are treated properly!' and turned away. The dogma of the radical operation has, it seems, died much more slowly in North America than here.

In Montreal I visited the Medical School of McGill University and the Osler Library, which I had last seen in Oxford with Lady Osler. This was a very happy visit, but in the almost entirely French city of Quebec we felt we were in a foreign country where we were not particularly welcome. The University officials who entertained me spoke chiefly among themselves in French, which I did not understand. I asked to see the University Library and it turned out to be part of a Jesuit college, where the black-habited students sat reading without ever raising their eyes as we passed. I was asked to give a lecture to the medical students and submitted a choice of subjects; 'The History of St. Bartholomew's Hospital' was chosen. I thought this an odd selection as it was not likely to be of much interest to the students. I had a number of illustrations to shew, and each time the lights were lowered I could see the men slipping out from the back rows. When I had finished the hall was nearly empty. The most rewarding moment in Quebec was when we stood outside the hotel entrance on a clear moon-lit night and watched a huge skein of geese flying at a great height in an arrowhead formation over the city, so high up that we heard no sound.

From Quebec we moved to Halifax, and seemed to have travelled from France to Scotland. The surgical staff in the medical school there were so much interested by my lecture on breast surgery that they asked to be allowed to print it in their journal, for which I was grateful. From Halifax we flew over the Rocky Mountains to the other end of the trail, at Van-couver, B.C., where I made a lasting friendship with Rocke Robertson, Professor of Surgery. We then travelled eastwards again, usually by road, visiting eight more medical schools but not staying anywhere for long enough to be able to establish any really meaningful contacts. I gave many lectures, attended many clinical sessions, met many distinguished colleagues, was given many enjoyable dinner parties, but did not feel confident that it had all been of very much use to anybody, except in Vancouver.

After the African tour I had made a long report to the College of Surgeons. Having returned from Canada I reported only that I had visited twice too many medical schools there: it should have been six instead of twelve. I did not say how astonished I had been at the commercialization of surgical practice in Canada.

———◆———

29

VISITS AND FAREWELLS

WHILE we were in North America late in 1956 my wife and I took the opportunity to visit not only the family of our son Stephen's Canadian wife Mary Hugessen, in Montreal, but also some close friends and relations in the United States. We stayed several days, for the last time, with Frances White Emerson in her seventeenth-century house in Brattle Street, Cambridge, Massachusetts. Mrs. Emerson had told me some time ago that she intended to give me before she died her father's copy of Blake's *Marriage of Heaven and Hell*. The time had now come and she handed me the book as we said a sad farewell. She also gave me Blake's manuscript Notebook, which her father had loaned to me on an earlier occasion, to keep as long as I wished for the verification of my text of Blake's writings and thereafter to hand over to the British Museum Manuscript Department. This I did about a year later, having used it, I thought, fruitfully. Much of it is very difficult to read.

A further Blake treasure came to me in New York when we went to see one of the leading American booksellers, John Fleming. He gave me part of a leaf from Blake's illuminated book *America*, telling me that he was grateful to me for my part in having made his career. As a boy he worked in the bookshop of the celebrated Dr. Rosenbach. He had been a close student of my *Bibliography* of Blake, and one day realized that an apparently perfect copy of Blake's *Poetical Sketches* (1783) which the Doctor had sold to one of his customers was in fact, from my description, lacking several leaves which had been replaced by excellent facsimiles. Rosy was so much impressed by the boy's acuteness that he immediately promoted him to the position of assistant in the shop; in due course John became his successor in the business, where he still reigns supreme.

In New York Margaret and I stayed, also for the last time, with out unforgettable friend, the famous diseuse Ruth Draper. She and I might have met in 1925, when we were both staying with Lady Osler in Oxford, I to begin work on William Harvey's books in Sir William Osler's library; but I had slipped out to breakfast elsewhere, and been reproached by Lady Osler not for my rudeness but for allowing myself to miss the chance of meeting this marvellous person. In 1925 Ruth Draper was no longer young (she was three years older than myself) and she was not then famous. But she possessed great beauty, with fine dark eyes, and was becoming known for her extraordinary gift for impersonation of a variety of characters. These she observed in different countries and surroundings with so sharp an understanding that she could fill, first a room and afterwards a stage, with scenes from real life by changes of voice and manner. The words were all her own, composed and stored in her mind so that she could reproduce one of the episodes in her repertory at will without preparation or properties other than a chair or table and without change of costume beyond adding a shawl, a hat, or other simple aid. I believe that I first saw her in a performance at the Aeolian Hall in London, perhaps in 1920, the year she began to appear professionally, and thereafter never missed seeing at least one of her stage appearances when she was working in London or occasionally in Cambridge.

I was simply one of her devotees, as was Margaret, until the happy day in November 1951 when, through some connexion with Margaret's American mother, Lady Maud Darwin, we were able to invite her to our house in Hampstead. In a letter dated 14 November 1951 to her sister Dorothy (wife of the younger Henry James, the novelist's nephew) she mentions that she took tea with us on one of her matinée days. She admired my collection of Blake drawings and books, describing me as 'a great brain surgeon', though this was a mistake. Later she came to stay with us at our country home in Brinkley and entertained us with some of her shorter sketches. In one she impersonated to the life (for my particular interest) a somewhat hyperthyroid lady talking on the telephone in tones of utter exhaustion to an unwelcome caller and then suddenly changing into extremes of excitement and delight when the next caller proved to be a favoured friend.

She also gave us an unexpurgated version of the royal occasion when at one of Lady Curzon's drawing-room parties King Alfonso of Spain, having manoeuvred her into a corner, tried to date her on his cuff. This was in 1919 before she had turned professional and was still rather shy. At first he pleaded his admiration in Spanish and she replied in French. Then he changed to German; she replied in Italian, and he tried English. She avoided this by answering in gibberish which she could manage in almost any tongue. (She gave us an example of her mastery of Swedish, a language she did not speak, but could imitate to perfection in meaningless sounds.) At this point her hostess, seeing her embarrassment, came to her rescue.

We could exchange accounts of conversations with Henry James (the novelist, that is) and Ruth contributed the now well-known story of his reply to her request for advice as to whether she should turn to writing or to acting. 'No,' he said, 'my dear young friend—you have made—my dear young friend, you have woven—my dear young friend, you have woven yourself a magic carpet—stand on it.'[1]

While she was with us at Brinkley another visitor arrived and met us in the garden. Ruth was an affectionate friend and made those she knew well conscious of her personality as she did on the stage. She was fully aware of this and could not help it. When Patrick Lindsay, David Crawford's son, whom she had met before, came into the garden, she suddenly focused the whole of her penetrating attention on the handsome intruder; never in my life have I felt so shamefully jealous of anyone as I did at that moment of my innocent young friend.

When we stayed with Ruth in New York, in December 1956, we saw in her house the map of the world made for her by her friends with a golden star marking every place at which she had performed throughout her life. She was about to give the

[1] See also *The Letters of Ruth Draper*, ed. Neilla Warren (1979), pp. 6–7; the volume forms a perfect picture in her own words of the warmth and beauty of Ruth's personality.

G.L.K. with Ruth Draper at Lammas House, *c.* 1955

last of several farewell performances (this time really to be the last one). She was tired, but as lovely as ever as she drove us round the city to see the Christmas decorations. We left the next day for Bermuda and heard later how she had died peacefully in her sleep on 29 December, utterly exhausted by her 'retirement'. It was what she would have wished. Her life was in her acting.

In Bermuda that December, we stayed for a fortnight with Toby Elmhirst, his wife Sheila, and their three children, Lyndon, Godric, and Peregrine. I took one look at Sheila and told her she was going to have twins; these materialized soon afterwards as Tristram and Orlando.

Edward Elmhirst, always known as Toby, had been a pupil of mine at Bart's and later became my House Surgeon. He was a man of few friends because there were few people whom he regarded as worthy of his confidence, but luckily I became one of these. He did not have the extrovert character which is so often the mark of the successful surgeon, but was a rather dreamy person with a delicate English beauty and grace of form, much given to romantic dreaming about the past fortunes of his family and how they lived. He became a deeply informed student of heraldry, much admired by his friend, Sir Anthony Wagner, Clarenceux King-of-Arms, and embarked on an investigation of the history of his family from before 1300 to his own time. In 1951 he published a book with the title *Peculiar Inheritance: A History of the Elmhirsts*, in which he took ten individual Elmhirsts, each representing a different generation, and reconstructed their lives in a brief, assiduously researched, narrative. He began his book with a Foreword in which he wrote:

> The dale of Worsbrough, lying south of the bleak black city of Barnsley in the West Riding of Yorkshire, is the scene on which this history was enacted. Today the land is treeless, coal trucks move far underground, opencast mining gnaws the surface and vomits back the earth, noise and dirty smuts gloom the air on an evil wind.
>
> Continuity seems out of place in such surroundings. Feudal lords and greedy Church long ago lost their holdings there to an all-powerful throne and its progeny of new-made squires; the industrial revolution supplanted these with its own grim spawn of ironmasters and traders grown rich with coal; now these in turn have loosed their grasp to drab anxious men who live in Worsbrough Hall and manage for the Welfare State. But in the valley the family of Elmhirst, one of the very few that has uninterruptedly held the place from which it got its name, alone is left alive to flourish and protect the land. . . .
>
> Everything that is written hereafter has been attempt at truth. During the five centuries spent journeying from serfdom to squiredom, there have been many temptations and opportunities for the family to exaggerate its own importance. The author, being of bastard descent, has had to resist the subtler temptation to mock at the true worth of the Elmhirsts of Elmhirst.

When I first knew Toby his name was Elmhirst-Baxter, but he soon afterwards shed the odious suffix by deed poll. He owned, as a token of the Elmhirst inheritance in Yorkshire, a small area of land occupied by a spoil heap from a coal mine. As the passage quoted shews, Toby was of a rather gloomy cast of mind, but an effective writer. He was fascinated by emblems of death, such as a funeral ring set with a tiny skull, but his taste and judgement were good and he had assembled a small collection of remarkable English portraits. He had an interesting mind and I greatly enjoyed his friendship.

By hard work Toby became a very competent surgeon and achieved the F.R.C.S. He obtained a subordinate surgical appointment at the Ipswich General Hospital, but there he seemed to get stuck fast and was unsuccessful in professional advancement. In the end he answered an advertisement for a surgeon to join a group of practitioners in Bermuda. He sent a photograph and was accepted. In Bermuda he was very happy, with interesting work, rewarded by a large untaxed income, and living in the genuine island Paradise, which I had known before only from Marvell's poems and as the ideal place in which George Berkeley, Bishop of Cloyne, decided to found his university for the education of the native population of the New World, so that they could participate in the culture brought to them from the Old. The Bishop was entirely correct in his ideas by hearsay of Bermuda's beauty and fertility, but he had failed to appreciate its remoteness from the mainland it was meant to serve, and his grand plan collapsed. Many years after our 1956 visit I discovered in a little-read book by Dr. Samuel Johnson an anecdote concerning a meeting between Johnson and Berkeley's son George, at which the bold young man berated the great lexicographer for his own *nescience* when he blamed the Bishop's *imprudence* in choosing Bermuda although he, Johnson, had not read what the Bishop had written about it. For once Johnson was silenced and gave his friends but lame reasons for having tried to put the young man down. The story was evidently so little known that I included it, as a bit of light relief, in my *Bibliography* of Bishop Berkeley (1976).

While staying in Toby's house we bathed from the beaches of silver sand on both Christmas and New Year's Days— necessarily in the sea, because the island has no water supply other than which falls from the sky, to be stored in tanks; yet there was no noticeable shortage. We last saw the Elmhirst family waving from the airport building. It seemed as if Toby's obsession with mortality had been premonitory, for six months later he was dead, killed by a lethal protozoal infection probably derived from rats.

The message of tragedy in Bermuda had come to me by telephone while I was staying at Felbrigg Hall in Norfolk, then the home of Wyndham Ketton-Cremer, with whom I had made contact many years before through our common interest in Sir Thomas Browne of Norwich and his works. Wyndham had a highly cultivated mind and was a fine writer who had become the acknowledged historian of the county of Norfolk. He had published magisterial biographies of Horace Walpole and Thomas Gray but his most attractive book among so many was perhaps his affectionate history of Felbrigg, his ancestral home, and its inhabitants. He lived there alone as a bachelor. He had had poor health since recovering as a schoolboy from rheumatic fever, and the maintenance of the estate and house was his chief preoccupation. Having no heir—his brother had died in the First World War—he planned to leave it all in a perfect state to the National Trust. For many years the large orangery with its huge camellia *trees* (no less) was in bad repair, but before he died Wyndham received a legacy which enabled him to put this right, as well as the splendid dovecot in the great walled garden. For me, Felbrigg with its unique Italianate façade of about 1600 is the most lovely of all the Stately Homes of Norfolk. Margaret and I stayed there as Wyndham's guests on many occasions.

The park at Felbrigg, with its lake and woodlands, covers six hundred acres, and for eight years in succession I camped with a variety of friends in the woods near, though out of sight of, the house. This allowed me to indulge my passion for living out of doors in the summer for ten days or a fortnight, sleeping on the ground protected by a tent six feet high and square, with a fly-sheet. I have used the same equipment in many other places, such as the island of Bryher next to Tresco in the Scillies, with my eldest son, Richard. It was there I once had a strange and unexplained experience. The channel between Bryher and Tresco is narrow, but can be walked over when the tide is low; at high tide it is filled with deep water and if one chooses to go on foot to Tresco to fetch a loaf of bread the walk back is made sufficiently alarming by the possibility that, if not enough time has been calculated for the return, one may be overwhelmed by the tide rushing swiftly in. It is difficult to hurry trudging in heavy gumboots over the wet sand, but we had safely done it. On another occasion we rowed over in our dinghy at deep water. I was at the oars looking backwards over Richard's, the steersman's, head, when I saw a huge brown hump emerging out of the water. It was not a previously un-noticed rock, because there were no rocks in this deep channel. It had no dorsal fin by which we could identify it as some well-known sea monster, and it did not move. We were accustomed to bathing with the seals, but this was something much, much larger. I was not eager to investigate and rowed on away from it as fast as I was able. We never had an explanation of what this object could have been.

Our time on Bryher was spoilt by the arrival of a troop of Boy Scouts who pitched their camp near by. The scoutmaster did not speak to us, but placed their incinerator so that its stinking smoke blew right over us and finally drove us away. Camping in Felbrigg Park, however, was very peaceful and en-tirely private. The surrounding woodland provided plentiful fuel for the fire that cooked our food and any Boy Scouts admitted by Wyndham's permission were a quarter of a mile away. Nearer to us were glorious stands of trees, huge beeches grouped so as to form arboreal cathedrals and magnificent sweet chestnuts hundreds of years old with twisted trunks from which some of the largest pillars in King Harold's pre-Conquest church at Waltham Abbey seem to have been copied. Wyndham had studied the science of forestry and cultivated his woodlands with the care of an expert, always having nurseries of saplings for replanting as his trees reached the end of their allotted term. He gave me several now growing in the copse at the bottom of my fields in Brinkley.

Life in Felbrigg Park was as simple as we cared to make it. We could get our fresh water from the house each morning, and buy our food in neighbouring villages on our way back from bathing on the wide beaches at Holkham. But it was not always simple. There could be a day when we had luncheon with the Cholmondeleys at Houghton Hall, the superb house built for Sir Robert Walpole in 1720 near King's Lynn, and dinner with Wyndham, who kept an excellent table.

The first time we visited another great house, Holkham Hall, Wyndham had arranged the occasion with Lord Leicester. We knocked at the side door of the huge Palladian mansion and it was opened by its owner. He said at once, 'I'm sorry I can't ask you to lunch. I am the only person in the house.' The days of the wealthy poor had come, when it was they who had to bear the hardships. Lord Leicester kindly took us round the rooms to see the pictures and then to the library, not usually seen by visitors, with all its shelves picked out in white and gold, filled with books and manuscripts of unimaginable splendour. But when I asked to see the Leonardo da Vinci manuscript his Lordship could not find the key of the box in which it was kept. As we left the house I remarked to Wyndham, 'I don't like the look of that man. I don't think he will live very long.' Sadly, I was much too good at diagnosing coronary trouble from people's faces. The unfortunate man was found dead at the foot of his staircase a week later. I have always felt as guilty as if I had murdered him.

Four years after my African tour as Sims Commonwealth Professor, Margaret and I decided to indulge ourselves, as we had always intended, with a second African experience. Many years earlier I had invested £500 in Premium Bonds and in 1960 had won the only dividend (£500) of any real value that has come my way in thirty-three years. Ernie is obviously biased and has decided never to look at the area where my interests lie, but on this occasion had generously stumped up enough to cover the expenses of an extended journey.

The opportunity arose from a long-standing friendship with Hamo Sassoon, nephew of Siegfried. I had first met him while visiting Heytesbury and he had stayed with us on many occasions. In 1960 he was working as a professional archaeologist under Bernard Fagg, curator of the museum in Jos, a small town in the middle of the tin-mining area of Northern Nigeria.

From London we flew to Kano and it was a further flight of only fifty minutes to Jos.

This was to be an entirely different African experience from the one in 1956, when I had the exhausting duty of trying to maintain the character of a VIP with constant appearances as lecturer, hospital inspector, surgical expert, and supposedly distinguished guest, in constantly changing surroundings. In Jos we lived quietly for nineteen days with Hamo and his family in a comfortable house formerly the home of a mining engineer, going out every day among the African people. Hamo had his various purposeful visits to pay in all directions. He was able to talk in Hausa wherever we went and we had an intimate view of African life without effort or embarrassment. It was all intensely interesting and enjoyable.

A somewhat incongruous incident was attending a large open-air meeting to hear the American evangelist Billy Graham. He spoke in English to a large African audience of Yoruba and Fulani, with a few whites. Beside him was a loudspeaker delivering his words in Hausa. We listened respectfully, but there was no enthusiasm. The Africans sniggered when he spoke of the sin of stealing another man's wife, and there were ill-suppressed cheers when he told us that in Paradise before the Fall there was *no work*. A vulture flew to and fro over the rostrum throughout the meeting.

Hamo's house was enlivened by the presence of a large cheetah kitten. It differed from a domestic cat in that it could not retract its claws, but was friendly and cheerful. It was incapable of learning polite habits. While lying on the sofa it would happily relieve itself without warning. It seems that the cheetah is unsuited for the post of domestic pet. In addition it always proves extremely difficult to give the animal the correct food to keep it in good health. Invariably they collapse with rickets, and that was what happened to our little friend Mopti after we had gone home.

Margaret and I left Africa with our feelings about the continent intensified, if that was possible. I had not gone there with any thought of collecting native art or anthropological specimens, but was pleased to carry in my luggage a large calabash, or native bowl, exquisitely decorated with an intricate incised pattern of stylized reptiles (snakes and another animal which might be a lizard or a turtle). We had visited a village, Fuskan Mata, to see an agricultural show of various products, prizes being given for the best in each class. Margaret was unexpectedly asked to give away the prizes. She was not called upon for a speech, but was embarrassed when she had to hand a bag of salt weighing forty pounds to a woman already burdened with a baby and other impedimenta, and still more so when she had to give a large fluttering cockerel to a small boy, rather smaller than the bird he had to carry. Hamo bought a three-foot monitor lizard for the Jos zoo. I was very satisfied to acquire my calabash for three shillings. It had lain unnoticed, a thing of beauty, among an assemblage of very ordinary bowls roughly ornamented with primitive poker-work. I was told that it is probably a ceremonial object only used on special occasions and not a thing that most families would wish to sell.

In that village and elsewhere I had also found skins of native-cured Niger morocco, some undyed, others dyed red. The Nigerian goat provides a lighter and finer-grained leather than the ordinary 'crushed morocco' used for binding conventional 'rare books' prized by conventional collectors, resplendent with far too much gold tooling. My skins, costing from 3/6 to 7/6 each, are now quietly occupying my shelves clothing the sides of some of my most special volumes, after they had passed through the workshops of John Gray and Son in Green Street, Cambridge, bound by the hands of their distinguished craftsmen, in particular the late Charlie Sanders, Ken Payne, George Bolton, and David Yates.

Little has been said about my companion in these and other journeys—my wife, born Margaret Darwin, three years younger than myself, who died in 1974. She was my friend as well as my wife, and we lived happily together for fifty-seven years. Margaret shared all my life's major events, except those in surgery, delighted in my friends as much as I did, and they all loved her. She had no special interest in Blake, but tolerated my obsession. Everything I wrote myself that really mattered, such as my *Life of Harvey*, was read to her to get her criticisms, always of value.

Our tastes in literature were very similar, and that gave Margaret the opportunity to indulge one of her particular and favourite talents—reading aloud. As a child she had enjoyed listening to reading by her father and her cousin, Bernard Darwin, and cultivated a high standard for herself. She had a beautiful speaking voice with a full appreciation of literary style, and these two qualities combined to make her a perfect medium for transmitting printed words to the ears of her listeners. She delighted to exercise this talent for the enjoyment of others, and was even able to read when travelling by motor car; she relieved the tedium of hundreds of drives from London to our country retreats and back, or our many drives to the North of England and Scotland. In this way I became familiar with all the novels of Jane Austen, many of Anthony Trollope's, all the short stories of Henry James, and all the books by Lucy M. Boston, supposed to be 'children's books' but so well written and constructed that they gave us both as much pleasure as any books aimed at adults. When I had to spend six terrible weeks in Bart's Hospital recovering from a serious operation which went wrong, Margaret came twice a day from Hampstead to read Jane Austen's *Emma* to me for the third or fourth time. My debt of gratitude to her could not be computed.

Margaret also had talents as a writer. Her friends delighted particularly in her letters, which were old-fashioned *real* letters expressing her humanity and outgoing warmth of feeling. She also kept delightful diaries of our journeys in Africa and Canada, usually written in bed after I had gone to sleep, tired out by the day's events. Another talent which she kept hidden away was for drawing. This she would hardly ever allow to be seen, chiefly, I think, lest she should appear to be trying to rival her sister, Gwen Raverat, whom she admired and respected, as we all did, but before whom she humbled herself as a younger sister.

Margaret's life as a child in the midst of her Darwin family was always in her mind; sometimes I felt she lived too much in the past and this made me feel rather jealous, but it was also an endearing feature of her conversation. In 1966 she was

Margaret Keynes aged 83, 1973

invited by the Master of Darwin College to write a short history of the Darwin home in Cambridge, Newnham Grange, which had been converted into Darwin College. She gladly agreed to do this, and it became the main occupation of the last eight years of her life. She possessed a mass of her parents' papers and letters on which she could base a minutely truthful account of the conversion of the building, interwoven with much local history concerning Cambridge and its inhabitants and with, inevitably, many of her own childhood memories. She took immense trouble to get everything right up to the standard of her grandfather's *Origin of Species*.

Margaret was of a worrying temperament, and when her mind began to fail she was in great anxiety about the publication of this book. Though it was not quite finished when she died of old age in December 1974, she died in the belief that it had been published, and was satisfied. It was left to me to see the book through the press, with the help of our sons. We gave it the title *A House by the River: Newnham Grange to Darwin College*. Though it formed a very pleasant sequel to Gwen Raverat's *Period Piece*, the publishers of that celebrated book refused to take it on, so I undertook to publish it myself with the imprint of Darwin College. I was given kind support by Heffer's bookshop, and an edition of about 950 copies was sold off within a year.

———◆◆◆———

30

TRIBUTES AND REASSESSMENTS

WHEN, on 25 March 1957, I reached my seventieth birthday, I had been much touched by the celebrations organized by my friends, in the afternoon of the next day in the Great Hall at Bart's and in the evening at a meeting of the Osler Club in the rooms of the Medical Society of London in Chandos Street. My feelings of pride, one of the Seven Deadly Sins, could only be stimulated by the many laudatory speeches to which I felt almost unable to reply in my embarrassment, though I warned the gatherings—advisedly, as it turned out—that they were incurring a risk by setting a precedent for what would have to be done again in twenty and perhaps even in thirty, years' time. Most of all I was moved by Sir Gordon Gordon-Taylor's beautifully phrased Oration in my praise. We had been friends since we met in France during the First World War and he had since proved himself one of the most distinguished surgeons of our time. He was older than I and we had been in profound disagreement over more than one surgical problem, yet he could not have been more generous in what he said. He had also laid out an exhibition of all the books I had published during the past forty-three years. It was most alarming looked at from the Deadly Sin point of view. Three years later the proceedings were printed as a 'Birthday Tribute' and published by the firm of Rupert Hart-Davis. Appended to the various proceedings was a check-list of my publications in books and periodicals compiled by William Le Fanu, amounting to 186 under the heading SURGERY, and 188 under GENERAL—and there are now (1980) 133 further entries to be added, with more in the pipe-line.

Some of the further entries came about because, as a senior retired member of my profession with time to spare, I was clearly vulnerable to requests for memorial lectures of various kinds.

In 1961 I was invited to deliver the Gideon de Laune Lecture at the Society of Apothecaries in their historic hall in Water Lane near Blackfriars Bridge. For many years I had been a member of the Board of Examiners for the qualifying degree of Licentiate of the Society (L.S.A.), generally regarded as the last resort for medical students who cannot manage to pass the examinations held by the Conjoint Boards of the Royal Colleges (M.R.C.S., L.R.C.P.), though the standards set by the two bodies seemed to me to be very much the same. The Apothecaries, who commemorated their patron saint, de Laune, inventor in the sixteenth century of a pill, the prototype of a confection famous in a later age as 'Beecham's pill', possessed a lovely house and meeting place with an enjoyable atmosphere of the seventeenth century, and I had worked there with great pleasure.

I chose for my subject the life and works of Dr. Timothie Bright (1550–1615). Bright had been born in Cambridge and qualified as Doctor of Medicine in 1578; he was a subsizar of Trinity College and was for a time a teacher of medicine in the University. He wrote several small books while living in Cambridge, but in 1585 was appointed, through private influence, physician to St. Bartholomew's Hospital, the third in succession after the refoundation of Bart's by King Henry VIII in 1546. Bright had outside interests, including a wish to become a clergyman, and six years after his appointment, in 1591, he was ignominiously dismissed from the hospital staff for gross neglect of his patients. I cannot blame Bright for having had outside interests, having been guilty of this myself, but he erred in letting himself upset the balance between duties and interests.

Bright's most interesting book was his *Treatise of Melancholie* (1586), a forerunner of Burton's more famous and much larger treatise. Bright's book was mentioned by Burton, but had the much greater distinction of being the source of several passages in *Hamlet*. Shakespeare had clearly read the book carefully and incorporated what he liked in his play. It has been doubted by some scholars, but I had the support of Professor Dover Wilson.

To the accepted passages I added a foreshadowing of the soliloquy, 'To be, or not to be', but Dover was not sure about this. Over many years Dover Wilson was a very favourite visitor at Lammas House. Margaret always cross-examined him concerning various problems in Shakespeare which puzzled her and he was infinitely patient. She also made him write for her an imitation of Shakespeare's signature, which he could do to perfection at a moment's notice. He was a lovely man.

Another of Timothie Bright's interests was shorthand. He was not, as is sometimes claimed, the first inventor of shorthand. In his book *Characterie, An Arte of short, swifte and secrete writing* (1588), he set out a new method invented by himself which he regarded as specially suitable for recording sermons. He wrote books on *Therapeutics* and a silly but attractive little volume on *The Sufficiencie of English Medicines* (1580). He was a nationalist in the matter of medicinal plants—any of them grown in England were just as good as those grown abroad; even a decoction of English frogs was the equal of that made from French ones. Since a large proportion of the contemporary pharmacopoeia was useless anyway, except as magic, I thought we might concede that Bright had made his point.

I had found the study of my predecessor's life and works was well worth the trouble. The lecture was printed with the addition of a full bibliography of Bright's books, and was published in 1962.

In 1966 I was invited to deliver a Fitzpatrick Lecture at the Royal College of Physicians, and chose for my subject John Woodall, a surgeon to Bart's Hospital and a colleague of Harvey. Woodall had, in my opinion, never received the recognition he deserved. He had been surgeon to the East India Company and organized a medical service for the Company's ships. He wrote an excellent book of instructions for the young men in the service—the first of its kind—and became the leading authority on the lethal disease called scurvy, now known to be due to lack of vitamins in the food given to sailors on long voyages. Woodall included in his collected works *The Surgeon's Mate* (1639), a masterly account of scurvy, its symptoms and treatment, all based on long experience and observation. He was fully aware of the value of limes, oranges, and lemons as the sovereign cure and preventive agent. Unfortunately the book must have been quickly used up, its value being fully realized during Woodall's lifetime. But after his death in 1643 both he and his book were soon forgotten—with disastrous results, particularly for the British Navy. Thousands of seamen died simply because the medical profession ignored Woodall's work.

The use of lemon juice had to be 'rediscovered' a hundred years later by a not very distinguished naval doctor, James Lind, who conducted a rather ludicrous 'controlled experiment' by taking twelve patients suffering from scurvy and giving six different supposed remedies to each of six pairs of men. Lind had never heard of Woodall and was gratified when the two men taking lemon juice quickly recovered and took over the duty of nursing the other ten who all got worse. He published an excellent book on the subject in 1753, dedicating it very suitably to Admiral Lord Anson, who in 1744 had lost 75 per cent of his men through Lind's ignorance of the elementary facts about scurvy. Ever since that time Lind has been given the entire credit for using lemons or limes to treat scurvy. I had been lucky to acquire a complete copy of *The Surgeon's Mate*, and the main object of my lecture was to place the laurels of credit on the head where they properly belong. The whole affair is a most extraordinary example of how easily important facts may be forgotten through failure to consult the history of medicine.

Woodall was also an original and competent surgeon. Among other innovations he introduced a modification of the conventional instrument, the trepan, used for removing a small circular piece of the skull. The operation had been done with instruments of flint since palaeolithic times, but the sixteenth-century trepan was a dangerous instrument, since it often went too far, with injury to the brain or its coverings. By tapering the blade of the instrument Woodall made this operation quite safe and I had often used his trephine while operating on fractured skulls during the First World War.

Yet another memorial lecture had been offered to me in

October 1965. It was to be given in a celebration at the Royal College of Surgeons of the one hundredth anniversary of the birth of Lord Moynihan of Leeds, in every sense the greatest surgeon of his time. 'His time' was also partly mine and he had occupied a very important place in my life. I was delighted to be given this chance to express in public my admiration of and gratitude to this brilliant man.

I had first met Moynihan during the First World War, when, as Army Consultant, he came breezing into the wards of our casualty clearing station in Flanders. At the time we were grossly overworked and extremely tired, but his very presence gave us new heart by his air of sympathy, interest, and confidence. Then, ten years later, George Gask's plan of taking his professorial surgical unit at Bart's to visit other clinics in the provinces took us to the Leeds Infirmary to see Sir Berkeley Moynihan at work. It was a lesson in method and quiet efficiency. In the next year, 1926, Moynihan, long since the leading surgeon in the North of England and the Midlands, decided to conquer London by extending his private practice to the metropolis, using Lady Carnarvon's Nursing Home in Portland Place as his headquarters. Initially he brought his own assistant, Digby Chamberlain, with him, since he could not know what the quality of the assistants would be in strange surroundings. He also came to visit the professorial unit at Bart's, and I was overcome with almost incredulous delight when he invited me to become his private assistant in London.

So began my close association with this surgical hero, a fine man in physical appearance, with a personality larger than life-size. Moynihan came of an Irish family. His grandfather, Malachi, was a soldier, who migrated from Ireland to York-shire. His father, Sergeant Andrew Moynihan, took part in the siege of Sevastopol and was awarded the Victoria Cross for bravery in rescuing wounded officers—one of the first to receive the decoration at the hands of the Queen. The manner of Berkeley Moynihan's birth was also distinguished, his mother being fifty-five years old at the time, beyond the age limit, it is commonly thought, for the production of a healthy child. The young Berkeley, well set up and lively, was destined for the Army, but he had made up his mind to enter the Royal Army

Medical Corps, telling his mother: 'The Moynihans have done enough killing. It's time they mended their ways, and I am going to be the first to do it.'

His medical career was one of uniform success. He never failed in an examination and won every prize open to him. As a student he worked fourteen hours a day, rising to sixteen before an examination. His memory was extraordinary and his energy, both mental and physical, was limitless. Having listened one day to an unbelievable tale of things accomplished, I stupidly asked, 'But, Sir, don't you sometimes get very tired?' Instantly the answer came, 'I have never been tired in my life.' The words rang out, almost with a note of indignation, certainly with all the force of conviction. I was left stunned, but filled with the sense that here was a man of unusual vitality and stamina, who, even if he were tired, was never going to admit it. This combination of physical and mental toughness with an iron will to drive on to the limit of human endurance, or beyond it, helped to explain Moynihan's achievement in a profession which demands everything that a man can give. Moynihan was proud to give it. He neither smoked nor drank and kept physically fit by regular exercise, preferably by swimming. *Hard work*, he maintained, were the key words for a surgeon.

Moynihan soon gave up all thoughts of the Army, and decided to shape his career in Leeds, working with two distinguished surgeons, Mayo-Robson and McGill. He came in on the crest of a wave of surgical advance and mastered all the techniques required in abdominal surgery with particular attention to the biliary system. He would say of himself in later years, 'I have never been busy, merely occupied.' He wrote easily and in the eighteen years 1896 to 1913 published 134 contributions to medical periodicals and one large book, *Abdominal Surgery* (1905), mostly written each day before breakfast.

His operating technique was beautiful to watch, deft, gentle, and seemingly quick. He deprecated working by the clock, but seemed to work quickly by making no unnecessary movements. He would say that the perfect surgeon should have the heart of a lion (meaning courage) and the hands of a lady, not the claws of a lion nor the heart of a sheep. He attended with the utmost care to the details of aseptic surgery, and pleased me by quoting William Blake: 'Art and Science cannot exist but in minutely organized particulars.' He often repeated his *mot*, first made in 1920: 'Every operation is an experiment in bacteriology.' He seemed to regard the operating theatre as a kind of temple with the operating table as the altar. This attitude may sound silly and affected, but exaggeration is always needed to make people pay attention. Visitors came from all over the world to see him at work, and there can be no doubt that his example of surgical technique exercised an enormous influence on the surgical world. He was not handicapped by any trace of modesty and this made his conversation racy and exciting. He enjoyed his reputation and success and liked telling about it.

Many of Moynihan's patients were interesting and distinguished people. When Noël Coward came into the nursing home to lose his appendix, Moynihan said he was sure I should enjoy meeting him. Indeed, we made friends and I visited Coward several times at his Sussex home near Lympne. His company was pure delight, with an uninterrupted flow of witty badinage—a deliberate façade, as he told me, to keep people happy. Moynihan, too, had the gift of words at a higher level. Any speech made in public was a work of art, a perfectly co-ordinated flow of *oratory*. I had never quite known what the word 'oratory' meant until I heard Moynihan producing it. I would go anywhere to hear him. He was very much aware of his gift and all his most impromptu speeches had been carefully rehearsed.

Like Sir William Osler, Moynihan was a good catalyst, bringing people together to work for a common cause. As President of the Royal College for eight years he made his influence felt in many spheres. By his initiative the *British Journal of Surgery* was founded and guided to success. It was his idea to start the Association of Surgeons, whose annual meeting has long been one of the main events in the surgical world.

As Moynihan's assistant I felt as a young sculptor might have felt finding himself unexpectedly apprenticed to Michelangelo. 'The human body', Moynihan would say, 'is a work of art and artistry is needed in dealing with its delicate tissues.' Sometimes he would put down his instruments and tell me to carry on, explaining to the onlookers that he liked to watch other people's hands at work (implying, if they came up to his standards).

Moynihan had specialized in biliary surgery and the treatment of chronic duodenal ulcer and there is an extraordinary law by which every surgeon is liable to have a dose of whatever condition by which he chiefly lives. (I have had my statutory thyroid operation.) And so it came about that Moynihan suffered a duodenal ulcer. He considered it carefully and decided he probably had a cancer of the stomach, but the physicians did not agree and diagnosed an ulcer. It seemed the ulcer had been bleeding to a dangerous degree and a blood transfusion was advised. I was asked to carry this out—a simple operation but an ordeal for the operator in view of the relation in which he stood to his patient. But I didn't worry and travelled up to the Ruthven Castle Nursing Home in North Wales, where he was being nursed, together with a student donor of the correct blood group.

Soon it was being whispered in the corridors that when the King of Duodenal Ulcers has one himself there is no one available to do the operation, and so he doesn't have one. But they were wrong. The patient had an acute ulcer, which usually responds well to medical treatment. He made a steady recovery without surgery, and never had a recurrence. When the crisis was over, he wrote me a charming letter: 'You have done me great service by coming to see me. I had a sense of complete security when I learned that you were willing to come.' He enclosed a blank cheque which I of course never filled in. I felt rather wounded that he could have thought that I would do so.

My association with this great-hearted man was one of the most exciting periods of my life. In February 1928, when I had been elected to the staff of Bart's, Moynihan wrote me the following letter:

My dear Keynes,

It was a very considerable pleasure to hear of your election. You now join, at Bart's, the 'Great Procession', the most distinguished that any hospital can shew, &, if you care, you may in 20 or 30 years time be hailed as one of the most eminent figures in it. Surgery now more than ever needs just such men as you: men in whom technical gifts of the highest order & the easy command of manual dexterity are the servants of intellectual gifts that would win distinction, even supremacy, in any field. It is a safe prediction that if devotion is added to your natural gifts you may rank above all contemporary surgeons when you reach your best.

My good wishes go with you always.

Ever sincerely,
BERKELEY MOYNIHAN

This letter gave me both pleasure and alarm. It was typical of Moynihan's generosity to his friends to suggest that any one of them might be like himself. But I knew that he was exaggerating my gifts and that I did not have the personality to reach such a position or even the wish to attain it with all its burdens. I wished to pursue my profession more peacefully than these predictions suggest. I liked indeed to have some recognition but not coupled with the burden of such 'eminence' as he suggested.

EPILOGUE

———◆———

As I come to the point of concluding these memoirs of my life soon after entering my ninety-fourth year, I cannot help wondering whether I have succeeded in satisfying my friends who said I must have known 'so many interesting people'. It seems to me that I have given them too much about myself and too little about the 'interesting people'. I can only plead that what I have had to tell has been largely due to the influence of those whose friendship I have been privileged to enjoy. I have described only a few; there have been many, many more who have had their part in shaping the pattern of my life, and my gratitude to them must go unspoken.

I have outlived the great majority of my contemporaries at school, university, and in my medical training. Of my almost exact contemporaries, only two remain. One of my school friends, Jim Cornwall, now General Sir James Marshall-Cornwall, is only three months younger than I, but more physically active, as I judge from our correspondence. The other, only two years younger, is Rupert Brooke's friend, Cathleen Nesbitt; she comes to stay at Lammas House, and is soon starting on a tour of several months in the United States as a character in Rex Harrison's production of *My Fair Lady*. In many respects, she is still the same as when we first met in Rupert's company.

At every stage of my life friendship has been the main source of my quite outrageously enjoyable existence. My sorrows, even though occasionally acute, have been few, and the enjoyment still goes on. A great many of my friends, both within and outside my family circle, are sixty or seventy years younger than myself. One of them, David Wynne, a friend of twenty-five years' standing, has given me an example of his art in sculpture, a miniature version of a large-scale creation of a boy astride a thoroughbred Arab stallion of breathtaking beauty.

The Tulip Tree at Lammas House with G.L.K., *aet.* 92, 1979

The sculptor models, as did William Blake in fashioning his vision of Chaucer's Canterbury Pilgrims, types true for all time, unspoilt by any modernistic affectation. Another friend, a Cambridge undergraduate, has addressed to me a hilarious Birthday Ode, which puts me firmly yet affectionately in my place—giving a verbal picture of a nonagenarian enjoying the last decade of an active life in pleasant surroundings, with a large garden making him completely self-sufficient in all the fruits of the earth. I am grateful to the author for expressing so gracefully the simple delights which I am able to enjoy. His Ode has a place in this book with the portrait of the Lammas House tulip tree (*Liriodendron tulipifera*), symbol of the fertility celebrated by the poet, exposing at the same time the smallness of the man.

FLORA'S FESTIVAL

Being A Tributary Ode compos'd upon the Occasion of THE 93ʳᵈ BIRTHDAY of Sir Geoffrey Keynes 25 MARCH 19 80

Hail sweetest Season! Fair and festive Spring!
By Wind and Wave Thy welcome Tribute bring:
Grace Albion's Acres with Thy healthful Smile
And wake to Warmth our friend northern Isle:
Cast general Joy throughout the wintry Land
And strew Thy Blessings with a bounteous Hand:
Yet save Thy Best for one Man's famed Estate
And heap Thy Pride at GEOFFREY'S Garden Gate!

More sweet Thy Show than Autumn's gaudy Gold
Which woos the Eye, yet heralds but the Cold:
Thou, Youthful Season, are apt Counterpart
To Him who is forever young at Heart!
With Blossom Throng invade His fair Domain
And there commence Thy long-awaited Reign
And as the Nations celebrate His Birth
Reflect their Joying in the eager Earth!

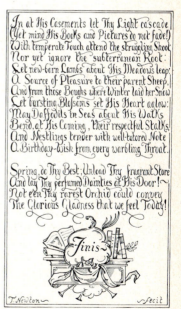

In at His Casements let Thy Light cascade
(Yet mind His Books and Pictures do not fade!)
With temperate Touch attend the struggling Shoot
Nor yet ignore the subterranean Root:
Let new-born Lambs about His Meadows leap:
A Source of Pleasure to their parent Sheep,
And from these Boughs where Winter laid her Snow
Let bursting Blossoms set His Heart aglow:
May Daffodils in Seas about His Walks
Bend, at His Coming, their respectful Stalks,
And Nestlings tender with well-tutored Note
A Birthday-Wish from every warbling Throat.

Spring, do Thy Best; Unload Thy fragrant Store
And lay Thy perfumed Dainties at His Door!—
Not e'en Thy rarest Orchid could convey
The Glorious Gladness that we feel Today!

Finis

T. Newton   fecit

APPENDICES
INDEX

———◆◆◆———

*RELIGIO BIBLIOGRAPHICI**

Presidential Address to the Bibliographical Society,
March 1953

———◆◆◆◆———

WHEN Sir Thomas Browne invented the title *Religio Medici* for
his engaging and revealing examination of his 'religion' he was
really, perhaps, writing an *apologia* for his profession rather than
an essay in theology. What the reader gathers from a perusal is
an idea of the writer's personality and attitude towards life, a
picture of a liberal and sensitive mind rather than an appreciation of a profound philosophical system. Ever since 1642, when
the title *Religio Medici* was first put into print, imitators have
adapted the form of it to their own purposes and a stream of
other *Religios* has poured from the press. Some have been frank
imitations of the prototype, many have had little in common
with it beyond the title. Every kind of profession has found its
apologist. Some have had more religion in them, others less;
occasionally politics have crept in. The assiduous collector and
bibliographer has amassed 110 titles (including some new
editions), and by now there is precedent, if not justification,
for using the mode in any sense one pleases, and I make no
further apology for adding one more, a *Religio Bibliographici*, to
the series. It will contain no theology, no intimate revelations
of personality, but will seek to examine the mysteries of bibliography in the light of over forty years' experience of, or if you
prefer to call it so, addiction to, the cult. Temporary elevation
to the presidential chair of this learned society has made me
acutely conscious of my merely amateur status as a bibliographer, and in that humble frame of mind I cannot expect a
partly professional audience to take my remarks very seriously.
An attempt to examine the question of what Bibliography
really is and why we take so much trouble to do what to so

* First published in *The Library*, Fifth Series, vol. VIII, no. 2 (June 1953).

many people seems to be nothing but aimless pedantry, may be found to degenerate into a recital of curious delights far removed from the serious purposes of the professional. If so you must forgive me. Obviously the amateur will only indulge in so seemingly desiccated a pursuit if he enjoys it, and in the end no further justification need really be demanded.

There may be those who can claim to have been bibliographers from their nursery days, collating their horn books or their modern equivalents while yet on their mother's knee. My own claim is more modest. I was seventeen when my close association at school with Rupert Brooke resulted in a spontaneous impulse to begin recording and collecting his poetical and literary output, thus preserving much material which could never have been recovered had it not been treasured by the piety of a hero-worshipper. It may lead in the end to a full-scale bibliography of Brooke.

And so, I fear, even at this early stage of my remarks, romance has crept into the discussion of so apparently unromantic a subject as bibliography. At this point I must diverge for a while from a personal *apologia* to consider the shadow which seems in recent years to have descended over our amiable bibliographical discipline as we have conceived it to be. In 1949 Fredson Bowers of the University of Virginia published his remarkable and, indeed, splendid book on the *Principles of Bibliographical Description*. This was an event of shattering importance to the little world of bibliography, because it brought home to our consciousness the fact that what we had thought in our innocence was a pleasant, if sometimes exacting, pastime, was in fact a prime example of 'pure scholarship', to be pursued with the mind of a detective, the spiritual temperature of an iceberg, and the precision of a machine. We had been used to looking up to the exalted stature of our own Sir Walter Greg, but we recognized that he necessarily moved on a different plane from the rest of us, devoting his life to the study of the printed word in its function of transmitting literature from author to reader. His dedicated purpose was the rescue of the original text, the actual words that the author wrote, from the garbled form in which it had been served up to the uncritical consumers. The garbling was due to the carelessness of the hired man, the compositor;

the lack of intelligence, combined with carelessness, of the proofreader; and the acquisitiveness of the greedy publisher who cared more for immediate profits than the purity of the author's text. Greg dealt with Shakespeare texts, with major Elizabethan poets, with the drama of the seventeenth century. All this was Literature of the highest importance, and had been transmitted from the era of casual printing and lack of respect for authors' manuscripts, which have mostly disappeared, so that acute intelligence, precise scholarship, and tireless industry were worthily directed to the task of reconstruction and purification. The exercise of scholarship on this scale is a task for the few, and those few will necessarily sharpen their tools to a fine edge so that their results may fully justify the expenditure of time and effort. Sir Walter Greg deserves, and has been given, our gratitude and admiration for his splendid achievement; but now the rest of us are inclined to feel that we have been chastised with scorpions because we are not all Gregs or even imitation Gregs. We must either fulfil the utmost demands of 'pure scholarship' or keep off it altogether. There is, it seems at first, no place for the humbler bibliographical practitioner dealing with problems of less transcendent importance.

Bowers rightly complains of the looseness of current usage of the term 'bibliography', whereby the briefest list of references is dignified with the name. A check-list of books is always the initial stage of bibliography, and I am sure it is often worth going to the length of printing the preliminary check-list, as this is a great convenience both to the bibliographer and to all of those whom he will call to his aid in finding the books that are his object, but let the check-list, or whatever you like to call it, preserve its identity and keep its proper place. It is *not* a bibliography.

What then is a bibliography? Bowers has the answer. A true bibliography is primarily an *analytical* bibliography. It is not concerned, he maintains, with such literary matters as correctness of a text, 'but endeavours on the evidence of printing to determine (without regard to the correctness or error) which form must have preceded the other. This examination based on the demonstrable evidence of a material object will frequently reverse normal literary judgement.' Bibliographers should therefore rigidly maintain 'a standard and uniform system of notation in all its details'. Anything else is pseudo-bibliography. Anyone who has not had a training in the technicalities of actual printing practice is unlikely to be anything but a pseudo-bibliographer, even though he may have acquired from Bowers's eloquent pages some idea that he is attempting the practice of pure scholarship.

I would now like to return to the point at which I was becoming distressingly romantic. I had mentioned hero-worship as one of the possible triggers activating the bibliographical impulse. I must blushingly confess that this has played a part in my own history. It began, as I have said, quite unwittingly through my having been a school-fellow of Rupert Brooke. It happened again when this school-fellow, now a fellow undergraduate at Cambridge, had convinced me that Dr. John Donne was one of the greatest poets of the first half of the seventeenth century. The third shock was the realization that Sir Thomas Browne was one of the greatest prose writers of all time as well as being a doctor. The fourth was a chance encounter with reproductions of William Blake's engravings for the Book of Job, this being the beginning of an entanglement in which I seem to be ever more unescapably enmeshed, even after the lapse of nearly fifty years. I see no cause for shame in the admission that the bibliographical impulse was aroused by admiration for the work of these great artists, by interest in their lives and personalities, and by the desire to know more of every aspect of the subjects than was to be found in the current books available in the shops and libraries. All this amounts to hero-worship, which might be foolish if directed to trivial and unworthy objects, but is not to be condemned when it finds heroes that *are* heroes and swans that will not turn out to be literary geese.

Another point that seems to me to call for comment is the fact that we never find the artists themselves turning to bibliography. It must be admitted that a taste for bibliography is not an indication of a creative mind, but rather of a turn for craftsmanship and for a certain tidiness—which is, indeed, often shared by the artist. 'Painting and musical composition', it has been said, 'depend equally on a sense of order and form which man instinctively finds satisfying.'[1] Bibliography demands a technique of a known kind rather than the originality of an artist, and so is being raised to the status of 'pure scholarship' in the minds of some of its exponents. This tendency to exaggerate the claims of bibliography until it comes to be an end rather than a means is perhaps to be recognized as a psychological frustration. If the ego cannot get satisfaction by creating something for itself, let it at least gain reflected glory by hanging on to the coat-tails of the true artists, until it may seem in its own eyes after all to have created something shining with the lustre of pure scholarship. It is not too pleasant to have to admit that the bibliographer may be, so to speak, a literary parasite, sucking his nourishment from the creations of the great dead—or even from the living. But personally I do not mind in the least. I am not an artist—I have devoted a lifetime to the craft of surgery, and have gained much additional satisfaction from the craft of bibliography. I am fully reconciled to the fact that I have no creative originality. It is impossible, however, not to feel some sympathy with the tendency we think we detect in academic bibliographers to exaggerate the claims of their craft. Finding themselves in the company of scholars, who need to be convinced that bibliography really has serious claims on their attention, they instinctively react by behaving as a small persecuted minority. They are forced to push their technical speciality in order to be taken seriously and to compel their institutions or universities to realize the necessity for acquiring first and early editions of the older books.

Although I have protested mildly against overstatement of the claims of bibliography, I do not mean to imply that it is an easy discipline acquired overnight by a perusal of McKerrow's treatise and a demonstration of how a piece of paper is folded once, twice, or three times to make a folio, quarto, or octavo volume. In fact, I see no way of becoming even a moderately expert bibliographer except by sitting down and laboriously compiling a bibliography, making all the possible mistakes, submitting to the harshest criticisms, admitting every one of the humiliating inadequacies, and starting all over again at the end of the first year's work. This, at any rate, was my experience

[1] H. Caudwell, *The Creative Impulse* (1951), p. 122.

and so I naturally think it normal and wholesome. Obviously the budding bibliographer can accelerate his training by an intensive study of works by the masters of his craft. But there are many different kinds of bibliography—not all of them, of course, admitted to the ranks of true bibliographies by the academic practitioner. There are bibliographies of a special type of literature such as Poetical Miscellanies, Song Books, Character Books, Plays. Or your 'unifying purpose' (one of many useful terms invented by Professor Bowers) may be applied to the productions of a particular press, or, best of all, to the works of a particular author. I say 'best of all' because so many of the other categories will not demand full descriptive bibliography, but will be admittedly little more than 'bibliographical catalogues', good in themselves but not meeting the 'high requirements' (Bowers) of true bibliography. A full 'author-bibliography' offers one of the best opportunities for the exercise of bibliographical ingenuity. The end for which you are using your technical means must surely be the full knowledge of your author's writings with a view to the establishment of an authentic text on the soundest possible basis.

I may be allowed, I hope, to illustrate this first by reference to the compilation of my *Bibliography of William Blake*, issued by the Grolier Club of New York in 1921. The hopeful medical student of the years 1909 to 1913 cannot, of course, have realized what he was undertaking. The compilation of a bibliography of the works of an original such as Blake— painter, engraver, poet, philosopher—could clearly be no simple task. His works first printed in normal typography amounted to only three—the others were engraved books, etched books, or manuscripts, with a large category of books containing engraved plates executed by him from his own designs or those of other artists. In addition to the later reprints of his writings, an immense literature, biographical and critical, had grown up around his name, and there were important appendages such as books containing his marginal annotations, letters, sale catalogues, and so forth. In the Blake *Bibliography* there were six main headings and twenty-four sub-headings. With such an unusual variety of material it was plain at the outset that an equally elastic technique had to be used in dealing with it. Much of the work would be, indeed, no more than bibliographical cataloguing, but the work as a whole, ranging from descriptions made in fullest detail to brief entries without collations, could claim, in the end, to be a *Bibliography* worthy of the attention of scholars even though the author's scholarship was not *pure*.

The enthusiasm of the beginner carried me along, as I thought, swimmingly, and early in 1910 I actually had the temerity to submit my work to the eye of the redoubtable Dr. John Sampson, Librarian to Liverpool University, and reputed to be a somewhat formidable personality. I have long wanted to pay a public tribute to the memory of that great man, and now take the opportunity of saying that his kindness and helpfulness to an unknown student was only equalled by his scholarship and by his eminence as philologist and bibliographer. His first letter to me, dated 10 February 1910, is a model of how to deal kindly but firmly with an ignorant, if enthusiastic, beginner. After a few sentences of encouragement he gives an unequivocal estimate of what the book is worth. 'I take it', he says,

> that in its present form it is merely the roughest of rough drafts and would be considerably rewritten and rearranged before being offered to the public. In my opinion no time or trouble should be grudged to make the book a perfect specimen of its kind. Remember that Bradshaw chose a motto for himself, and incidentally for other bibliographers: 'Whatsoever thy hand findeth to do, do it with thy might; for there is no work, nor device, nor knowledge, nor wisdom, in the grave, whither thou goest.'

He then made a series of practical suggestions for the improvement of the work before setting to his letter the characteristic signature which came to mean so much to me during the next ten years. This letter could only have one meaning and one effect, and I immediately started to rewrite the whole bibliography on a different and larger plan.

I blush now to say that it was only a year later that the completed work was submitted for publication to the Cambridge University Press, who in their turn submitted it to Dr. John Sampson. His detailed report was dated February 1911, and with his permission I was allowed to see it. It was, indeed, painful, if salutary, reading. The first sentence put it in its place. 'Only in a strangely limited sense can the work be described as a Bibliography of William Blake.' This is under the heading 'Content'. Under 'Arrangement', the criticism begins, 'Mr. Keynes's arrangement cannot be described as happy'; but there was far worse to come under 'Method'. 'Mr. Keynes's descriptions of books show throughout a lack of familiarity with the methods of exact bibliography, and in this regard he might be advised to study the best models.' Finally, under 'Sources and Acknowledgements', he wrote, 'In many cases Mr. Keynes seems to have taken his facts from other bibliographers, obviating the necessity of acknowledgement by restating them in his own fashion, though not always, perhaps, more lucidly and sometimes even with positive misunderstanding.' This last hit was, in fact, unjust, as my attempted descriptions were made quite independently of Dr. Sampson's and the ineptitudes were all my own, though he could not know that. The report was of considerable length and, of course, extremely helpful. However much the wounds might smart, I accepted them humbly, and immediately set out to rewrite the whole book for the third time.

I am glad to say that a somewhat longer interval now elapsed, and it was not until July 1914 that the third version was submitted to the delegates of the Clarendon Press, who in turn submitted it to Dr. John Sampson. During the three years that were occupied by this revision important advances had been made. The greater part of Blake's output was in the form of the Illuminated Books, printed in monochrome or in colours from etched copper-plates and usually painted by hand with water-colours. The books were not published in any ordinary sense, but were sold by the author to his friends and acquaintances, copies being printed and coloured as they were called for. There was thus no 'edition' of any particular number of copies, and no two copies were alike, differing in the colouring, arrangement, and even in the number of plates included. There was, therefore, no alternative to making the attempt to locate and describe every copy of each book that could be discovered, and a special technique had to be used in the descriptions. The method was naturally based on the beginning already made by Dr. Sampson in his edition of Blake's *Poetical Works*, 1905. First an imaginary 'ideal copy' had to be fixed and collated. Then every page had to be described in detail, giving the first line of text. Lastly every existing copy, as far as was known, was described in detail with its full provenance, including the sale records. With this information every copy was identifiable by future researchers, and a basis established for a full knowledge of Blake's texts—an end acknowledged by Bowers to be one of the objects of true bibliography—though in this instance the particular technique elaborated by him happened not to be applicable to the peculiar conditions of Blake's work.

The description of Blake's etched books could only be satisfactorily done by personal examination of each one, and this demanded many journeys in England and Scotland as well as an expert collaborator in the United States, who was found in the person of Miss Henrietta Bartlett of New York. A printed leaflet with a list of questions covering the main points was also sent to the more inaccessible owners, and proved useful although never as good as personal examination.

Much time and labour were expended on this pursuit of the Illuminated Books, and every other section of the *Bibliography* —I shall persist in dignifying it by this name—was extended, verified, and rewritten. But the time had not been wasted, and on this occasion Dr. Sampson was distinctly respectful. His report was written from Merionethshire and was couched in almost flattering terms.

> Since I read the work three years ago it has evidently been rewritten with wider knowledge and regard for bibliographical conventions, and is practically a different book. As it now stands, it strikes me as a really valuable addition to what is known of Blake's writings. The general plan and arrangement leave little to be desired and show familiarity with the system adopted in standard bibliographies of this class. There is much that is new. Mr. Keynes has evidently sought out, examined and collated more copies of Blake's scattered works—no light task!—than any of his predecessors, and the result is not only interesting in itself, but should prove of

much service to any future editor or student of Blake. This is especially the case in issues of the Prophetic Books, and his lists and collations of copies known attest industry and care.

This was indeed an advance and at last the dawn seemed to be at hand after the long night of endeavour. But Dr. Sampson's report was dated 29 July 1914. Within three weeks I was with the Expeditionary Force in France, and bibliographical research was almost at a standstill—not completely, for during the next four years of active service abroad I was able to lay the foundations of a monograph on William Pickering, the publisher, and of a bibliography of John Evelyn, two more literary heroes who had been added to my list. Bibliographical method had also been developed by the compilation of the first edition of the *Bibliography of Dr. John Donne*, printed for the Baskerville Club at Cambridge and published in September 1914, shortly after the outbreak of war.

Blake, at any rate, was shelved, and it was not until seven years later that the book was ultimately issued by the Grolier Club of New York as a sumptuous volume limited to 250 copies. The Publications Committee of the Grolier Club had generously left the entire production in my hands, little knowing how small was my experience of typographical design and layout; but with the guidance of the experts of the Chiswick Press a reasonably good-looking result was obtained. Any merits the book might have were largely due to the kindly criticisms of Dr. Sampson. In a letter dated 15 March 1915 he wrote: 'I was glad, my dear Keynes, that my notes on your revised Bibliography did not—to borrow a feline figure—get your back up. Certainly it was written in a spirit of sympathy, though, more and more, perhaps too much, I have got to feel that the only way in which an opinion can be helpful is just to blurt it out, and let it go at that.'

I hope I have not wearied you with too long a recital of the evolution of the *Bibliography of Blake*; but I had an object in dealing with this in some detail. As I have already said, the 'pure' bibliographical scholar is not concerned with literary matters of content but only with 'the evidence of printing to determine which form must have preceded the other'. I must plead guilty to being horribly impure, for I believe that bibliography becomes the more worthwhile the wider its scope and the more elastic its technique. I must admit with pleasure that Professor Bowers lays down the principle that 'bibliographical work cannot be ground out to schedule and should not be engaged in unless the writer is willing to allow considerably more time than he originally estimated for its production'. In other words 'no hurry', a most salutary basis for bibliographical work, which will always be the more finished the longer it takes. Ten to sixteen years is for me the normal period of gestation for a book of this kind. As John Ray wrote in 1691, we should not be 'too hasty in huddling up and tumbling out books', adding that 'the longer a book lies by me, the perfecter it becomes'. Bowers has also said that 'after certain basic requirements have been met' bibliographical method 'should be adjusted to the expressed purpose of the bibliography', and also that 'the subject and purpose of the bibliography may have some effect on the choice of detail'. So there is some room for individual judgement after all, and it is unfair to give the impression that 'pure scholarship' is utterly unyielding. Yet for me bibliography must be a fundamentally humane pursuit, shedding light not only on an author's printed texts, but also on his literary history, his life in general, his personality, and should often have as its main objective the establishment of the basic and final text of all his writings.

It is an extraordinary fact that in 1921 only certain portions of Blake's writings had been established with any sort of accuracy. Dr. Sampson's edition of the *Poetical Works* was, of course, well known, and almost entirely trustworthy, but very many of the poems which he included had been forcibly extracted from their context and thereby deprived of much of their value and meaning. On the other hand, most of the texts edited by the enthusiasm of the Pre-Raphaelites and by the combined efforts of E. J. Ellis and W. B. Yeats were extremely inaccurate, though in many instances these were the only available texts. D. G. Rossetti even introduced deliberate falsifications, or 'improvements' as he believed them to be, and these corrupt texts were still current and being copied from one edition to another when my *Bibliography* appeared. As a consequence of the labour expended on this book, I was possessed of a more complete knowledge of the original sources of Blake's writings than anyone else, with the almost inevitable *sequela* (as we say in medicine) that the urge to edit them in their entirety became apparent. Or was it a suggestion from Sir Francis Meynell, who saw in it a chance for an important development in the policy of the Nonesuch Press, which up to 1925 had concentrated mainly on reprints of older books? The answer to this question does not now matter. The point I wish to make is that my most impure bibliography, with its mixture of methods and its sorry fumblings over so many years, had led directly to the establishment of the first complete and accurate text of one of our major poets and philosophers. This was published by the Nonesuch Press in 1925 in three magnificent volumes, and in 1927 was compressed, mainly by the omission of variorum readings, into one volume, the first of the compendious Nonesuch books, and this has been the standard text ever since. A revised and enlarged edition of the *Census of the Illuminated Books* is about to be published by the Grolier Club of New York.

I do not wish it to be thought that I am in any way trying to belittle the value of analytical bibliography, which obviously must be of paramount importance in establishing the texts of writers whose works have survived only in the ordinary printed forms, the original manuscript having entirely disappeared; but here is an instance of a major author whose writings were still accessible in manuscript or in unorthodox forms resistant to the usual technique of the analytical specialist. In other words, the purpose of the practitioner of the less pure forms of bibliography may sometimes be just as 'high' as those of his academic brethren. It may well be that, as Professor Bowers says in his most illuminating paper on 'Bibliography, Pure Bibliography and Literary Studies',[1] there is still some 'nostalgia for the good old days before the tabby cat of bibliography grew into a tiger', but I wish to maintain that even a 'tyger, tyger, burning bright' in the bibliographical forests is not the only beacon that beckons the contemporary bibliographer. The old

[1] *Papers of the Bibliographical Society of America* (1952), vol. 46.

tabby cat, innocent of streamlined brilliance, can still be well worth stroking by our firesides. It all depends on the kind of material that happens to be our object at the moment.

I have already mentioned that Sir Thomas Browne was one of my earliest literary heroes and, with the collaboration of Cosmo Gordon and the comforting friendship and encouragement of Sir William Osler, a Browne *Bibliography* was slowly taking shape from the year 1908 onwards. It was not published until 1924, by which time the conviction had formed in my mind that again so much familiarity with the writings and personality of Browne could only end in a new edition of the whole of his works, which was in fact published in six volumes in the years 1928–31. The material was more orthodox than it had been with Blake, such works as had not survived in the author's manuscript being contained in ordinary printed volumes, but again most of these did not demand any very advanced technique for their description, π and χ had been invented but were not in general use, and most users of the book do not appear to have been dissatisfied. The old cat was still purring. I may confess, having already done so in public, that an attempt to reverse the accepted order of the two unauthorized editions of the *Religio Medici* on purely physical grounds was quite unsuccessful. I had relied on a comparison of the impressions of the engraved title-pages in unsophisticated copies of the two books, but it was demonstrated some years later, after the commercial dovecots had been considerably fluttered, that the original order was correct. My criticisms had been based on chance factors of inking and distribution of sheets which had to give way before Miss Elizabeth Cook's reasoned evidence derived from typography and variant readings.[1] None, I think, of Professor Bowers's newly forged weapons could have settled the question of priority in ten minutes. It could only be done by a laborious collation of the texts.

The effect of my mistake was seen repeatedly in the sale-rooms, the previous 'first' dropping in value below the supposed new 'first' by an appreciable number of dollars. I have not yet been sued in the courts for malicious defamation of the book's

---

[1] *Harvard Library Bulletin*, 1948, no. 2, 22–31.

character, but it illustrates how bibliography is not only 'the handmaid of literature', but may also be the 'mistress of the ring' (if the sale-room may be likened to a boxing match).

It is only comparatively recently that the importance of bibliography to literature and scholarship has come to be realized. Pollard's work on the Shakespeare quartos had, indeed, been fully appreciated for many years, but, in general, bibliography was regarded as chiefly valuable to librarians, booksellers, and collectors, and for this very reason was too much neglected by scholars. During the last twenty-five or thirty years this misconception has been redressed, and it is, of course, the laudable desire to be of the maximum service to literary criticism that has prompted the emergence of the higher flights of academic bibliography. Of this high aim no one need complain—provided that the supposed needs of the few do not result in rendering the rigidly abbreviated formularies unintelligible to the many. Librarians, booksellers, and even collectors, are decent and deserving people, whose needs should be considered; obviously their training in bibliography cannot equal that of the specialized analytical bibliographer, and collations and descriptions should be kept within their comprehensions, even if brevity has to be sacrificed in order to do so.

I should like now to examine a little more closely the relation of bibliography to book collecting. In the past collectors have often had only the most rudimentary knowledge of the physical make-up of their quarry, and have sometimes had to pay heavily for their ignorance. They are now getting wiser and the growing number of author-bibliographies is helping them to acquire their knowledge more easily than in the past: I am not ashamed of the part I happen to have played in this process, because I am a collector myself, and am not ashamed of that either. I have long felt, however (and this may be a somewhat priggish sentiment), that, as I recently told the young 'Oxford Bibliophiles', *bibliophily is not enough*. Stamp collecting is an amusing game, but it is essentially sterile. Book collecting is sometimes little better, though most books have more intellectual and humane meaning than any stamp can possess. Rarity value has an influence on the market price of both, this being especially obvious, if I dare say so in this company, in the collecting of incunabula, though this cannot easily be disentangled from their importance in the history of printing. It is also seen to some extent in the values attached to sixteenth-century English books, but from 1600 onwards historical or literary importance gets the upper hand, and many books possessing the highest market values are not particularly rare. It was perhaps the gibes of the friends of my youth that may have helped to determine my aims as a collector. I must have written something about it to Rupert Brooke, for in March 1911, when I was already collecting books by Donne and Browne, he wrote me a long letter beginning:

> Your defence of stamp collecting was magnificent, but not war, that is to say it was unprovoked. A guilty conscience! Hast no drug therefor? Can neither balsamum nor mandragora cure the sinful soul? Physician heal thyself! Yes; I am quite ready to attack the antiquarian, the bibliophile. . . . Only—I did not. I merely attacked the people who like 'quaintness' in works of art. There are points of resemblance, I admit. Both quietudes are essentially Evasions. But I was not thinking [e.g.] in what *edition* you read Donne; but whether you read him for poetry or for 'prithees' and 'quothas'. . . . Have you ever seen Americans in a picture-gallery? They're out for quaintness. You've surely found people who like even Blake's prints that way? And Chaucer, and the Ballads, and 18th century prose. Oh my God! I could write for hours about it. But I won't. 'What in my youth I used to call not caring about literature.' My Gyff, it's the Last Leprosy.

I fancy there was a touch of guilty conscience somewhere. Anyway I determined from an early stage that book collecting must always have, if possible, an object in view, that it should not be a 'quietude which was essentially an Evasion', and there grew a determination that collecting should always try to add to the sum of knowledge. Author-bibliographies were the inevitable consequence, and the resulting satisfaction has been compounded from the joys of hero-worship, collecting, and bibliography. The bibliographer whose life is spent in a public library will usually have less need to collect for himself; but for the amateur there can be no better way to work than by acquiring his basic knowledge as a collector. I do not wish to enlarge on the advantages his special knowledge gives him in the open market, but they can be spectacular. In the end, of course, when his knowledge is published in a printed book the trend is in the other direction, but by then he already has most of the books he wants, and can be content to see the others, the latecomers, scramble for what remains.

Sometimes the compilation of an author-bibliography may have consequences that no one could have foreseen. I have already mentioned my interest in John Evelyn and his books, which arose as a relief from the realities of war in France and Flanders. Apart from his diary, John Evelyn's numerous books seemed to have been very much neglected. As soon as the war was over this investigation naturally led to a wish to visit Evelyn's library in his home at Wotton, and I was luckily able to achieve this through knowing friends of the family. For more than half a century the library had been virtually inaccessible, even scholars being suspect owing to the notorious depredations of William Upcott, the first editor of the diary, early in the nineteenth century. My immediate object was to see Evelyn's books and bindings, but having once penetrated the stronghold, the wish for a sight of the manuscript of the famous diary naturally arose. This had been so closely guarded that no edition published after the first could be regarded as much of an improvement on the second Bray–Upcott text published in 1819. The John Evelyn of 1921 proved, nevertheless, to be amenable to reason, and, indeed, anxious to do what was best. As the result of our conversations the manuscript was deposited in the Bodleian for ten years in order that a complete new transcript might be made. Mr. Esmond de Beer afterwards undertook the task of editing the diary, and this will presently be published by the Oxford University Press.

My investigations at Wotton on this and several other occasions provided material for the Sandars Lectures of 1933–4, and later for a full-scale *Bibliography* of Evelyn's works with a study of his character as a bibliophile, writer, and horticulturist. The book was finely produced by the Cambridge University Press and issued by them jointly with the Grolier Club of New York in 1937. This book has seemed to me to be one of the most readable of the bibliographies that bear my name, and it brings me to the point of discussing the so-called bio-bibliography.

Recently in Harvey Cushing's work on Vesalius and in W. R. Le Fanu's work on Jenner's writings, the term bio-bibliography has actually appeared on the title-page. I am not quite sure of the propriety of this usage, though I am quite sure of the rightness of giving a bibliography a biographical bias, so that it becomes much more than a dry record of the physical constitution of the author's books. His books were, after all, an important part of his life. 'Historical bibliography', regarded by Bowers as one of the more important categories of the discipline, does not quite cover the so-called bio-bibliography, since 'history' is defined as comprising inquiries into the evolution of printing, binding, book-ownership, and book-selling. This seems to leave out any consideration of the author himself and to make of his book a thing apart. I should, therefore, like to add to Bowers's five compartments into which he divides bibliography (enumerative, historical, analytical, descriptive, and critical) a sixth, the biographical, though, like the others, this compartment is far from water-tight, and, indeed, the ideal bibliography should, I believe, contain an admixture of them all.

My devotion to bibliography is, in fact, given in the belief that it serves the humanities and I do not see why it should be subjected to any restrictions, limiting its usefulness to any arbitrary kind of scholar. Naturally a bibliographer, before setting out on his task, will like to have some definite limitations in view—though I must confess that I have not myself consciously thought out any such plan. I have not modelled my books to follow exactly anyone else's method, and have tried only to make them of the maximum usefulness to people who want to know the same sort of things as I want to know myself. This may seem to a purist to be a serious fault, but I am not prepared to admit it. A bibliography with a human interest can still be a source of accurate information on purely biblio-graphical points, and I believe most users of the book are grateful for the added interest that it gives them when they have occasion to refer to it.

My recently published *Bibliography of John Ray* is, I believe, a fairly satisfactory example of the principle. It deals in detail with the physical constitution of every edition of every one of his works. It gives an idea of the purpose of each book and of its relative importance in the history of the various subjects, theological, botanical, biological, and philological, of which Ray wrote. By using the information provided by Ray's letters to his friends much of the printing history of his books is recorded. Lastly, Ray's modest, lovable, and utterly honest character is portrayed without, I hope, obtruding the biographical element beyond what the book should carry. It is printed, I must own, on extremely peculiar paper, but that was the publisher's affair and does not reflect on Ray's character or my own.

Bibliographies of Dr. William Harvey, Jane Austen, and William Hazlitt have each provided their individual problems and pleasures, with the biographical side developed to varying degrees. The Harvey and Hazlitt led, as usual, to editing new texts of some of their writings, but the discovery that Jane Austen had made revisions in the text of *Mansfield Park* did not lead to any editing by me, as I soon found that Dr. R. W. Chapman was already hot on the scent. In each of these books the bibliographical pill is coated with a certain amount of sugar in the form of portraits of the author, examples of his handwriting, and such other illustrations as may have a bearing on the subject. I am also a strong believer in having as many good line-block reproductions of title-pages and other relevant matter as possible. They enliven the pages of the book, are of interest as typographical specimens, and make plain, without further explanation, the plan upon which title-pages have been transcribed. They do not preclude the necessity of transcriptions, unless *every* title-page is reproduced, which is usually impossible for a variety of reasons.

There is another, lower, reason for giving a bibliography these embellishments—they help to sell the book! The time is long past when all bibliographies had to be published by subscription, or at the charges of a learned society such as our own. These books are now undertaken by ordinary publishing houses as evidenced recently by Macdonald's *Dryden*, Sadleir's *Nineteenth Century Fiction*, Gallup's *T. S. Eliot*, and the 'Soho Bibliographies' in course of production by the firm of Rupert Hart-Davis. These books may not be immediately profitable, but they bring, at any rate, prestige, and profit follows in the long run. Most of my bibliographies after Blake have come to birth in this way. That of William Harvey has just gone into a second edition, and that of John Donne may, I hope, before long reach a third. There is every reason, therefore, for making a bibliography as attractive as possible so that it may take its place on the publisher's list and justify the rather high price which has to be charged for a book with a necessarily limited sale.

In 1645 Sir George Mackenzie, the Scottish lawyer, wrote *A Moral Essay preferring Solitude to Public Employment*. Two years later John Evelyn produced a counterblast, *Public Employment and an Active Life Prefer'd to Solitude*. Evelyn was perhaps somewhat disingenuous since really he liked both Solitude and an Active Life, each in its proper place. His attack, therefore, was without rancour and reconciliation was almost simultaneous. Polite letters passed shortly afterwards in which Mackenzie said Evelyn's book was 'rarely weel writ', and Evelyn that Mackenzie was a person 'infinitely obliging' to him.

If I have seemed in the course of this *apologia* to attack the school of Professor Bowers, I hope he will be able to regard my remarks as little wounding as Mackenzie did Evelyn's. In fact I have immense respect for Professor Bowers's single-minded efforts to improve the standard of bibliographical research, and even if he cannot say that my paper was 'rarely weel writ' (which indeed it is not) I can fervently assert that he is a person 'infinitely obliging' to me. I have only tried, in this statement of my aims and beliefs as an amateur, to justify my status and assert my belief that there is a place for more than one kind of bibliographer. Each kind must maintain the highest standards of his craft and contribute his quota to the sum of knowledge. There should be no reason for any serious disagreement between them.

THE OSLERIAN TRADITION*

The first Oslerian oration delivered at
the Royal College of Physicians,
16 October 1968

———•••••———

SIR WILLIAM OSLER died on 29 December 1919, nearly fifty years ago. He was born in Canada in July 1849, so that his life spanned the reigns of Queen Victoria, King Edward, and King George. Anyone, therefore, who enjoyed his friendship during the last fourteen years of his life in Oxford is likely to be eighty years old or more. I was privileged to be one of these, and it is probably for this reason that our President has asked me to deliver this oration. He had, indeed, little choice if he wished to employ one of Osler's friends for the task. I think he should really have asked our revered friend Sir Arthur MacNalty to call upon his memories, for he knew Osler for several years before he came into my life. However, I could not refuse so honourable an assignment, and I will do my best to give some idea of Osler as I knew him, and to suggest why the Oslerian Tradition is still so lively an inspiration to medical men in the English-speaking world.

In 1908 I was a second-year undergraduate at Pembroke College, Cambridge, reading for the Natural Sciences Tripos, and could have no claim on the notice of the Regius Professor of Medicine at Oxford, except that we had a particular interest in common—the life and writings of Sir Thomas Browne, of Norwich. In that year my friend Cosmo Gordon, of King's College, and I conceived the idea of compiling a bibliography of Browne's works, both of us having already begun to form collections of the books. In those days it was still possible for impecunious students to make significant collections of early writers, even incunabula, the cradle books of the printed word, being readily obtainable at a bookstall in the Cambridge market-place. Gordon and I realized that it would take years

* Published in the *British Medical Journal* (7 December 1968).

to produce an adequate bibliography, and that it would have to be founded on other collections besides our own. It was well known that Osler possessed the largest Browne collection in existence. He had been introduced to Browne's influence while a schoolboy in 1866, and bought his first copy of *Religio Medici*, the Boston edition of 1862, in 1867—the very same book that lay on his coffin in Christ Church chapel through the last night of 1919. Sir Thomas Browne, physician and humanist, was the lifelong hero of Osler, another physician and humanist, both Fellows of this Royal College, to whom their successors can look for inspiration as long as the college may survive.

It was in 1909 that Gordon and I wrote to Osler asking for permission to see his library, using our projected bibliography as the excuse for our temerity. Kindness to one's juniors is an important element in the Oslerian Tradition, and so, of course, our request was met by an invitation to stay at 13 Norham Gardens, the house in Oxford known to medical men all over the world as 'The Open Arms'. Osler had recently been visiting Italy, and had written to a friend in Philadelphia:

> I enclose you a little prayer to St. Cosmas and St. Damian, our patron Saints, which may be useful. I have made a pilgrimage to their mother church, and have burnt a candle —a small one—for my surgical colleagues. The instruments, with which they cut off a leg which had a cancer and transplanted the sound leg of a just-dead man, are carefully preserved in the church, with an arm of each Saint and a bottle of milk of the Virgin Mary.

Back in Oxford, Osler still possessed, when we came to his house, some gaudy coloured prints of the saints, whose rather juvenile features he pretended bore a resemblance to those of Cosmo Gordon and myself. Cosmo's name suggested a closer relationship, and we were immediately dubbed St. Cosmas and St. Damian. Osler often thereafter addressed me in his letters as Damian. My sanctification has always been accepted in Oslerian circles, little as I have deserved it, having never during my surgical career transplanted any human tissue more complex than blood. It has fallen to others to transcend more recently the miracles of the saints.

Thomas Browne's Influence

It was not surprising that Osler was so taken with the prospect of our *Bibliography of Sir Thomas Browne*. He had said in 1902 to the Association of Medical Librarians that 'we desire to foster among our members and in the profession at large a proper love of books'. He remarked that, strictly speaking, 'bibliography' means the science of everything relating to the book itself, and has nothing to do with its contents, but later in the same address he added that the 'true bibliophil cares not so much for the book as for the man whose life and mind are illustrated in it', and, of course, Osler himself in addition valued highly the historical associations of a book. Browne's writings, in particular the *Religio Medici*, were ever in his mind. Quotations from Browne were constantly springing to his lips. His literary style frequently showed plain signs of being modelled on Browne's, and some of his addresses were Brunonian in their aphoristic and moralistic content. But compilation of a bibliography is a slow process, particularly when it has to be done in the spare moments of a medical training, and is subjected to the distractions introduced by a world war. Osler sometimes felt impatient, and one of his last postcards to me, written on his death-bed, asked reproachfully when the book would be done. But, alas, he never saw it. It had been incubated for nearly sixteen years, and when it was finally published in 1924 I could only dedicate it to his memory—and what memories this held for me! I was granted the friendship of a man thirty-eight years my senior, the holder of four successive chairs in famous schools of medicine, the author of one of the most successful textbooks of medicine ever written, an outstanding teacher and clinician, and a book collector of width tempered by discrimination, who used his books fruitfully and with generous consideration of the needs of others.

Osler's generosity was notorious. If an important book which he already possessed came to his notice he at once began to think what other medical library might lack it, so that he could fill the gap. Thus several copies of Harvey's *De Motu Cordis* passed through his hands, and he could never resist buying the first edition of the anatomical *Fabrica* of Vesalius, knowing that he could always find a willing recipient. In fact, he bought so many copies that he could not always remember where they had gone. In 1903 he bought three copies, saying it was not a book that should ever be left on the shelves of a bookseller, and sent one to McGill University. Six years later, when in Rome, he sent another copy to the same library. This reckless generosity sometimes left him so short of money when abroad that he had difficulty in paying his fare for the return home. As a tradition, Osler's attitude is hard for us to imitate, for, partly owing to his example, the books have largely disappeared from the market.

Belief in 'Culture'

A tradition of Osler's use and love of books can, however, still influence our minds. He believed that 'culture', the word that made Hermann Goering reach for his gun, was of the utmost value to medical men. 'In no profession,' he said, 'does culture count for so much as in medicine, and no man needs it more than the general practitioner, working among all sorts and conditions of men, many of whom are influenced quite as much by his general ability, which they can appreciate, as by his learning, of which they have no measure.' The practice of physic should no longer be as by Dr. Johnson's friend, Robert Levett, 'obscurely wise and coarsely kind'. The poorer the conditions in which a doctor has to work the more necessary is it for him to keep his mind free and filled with the liberal spirit necessary for the proper attitude to our human problems. Wide reading, he maintained, was possible even though the time for it was restricted to half an hour in bed before going to sleep and an open book on the dressing-table in the morning.

Sir Thomas Browne, advising a student what to read, was in favour of deep learning—Hippocrates, Galen, Vesalius, Spigelius and Bartholinus, the Herbalists, the Apothecaries, Fallopius, Fabricius, Paré, Vigo, the Chemists, 'and be sure you make yourself master of Dr. Harvey's piece, *De circulatione sanguinis*, which discovery I prefer to that of Columbus'—an opinion which I have seen Osler taste with particular delight. His prescription for his students was somewhat lighter fare—the Bible, Shakespeare, Montaigne, Plutarch, Marcus Aurelius, Epictetus, *Religio Medici*, *Don Quixote*, Emerson, and Oliver Wendell Holmes. He might well have included *Sherlock Holmes*.

Dedicated Teacher

To students, Osler's reputation is an important element in the tradition of their training. He was a dedicated teacher, and it may seem extraordinary that he said of himself that he wished to have as his epitaph: 'Here lies the man who admitted students to the wards.' He was addressing the New York Academy of Medicine in December 1902, and quoted John Abernethy of St. Bartholomew's as saying that 'the Hospital is the only proper college in which to rear a true disciple of Aesculapius'. He had to say this because at that date in most New York hospitals and in other places students were admitted to demonstrations in lecture halls but not to the wards, where their presence was regarded 'as hurtful to the best interests of the patients'. This had been the rule in Philadelphia when he went there. Osler had insisted that contact with patients in the hospital wards was of fundamental importance.

It is what may be called the natural method of teaching, the student begins with the patient, continues with the patient, and ends his studies with the patient, using books and lectures as tools, as means to an end. The student should start, in fact, as a practitioner, as an observer of disordered machines, with the structure and orderly functions of which he is perfectly familiar. It is a safe rule for the junior student in medicine and surgery to have no teaching without a patient for a text, and the best teaching is that taught by the patient himself.

I am emphasizing this seeming truism with memories of recent rumblings from patients who have objected to allowing themselves to be examined by students. This attitude has somehow become mixed up with the idea that hospital patients are guinea-pigs, the subjects of experiment. Respect for the personality of the patient must indeed never be compromised or forgotten, and Osler was the last to overlook this principle. I was never myself able to see Osler teaching in the wards, but I have the assurance of others who did so.

Osler at Johns Hopkins adopted a somewhat flamboyant approach to his ward rounds. He was punctual in attendance, but arrived at the hospital building in a rush with coat-tails flying, his arms thrown wide in a welcome to his attendant group of juniors and students. Some of his colleagues disapproved of this, regarding it as an exaggerated sense of showmanship, unbecoming in a Professor of Medicine. I have indeed heard two of our most senior medical scientists criticize this side of Osler's irrepressible enthusiasm; they were both struck by his being too evidently a 'showman' to suit their own more restrained and scientific approach. Yet Osler, having reached the patient's bedside, was the perfect exponent of clinical tact and consideration. In person he was small, with a drooping moustache and an 'olivaster' complexion, which he shared with William Harvey; but his eyes, though dark, were brilliant, and he would keep their sympathetic gaze fixed on the patient's face throughout the questioning. The patient was made to feel that he was the most important person present. Osler addressed him by his name with friendly interest, and gave him confidence. In Harvey Cushing's *Life of Osler* there is an admirable page of bedside snapshots labelled Inspection, Palpation, Auscultation, and finally Contemplation, the last one illustrating Osler posed characteristically in mental summation of all that he had observed. I do not mean to imply that Osler was exceptional in this sort of bedside behaviour—far from it; but he was so immensely popular and successful as a teacher that his example could not fail to create a tradition calculated to inspire others even beyond the generations of students immediately affected.

An Opinion on Ageing

As a teacher Osler had a somewhat exaggerated belief in the inevitable deterioration of the human brain as age advances. He thought that by the age of forty most men were losing their power of adaptation. Silvering of the hair, or loss of it, indicated a probable inability to accept readily any new ideas. He claimed Harvey as a supporter of this opinion, quoting his complaint that few men above forty seemed able to receive the doctrine of the circulation of the blood. He noted also how, in his own time, the bacterial origin of disease could gain easy

acceptance only by the generation in whose time it was announced. The warning was wholesome, but retirement of all
teachers at this age was scarcely practicable. He repeated this
idea in his valedictory address at Baltimore, when he himself
was fifty-five years old. He called it a harmless obsession, yet
extended it to the thesis that men over sixty were useless in
commercial, political, and professional life, concluding with a
humorous reference to Anthony Trollope's suggestion of an
institute to which men aged sixty retired for a year's quiet
contemplation before 'a peaceful departure by chloroform'. He
admitted that he felt somewhat dubious about this, as he was
himself nearing the limit set. The faculty at Baltimore fully
understood the spirit in which Osler had spoken, but nevertheless the storm broke in the newspapers next morning, and it was
a long time before this unfortunate pseudotradition, called
'Oslerization', was allowed to die down.

Osler's belief in the value of young and adaptable minds as
the prime source of advances in scientific medicine was perfectly genuine; yet he certainly underrated the worth of experience in research, though he admitted its importance in the
practice of medicine.

Primarily a Clinician

I am told that an eminent scientific physician of a later generation criticized Osler as having no claim to be an 'original
thinker' (such as himself). Osler was, he said, merely a 'collector' who accumulated lists of symptoms referable to diseases
already recognized. It is true that Osler was not an 'original
thinker' in the sense that he had advanced new theories of
disease or even described many previously unrecognized conditions. His name is generally found as an eponym for only one
disorder, the polycythaemia rubra of Vaquez.[1] He did not
carry out any laboratory research other than intense application to morbid anatomy at McGill. He would not have

---

[1] Sir Archibald Garrod in 1921 suggested that Osler's name should also
be attached to a hereditary malady characterized by multiple telangi-
ectases associated with haemorrhages. This would certainly have been a
useful short-cut in nomenclature.

complained that his work had gone unrecognized, since his strength did not lie in work at the laboratory bench.

The Oslerian Tradition in medical advances insisted on the importance of careful and expert clinical observation coupled with wide knowledge of the symptoms of disease, these two forms of 'collecting', if you like to call them so, being co-ordinated to form the basis of accurate diagnosis. His own way of putting this was in the words: 'It is only by persistent intel-ligent study of disease upon a methodical plan of examination that a man gradually learns to correlate his daily lessons with the facts of his previous experience and that of his fellows, and so acquires clinical wisdom.' In another passage Osler said: 'In the fight which we have to wage incessantly against ignor-ance and quackery among the masses and follies of all sorts among the classes, *diagnosis*, not *drugging*, is our chief weapon of offence.'

Osler was, in fact, primarily a clinician, intent on establishing the surest means of arriving at a sound diagnosis, utilizing every form of clinical aid offered by the laboratory, but not presuming to elevate his function to the level of a pure science. He could admire and appreciate the great value of 'original thinking' to the advance of medicine, but his own thought was directed to another goal—the relief of suffering by hitting the bull's-eye in the diagnostic target as often and as quickly as possible. The tradition of this goal in medicine is surely not to be despised. Moreover, the theories of the 'original thinker' frequently do not stand the test of time, and may touch only a restricted field. They may have helped science on its way, but can suffer eclipse when another 'original thinker' makes another better theory or more fruitful experiments. Osler would be content with his anonymity. The ripples of his influence would spread widely and for an indefinite time, carried first by the students he had trained himself and then unknowingly by their successors. In addition let it not be forgotten that he was elected a Fellow of the Royal Society of London in 1898, at about the same time as J. S. Haldane, Henry Head, and E. S. Starling.

One of Osler's claims to fame is still recognized to be the textbook entitled *The Principles and Practice of Medicine*, written during his early years at Johns Hopkins and first published in

1892. The book was instantly welcomed as a masterpiece in its own line, and has passed through innumerable editions and revisions by Osler and his successors, but the day of the comprehensive textbook written by one man is quickly passing, and *The Principles and Practice* has been largely superseded. Its method was based on the author's pre-eminence as a 'collector'. Each disease was analysed under headings: Definition, Etiology, Morbid Anatomy, Symptoms, Diagnosis, Prognosis, and Treatment. It was a *tour de force* for a single writer to cover the field, but as knowledge increases its accomplishment becomes impossible. Osler carried it through by writing in a clear sober style based on vast experience and a prodigious memory. In the first edition it filled over a thousand large pages, and Osler himself would have been the last to recommend any student to read it through. It was intended to supplement the tradition of his teaching, the student using it as a book of reference while he accumulated clinical experience. The book is itself traditional chiefly as a pattern of exposition of clinical facts and their implications. Moreover, it is well known that a literary authority at Oxford made the pronouncement that Osler had 'succeeded in making a scientific treatise literature.'

Wilder Penfield's book *The Epic of Alan Gregg* supplies an important sidelight on the consequences of Osler's method of exposition. Frederick Gates, an administrator who had been deeply concerned in the affairs of the University of Chicago, was asked by John D. Rockefeller to advise him in the disposal of the important benefaction he wished to make to medicine. Gates had read *The Principles and Practice* in 1897 and perceived that Osler had set aside the traditional and unproved forms of treatment of disease. He had been called a 'therapeutic nihilist', or, more accurately, an 'iconoclast', since he was introducing for each patient the exhaustive pathological study in which German scientists had excelled. To this he was adding a method of bedside teaching derived from the Edinburgh school of clinicians, developed further by him at the Montreal General Hospital. It was the beginning of a new era of specific tests and therapy in medicine throughout the world. Osler was clearing out the dead wood and making a way for the advent of scientific medicine. Frederick Gates saw in his honest scholarly writing the promise of a great advance, and as a result the Osler Tradition was largely responsible for the advice given by Gates in the vast benefactions of the Rockefeller Foundation.

Osler's Historical Sense

It is noticeable that on the first page of *The Principles and Practice* the section on typhoid fever is given a long Historical Note, but thereafter this heading is seldom used. Osler's historical sense was so strong that this abstinence must have been dictated by realization that systematic 'Historical Notes' would have added too much to an already unwieldy volume, but it must have been a hard decision. Indeed, the Oslerian Tradition is, I suppose, now centred more on his doctrine of the value of medical history in teaching and in practice than on anything else. His deep interest in the story of Dr. William Beaumont and Alexis St. Martin, the soldier with a hole in his stomach, is well known. It was one of the most dramatic chapters in the history of gastric physiology, and Osler made no secret of the fact that after the death of St. Martin he expected that his stomach would be deposited in the United States Army Museum in Washington. But St. Martin was French Canadian, and when he died Osler was warned that if he attempted to hold a postmortem he would be killed. For some time the dead man's grave was guarded every night by a number of his compatriots armed with rifles.

The Historical Club at Johns Hopkins was initiated by three men, John S. Billings, Welch, and Osler, who attended its meetings regularly for fifteen years, regarding this as a most important element in the education provided by the medical school. He prescribed a grounding in medical history not only for the students but also for his colleagues. A course was mapped out for the Historical Club to devote successive sessions to the systematic study of the great figures of the past, beginning with Aesculapius and Hippocrates. The club almost met its Waterloo when it came to Galen. The morsel was too large to swallow, and nearly choked the assembled devotees of the Muse Clio. Nevertheless the club survived, and Osler concentrated on the study of Plato, whose definition of medicine was prefixed to *The Principles and Practice*: 'This is an art which considers the constitution of the patient, and has principles of action and reasons in each case.' It was, indeed, remarked that at this time Osler's addresses contained almost as many references to Plato as to Sir Thomas Browne—a notable change.

Osler delighted his audiences by painting eloquent word pictures of supposed climactic events in medical history, as, for instance, in his Harveian Oration of 1906. He was anxious to get the full effect of describing what he called a *dies mirabilis* in the history of this college, beginning:

> At ten o'clock on a bright spring morning, April 17, 1616, an unusually large company was attracted to the new Anatomy Theatre of the Physicians' College, Amen Street. The second Lumleian Lecture of the annual course given that year by a new man had drawn a larger gathering than usual, due in part to the brilliancy of the demonstration on the previous day, but also it may be because rumours had spread abroad about strange views to be propounded by the lecturer,

and so forth. But this semi-fictional method of dispensing medical or any other sort of history is dangerous. We now know that Harvey made no startling revelation on 'that bright spring morning', nor for many years afterwards. However, some licence must be allowed to the man who so successfully popularized and established the significance of medical history to all concerned in its practice. It is, I think, true to say that a growing interest in medical history has played a large part in stimulating the deep and widespread cultivation of the history of science in general that we see today. The Oslerian Tradition has asserted itself in a way that would have gratified its originator.

There can be no doubt that Osler acquired his knowledge of medical men and their writings in the hard way—by solid reading. He was not one to employ a literary ghost who would provide him with apt quotations with which to pepper his addresses in order to give them a false literary glitter. His knowledge was profound, his memory phenomenal, and his use of these faculties was entirely convincing. It could also be embarrassing to his friends. Imagine receiving a postcard asking: 'Has the poem of Ariphron on Health—Athenaeus xv.63,702a, ever been translated? Rabelais refers to it—introduction to bk. iv. If not translated why not do it?' This was written in February 1919, when he was already sickening for his last illness.

An Astonishing Performance

In the last year of his life Osler, to his surprise and delight, was elected president of the Classical Association in Oxford. He afterwards told his friend Welch, from Johns Hopkins, that he took more trouble over this presidential address than over any other of his career, and it was an astonishing performance for a man so stricken with years and multifarious duties. Its style has much of the flavour of Sir Thomas Browne, it carries lightly a heavy burden of classical learning and allusion, it satirizes humorously and without offence the rather antiquated character of the Oxford school and its Greats, and it advances a powerful plea for the greater recognition of the claims of science and modern learning in the University. Osler even twitted the classical dons on their scant knowledge of the great classical forerunners of modern science. 'In the only school', he said,

> dealing with the philosophy of modern thought, the sources of the new science that have made a new world are practically ignored. One gets an impression of neglect in the Schools, or at any rate of scant treatment, of the Ionian philosophers, the very fathers of your fathers. Few 'Greats' men, I fear, can tell why Hippocrates is a living force today, or why [he continued] a modern scientific physician would feel more at home with Erasistratus and Herophilus at Alexandria, or with Galen at Pergamos, than at any period in our story up to, say, Harvey. Except as a delineator of character, what does the Oxford scholar know of Theophrastus, the founder of modern botany, and a living force in one of the two departments of biology?

It was not only the division of 'the two cultures' that he deplored. 'It is not the dominance', he said,

> but the unequal dominance that is a cause of just complaint. As to methods of teaching—by their fruits ye shall know them. The product of 'Greats' needs no description in this

place. Many deny the art to find the mind's construction in the face, but surely not the possibility of diagnosing at a glance a 'first in Greats'! Only in him is seen that altogether superior expression, that self-consciousness of having reached life's goal, of having, in that pickled sentence of Dean Gaisford's Christmas sermon, done something that not only elevates above the common herd, but leads not unfrequently to positions of considerable emolument. . . . As a discipline for the mind for the few, the system should not be touched, and we should be ready to sacrifice a holocaust of undergraduates every year to produce in each generation a scholar of the type of, say, Ingram Bywater. 'Tis Nature's method—does it not cost some thousands of eggs and fry to produce one salmon?

He even dared to accuse the classical scholars of virtually ignoring Aristotle as the founder of modern biology, and of making an unfortunate break in the Humanities by their treatment of Lucretius, 'the greatest nature-poet in literature'. To be fair, he also deprecated the overspecialization of the scientists, whose salvation lay in recognition of a new philosophy—the *scientia scientiarum* of which Plato speaks; though here Osler admitted a hesitant approach through being like Dr. Johnson's friend Oliver Edwards—he never succeeded in mastering philosophy; cheerfulness was always breaking in.

Teacher and Friend

I mentioned at the outset of this address that kindness to one's juniors was an important feature of the Oslerian Tradition. This kindness he extended to all the students who ever came into his sphere of influence, and keeping up with old pupils in later life was partly responsible for his habit of corresponding largely on postcards. Receipt of a postcard from Osler was not a sign that the communication was trivial; it was simply the result of the physical impossibility of writing all the letters needed to keep his innumerable friendships green. Each student was made to feel that his teacher was his friend, and Osler was at his best when addressing student bodies. In some degree he tended to speak as a lay preacher, though he could preach without pomposity, and tempered the austerity of his view of how a student's life should be regulated with a tolerant humanity and often with humour. In his celebrated address on 'The Student Life', when saying farewell to American and Canadian medical students in 1905, he remarked that he once asked a well-known story-writer what time he found best for work, and was told: 'Not in the evening and never between meals.' This Osler thought might appeal to some of his hearers. He went on to say that during a visit to Bedlam the physician in charge had mentioned two great groups of patients, those who were depressed in the morning and those who were cheerful, suggesting that spirits rose and fell with the body temperature. This, Osler suggested, was the explanation of the extraordinary difference in the habits of students concerning the best time for work.

'Outside of the asylum', he said,

> there are the two great types, the student-lark who loves to see the sun rise, who comes to breakfast with a cheerful morning face, never so fit as at 6 a.m. What a contrast to the student-owl with his saturnine morning face, thoroughly unhappy, cheated by the breakfast bell of the best two hours of the day for sleep, no appetite, and permeated with an unspeakable hostility to his vis-à-vis, whose morning garrulity and good humour are equally offensive. Only gradually, as the day wears on and his temperature rises, does he become endurable to himself and others. But see him really awake at 10 p.m. while our blithe lark is in hopeless coma over his books, from which it is hard to rouse him sufficiently to get his boots off for bed; our lean owl-friend, Saturn no longer in the ascendant, with bright eyes and cheery face, is ready for four hours of anything you wish—deep study or 'Heart-affluence in discursive talk'—and by 2 a.m. he will undertake to unsphere the spirit of Plato. In neither a virtue, in neither a fault, we must recognize these two types of students differently constituted, owing possibly to thermal peculiarities.

Osler's tolerance did not, however, prevent him from speaking very forcibly, even in public, when the occasion seemed to him to demand it. Yet, somehow, when he did so, it did not give offence and was effective. In personal relations, also, he could never quarrel with anyone. His senior colleague at Philadelphia, when he first went there, was William Pepper. His very name suggests he was not an easy man to live with, and Osler by his reforming zeal and enthusiasm no doubt provided a wholesome amount of irritation calculated to stimulate petty reaction. Osler delivered a generous tribute to him after his death, yet Osler's biographer, Harvey Cushing, lifted a corner of the veil over their relations when he recorded that Osler 'never heeded pinpricks. He had lived for five years in Philadelphia with Pepper and kept on the friendliest terms, and would not have recognized Jealousy had he met her, green eyes and all. She and Gossip were almost the only people who never sat at his table or sojourned under his roof. "He that speaketh a matter separateth many friends." '

Osler was always pleased to recall William Harvey's last exhortation to the Fellows of this college, 'to search out and study the secrets of Nature by way of experiment, and also for the honour of the Profession to continue mutual love and affection amongst themselves without which neither the dignity of the College can be preserved nor yet particular men receive that benefit by their admission to the College which else they might expect.' It was no doubt this unfailing friendliness and equanimity that was an important element in another large section of the Oslerian Tradition—his quite extraordinary capacity for overcoming discordant feelings among his friends and acquaintances, while inducing them to unite in forwarding some common cause. He was an incomparable stimulator of the formation of clubs and societies, particularly, of course, for the study of medical history. He not only 'mixed' well himself, he also caused others to 'mix' harmoniously. The outstanding example of this faculty was the successful amalgamation of a large number of medical societies in London into a single institution under one roof, this being the enlarged Royal Society of Medicine. Many other people, Sir John MacAlister most notable among them, played prominent parts in bringing this about. In fact, Osler's name was not mentioned in the medical journals at the time, though in reality it was he who had been the anonymous catalytic agent. He had stood at MacAlister's shoulder with suggestions and encouragement and had dropped hints in many other quarters where they were needed. He was never eager to take credit, being perfectly content to enjoy the result of his influence and witness the satisfaction of others.

It was most appropriate that in 1928 two young men, then students at Bart's, should found a society, the Osler Club of London, 'to encourage the study of the history of medicine and to keep green the memory of Osler.' Forty years later Dr. Alfred White Franklin and Dr. W. R. Bett can look back with satisfaction on what they have achieved. The Osler Club has gone from strength to strength and is now the premier society of its kind in Great Britain. I can remember early meetings when the gathering consisted of perhaps eight distinguished visitors and five members of the club, the flame being kept burning by the enthusiasm of the two founders and their conviction that the Oslerian Tradition was a real thing to be kept in memory for all time. I am proud to have been designated a Friend of the Osler Club, a special order of chivalry instituted for older, and, I fear, elderly, members.

Collected Papers

There are two well-known volumes of Osler's collected papers. One, *An Alabama Student*, consists of a series of biographical studies, including, of course, William Beaumont and Sir Thomas Browne; the other, *Aequanimitas*, gives eighteen addresses delivered on a variety of occasions in America and Great Britain. The title of the second book is taken from the first address given as a valediction primarily to his students when he was leaving Philadelphia for Baltimore in 1889. He stressed first the value of imperturbability in both physician and surgeon, meaning coolness and presence of mind under all circumstances, calmness amid storm, clearness of judgement in moments of grave peril, immobility, impassiveness, or, to use an old and expressive word, *phlegm*. Though often misunderstood by the laity, it is a quality greatly appreciated by them. This Osler regarded as a bodily virtue. Equally important was the mental equivalent, *aequanimitas*, a quality so liable to be upset by the uncertainty which pertains not alone to our science and art, but to the very hopes and fears which make us men. In seeking absolute truth we aim at the unattainable and must be content with finding broken portions. He quoted the cynic who said that in prosperity our equanimity was chiefly exercised in enabling us to bear with composure the misfortunes of our neighbours. Yet he warned his hearers against the trials of the day that might come to some owing to large and successful practice. Over-engrossed in professional cares, they might discover too late that there was no place in their habit-stricken souls for those gentle influences which make life worth living.

He also issued the warning that we are apt to live too much for the present and too much in the future. It were better to think more of the past and recall with gratitude the men whose labours in the past have made the present possible. Twenty-five years later at Yale he modified this precept, though not in any way depreciating the value of the historical sense. He was offering what he called 'A Way of Life', and it was summed up as 'the practice of living for the day only, and for the day's work, *life in day-tight compartments*'. This he claimed as a plain man whose life had never been worried by any philosophy higher than that of the shepherd in *As You Like It*:

> Sir, I am a true Labourer, I earne that I eate; get that I weare; owe no man hate, envie no man happiness; glad of other mens good content with my harme: and the greatest of my pride, is to see my Ewes graze and my Lambes suck.

A man's duty, he believed, was always to do what is clearly at hand. Let the dead part of our personal lives bury its dead. Retrospection and introspection handicapped the lives of many men, the mistakes of yesterday paralysing the efforts of today.

As a philosophy this sounds superficial and therefore easy; yet in practice it is difficult. Osler claimed that any success he had attained depended on this principle. He illustrated it with examples from Aristotle, from Plato, from the life of Christ, from Bunyan, from Dr. Johnson, and finally from Walt Whitman, whose physician he had been for many years. He recalled a summer's afternoon when they were sitting together in the window of Whitman's home; they saw a passing group of workmen, whom the poet greeted in a friendly way. He then said: 'Ah! the glory of the day's work, whether with hand or brain. I have tried "To exalt the present and the real,/To teach the average man the glory of his daily work or trade." ' In this way of life, that was Osler's, each one, he hoped, might learn to drive the straight furrow and so come to the true measure of a man.

A Solid Monument

The main theme of this address has been the Oslerian Tradition —that is, the influence that Osler's life and personality may have upon the outlook of succeeding generations of medical men when the man himself is gone. This is impalpable and elusive and therefore impossible to convey except in words. But he also left a more solid monument in the shape of a large library, which passed at his death to McGill University, Montreal. This library was formed over the years with a very definite end in view—that is, to illustrate and record with books and manuscripts the whole history of medical science. It was no haphazard collection formed by the mind of a magpie. Its aim was to direct the student to every aspect of the subject through a balanced selection of material. Osler had, of course, his special obsessions, such as Sir Thomas Browne, but in general his survey was sane and serious. This was demonstrated by the highly organized and original plan of the catalogue carefully laid down for the guidance of the two scholars, his cousin Bill Francis and R. H. Hill of the Bodleian, who were designated to carry it into effect, under the direction, as it turned out, of Lady Osler.

The first section was entitled *Bibliotheca Prima*, to include the works of primary importance produced by the ancient civilizations of the East and by the greatest of the Greeks and the Arabians; by the middle ages, giving only the name of Roger Bacon; and by the sixteenth to the nineteenth centuries, including a special section on anaesthesia. This is followed by the *Bibliotheca Secunda*, with the names of lesser lights, though still important; then the *Bibliotheca Literaria* with Browne and Burton in the forefront, followed by the *Bibliotheca Historica*, *Biographica*, and *Bibliographica*, and ending with *Incunabula* and manuscripts. The organic whole, entitled *Bibliotheca Osleriana*, contains nearly 8,000 entries, and provides an extraordinary panorama of medical history in an easily assimilated form, a mirror of the mind that produced it. Osler, with the broad sweep of his multifarious interests and duties, could not provide the detailed scholarship needed for the minutiae of accurate annotation. This was supplied in full measure by the meticulous mind of Bill Francis—so full, indeed, was the measure that the years passed and it was not for a decade after Osler's death that the book was published. Lady Osler, compelled to continue living in 'The Open Arms' together with the library for much longer than she liked, used to sigh and ask me in despairing tones would this man *ever* finish his task? But she realized that the foibles of a perfectionist must be respected and that Sir William would have approved. The catalogue as we have it is a monument to all the great physicians that have ever lived and the printed testimony to the value of the Tradition I have tried to define.

INDEX

———◆◆◆———

(Compiled, with the author's 'help' and gratitude, by Frank Collieson)